Aging in America
A to Z

Aging
in America
A to Z

Adriel Bettelheim

CQ PRESS

A DIVISION OF CONGRESSIONAL QUARTERLY INC.
WASHINGTON, D.C.

V

CQ Press
A Division of Congressional Quarterly Inc.
1414 22nd Street, N.W.
Washington, D.C. 20037
202-822-1475; 800-638-1710
www.cqpress.com

♾ The paper used in this publication meets the minimum requirements of the American National Standard for Information Sciences—Permanence of Paper for Printed Library Materials, ANSI Z39.48-1992.

Aging in America A to Z was designed and typeset by Paul Hotvedt of Blue Heron Typesetters, Inc.

Cover Design: Karen Doody

Printed and bound in the United States of America

05 04 03 02 01   5 4 3 2 1

Library of Congress Cataloging-in-Publication Data

   in process

To my mother and father

Contents

x   **Contents**

Preface

The idea for a book about politics and aging originated with a series of reports I wrote for the *CQ Researcher* in 1998 dealing with Social Security, Medicare, and the challenges facing entitlement programs primarily directed at elderly people.

As a reporter who spent five years covering Washington for a large regional newspaper, I already had a passing acquaintance with these matters, usually in the context of how budget cuts to particular programs affected local hospitals and other health-care providers. Writing the longer pieces gave me a deeper appreciation of the enormously complex task the government faces in addressing aging issues and of the intense political pressures that interest groups, blocs of voters, and other parties bring to bear on the process.

This book attempts to lay out some of the most important policy questions that come under the aging rubric and to identify key players in current and past debates. The hope is that it will provide a valuable reference as Congress ponders making structural changes to programs directed at the elderly; as the graying U.S. population forces retrenchments in the health-care, insurance, and financial services industries; and as scientific research reveals a new understanding about afflictions that most often strike elders.

Much space is devoted to Social Security, the oft-debated New Deal program that many regard as the nation's greatest social policy achievement. Skeptics in recent years have questioned how long the program can remain solvent with the anticipat-

ed surge of retiring baby boomers and whether this pay-as-you-go system places a disproportionate burden on younger workers, who must fund retirees' benefits. Defenders of the program believe it must be kept in its present form to preserve a vital intergenerational contract. Various entries explore the debate over privatizing the system—an issue that played a prominent role in the 2000 presidential elections and in the first-year agenda of President George W. Bush and his administration.

Medicare and Medicaid also factor into many entries and policy discussions. Medicare, the giant health-insurance program for the elderly, pays primarily for hospital and surgical care and the medically necessary rehabilitation that follows. But other health needs, such as long-term care and outpatient prescription drugs, are left uncovered. Policymakers continue to debate whether to expand the program's package of benefits—and how such a move could affect the solvency of the Medicare trust funds.

Similar difficult questions face Medicaid, the complex federal-state program that provides health care for the poor, which also has become the main source of public funding for nursing home care. Although the elderly and disabled make up less than one-third of Medicaid recipients, they account for about 64 percent of program spending. Policy experts worry that rising health-care costs and the growing elderly population will lead to even greater disparities.

Another focus of the book is on eldercare and

whether America is equipped to offer a "continuum of care" for its aging population. The book explores how health-care providers are developing alternatives to institutional settings, such as traditional nursing homes, and how improved medical technologies and innovations in ergonomics are making it easier to care for elders in the setting they appear to most prefer—their own homes. The book covers recent developments in senior living, including the advent of continuing care retirement communities, where elders can receive varying levels of care without having to move.

One more aspect of eldercare is society's increased understanding of the afflictions that commonly plague older persons. Only a few decades ago, conditions such as dementia or hearing loss were accepted as normal by-products of aging, even by health professionals. The recent decoding of the human genome and other scientific advances are yielding a greater understanding of the biological underpinnings of many afflictions. One example is Alzheimer's disease, little understood as recently as the 1970s but now the focus of billions of dollars in biomedical research. The book explores diseases that are more likely to strike elderly people, government agencies such as the National Institutes of Health that oversee much of the research into causes and treatments, and the politics and interest groups that drive the federal effort.

Although most of the book is focused on policy and politics, it also takes up society's perceptions of what it means to age. Entries explore different perspectives on aging through the eyes of baby boomers, Generation Xers, gays and lesbians, and other demographic groups. The book also explains how attitudes about aging and society affect trends in early retirement, consumer spending, housing, and investing. And it details how federal policymakers have responded to these developments by lifting certain income restrictions on working seniors and by changing laws to create new varieties of pensions and investments.

Because the numerous aging issues covered in these pages are always changing, this book can offer only a snapshot of the state of public policy at the beginning of the twenty-first century. Any omissions or mistakes are my responsibility alone, and constructive comments are appreciated. Those readers seeking a more detailed discussion of various issues can draw on a variety of primary source material. A government publication that may prove particularly helpful is the *Green Book,* a biannual publication of the House Ways and Means Committee that provides background information and statistics on Social Security, Medicare, and other programs that come under the committee's jurisdiction. Another useful volume is *Developments in Aging,* published by the Senate Special Committee on Aging, which contains detailed discussions about entitlements, pension law, long-term care, social services, and other aging-related issues that have come before that committee.

Many people have provided help and encouragement during the preparation of this book. At CQ Press, thanks go to Patricia Gallagher, who first approached me about doing this project, and David Tarr, who shepherded the book to completion. Thanks also go to Kathryn L. Krug, who copyedited the text, and Talia Greenberg, who researched and acquired the photographs. And I owe special thanks to Paul Kleyman, editor of *Aging Today* and one of the preeminent journalists on the aging beat, who pored over the rough draft of the manuscript and offered many valuable suggestions.

At Congressional Quarterly's *CQ Researcher,* Sandra Stencel and Thomas Colin supervised and helped shape most of the early reporting that provided a foundation for this book. At *CQ Weekly* magazine, fellow reporters Mary Agnes Carey and David Nather gave generously of their time in helping me grasp some of the vagaries of social policy.

Most of all, I owe my deepest gratitude to my wife, Jennifer Gavin, who put up with disruptions in our routine and read and edited early versions of this manuscript. Her love and encouragement are the greatest gifts I possess.

Aging in America
AtoZ

AARP

The AARP, a trademark that formerly stood for the American Association of Retired Persons, is an influential national advocacy group for elderly people. Founded in 1958 by retired educator Ethel Percy Andrus, the organization initially sold group health insurance and offered members travel discounts. Today, AARP is a huge nonprofit entity that runs community-service and legal-assistance programs, sponsors educational forums, operates on-line shopping services, and publishes *Modern Maturity* magazine. AARP's activities are estimated to generate in excess of $5 billion per year for the organization and various partners.

AARP's significant operations include its Public Policy Institute, which produces policy analysis reports written by a highly respected staff on topics ranging from SOCIAL SECURITY and MEDICARE to issues for older workers and the intricacies of tax policy proposals. A second area of activity—and one of concern to the organization's critics—is AARP's selling of insurance and financial investment products to its members. Questions have been raised from both the political right and left about the organization's apparent split personality as a defender of traditional social programs, but also as a merchandiser of financial and insurance products that call some of its more centrist stands into question. Some critics from the left have questioned whether AARP's supporting of some limited Social Security PRIVATIZATION, particularly government-controlled investments, instead of opposing all reform efforts, comes from the interest in selling more retirement investment plans.

Politics, of course, is what AARP is best known for—especially its ability to mobilize its thirty-four million members for or against various causes. Until the late 1990s, pressure from the group discouraged lawmakers from considering major structural changes to the Social Security system, despite financial projections showing that the retirement system in its present form will run out of cash to pay all its obligations by the middle of the twenty-first century. The organization's hardball tactics were also evident during contentious congressional negotiations over the 1997 BALANCED BUDGET ACT (PL 105-33). At that time, AARP set up a toll-free phone line that connected senior citizens to their representatives' offices in Congress and helped convince lawmakers to drop provisions that would have made important changes to Medicare, the federal health-care program for the elderly. The proposed changes would have raised the eligibility age and increased the cost of coverage for some affluent seniors.

AARP has also drawn criticism for what some see as a left-leaning, pro-taxation bias, and for taking positions that don't always reflect the majority of members' sentiments. Some Republicans have questioned why the organization did not more vocally oppose President Bill Clinton's 1993 budget, which expanded taxation of Social Secu-

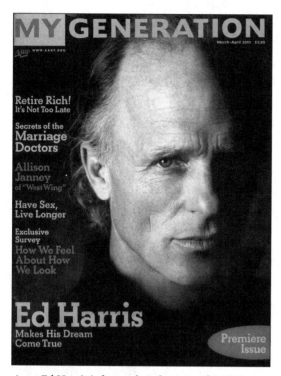

Actor Ed Harris is featured on the cover of AARP's newest publication, My Generation, *a magazine aimed at baby boomers that hit newsstands February 8, 2001. The magazine was created for "people turning 50 who are not thinking about retirement, but looking forward to a healthy, long, active life." Source: AARP Publications*

decentralize its operations away from its Washington headquarters, take a generally lower profile on issues, and focus on building up its state organizations, which constitute the heart of its membership. This is seen, in part, as an effort not to overstep its bounds with a politically diffused membership.

To bolster its ranks with younger members, AARP is intensifying its recruiting efforts among members of the post–World War II BABY BOOM cohort now turning fifty. Responding to a 1998 survey it commissioned from Roper Starch Worldwide that showed about 80 percent of baby boomers expect to work during retirement—about one-third because they expect to need the income—AARP says it will advocate changes to the tax code, to health insurance practices, and to employment laws to make it easier for people to work longer. It also is pressing large corporations to offer continued training for workers so their skills can keep pace with the changing job market.

rity benefits for middle-income singles and couples. At the same time, liberals complain AARP is too soft on private-investment retirement concepts that seem to emanate from the right.

In 1998, AARP joined with the CONCORD COALITION and the Clinton administration to organize a nationwide series of forums on the future of Social Security. Some viewed the move as an attempt to shift AARP's role to that of a consensus-builder—and to mollify Republicans who control Congress in advance of the 2000 elections. Simultaneously, AARP has also moved to

Accelerated death benefit

An accelerated death benefit, or living benefit, is a type of viatical settlement available in some life insurance policies that allows the insured person to collect part of the death benefit before he or she actually dies. First introduced in the late 1980s for persons dying of AIDS, accelerated benefits have become popular among elderly people with terminal illnesses—most often CANCER, HEART DISEASE, or kidney failure. The American Council of Life Insurance reports there were 39.9 million policies with an accelerated death benefit clause or option at the beginning of 1998, compared with 18.1 million in 1994.

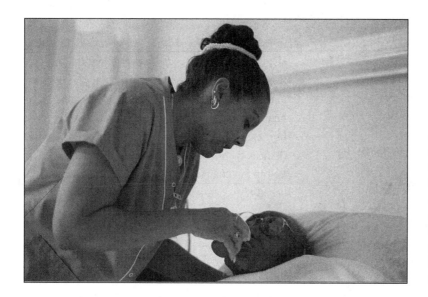

A young nursing assistant lifts a drink to the lips of a ninety-year-old patient at Greenbrook Manor Nursing Home in Monroe, Michigan. Feeding patients during a typical eight-hour shift requires patience, a gentle hand, and determination.
Source: Travis Hartman, AP Photo

Most accelerated death benefits are conditioned on the insured person not being expected to live more than twelve more months. A portion of the life insurance is advanced, either in a lump sum or in periodic payments. The remainder is treated like a conventional life insurance policy and paid to the beneficiaries after the insured person dies. Many companies limit the amount of money that can be advanced to something like $100,000 or $250,000. Accelerated benefits aren't subject to federal income taxes under the Health Insurance Portability and Accountability Act of 1996 (PL 104-191), and some states also exempt the benefits from state taxes. Fees for accelerated death benefits vary, with some insurers charging a percentage of the death benefit as a processing fee. The accelerated benefits are offered as an option with some policies and built into the standard language of others, again depending on the insurer.

Activities of daily living

Activities of daily living, or ADL, is a measurement of the extent of disability for a person who requires long-term medical care. There are five "core" ADLs: eating, getting in or out of bed, dressing, bathing, and using the bathroom. ADL limitations have been included in congressional bills to determine the eligibility of MEDICARE beneficiaries for LONG-TERM CARE benefits, beginning with the so-called Pepper Bill, named for the late Rep. CLAUDE PEPPER, D-Fla., in the 100th Congress.

Individuals typically are considered disabled if they need help with three or more of the five ADLs. A second kind of measurement, Instrumental Activities of Daily Living, or IADL, considers higher-level daily tasks that people must perform to remain independent. These include shopping, cooking, paying bills, taking medication, and doing routine housework. Approximately one-quarter of all senior citizens need help with at least one ADL or IADL, and the number is expected to increase as the number of aging BABY BOOMERS rises.

Administration on Aging

The Administration on Aging, a division of the U.S. Department of HEALTH AND HUMAN SERVICES was established by the OLDER AMERICANS ACT OF 1965 (PL 89-73) to administer a host of federal programs for elderly people that were created by the act. These include grants for transportation, senior centers, nutrition and health programs, as well as LEGAL SERVICES and ELDER ABUSE prevention programs. The agency has an annual budget of about $1 billion. A separate amount is allocated under the act to the U.S. Department of Labor's Senior Community Service Employment Program for various job training efforts and job placement services for seniors.

The Administration on Aging is headed by an assistant secretary for aging, who customarily is the executive branch's leading advocate for older citizens and their concerns. The job also entails coordinating outreach efforts among the myriad local agencies across the country that serve elderly people; the Older Americans Act grant programs support 57 state agencies on aging, 660 county or area agencies on aging, and more than 27,000 service providers. One key focus is administering the act's Title III services for lower-income individuals age sixty and over, particularly indigent minority persons. The largest of these services is a nutrition program that provides meals to more than three million people annually, usually in senior centers and schools, but also delivered to the frail elders in their homes. This program receives annual funding in excess of $625 million.

While service programs represent the bulk of the Administration on Aging's work, the agency also is deeply involved in developing demonstration projects to better address the needs of elderly people. In recent years, new programs have helped train paralegals to provide counseling, and home health aides to tend to frail elders. Some demonstration program money also is directed at helping agencies improve home and community-based LONG-TERM CARE programs.

Adult day care

Adult day care is a supervised setting that provides elderly people with social services, recreational opportunities, and some medical care. The programs allow families to keep an elder at home and out of an institutional setting for as long as possible. More structured than a local senior center but less restrictive than ASSISTED LIVING facilities or NURSING HOMES, adult day care centers take many forms. Some are stand-alone facilities located in neighborhood settings, such as shopping malls, while others are connected to medical centers or LONG-TERM CARE facilities. There are no federal standards for adult day care facilities, though many states have licensing requirements. The facilities also may voluntarily choose to be accredited under the NATIONAL COUNCIL ON THE AGING's national standards to assure quality care.

The centers cater to people over age sixty-five who need help with daily tasks, such as eating or grooming, but still are capable of living at home or with family. Transportation to and from the site is often provided, and centers typically provide a daily meal. MEDICAID and VETERAN'S BEN-

An eighty-three-year-old art enthusiast works at a watercolor at Senior Adult Services, an adult day care center in Carbondale, Illinois. Source: Joe Jines, AP Photo

EFITS may be available to offset the cost to patients, depending on eligibility and services provided.

Advance directive

An advance directive is a legal document recognized by state law that outlines how a person wants to be treated if he or she becomes medically incapacitated. The two most common varieties are LIVING WILLS and MEDICAL POWERS OF AT-TORNEY. The forms address such situations as when a person is in a coma, or suffering from terminal illness, and would die without supplied respiration, tube-feeding, or similar medical intervention. Advance directives may include "DO NOT" ORDERS that explicitly instruct physicians not to resuscitate a patient in the event of a heart attack or forbid administering other kinds of critical care.

A living will outlines specific directions for medical treatment and those conditions under which a person may wish to be kept alive, and it designates a surrogate to carry out the person's wishes, if the person cannot express them. A medical power of attorney designates a surrogate— with the general understanding that that person will make decisions about treatment options, applying for government benefits, and transferring a patient to or from a health care facility when applicable.

Advance directives gained nationwide attention during the 1990 U.S. Supreme Court case *Cruzan by Cruzan v. Director, Missouri Department of Health.* The high court upheld a Missouri decision refusing the request of the parents of a woman left in a persistent vegetative state as the result of an automobile accident to terminate the medical care that prolonged their daughter's life. Congress that year enacted the PATIENT SELF-DE-TERMINATION ACT, requiring health care facilities that receive MEDICARE or MEDICAID funds to inform patients about advance directives and, if they have not already done so, give them the option to execute one. While credited with strengthening patient rights, advance directives have created problems because of state-by-state variations in format and rules. Some patients with an advance directive completed in one state may find that another state places restrictions on how the document is enforced.

Age discrimination

Age discrimination is a central focus of employment law—a subject that has received increased public attention over the past three decades as corporate downsizing affected a large number of older workers. The U.S. ADMINISTRATION ON AGING attributes many age-discrimination cases to long-held assumptions that older workers must step aside and make room for younger workers with families, or that it isn't financially practical for a company to retrain aging employees for new jobs.

The term is somewhat broadly defined because discrimination can take many forms. Essentially it reflects unfair treatment in the workplace, based strictly on a person's age. This might entail something as straightforward as a company filling a vacancy with a thirty-year-old instead of an equally qualified fifty-five-year-old, or repeatedly passing over an older worker for promotions. Age discrimination can also take more subtle forms, such as singling out employees in their fifties and sixties for special buyouts meant to thin out their ranks—a practice sometimes referred to as offering "golden handshakes."

Congress has taken a number of steps to address the issue. The most notable was passage of the Age Discrimination in Employment Act of 1967 (ADEA; PL 90-202), which expanded protections guaranteed to certain groups in the Civil Rights Act of 1964 to workers and job applicants aged forty and older. The law originated with a 1964 executive order issued by President Lyndon B. Johnson and prohibits employers from mentioning age preferences in job notices or advertisements, or from discriminating by age in apprenticeship programs. Exemptions have been granted only when age is a "bona fide qualification for the job," such as with airline pilots or police officers.

In the years since its passage, the ADEA has prompted many legal disputes over the way it creates a protected age group, and whether that implies employers must give the group preferential treatment. The U.S. Supreme Court has held that age isn't in the same class as gender or race in discrimination suits, in essence because everyone ages. Those who charge age discrimination must prove there was no rational basis for the alleged discrimination.

Several other federal laws have dealt with age discrimination. The Age Discrimination Act of 1975 prohibited age bias in any program or activity involving federal funding, including housing or educational programs, health care services, and welfare. The 1982 Tax Equity and Fiscal Responsibility Act (TEFRA; PL 97-248) required employers to keep workers over age sixty-five on company health plans instead of automatically shifting them to MEDICARE. The 1990 OLDER WORKERS BENEFIT PROTECTION ACT (PL 101-433) banned age discrimination with respect to employee benefits, except in those cases where benefit differences were due to age-based differences in cost, such as with retiree health benefits. The law came in response to a 1989 U.S. Supreme Court decision in *Public Employee Retirement System of Ohio v. Betts* that ruled that the ADEA's prohibitions against bias didn't extend to employee benefits.

The Supreme Court currently is weighing whether people who sue under the ADEA must provide direct evidence of discrimination in order to win their cases. Senior advocates complain that circuit courts have raised the burden of proof

The Age Discrimination in Employment Act of 1967 originated with a 1964 executive order issued by President Lyndon B. Johnson that prohibits employers from mentioning age preferences in job notices or advertisements, or from discriminating by age in apprenticeship programs. Source: Senate Historical Office

unreasonably, and hope justices will give lower courts guidance on how to rule in such cases. The high court in January 1999 ruled in a separate case that state employees cannot sue in federal or state courts under the ADEA. The justices ruled in a 5–4 decision that Congress doesn't have the authority to revoke a state's immunity from being sued without prior consent for violating a federal law—an immunity guaranteed by the Eleventh Amendment. The decision was cheered by states'-rights advocates, who support a reduced federal role in judicial decisions. However, advocates for the elderly said the decision leaves state employees with virtually no legal protection against age discrimination. The decision doesn't affect em-

ployees of private businesses, who can still sue under the law.

Individuals who believe they are victims of age discrimination have several options beside private suits. They can file charges under state age-bias laws, though those laws are regarded as something of a patchwork and vary in strength, depending on the state. At the federal level, individuals can press a complaint with the EQUAL EMPLOYMENT OPPORTUNITY COMMISSION (EEOC), the federal agency responsible for enforcing ADEA and investigating allegations. If the EEOC finds discrimination took place, it can then mediate the dispute and assist in striking a financial settlement. The EEOC dismisses the charges if its investigation doesn't back up the allegations. Remedies available to people who are found to have suffered from age discrimination include back pay, reinstatement, promotion, "reasonable accommodation," or other steps that make the person "whole," including attorneys' fees and court costs. However, civil-rights experts complain the EEOC is too short-staffed and lacks the budget to enforce the ADEA by itself.

Ageism

"Ageism" is a term popularized by Dr. ROBERT N. BUTLER in the 1970s. It is generally understood to mean prejudice against old age. Like racism and sexism, it is often characterized by negative stereotypes, such as the perception that the elderly take disproportionate benefits, shortchanging younger generations. Advocates for the elderly say these perceptions affect the provision of care for older people and erode support for their CARE-

GIVERS. Many say avoiding contact with elderly people is a subtle form of ageism.

Explanations for ageism vary. One psychological analysis is that individuals, in denying they are aging, try to avoid acknowledging its effects in other people. Another interpretation is that young people in society don't have enough personal experience with the elderly to know about their behavior. Authorities in aging hold that younger individuals, especially those training for medical or other service careers, need direct experience with elders in order to understand the ramifications of older age and its positive advantages. For example, some of these experts believe periodic calls to pull the driver's licenses of elderly people—who tend to be blamed for causing more traffic accidents—do not take into account such things as the gradual loss of a "useful field of vision," and special training that can help seniors with this condition be safer drivers.

The term ageism is increasingly working its way into politics, though it is sometimes used interchangeably with AGE DISCRIMINATION. British Prime Minister Tony Blair vowed to enact legal measures against ageism in the workplace during his 1997 Labour Party campaign. The British government subsequently drafted a voluntary code of employment practice designed to discourage businesses from turning away older job applicants.

"Aging in place"

The term "aging in place" means allowing an elderly person to remain in his or her home, despite the physical and mental ailments that are common with aging. It is increasingly used in marketing for senior housing, especially CONTINUING-CARE RETIREMENT COMMUNITIES, which offer multiple levels of elder care in a single location.

Aging in place more accurately might refer to the situation of a senior citizen who has lived in the same house or apartment for decades and now receives a full range of health services delivered on site, including full- or part-time nursing care. Studies by AARP and other organizations show this is the preferred setting for most elderly people; only 7 percent move to an organized retirement community when they turn sixty-five or retire.

Allowing an elderly person to live at home indefinitely often involves remodeling living quarters. Some people renovate the lower level of a single-family home for one-level living so stairs can be avoided. Installing grab bars in showers, tubs, and toilets, renovating kitchen cabinets to offer pullout shelves and lazy susans, and installing programmable thermostats can help make an existing home more friendly to an elderly resident.

When an apartment building or condominium has a majority of residents who are elderly, it is referred to as a "Naturally Occurring Retirement Community," or NORC. The Fair Housing Amendments Act of 1988 allows communities to be restricted to older persons if at least 80 percent of the units are occupied by at least one person aged fifty-five or older and there are adequate facilities to meet the physical and social needs of older persons.

Professionals in aging also discuss ways in which communities can become more friendly to those who want to age in place. Ergonomic changes as simple as curb cuts or as sophisticated as talking traffic lights are examples. For example, a 1999 Florida State University study showed that ambient lighting in public places from airports to restaurants is far below recommended minimums set by the Illuminating Engineering Society of North America. Improvements could help everyone's eyes. Additionally, businesses such as supermarkets and banks can adopt elder-friendly policies that include better lighting in aisles and stairways and staff trained to be more patient with elders. (See also GEROERGONOMICS.)

Alcohol abuse

Alcohol abuse is an underdiagnosed but prevalent health problem among the elderly. The AMERICAN MEDICAL ASSOCIATION (AMA) estimates that as many as 3 million people over the age of sixty have problems with drinking, and various studies indicate that 6 to 11 percent of patients age sixty-five and over who are admitted to hospitals exhibit some symptoms of alcoholism. However, many cases go unnoticed because doctors frequently don't quiz their elderly patients about drinking, and because most older problem drinkers are unemployed and don't receive job-related referrals for treatment.

Health experts say many of the cases involve "late-onset drinkers" whose habits are linked to psychological or physical problems. These may include DEPRESSION and loneliness due to the loss of a spouse or close friends, or the boredom that sometimes accompanies retirement. Some also drink to relieve the pain from such chronic diseases as OSTEOARTHRITIS. Elderly alcohol abusers typically are less likely to get in trouble with the law and more likely to be living alone than younger alcoholics are.

The aging process doesn't change the way the body metabolizes alcohol but makes older alcoholics more vulnerable to health problems. It takes longer for alcohol to break down in an older person's body because liver enzymes are less efficient, meaning the person is impaired longer and more vulnerable to accidents or injury. Alcohol also can slow down the heart, exacerbating conditions like hypertension. Long-term alcohol consumption additionally activates enzymes in the body that can break down common prescription drugs, potentially reducing the effectiveness of those medicines. Certain other antianxiety drugs or sedatives can be dangerous or fatal when mixed with alcohol. The American Medical Association in 1999 released guidelines for physicians on how to better identify older patients with alcohol problems, and what to do to help them.

Alliance for Aging Research

The Washington-based Alliance for Aging Research is an independent, not-for-profit organization founded in 1986 to promote biomedical research into aging. In addition to lobbying Congress for more funding, the group administers grants and programs promoting the practice of geriatric medicine and basic research on aging, including the $200,000 AlliedSignal Award for Research on Aging.

In recent years the group spearheaded the Task Force for Aging Research Funding, a coalition of more than fifty patient and health care groups that has pressed Congress and the White House to increase the budget of the NATIONAL INSTITUTES OF HEALTH. Separately, the alliance has called for a reexamination of MEDICAID policies, contending the program makes it difficult for the elderly to obtain LONG-TERM CARE.

Recently the group has become one of the prime drivers behind Patients' CURe, a coalition of more than two dozen patient organizations advocating federal funding for stem-cell research. Stem cells are early-development cells found in embryos and aborted fetuses that researchers believe can be harnessed for a new generation of antiaging drugs. However, the research is controversial because some abortion foes believe it violates a 1995 congressional ban on embryo research. Patients' CURe has tried to downplay the abortion politics while urging patient and research organizations to lobby Congress. The alliance argues the research can help patients with chronic disabilities and diseases, who fare poorly in a health system currently oriented to curing acute illnesses.

Alternative health care

"Alternative health care" is a general term referring to round-the-clock care that is more extensive than what can usually be offered at home, but not equivalent to the level offered by a NURSING HOME. Such care is sought for elderly persons suffering from certain chronic diseases, or those whose health conditions render them incapable of performing ACTIVITIES OF DAILY LIVING. This setting may also be appropriate for deaf or blind seniors.

A HOSPICE is one obvious example of an alternative care facility. Others include outpatient surgical clinics that provide twenty-four-hour care in one location as an alternative to admitting a patient to a hospital. Alternative care facilities typically have specially trained attendants on hand at all times, serve three meals per day, and are licensed and accredited. The facilities also should have arrangements to summon doctors or nurses at all hours in the event of medical emergencies.

Alzheimer's Association

The Chicago-based Alzheimer's Association was founded in 1980 as the Alzheimer's Disease and Related Disorders Association and has grown into a prominent health-care lobbying group with two hundred local chapters and a budget of $100 million. It promotes research to identify causes and diagnose symptoms of ALZHEIMER'S DISEASE and lobbies Congress for long-term health care, NURSING HOME reform, and RESPITE CARE for family members of Alzheimer's patients.

The group grew out of a meeting of families, physicians, and health care professionals sponsored by the NATIONAL INSTITUTES OF HEALTH. Beginning in 1990, the association's Washington, D.C., public policy office spurred significant increases in annual funding for Alzheimer's research, winning the support of lawmakers including senators Mark O. Hatfield, R-Ore., and Tom Harkin, D-Iowa, by arguing the disease represented a looming public health threat. The organization also weighed in on congressional attempts to restructure the MEDICARE program, arguing for increased benefits for recipients with chronic-care needs.

Estimates of Any Alzheimer's Disease and Moderate or Severe Alzheimer's Disease for Americans Sixty-five Years of Age or Older in 1995

Age	Any Alzheimer's disease		Moderate or severe Alzheimer's disease	
	Number	Percent	Number	Percent
65–69	104,785	1.1	61,815	0.6
70–74	194,716	2.2	111,111	1.3
75–79	304,399	4.6	169,549	2.5
80–84	411,363	9.2	227,757	5.1
85–89	412,764	17.8	232,726	10.0
90–94	312,509	31.5	185,516	18.7
95+	166,287	52.5	110,595	34.9
Total	1,906,822	5.7	1,099,069	3.3

* Our integration of prevalence rates from eighteen studies in the literature and the U.S. Bureau of the Census population estimates in *Statistical Abstract of the United States: 1996* (Washington, D.C.: 1996).

Source: United States General Accounting Office, "Alzheimer's Disease: Estimates of Prevalence in the United States (January 1998).

Alzheimer's disease

Alzheimer's disease is a long-observed but only recently understood degenerative condition that destroys brain cells controlling a person's ability to remember, reason, and perform basic motor functions. An estimated four million Americans suffer from some form of the disease, and the U.S. General Accounting Office estimates that, after the age of sixty-five, the prevalence of the disease in men and women doubles every five years. Health care experts worry that the surge of aging BABY BOOMERS will bring many more cases of the disease and increase financial stresses on the nation's health care system. The average annual cost of caring for a pa-

tient with a moderate case of Alzheimer's is $30,096, according to the NATIONAL INSTITUTE ON AGING, which estimates that the annual national cost of caring for Alzheimer's patients at home or in nursing homes now exceeds $50 billion.

Because many Alzheimer's patients live a decade or longer after their initial diagnosis, families often use up savings on care, even if they qualify for home health care benefits under MEDICARE. They then have to turn to MEDICAID, the health care program for the poor. Advocates have lobbied for more federal funding of respite- and family-caregiver support programs, arguing that delaying placement of an Alzheimer's patient in a NURSING HOME for just one month will save more than $1 billion annually. Others have called for

Transcript of Letter from Ronald Reagan to the American People

My Fellow Americans,

I have recently been told that I am one of the millions of Americans who will be afflicted with Alzheimer's Disease.

Upon learning this news, Nancy and I had to decide whether as private citizens we would keep this a private matter or whether we would make this news known in a public way.

In the past Nancy suffered from breast cancer and I had my cancer surgeries. We found through our open disclosures we were able to raise public awareness. We were happy that as a result many more people underwent testing. They were treated in early stages and able to return to normal, healthy lives.

So now, we feel it is important to share it with you. In opening our hearts, we hope this might promote greater awareness of this condition. Perhaps it will encourage a clearer understanding of the individuals and families who are affected by it.

At the moment I feel just fine. I intend to live the remainder of the years God gives me on this earth doing the things I have always done. I will continue to share life's journey with my beloved Nancy and my family. I plan to enjoy the great outdoors and stay in touch with my friends and supporters.

Unfortunately, as Alzheimer's Disease progresses, the family often bears a heavy burden. I only wish there was some way I could spare Nancy from this painful experience. When the time comes I am confident that with your help she will face it with faith and courage.

In closing let me thank you, the American people, for giving me the great honor of allowing me to serve as your President. When the Lord calls me home, whenever that may be, I will leave with the greatest love for this country of ours and eternal optimism for its future.

I now begin the journey that will lead me into the sunset of my life. I know that for America there will always be a bright dawn ahead.

Thank you my friends. May God always bless you.

Sincerely,
Ronald Reagan

On November 5, 1994, former president Ronald Reagan disclosed in a handwritten letter to the American public that he was suffering from the early stages of Alzheimer's disease (see page 13). Source: Office of Ronald Reagan

RONALD REAGAN

Nov. 5, 1994

My Fellow Americans,

I have recently been told that I am one of the millions of Americans who will be afflicted with Alzheimer's Disease.

Upon learning this news, Nancy & I had to decide whether as private citizens we would keep this a private matter or whether we would make this news known in a public way.

In the past Nancy suffered from breast cancer and I had my cancer surgeries. We found through our open disclosures we were able to raise public awareness. We were happy that as a result many more people underwent testing. They were treated in early stages and able to return to normal, healthy lives.

So now, we feel it is important to share it with you. In opening our hearts, we hope this might promote greater awareness of this condition. Perhaps it will encourage a clearer understanding of the individuals and families who are affected by it.

At the moment I feel just fine. I intend to live the remainder of the years God gives me on this earth doing the things I have always done. I will continue to share life's journey with my beloved Nancy and my family. I plan to enjoy the great outdoors and stay in touch with my friends and supporters.

Unfortunately, as Alzheimer's Disease progresses, the family often bears a heavy burden. I only wish there was some way I could spare Nancy from this painful experience. When the time comes I am confident that with your help she will face it with faith and courage.

In closing let me thank you, the American people for giving me the great honor of allowing me to serve as your President. When the Lord calls me home, whenever that may be, I will leave with the greatest love for this country of ours and eternal optimism for its future.

I now begin the journey that will lead me into the sunset of my life. I know that for America there will always be a bright dawn ahead.

Thank you my friends. May God always bless you.

Sincerely,
Ronald Reagan

expanded HOME HEALTH BENEFITS under Medicare, which now is heavily weighted to providing acute care and doesn't pay for the LONG-TERM CARE many Alzheimer's patients require unless there is a coexisting illness.

Alzheimer's was first observed by the ancient Greeks and Romans and clinically diagnosed in 1906 by the German neuropathologist Alois Alzheimer. Scientists for most of the twentieth century viewed the disease as a mysterious by-product of aging. Increased life expectancies and advances in molecular biology led researchers to reexamine the disease in the 1960s and 1970s, then begin to identify mutant genes that might make certain individuals predisposed to the condition. They also made advances in identifying early stages of the disease, and slowing down the progression of its symptoms. The National Institute on Aging inaugurated an Alzheimer's program in 1978 and now devotes about half of its budget to improving screening and developing therapies. Other major federal institutions involved in Alzheimer's research include the National Institute of Neurological Diseases and Stroke and the National Institute of Mental Health.

There are two major types of Alzheimer's disease—a familial form that is inherited, and the more common late-onset Alzheimer's that typically strikes individuals over the age of sixty-five. The disease first destroys memory-controlling neurons in the hippocampus portion of the brain, then spreads to the cerebral cortex, which controls language and reasoning. Patients at this stage may exhibit bizarre, disturbing behavior, including sometimes violent emotional outbursts. Eventually the disease affects other areas of the brain, causing the organ to atrophy. Patients become bedridden, incontinent, and increasingly helpless, though they don't actually die from the condition but from health complications stemming from the disease.

Public interest in Alzheimer's reached new levels with former president RONALD REAGAN's 1994 disclosure that he had been diagnosed as suffering from early stages of the disease. Reagan was but the latest high-profile victim of the disease; other sufferers included actress Rita Hayworth, illustrator Norman Rockwell, welterweight boxing champion Sugar Ray Robinson, and humorist E. B. White. Advocacy groups such as the Chicago-based ALZHEIMER'S ASSOCIATION pressed lawmakers for increased funding, and by 1999 the federal government had earmarked $400 million annually on preventing the disease. Alzheimer's now is the fourth-most-funded affliction, after cancer, HIV/AIDS, and heart disease. But despite federal expenditures of more than $3 billion on Alzheimer's research since 1976, scientists have only developed two Food and Drug Administration–approved drugs that slow the disease's telltale breakdown of the brain chemical acetylcholine. Neither drug can restore memory or stop the disease's pattern of destroying brain cells.

Several genes are associated with increased risk of Alzheimer's. Duke University researchers in 1993 associated a variant of a gene called APOE with increased risk of Alzheimer's after age sixty-five. The gene normally directs production of a protein that carries blood cholesterol. The brain protein tau more recently has been implicated in Alzheimer's and several other forms of DEMENTIA.

President Bill Clinton and Congress raised federal funding specifically earmarked for Alzheimer's research from $349.2 million to $400 million in the fiscal 1999 federal budget. Congress instructed the National Institute on Aging and other federal agencies to use the extra money to

collaborate and develop new treatments that delay or prevent the onset of Alzheimer's. Congress continues to debate other Alzheimer's-related measures, including a proposed tax credit for caregivers.

American Medical Association

The Chicago-based American Medical Association (AMA) is a powerful doctors' group that lobbies on health-care issues and represents approximately 300,000 members, though this is less than half of the nation's physicians. Founded in 1847 to promote science, medicine, and public health, today it is a significant political force and a major donor to candidates. The AMA's political action committee contributed more than $2.3 million during the 1997–1998 election cycle, according to the Center for Responsive Politics, a Washington watchdog group. Taking a new tack, the AMA branched into presidential politics during the 2000 elections, sponsoring a campaign called "National House Call," in which members in a motor home followed candidates to key states and pressed them for their views on key health topics. The questions included how the candidates would overhaul MEDICARE and provide health coverage for uninsured individuals, and whether insurance companies should be sued for influencing medical treatment decisions that harm patients.

The AMA historically has leaned to the political right, opposing the creation of national health insurance and the Medicare program. It also fought President Bill Clinton's failed health-care reform plan in 1993 and 1994. Though the organization supported congressional Republicans' efforts to slow down spending on Medicare and MEDICAID in the mid-1990s, it broke with the

GOP in 1998 and strongly supported Clinton's proposed Patients' Bill of Rights, which would impose new federal rules on managed-care firms and other health insurers and give patients the right to sue their health plans over treatment decisions. The AMA has been strongly opposed to managed-care strategies for controlling medical decisions, such as pressuring doctors to spend less time with patients. Backing the bill of rights reflected doctors' increased frustration at having their decisions second-guessed by cost-conscious insurance companies. But it pitted the AMA against a well-heeled coalition of insurance companies and major employers intent on limiting health plans' exposure to patient suits.

American Society on Aging

Founded in 1954 as the Western Gerontological Society, the San Francisco–based American Society on Aging (ASA) is a nonprofit professional membership association that offers education and training about services for the elderly and other issues affecting their quality of life. The organization, which does not engage in political lobbying, sponsors training workshops and conferences on gerontology and elder care and publishes *Generations* magazine and the newspaper *Aging Today*. It also sponsors a large annual meeting for professionals in the aging field that focuses on medical research, developments in health-service delivery and public-policy initiatives, and serves as a forum for more than seven hundred papers in forty subject areas. ASA has eight niche groups focusing on emerging areas of importance in an aging society, such as the Business Forum on Aging; the Forum on Religion, Spirituality,

and Aging; the Lesbian and Gay Aging Network; the Mental Health and Aging Network; and the Multicultural Aging Network.

Americans with Disabilities Act of 1990

Though not specifically aging legislation, the Americans with Disabilities Act (ADA; PL 101-336) is a landmark law that offers protections against discrimination in employment and public accommodation to the estimated forty-three million disabled people in the United States. Among the provisions affecting seniors, the law requires buses and trains to be accessible to wheelchair-bound individuals, and mandates that telecommunications companies operate special relay systems allowing speech- and hearing-impaired people to use telephone service. It also requires localities and transit agencies to offer paratransit services with wheelchair lifts in areas where bus, subway, or train service already is available. The law additionally requires that bus and train stations and public elevators be able to accommodate people with disabilities, including those who use wheelchairs.

Signed by President George Bush on July 26, 1990, the law extends to the disabled the protections against discrimination originally contained in the Civil Rights Act of 1964. The ADA was conceived and promoted by several members of Congress who suffered disabilities or had close relatives who were disabled. Among these were former senator Bob Dole, R-Kan., whose right arm was severely injured in World War II, former senator Lowell Weicker, R-Conn., who had a child with a birth defect, and Sen. Tom Harkin, D-Iowa, whose brother was deaf.

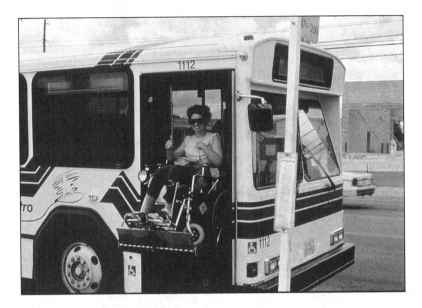

The Americans with Disabilities Act of 1990 requires buses and trains to be accessible to wheelchair-bound patrons.
Source: File photo

The law defines a disability as any physical or mental impairment that substantially limits a person's significant life activities. Employers must try to make "reasonable accommodations" for disabled people, including allowing them to work at home, obtaining special office equipment, or hiring readers or interpreters, as long as such steps don't cause "undue hardship" for the business. Most lawsuits brought under ADA revolve around whether an employer has made such accommodations, not whether the plaintiff is able work without them. While virtually no one has questioned the positive intentions of the law, congressional debate over its passage was contentious, and critics continue to question how it is applied. Some small businesses have complained that it forces them to make unreasonably costly renovations, such as installing wheelchair ramps, to avoid being sued. Restaurateurs also initially worried that the law would force them to keep workers with contagious diseases in food-handling jobs. However, the law includes language allowing exemptions for individuals who pose a direct threat to the health and safety of others.

A person who receives reasonable accommodations under ADA may still file for SOCIAL SECURITY disability benefits. The Social Security system determines eligibility based on presumptions about whether certain physical conditions limit a person's ability to work, not whether an employer has taken reasonable steps to help the individual. Social Security also recognizes that a disability can worsen over time, eventually rendering a person incapable of holding a job.

Annuity

An annuity is a hybrid insurance contract and retirement investment that can offer attractive returns and the ability to defer taxes on investment income. Marketed as an alternative to 401(K) PLANS or IRAS, annuities have surged in popularity in the 1990s, with annual sales now in excess of $100 billion. But some financial experts dislike the products because fees typically are higher than for some other investments, and because there are "surrender charges" if an investor withdraws money before age 59 1/2.

The annuity essentially is a contract with an insurance company. There are two major types. A fixed-rate annuity guarantees a stated return over time on the principal that is invested, meaning the insurance company assumes the investment risk. The more popular variable-rate annuity invests the principal in mutual funds or similar instruments and shelters any gains from taxes until the investor begins withdrawing the money. At that point, the withdrawal is taxed at normal income tax rates—not the lower capital-gains tax rates one pays on investments in stocks or mutual funds. Investors face the possibility of losing the principal they placed in a variable-rate annuity if they make the wrong investment decisions. But over the life of the annuity they have the flexibility of reallocating the money within different funds without having to pay taxes. They also can restructure the annuity into a death benefit, meaning their heirs, at a minimum, will be able to collect the original amount invested without having to go through the probate process.

The giant university teachers' pension fund TIAA-CREF pioneered variable-rate annuities in 1952 but only sold the products to educators and employees of nonprofit research institutions due to a longtime congressional tax exemption. After investment firms and insurers complained that TIAA-CREF enjoyed an unfair advantage over insurers and investment companies, Congress in 1997 lifted the exemption. Since then, TIAA-CREF has begun selling some of its annuity products to the general public. However, direct sales of

annuities lagged in the late 1990s because investors flocked to mutual funds or individual stocks, whose values soared with the strong stock market. A plan by Hartford Life and Pacific Life to market annuities to members of AARP was halted in 1999 because of low sales.

Antioxidants

Antioxidants are a class of compounds that have been heavily marketed as nutritional supplements to fight HEART DISEASE, CANCER, DIABETES, ALZHEIMER'S DISEASE, and various other age-related ailments. Examples include vitamin E, vitamin C, beta carotene, MELATONIN, green tea, and selenium. While some, like vitamin E, have been shown to reduce heart disease in some studies, the products generally have not been tested sufficiently in humans to prove they actually fight disease.

Antioxidants work by eliminating so-called FREE RADICALS—oxygen molecules that are missing an electron and, as a result, are in a highly reactive state because electrons prefer to exist in pairs. To gain an additional electron, the free radicals attack the body's cells. Free radicals are a byproduct of the body's normal metabolization of proteins, fats, and carbohydrates. The body produces its own antioxidants that usually keep free radicals in check. However, cells that are weakened by the aging process are more vulnerable to free radical attacks. Additionally, smoking, alcohol consumption, eating excessive amounts of fat, and overexposure to the sun are believed to release more free radicals.

Antioxidants are frequently mentioned in conjunction with hardening of the arteries and heart disease because when free radicals attack low-

Antioxidants are popular nutritional supplements, but their effectiveness in fighting disease has not yet been confirmed. Source: File photo

density lipoprotein, the body responds by creating plaques inside blood vessels, a key factor behind clogged arteries. However, health professionals advise against putting too much faith in these products, saying it may be more advisable to take steps like adopting a lower-fat diet.

Arthritis

"Arthritis" is a general term referring to more than a hundred rheumatic diseases that cause inflammation and pain in the body's joints. The most common forms in elderly people are os-

TEOARTHRITIS, rheumatoid arthritis, and gout. More than 40 million Americans suffer from some form of arthritis, and the U.S. Centers for Disease Control and Prevention estimates the number affected will rise to 59.4 million, or about one in five, by 2020, as a result of the number of aging BABY BOOMERS.

Arthritis is possibly the most prevalent chronic disease affecting older Americans, preventing many from doing daily tasks, exercising, and, if the pain is especially intense, sleeping and getting out of bed. It is especially debilitating because it tends to attack weight-bearing joints, such as the knees and hips. Public health officials estimate the conditions collectively account for more than

$100 billion of medical costs annually but don't completely understand the biological roots of the diseases. General characteristics include inflammation of the tissue that lines the joints, swollen ligaments and tendons, muscle strain, and general fatigue. The degree of pain varies greatly depending on the amount of swelling, whether there is existing damage to the joint, and the individual's personal pain tolerance.

Arthritic conditions are usually treated by rheumatologists or orthopedic surgeons, as well as physical therapists. Osteoarthritis, the most common form of arthritis, is usually treated with acetaminophen (Tylenol) or other pain relievers. Rheumatoid arthritis is the most disabling form of the disease and affects women about three times more often than men. It is believed to be caused by a breakdown in the body's immune system and is characterized by more intense swelling than osteoarthritis. The condition is treated with anti-inflammatory drugs such as Motrin or Advil, or by more powerful corticosteroids administered orally or by injection. Other medical treatments include electrical nerve stimulation, heat and cold therapy, therapeutic massage, and splints or braces that are used to rest or protect affected joints. In extreme cases, doctors can operate to realign joints or replace damaged joints with artificial ones.

In recent years, many creams, lotions, dietary supplements, and unproven remedies such as copper bracelets have been aggressively marketed at sufferers. The NATIONAL INSTITUTE ON AGING warns that, because arthritis symptoms may go away by themselves only to return weeks or months later, people with arthritis may be quick to try such cures instead of seeking medical help. Some treatments may, indeed, be harmless and help patients cope with the chronic pain arising from their conditions. However, health professionals say there is no research showing such alternative therapies help, and some may prove dangerous.

The federal arthritis research effort is centered around the National Institute on Aging and the National Institute of Arthritis and Musculoskeletal and Skin Diseases (NIAMS), both part of the NATIONAL INSTITUTES OF HEALTH in Bethesda, Maryland. Congressional funding for NIAMS rose steadily through the 1990s and stood at $309.9 million in fiscal 2000. Additionally, various members of Congress have sought to amend the Public Health Service Act of 1944 and increase funding for specific arthritic conditions. Rep. Carrie Meek, D-Fla., has pressed for increased funding to study lupus, which has been observed to hit a disproportionately large number of African Americans, while Sen. Ron Wyden, D-Ore., has similarly championed efforts to study pain management. But because arthritis is nonfatal, funding for arthritis research lags far behind sums earmarked for major killers, such as HEART DISEASE, CANCER, and HIV/AIDS.

Federally funded researchers are focusing on investigating possible gene-based causes of arthritis, understanding how the disease progresses, and developing new diagnostics and therapies. Some recent NIAMS studies suggest that several compounds known as neuropeptides, produced by cells in the nervous system, are found at elevated levels in arthritic joints. One neuropeptide called "substance P" is being studied in the spines of animals with chronic arthritis to determine whether it can be used to develop drugs for chronic pain. Researchers also are examining how injuries to one joint can affect other joints, as well as analyzing the effects of pain and pain relievers on walking.

The Centers for Disease Control separately participates in a public-private partnership called the National Arthritis Action Plan to increase

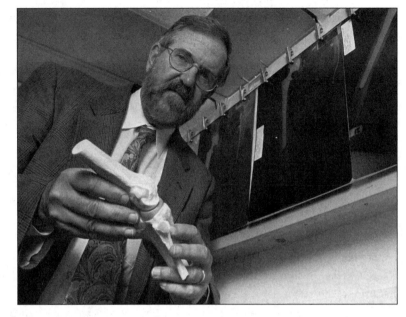

Orthopedic surgeon David S. Hungerford, head of arthritis surgery at Johns Hopkins University, poses in front of an X-ray light table holding a model of a knee joint. In extreme cases, doctors can operate to realign joints or replace damaged joints with artificial ones. Source: Gail Burton, AP Photo

public awareness of the disease and better characterize and treat its symptoms. The major private advocacy group devoted to arthritis is the Atlanta-based Arthritis Foundation, which has local chapters and publishes a monthly magazine on the disease.

Asset dumping

Asset dumping is one example of "spending down" one's savings and refers specifically to individuals who have assets and must divest them in order to qualify for MEDICAID and its LONG-TERM CARE benefits. This dramatic step became increasingly prevalent in the 1990s as average out-of-pocket costs for NURSING HOMES rose above $40,000 per year and MEDICARE payments for long-term care remained low because the national health program for the elderly primarily focuses on acute care. Asset dumping has caused concern

for policymakers because it has made Medicaid a de facto safety net for middle- and upper-income individuals. Some politicians contend Medicaid's core mission is being thwarted by wealthy individuals, who, in some instances, carefully transfer homes, cars, and other possessions to their heirs as they become disabled so they can fall below a state's Medicaid poverty line.

State agencies that administer Medicaid have thirty-six-month reviews of asset transfers to guard against fraud, but cases still slip through the cracks. Congress tried to discourage asset dumping in the Health Insurance and Portability Act of 1996 by criminalizing instances where people "knowingly and willfully" dispose of assets with imposing fines of up to $10,000 or one year in prison. Uncertainty over how aggressively to enforce the law led to changes in the BALANCED BUDGET ACT OF 1997 that removed legal sanctions against individuals but instead punished lawyers or financial advisors who urged clients to spend down their assets. Some have criticized the revisions as a "gag rule" on these professionals.

Many elderly people unwillingly deplete their assets on long-term care. Varying estimates show between one in four and one in five individuals who enter nursing homes as private payers have to convert to Medicaid before they are discharged. One possible option is to purchase long-term care insurance from private insurers to finance future health-care costs, but such policies are expensive and provide only a partial solution to the nation's lack of a coherent LONG-TERM CARE system.

Assisted living

"Assisted living" is a general term the definition of which varies widely from state to state. It can most accurately be described as a level of care for elderly people that falls somewhere between independent living and a NURSING HOME. The National Center for Assisted Living, a branch of the American Health Care Association, describes the "typical" assisted-living resident as an eighty-three-year-old woman who is capable of getting around but who needs assistance with one or two ACTIVITIES OF DAILY LIVING. Federal and private estimates indicate there are approximately 1.15 million people living in assisted living residences, 74 percent of whom are women. The facilities are referred to by a variety of names, including CONGREGATE HOUSING and retirement homes.

Assisted living residences aren't regulated by the federal government, but are usually licensed by states and subject to state and local laws. Services provided at the facilities aren't covered by MEDICARE. However, some states choose to pay for the services under MEDICAID, and certain costs are covered by SUPPLEMENTAL SECURITY INCOME (SSI) and SOCIAL SERVICES BLOCK GRANTS.

Assisted living facilities have become an increasingly popular alternative to more institutionalized settings, such as nursing homes, since emerging in the United States in the mid-1980s. Based on an elder-care model popular in Scandinavia, they feature congregate housing with private or semi-private rooms and a twenty-four-hour staff with nurses. The facilities usually have congregate dining halls, religious chapels, and recreational facilities. Some are located near SKILLED NURSING FACILITIES or hospitals. Doctors, dietitians, physical therapists, and podiatrists are under contract to the facilities, make regular visits, and remain on call. The environment is designed to accommodate individual needs as much as possible, meaning that visiting hours are flexible and residents are allowed to keep pets. The facilities vary in size from fewer than a dozen residents to more than one hundred and tend to charge between $1,000 and $3,000 per month in rent and fees. Generally, they are too expensive for most middle-income elders.

Policymakers increasingly have recognized the value of assisted living as an alternative to nursing homes but also have had to grapple with problems of balancing between protecting the personal safety of the more frail residents and protecting their privacy. One potential solution is the CONTINUING-CARE RETIREMENT COMMUNITY (CCRC), which provides multiple levels of care and different housing options in the same location. This could allow a person with increasingly acute health problems to receive the treatment he or she needs without having to be moved to a more institutional setting.

Because of variations in the levels of care provided, senior advocates suggest carefully assessing needs, legal documents, and costs before entering into any assisted living arrangements. Among the issues of special importance are whether the facility's contractual agreement discloses all healthcare and supportive services, in addition to admission and discharge provisions. Facilities also should be willing to disclose whether they have a process for assessing the need for services, and whether they draft a written plan for care for each resident.

Australian private pension plans

Australia's old-age pension system has been held up as a model by advocates of privatizing the American SOCIAL SECURITY system. The Australian system, implemented between 1986 and 1992 by the center-left Labor government, is notable because it forces workers to set aside a portion of their income in "superannuation funds," which they then draw on when they retire. The mandated contribution is currently 8 percent of income and will rise to 9 percent when the program is fully phased in, in 2002. Already, this form of mandatory savings is credited with increasing the overall national savings rate and providing retirees with more income. It also relieved financial stresses on the country's old Social Security system, which still provides taxpayer-financed pensions to some citizens.

However, it remains unclear whether the system is helping people save enough for retirement. Although projections made in 2000 by the Reserve Bank of Australia indicated that the pension system would improve the country's savings, nationwide private savings have not reflected the increase in compulsory contributions to the superannuation funds of the pension system. There could be several reasons: leakage of savings due to early retirement, generally less voluntary saving, or the fact that capital gains are not included in measurements of savings. For whatever reasons, overall savings remain roughly where average levels were in the 1980s. In addition, numerous rules changes and a complex taxation scheme for superannuation funds may be cooling public attitudes in Australia to the system. The Australian system remains a favorite case study for politically conservative reform advocates in the United States, in part because it relies on mandated savings, not expanding government programs.

Average Indexed Monthly Earnings (AIME)

Average Indexed Monthly Earnings (AIME) is a calculation that is used to determine a person's SOCIAL SECURITY retirement benefits. It reflects the past earnings on which a person paid Social Security taxes, indexed for inflation. For workers born after 1929, the AIME reflects the thirty-five years (not necessarily consecutive) in which a person's wages were highest. The wages are indexed to changes in wage levels, added up, then divided by 420 months, with the result being the AIME. The figure is then used in a formula to determine the Primary Insurance Amount, the basic Social Security benefit a person receives at full retirement age, usually age sixty-five. The inflation factor used in the indexing is adjusted annually by the SOCIAL SECURITY ADMINISTRATION.

B

Baby boomers

The term "baby boomers" refers to the group of Americans born between 1946 and 1964. Products of the unprecedented population growth that followed World War II, baby boomers today are frequently the focus of policy discussions about the long-term financial health of federal programs for the elderly, especially MEDICARE and SOCIAL SECURITY. Advocates of entitlement reform say the prospect of anywhere from 64 million to 69 million baby boomers retiring early in this century will put severe financial stresses on the programs, because the government will be forced to pay out more in benefits than it takes in from payroll taxes and interest income. However, many respected observers contend the reform advocates are manufacturing a false crisis atmosphere, and that the worker-to-beneficiary ratio will be no worse than it was in the 1960s and 1970s. Additionally, sustained economic growth has brightened the outlook for the Social Security TRUST FUNDS; the Medicare HOSPITAL INSURANCE trust fund is now projected to pay benefits until 2025, while the Social Security trust funds are expected to be adequately financed until at least 2037.

The baby boomer generation was no DEMOGRAPHIC accident. American men returned home from war to find a prosperous economy, numerous well-paying jobs, and new housing opportunities in cities and suburbs. As a result, millions started new families. U.S. Census Bureau figures show the number of marriages in the United States doubled from 1945 to 1946, to more than 2.2 million, and the number of babies born in 1946 increased 20 percent, to 3.4 million. In 1954, the number of births in a single year exceeded 4 million for the first time in American history, and the figure continued to rise through the early 1960s.

Because they grew up in generally prosperous times and faced fewer hardships than their parents, baby boomers are often depicted as pampered and profligate, with greater freedom to indulge themselves and pioneer new social trends. They are credited with—or alternately blamed for—the student protests of the 1960s, the sexual revolution, the surge in consumer spending in the 1970s and 1980s, an increased focus on physical fitness and lately the use of antiaging remedies and so-called lifestyle drugs such as VIAGRA. Having reaped the benefits of the long-running postwar economic expansion, baby boomers are sometimes characterized as self-centered, or ill equipped to make the sacrifices the previous generation encountered during the Great Depression and World War II. Some social commentators contend baby boomers also have different attitudes about aging than their parents have, tending not to accept old age with grace or resignation, but instead trying to fight the clock and redefine their concept of mortality.

The truth may not entirely fit this picture. First, the nineteen-year span attributed to baby boomers is considered somewhat long by demog-

A family watches the Rolling Stones in concert at Soldier Field in Chicago. In a rare event with all age groups sharing the same interest, Baby Boomers, Generations Xers, and elementary schoolers help cheer the popular band.
Source: Beth A. Kaiser, AP Photo

raphers. Studies have shown attitudinal break-downs and behavioral differences that suggest "younger" and "older" boomers save differently and have different philosophies about life. In short, this demographic group may be difficult to depict in broad brush strokes. Second, in the boom economy at the millennium, government economic forecasting considers much of what is not counted as savings—such as stock invest-ments—as spending, giving a somewhat skewed picture of boomers' apparent lack of frugality.

These concerns notwithstanding, baby boomers' apparent affluence and large numbers make them one of the most courted consumer segments in American society, as evidenced by the profusion of "oldies" radio stations, new varieties of retirement plans, and commercials touting high-priced cars, cruises, and real estate. Nine-teen-ninety Census surveys of baby boomers then aged twenty-six to forty-four showed a large ma-jority (76.1 percent) lived in or near cities and nearly 85 percent had at least a high-school diploma. Their median household income in 1989 stood at $34,601.

But strength in numbers may not necessarily ensure that boomers are financially secure in their retirements. Increased life expectancies arising from medical breakthroughs and an increased focus on healthy living mean baby boomers likely will live longer and spend more of their lives in retirement. Faced with the possibility of reduced payments from government programs, boomers will have to stash more money in retirement savings to make ends meet. To further complicate matters, baby boomers' assets, particularly real estate, aren't expected to appreciate as quickly as their parents', because demand won't be as great.

Recent surveys of baby boomers suggest they are aware of the potential problems. Many plan to keep working part-time after they retire, both to remain active and to help make ends meet. Other studies show that while a significant number of boomers are investing in retirement plans like IRAS, many are not feeling secure about the golden years and do not think Social Security will continue to survive in its present form. The national political debate will increasingly be characterized by appeals to baby boomers' concerns about income security. Both Republicans and Democrats have offered proposals for LONG-TERM CARE, to alleviate stresses on baby boomers faced with caring for aging parents. The Clinton administration and the Republican Congress repeatedly sparred over how to best preserve current Social Security surpluses, after President Bill Clinton in his 1998 State of the Union address called on lawmakers to "save Social Security first." But lawmakers so far haven't come to a consensus on whether to allow individuals to invest part of the Social Security payroll tax in private accounts,

mindful that the majority of older baby boomers oppose the idea. The White House and Congress in early 2000 did agree to scrap Social Security's earnings limit—a move that will allow baby boomers between the ages of sixty-five and seventy the freedom to make as much income as they want without having to sacrifice any Social Security benefits.

Balanced Budget Act of 1997

The Balanced Budget Act of 1997 (BBA) is one of a series of congressional budget-reconciliation bills that were designed to make permanently authorized programs like MEDICARE and MEDICAID conform with annual budget resolutions. The 1997 act was especially notable because it was the first to operate under the assumption of a balanced federal budget, meaning spending and savings on the programs had to cancel each other out.

The result was a series of dramatic changes to health-care programs affecting the elderly. Medicare was targeted for an unparalleled $115 billion in cuts over five years. In addition, lawmakers ordered the HEALTH CARE FINANCING ADMINISTRATION, which runs the program, to make significant changes to the way it pays for HOME HEALTH CARE, NURSING HOME care, and hospital OUTPATIENT SERVICES. It also created a new program called MEDICARE . CHOICE that was designed to entice Medicare beneficiaries to join managed-care plans. Changes to Medicaid included reduced payments to hospitals that treat a disproportionate number of low-income and uninsured patients and new rules that made it easier for

House Speaker Newt Gingrich announces the Republican budget plan in Washington on May 2, 1997, as fellow GOP lawmakers look on. Efforts to make permanently authorized programs like Medicare conform with budget resolutions brought sweeping changes to programs affecting the elderly.
Source: Joe Marquette, AP Photo

states to move Medicaid beneficiaries into managed care.

The changes prompted howls of protest from health-care providers, who complained the cuts went deeper than lawmakers anticipated. Because studies showed Medicare spending was lower than expected, Congress in 1999 restored $16 billion of the cuts over five years in a "givebacks" package that especially helped hospitals, nursing homes, managed-care plans, and home health agencies. Home health agencies won a temporary reprieve from a 15 percent cut in payments that was due to go into effect in October 2000. The relief package also temporarily raised the reimbursements that SKILLED NURSING FACILITIES receive for fifteen categories of high-cost patients. Price caps that limited the cost of physical, speech, and occupational therapy were also lifted. The relief package did not address more fundamental problems associated with Medicare as a whole, which some say faces insolvency by about 2015.

Ball, Robert

Robert Ball served as commissioner of SOCIAL SECURITY from 1962 to 1973 and in recent years has been a staunch defender of the government's pension system in the face of increased calls to overhaul or "privatize" it. Like other public policy experts, Ball has grappled with ways to increase funding for the system without making significant changes to its structure or putting beneficiaries at financial risk.

Ball's solution would be to have the government invest about 40 percent of the money in the Social Security TRUST FUNDS in stocks, 30 percent in corporate bonds, and the rest in government debt. Currently the entire trust fund is invested in government debt. The proposal is modeled on the way PRIVATE PENSION funds invest and would take advantage of surging financial markets to earn higher returns on Social Security's reserves. In contrast to many conservative economists and policy analysts, Ball maintains there is no financial crisis in Social Security, but that the system needs adjustments.

Ball's plan would make the U.S. government the world's largest investor—a situation that is problematic to some observers, who believe stock and bond prices could fluctuate every time government investment managers decide to buy or sell some holdings.

Benefits

Benefits, within the context of federal entitlements, are generally understood to refer to the payments that government ENTITLEMENT PROGRAMS like SOCIAL SECURITY, MEDICARE, and MEDICAID distribute to individuals who meet the programs' eligibility requirements. Recipients are legally entitled to these payments and can sue if they are denied.

In the case of Social Security, benefits are based on the average earnings over most of a worker's lifetime, indexed for inflation. The amount varies, depending on whether a worker chooses early retirement or decides to work beyond the legal retirement age. Individuals can begin collecting reduced benefits as early as age sixty-two.

Medicare, the federal health program for the elderly, pays benefits for what it defines as "medically necessary care" for individuals sixty-five and older. A key distinction is that Medicare benefits currently don't cover outpatient prescription drugs, dental, vision, or hearing care, as well as most forms of LONG-TERM CARE unless there is a concurrent acute medical condition. Medicare benefits were expanded under the 1997 BALANCED BUDGET ACT to cover more preventive services, such as Pap smears, mammograms, and prostate cancer screening. But beneficiaries still pay a significant portion of their medical bills out of pocket.

Medicaid, a jointly administered federal-state program for the poor, distributes more than 60 percent of its benefits to elderly and disabled people, even though they make up just more than one-quarter of its recipients. That is because most elderly beneficiaries tend to require long-term care services that are more expensive than the primary care targeted at younger individuals.

Bipartisan Medicare reform

Faced with projections that the MEDICARE Part A TRUST FUND would be insolvent as early as 2008, federal lawmakers in August 1997 created a seventeen-member National Bipartisan Commission on the Future of Medicare to solve the long-term financial problems surrounding this health-care program for the elderly. Commission members appointed by the Clinton administration and Democratic and Republican congressional leaders were supposed to issue recommendations to Congress, eliminating some of the political unpleasantness of overhauling one of America's cornerstone social programs. However, the panel fell one vote short of producing the supermajority of eleven votes needed to formally approve the recommendations, and went out of business in March 1999.

The bipartisan commission was chaired by Sen. John B. Breaux, D-La., and Rep. Bill Thomas, R-Calif. Its most-remembered recommendation was that Medicare halt its practice of setting prices for medical services and reimbursing doctors and health-care providers. Instead, Breaux

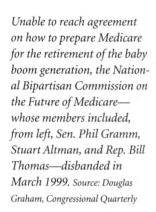

Unable to reach agreement on how to prepare Medicare for the retirement of the baby boom generation, the National Bipartisan Commission on the Future of Medicare—whose members included, from left, Sen. Phil Gramm, Stuart Altman, and Rep. Bill Thomas—disbanded in March 1999. Source: Douglas Graham, Congressional Quarterly

and Thomas proposed an approach that came to be known as "premium support," in which the government would give Medicare recipients a fixed amount of money that they could then spend on health insurance from competing private plans or the government. The reasoning was beneficiaries would save money because they would be more sensitive to prices and the scope of coverage. However, many Democrats insisted that any restructured Medicare program provide PRE-SCRIPTION DRUG BENEFITS to the elderly—a demand Republicans rejected, saying it wouldn't save any money. Former HEALTH CARE FINANCING ADMINISTRATION director Bruce C. Vladeck, one of seven panel members who voted against the recommendations, delivered blistering criticism of premium support as little more than an insurance-industry subsidy that would leave many low-income elders unable to cover their costs.

The failure of the commission prompted political recriminations, with Democrats accusing Re-

publicans of jeopardizing seniors' well-being, and the GOP responding that Democrats were unwilling to reform an inefficient government bureaucracy. Some lawmakers were particularly critical of President Bill Clinton, who refused to broker a last-minute deal and instead appeared less than an hour before the panel met for its pivotal final vote, saying he disapproved of its recommendations. Analysts of both political stripes generally agree that the commission succeeded in elevating the place of Medicare's financial problems in the national political debate, and in focusing on the controversial issue of prescription drug prices. It also took up more detailed health-care issues, such as whether Medicare reimbursements should be based on regional rather than national health-care costs.

Bismarck, Otto von

Germany's "Iron Chancellor," Otto von Bismarck, established the first SOCIAL SECURITY system in 1889, in part to ease the financial pain of unemployment in his rapidly industrializing nation. Many historians suggest the move was less out of compassion for displaced workers than to blunt Social Democratic critics of his military buildup. Whatever the reason, and despite his right-wing politics, Bismarck for years was labeled a socialist for introducing the program.

The German system was mandatory and collected contributions from workers, employers, and the government. It paid out retirement and disability benefits, which, combined with already existing workers' compensation and national health insurance, provided a comprehensive safety net. Germany added unemployment insurance to complete its income security system in 1927. The system was copied in European and South American nations in the late nineteenth and early twentieth centuries, but was at first viewed suspiciously in the United States, where many clung to Jeffersonian philosophies of self-reliance and minimal government.

The German system was to provide a model for U.S. policy planners in the administration of FRANKLIN D. ROOSEVELT, who were given the responsibility of designing the American social security system in the wake of the Great Depression. However, it contributed to a myth concerning the selection of age sixty-five as the retirement age. Some believe the milestone was selected because that was Bismarck's age when the program was implemented—and that American policy planners simply followed suit. In fact, the SOCIAL SECURITY ADMINISTRATION notes, Germany ini-

Otto von Bismarck, Germany's "Iron Chancellor," established the world's first social security system in 1889.
Source: Corbis/Bettmann

tially set its retirement age at seventy (Bismarck was seventy-four at the time), and lowered the age to sixty-five in 1916, when Bismarck had already been dead for eighteen years.

Bureau of Labor Statistics

The Bureau of Labor Statistics is a branch of the U.S. Department of LABOR that is responsible for tracking key economic indicators, including unemployment, consumer prices, productivity, and health-care spending. The bureau's oft-cited CONSUMER PRICE INDEX is used to calculate SOCIAL SECURITY benefits, as well as the annual COST-OF-LIVING ADJUSTMENTS in the payments retirees receive.

The bureau's ability to track the number of people employed or looking for work has yielded intriguing insights into the work habits of older Americans, particularly as they relate to trends such as EARLY RETIREMENT. Bureau studies show that, in 1955, 45 percent of all men aged sixty-five and older were still in the work force. Today, more than two-thirds drop out of the work force before they reach sixty-five. The bureau says its surveys show that, for both men and women, participation in the labor force begins declining rapidly after age fifty-four. Reasons for this trend include the availability of Social Security benefits beginning at age sixty-two and tax laws that can penalize some Social Security recipients if they continue to draw salaries.

Butler, Robert N.

Few health professionals have had a greater impact on the field of geriatric care than Dr. Robert N. Butler, founder of the International Longevity Center—which operates under the auspices of Mount Sinai Medical Center in New York City—and winner of the 1976 Pulitzer Prize for nonfiction for his book *Why Survive? Being Old in America*. A leading advocate of increased federal research spending on aging, Butler is widely credited with helping establish that senility is a consequence of disease, not simply a by-product of aging, and for being one of the first to tar-

get ALZHEIMER'S DISEASE as a national research priority. He also coined the term "AGEISM" to describe pervasive social bias against older people.

Butler was the founding director of the NATIONAL INSTITUTE ON AGING at the NATIONAL INSTITUTES OF HEALTH in Bethesda, Maryland, and later became the director of the first GERIATRICS department at a U.S. medical school, at Mount Sinai. His work with the longevity center, which he founded in 1990, has centered on the effects of increased life expectancy on social institutions. Butler argues that elderly people are an underutilized work force and mistakenly and unfairly depicted as an economic drain on the U.S. social safety net and its ENTITLEMENT system. He also has spoken out against assisted SUICIDE, called for improved HOSPICE care and for better training of young physicians, who may not be equipped to deal with pain relief and other special needs of older patients.

Buy-in (Medicare)

The phrase "buy-in" is often used in connection with a proposal to allow workers as young as fifty-five to buy into the federal MEDICARE program, which now provides health coverage to Americans aged sixty-five and older. The proposal originated in the Clinton administration and has been taken up mostly by Democratic politicians as a remedy to reduce the number of uninsured Americans.

The proposal is aimed at baby boomers near the end of their working careers who fall into a demographic "Catch 22" because they are too young for Medicare but have trouble obtaining private health coverage because they may have preexisting medical conditions. Indeed, studies show fifty-five- to sixty-four-year-olds are the fastest-growing segment of the approximately 44 million uninsured Americans. Because buy-in premiums would cost between $300 to $400 per month, they only would provide coverage for the approximately 300,000 of these individuals who could afford the option. However, the premiums still would be preferable to buying private individual health coverage, which can cost older workers as much as $1,000 per month, if they qualify. Various legislative proposals take different approaches to buy-ins. Some would allow people in their early sixties to pay an up-front base premium to join Medicare, then pay another premium when they turn sixty-five as a kind of add-on to their Medicare Part B premium. The same option would apply to individuals over age fifty-five who are laid off or otherwise displaced from their jobs. Other proposals would allow early retirees aged fifty-five and older to buy into their former employer's health plan.

The buy-in concept has been criticized by Republicans in Congress, who contend it would cost billions or dollars and intensify financial pressures on the already strapped Medicare TRUST FUND. Some policy experts sympathetic to the idea of helping the uninsured say a better idea may be allowing them to buy into the Federal Employees Health Benefit Program, the health program for government workers that is on more solid financial footing. However, defenders of buy-ins say the proposal wouldn't threaten the Medicare TRUST FUND because those exercising the option would be paying for the coverage out of their own pockets, and because anti-fraud provisions are making the program work more efficiently. These defenders say Republicans are using the trust fund as a straw man because they don't want to provide health care to millions of people who need it.

Buy-outs

See LUMP-SUM BUYOUTS.

C

Cancer

"Cancer" is a general term referring to dozens of diseases that share the characteristic of uncontrolled cell growth and require a combination of therapies. The most lethal killers are lung, PROSTATE, breast, and colon/rectum cancer. Each year, approximately 1.2 million Americans are diagnosed with cancer, and studies show individuals over the age of fifty are at particular risk for some varieties. However, despite federal expenditures of more than $30 billion on cancer research since the early 1970s, scientists are only beginning to understand how the diseases progress. Most cancers, in fact, remain almost as incurable as they were in 1971, when President Richard M. Nixon proclaimed war on the disease. More than 563,000 Americans die of cancer each year, according to public health experts.

Cancers are caused by changes to genes that control cell behavior and growth. Older people may be at particular risk because the aging process weakens the cell's internal repair mechanisms. Elderly people also may suffer from the years-long cumulative effects of external factors—smoking, exposure to ultraviolet light, or a diet heavy in fats—that can trigger gene-based responses that give rise to cancer. The key to controlling cancer is early detection, which is accomplished through screening. MEDICARE in 1998 began paying for annual mammograms, or x-rays of the breast, to detect breast cancer, as well as screening for colorectal cancer. Medicare also covers pelvic examinations and Pap smears once every three years for women with an average risk of contracting cervical cancer, and annual screening for women with higher risk. For prostate cancer, Medicare covers an annual screening that may include a digital rectal exam or a PSA (prostate-specific antigen) test. High PSA levels in the blood could be a sign of cancer, or of an enlarged prostate, which is common in men over the age of fifty. However, evidence suggests few elderly Americans are taking advantage of some of these preventive services. The U.S. General Accounting Office reported that only 14 percent of Americans over age sixty-five got one of four varieties of colon cancer tests through Medicare in 1999, either because they don't know Medicare covers the tests, they are embarrassed to ask, or are afraid the tests will be uncomfortable.

Researchers now are using their new knowledge of cancer cells to devise therapies intended to mend faulty genes or introduce new genes that make cancer cells sensitive to drugs. Some novel "immunotherapies" can home in on particular molecules on cancer cells that are believed to promote tumor growth, and attract immune cells that can kill the cancer cells. One such targeted molecule is the Her2 protein on prostate cancer cells that, in some cases, has been shown to promote the spread of the disease. But lawmakers are divided over how much access patients should have to experimental treatments. Medicare in

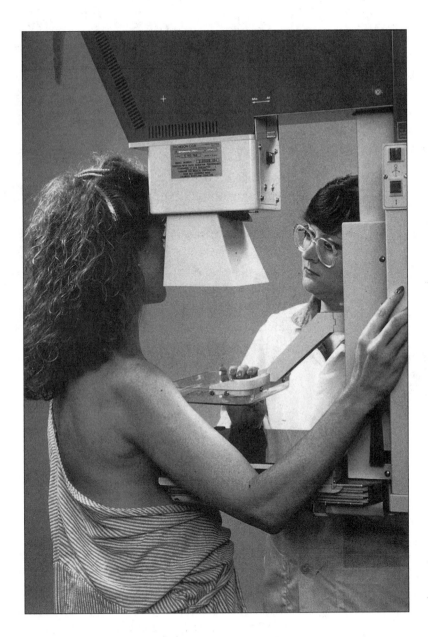

In 1998 Medicare began paying for annual mammograms for women. Source: National Cancer Institute

1998 began paying for some experimental cancer treatments for seniors, under a three-year pilot program that restricts seniors to clinical trials sponsored by the NATIONAL INSTITUTES OF HEALTH. But some lawmakers, such as Sen. Edward M. Kennedy, D-Mass., want to force man-

aged-care companies to provide access to more treatments. Managed-care companies say they shouldn't have to cover some experimental treatments because they almost always are more expensive than conventional treatments and may be harmful, or of no particular value, to the patient.

Some have suggested that drug companies running the clinical trials should cover the disputed costs. But oncologists and cancer-research advocates say the onus should be on health insurers, who they contend are denying coverage for high-quality therapy in clinical studies.

Cancer remains the nation's most publicly funded affliction, in part due to personal crusades by some influential members of Congress. Former senator Connie Mack, R-Fla., a victim of melanoma whose brother died of the disease and whose wife and daughter struggled with cancer, has been instrumental in earmarking funds for research. Another lawmaker with a personal connection to the disease is SENATE APPROPRIATIONS COMMITTEE chairman Ted Stevens, R-Alaska, a prostate cancer survivor whose committee controls discretionary spending in the federal budget. Proposed funding for the National Cancer Institute totaled $2.97 billion in fiscal 2000, compared to $2.9 billion in 1999.

As the population ages, researchers are noticing new trends in cancer incidence and death rates. Stomach cancer, once a leading killer, declined about 40 percent from the early 1970s to the early 1990s and continues to be on the wane because diets are healthier. Lung-cancer deaths have skyrocketed in women, largely because more women smoke. Prostate-cancer deaths in men have declined more than 20 percent since the early 1970s, in part because of increased and improved screening techniques. Despite some encouraging signs, the National Cancer Institute projects that, by the middle of the decade, cancer will have passed heart disease as the nation's No. 1 killer, both because of the rise in new cancer cases and because of declining mortality levels from heart disease.

Caregiver

A caregiver usually is defined as someone who provides unpaid care to an elderly person who can no longer perform some ACTIVITIES OF DAILY LIVING (sometimes the term also is used to refer to paid home-care aides and similar health professionals). The role of the unpaid caregiver in American society has come under increased scrutiny, as politicians and public policy experts ponder the effects of ALZHEIMER'S DISEASE and other chronic health conditions. Some lawmakers have suggested that caregivers receive tax credits, free RESPITE CARE, or other forms of compensation. The federal MEDICARE program does not pay for the services a caregiver provides, viewing them as custodial care except if there is an underlying acute medical condition, such as a STROKE or heart attack.

More often than not, the caregiver is a middle-aged offspring of the elderly person. A 1997 survey by AARP and the National Caregiving Alliance of Bethesda, Maryland, showed more than twenty-two million households have caregivers fifty years of age or older, and that about 73 percent of these are women. Various studies show a caregiver's annual cost of providing LONG-TERM CARE ranges from $4,000 to more than $10,000, depending on the elderly person's medical condition. Some caregivers exhaust most or all of their personal savings and are then forced to seek long-term care for their loved one under the federal-state MEDICAID program. Caregivers also have to deal with emotional and psychological burdens, such as watching an elderly parent's mental capacities decline, or deciding when the parent must be institutionalized. Another issue that distinguishes much of today's caregiving burden on

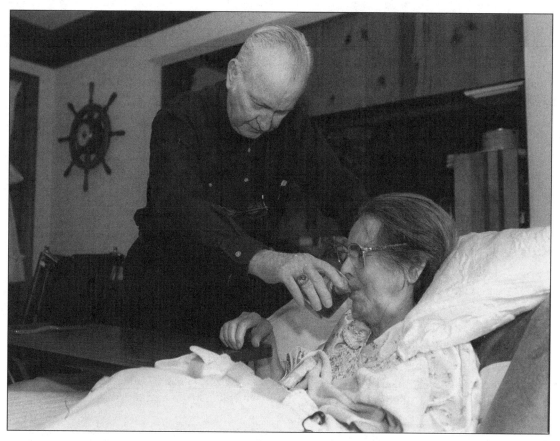

Caregivers are usually unpaid family members of the elderly person. Here a husband tends to his ailing wife.
Source: Scott J. Ferrell, Congressional Quarterly

families from traditional care at home in the past is the high-tech home care now in use, often requiring a family member to master techniques such as catheterization, ventilation, and tube-feeding.

There are steps caregivers can take to alleviate some financial stresses. The elderly person receiving care can be declared a dependent, which makes the caregiver eligible for a personal tax exemption. However, the older person's income must not exceed the personal exemption that can be taken on one's taxes—a regulation that elimi-

nates the benefit for many, because most older people receive SOCIAL SECURITY benefits.

The Health Insurance Portability and Accountability Act of 1996 (PL 104-191) allows certain long-term medical expenses to be deducted, if they total more than 7.5 percent of the caregiver's adjusted gross income. The FAMILY AND MEDICAL LEAVE ACT OF 1993 (PL 103-3) also allows caregivers who work for companies with more than fifty employees to take up to twelve weeks per year to care for an ill parent, though the law doesn't require the company to pay for the time off.

Carter, Jimmy

The former president and his wife, Rosalynn, are frequently praised by senior advocates for setting a combined personal example of a healthy, active retirement. When Jimmy Carter left office in 1981, at age fifty-six, he was one of the youngest ex-presidents. He soon founded the nonpartisan Carter Center in Atlanta, which advocates for human rights and improved health care around the world. Since then, Carter has traveled the world, monitoring elections, advocating to eradicate world hunger and prevent diseases, and helping negotiate international treaties. He has written fourteen books, including *Everything to Gain: Making the Most of the Rest of Your Life*, and the 1998 opus *The Virtues of Aging*, in which he outlined his energetic approach to the golden years, shared homey tales of teaching his grandchildren to fly fish, and even discussed the once-taboo subject of sex among elderly people.

Carter has described coping with the despair of losing the White House to RONALD REAGAN and confronting a potentially empty life. In a 2000 interview with the *New York Times*, the former president, a born-again Christian, described how he chose to apply his energy to helping the less fortunate, spending quality time with his family, and remaining engaged in public life. Carter is a distinguished professor at Emory University in Atlanta, where he lectures on political science and health issues. He also helps build homes for the charitable organization Habitat for Humanity and continues to play softball and tennis and jog. At age sixty-four, he climbed Mount Kilimanjaro. In 1999, the AMERICAN SOCIETY ON AGING awarded Carter its President's Award for being a champion of health and human rights.

Former president Jimmy Carter holds the Lions Humanitarian Award for outstanding humanitarian achievements. Carter has set a much-lauded example of healthy, active retirement. Source: *Paul Chiasson, AP Photo*

Cash-balance pension

The cash-balance pension is a controversial type of retirement plan that has attracted attention and comment because of the way it accrues BENEFITS. Critics contend cash-balance plans penalize older workers, because cash-balance retirement benefits accumulate in a more even fashion over a worker's career. By contrast, traditional pension plans' benefits build up faster in the later, highest-paying years on the job. Defenders of cash-balance plans say they more accurately reflect the changing nature of the workforce. Currently, employees switch jobs more frequently, and don't expect to spend their entire careers with one company. Women also may benefit under cash-balance plans because they aren't penalized as much for leaving the workforce to have children.

The plans essentially are a cross between a 401(k) and a traditional defined-benefit plan. Cash-balance plans promise a worker a specific payout, and workers who leave their jobs can roll the balance into an IRA (INDIVIDUAL RETIRE-MENT ACCOUNT), making the benefit "portable." As is the case with traditional pensions, employers make the contributions to the plan and are responsible for managing the investment. Cash-balance plans often promise returns similar to those of long-term Treasury bonds. If the plan doesn't meet its goal, the employer makes up the difference.

Employers' interest in the plans picked up in the early 1990s, after the federal government began penalizing cash-strapped companies that terminated pension plans so the firms could use surplus assets. Cash-balance plans legally allowed the companies to reduce their retirement obligations, because they fund a smaller benefit for older workers. But that doesn't sit well with older workers—especially when companies switch from traditional plans to cash-balance plans and don't give employees the option of sticking with their old plan. Workers in their fifties, who may be expecting the bulk of their benefits to accrue in their final years of employment—or who are planning to retire early—may lose out if they aren't informed. IBM Corporation was forced to backtrack on one such planned conversion in early 1999 after older workers mounted angry protests and the Communications Workers of America used the incident to try to organize the company's nonunion labor force. The EQUAL EMPLOYMENT OPPORTUNITY COMMISSION has received more

than a hundred complaints about cash-balance switchovers from older workers, and is weighing whether conversions may violate the Age Discrimination in Employment Act. Benefits consultants say about one-third of the companies that have converted to cash-balance plans have allowed workers to keep their old pension systems.

Though pension law only protects accrued benefits, and not those promised under existing plans, the INTERNAL REVENUE SERVICE—which oversees the financing of pension plans—has stopped approving conversions so it, too, can review older workers' complaints. If the complaints continue, some observers believe Congress could take such steps as penalizing companies that convert to cash-balance plans without informing their employees.

Census

The census is an important instrument in the federal government's allocation of formula grants for programs for elderly people. Senior advocates were particularly vocal about encouraging participation in Census 2000, noting that in recent decades fewer people have mailed back their census forms. That has resulted in underrepresentation of certain groups, particularly minority individuals. Advocates say this could result in less funding for bilingual programs or outreach efforts targeting diverse ethnic communities. The effects of undercounting can be amplified because states often match the amount of federal dollars that come in the form of grants.

The census factors particularly strongly in spending on so-called Title III programs under the OLDER AMERICANS ACT of 1965, including MEALS

For the 2000 census, the Census Bureau established committees to advise on the design of advertising materials designed for specific groups. This poster, tailored to young and elderly Americans of Asian descent, was approved by the full Race and Ethnic Advisory Committee. Source: U.S. Bureau of the Census

ON WHEELS and supportive services, such as in-home care and disease prevention. Census counts do not affect overall spending on the programs, just the share each state receives. For that reason, states with some of the fastest-growing populations of elderly individuals—California, Florida, Texas, New York, and Pennsylvania, for example—stand to lose the most from inaccurate counts.

Census 2000 also attempted to factor in new roles for elders in society. The Census 2000 long forms, mailed to one in six individuals, included a new category added for "grandparents as caregivers" to reflect the growing number of elderly people, particularly immigrants, who are called on to care for children while the parents work.

Certification

Certification, in the context of elder care, refers to the credentials of NURSING HOMES. All nursing homes need a state permit to operate. But in order to receive payments from the federal MEDICARE and MEDICAID programs, the facilities also must obtain certification confirming they have appropriate staff and suitable food and toilet facilities, and have made necessary steps to reduce the chance that residents become sick or get injured. The certification process is overseen by the HEALTH CARE FINANCING ADMINISTRATION, with state officials usually conducting the surveys.

General Augusto Pinochet installed the world's first privatized national pension system in Chile in 1981. Source: Santiago Llanquin, AP Photo

The certification process was defined by the Omnibus Budget Reconciliation Act of 1987 (see OMNIBUS RECONCILIATION BILL), which set new standards for LONG-TERM CARE facilities that receive federal Medicare and Medicaid payments. The act requires unannounced surveys every year on average, as well as follow-up checks if problems are found. The nursing homes also must submit to special surveys if complaints about care are lodged with the appropriate state or federal authorities. Most general surveys assess the mix of cases in a nursing home's residential population, the quality of care, written plans for care and assessments of residents, and the facility's compliance with patients' rights.

Chilean pension system

General Augusto Pinochet installed the world's first privatized national pension system in Chile in 1981, requiring individuals who entered the workforce after 1981 to automatically place at least 10 percent of their wages in individual retirement accounts invested in stocks, bonds, and other securities and not taxed until withdrawal. Workers have the option of shifting their money among about a dozen accounts. Older workers had the option of remaining in a traditional social security system. Those workers who switched from the old to the new system were given "recognition bonds" that credited past contributions and matured upon the workers' retirements.

The Chilean system was the brainchild of a group of American-educated economists, led by José Piñera. The system has been widely copied in nations such as Mexico, Peru, and Argentina, and hailed by advocates who favor privatizing the U.S. SOCIAL SECURITY system. The advocates point to the fact that the old Chilean PAY-AS-YOU-GO SYSTEM had high payroll taxes yet still operated in the red and paid benefits that were significantly below what workers could have earned by saving and investing on their own. Switching to a privatized system boosted the national savings rate and helped solidify the nation's capital markets—goals PRIVATIZATION advocates say can be accomplished in the United States if American workers are allowed to divert some payroll taxes to private retirement accounts.

Chile's retirement accounts had accumulated more than $30 billion by the late 1990s. But the pension system's track record was hindered by a recession in 1998 and 1999 brought on by weak prices for copper, a major Chilean export, and reduced trade with Asia. As Chile's stock market slumped, retirement funds tied to stock performance lost value. The experience pointed to the fundamental risk of tying pension savings to equity markets. In addition, the Chilean system required heavy public expenditures on transition costs from the start. Despite this, many experts believe Chile's innovations—like privatization experiments in other nations, such as Australia—may be cited in future discussions over whether to privatize Social Security in the U.S.

Chronic care

See ASSISTED LIVING; CAREGIVER; CONTINUING-CARE RETIREMENT COMMUNITY; HOSPICE; LONG-TERM CARE; NURSING HOME.

Cohen, Wilbur J.

Wilbur J. Cohen, a pioneering figure in U.S. ENTITLEMENT PROGRAMS, played a major role in both President FRANKLIN D. ROOSEVELT's "New Deal" and President Lyndon B. Johnson's "Great Society" programs. Cohen (1913–1987) joined Roosevelt's cabinet-level Committee on Economic Security fresh out of the University of Wisconsin, and in 1935 helped draft the SOCIAL SECURITY ACT. After passage of the act, he became the first employee of the Social Security Board and the agency's key liaison to Congress. Over the next two decades, Cohen was involved in major expansions of the program, helping add survivors' benefits in 1939 and increasing SOCIAL SECURITY benefits for the first time with the 1950 amendments to the act.

Cohen left government in 1956 but was lured back by the administration of President John F. Kennedy in 1961. He became assistant secretary for legislation at the Department of Health, Education, and Welfare and, during the Lyndon Johnson administration, advanced to secretary of health, education, and welfare. It was from this post that Cohen spearheaded passage of the MEDICARE program in 1965. Helped by the Democratic landslide in the 1964 elections and his expertise with tax and entitlement issues, Cohen worked with figures such as HOUSE WAYS AND MEANS COMMITTEE chairman WILBUR MILLS to design a giant health insurance program for the elderly, then secured political victory for the legislation. Cohen retired from government again after the Johnson administration but continued to lobby for the Social Security system, founding the Save Our Security coalition and defending the program against proposed cuts during the first term of the RONALD REAGAN administration.

Commissioner of Internal Revenue v. Schleier

In June of 1995, the U.S. Supreme Court ruled that back pay and liquidated damages recovered under the Age Discrimination in Employment Act (ADEA) cannot be excluded from gross income for federal tax purposes. The ruling, in the matter *Commissioner of Internal Revenue v. Schleier,* concluded a dispute between the INTERNAL REVENUE SERVICE and a former pilot for a major U.S. airline who had received both back pay and damages through a class-action lawsuit against the airline, which alleged violation of the ADEA.

The former pilot, who had been forced to retire at age sixty, reported the back pay he received through the class action as income to the IRS, but did not report his liquidated damages award. The IRS issued a notice of deficiency, which was challenged by Schleier in U.S. Tax Court. He argued that both awards should be excludable from his income under the federal tax code's Section 104(a)2. His view was supported by the tax court on the ground that age-bias remedies resemble tort injuries, which are excludable from income under the code section Schleier cited. Courts in the Fifth and Ninth Circuits agreed with that view, while the Seventh Circuit disagreed.

Voting 6–3, the U.S. Supreme Court found that Section 104(a)2 excludes damages received due to personal injury or sickness, but not the type of damages Schleier was awarded, which Justice John Paul Stevens termed "completely independent of the existence or extent of any personal injury." The high court decision relied heavily on precedent set in the 1992 case *U.S. v. Burke,* the outcome of which rested on the rationale that back pay redresses economic injury rather than the personal type of injury typically addressed through tort law. (See also AGE DISCRIMINATION.)

Community-based services

Community-based services, also known as home- and community-based services (HCBS), generally refer to locally based programs that provide seniors with housekeeping, cooking, shopping, minor home repairs, and other forms of assistance to allow them to continue living in their homes. The programs are often limited in scope and depend on volunteers and local sources of funding. Implicit is the belief that in-home assistance helps elderly people maintain a sense of independence and self-respect. The services are not intended to serve as a substitute for ASSISTED LIVING, however.

In some communities, services include free shuttle buses to local senior centers or arrangements that allow elderly people to take college courses tuition-free. Other localities provide referral centers that can help an elderly person find transportation options if he or she decides to stop driving. These centers also can assist seniors in finding forms of health care. Community services frequently rely on state and local grants because the lion's share of federal money in this area is directed to subsidize ADULT DAY CARE and provide nutritional programs like MEALS ON WHEELS. Catholic Charities, Volunteers of America, and similar groups support the community-based programs.

Comprehensive Employment and Training Act (CETA)

The Comprehensive Employment and Training Act (CETA) was passed by Congress and signed into law by President Richard M. Nixon in 1973 as part of his "New Federalism" program. While the legislation was not targeted specifically at the elderly, it gave state and local governments hundreds of millions of dollars to run job-training programs aimed at reducing unemployment and poverty among low-income people, including older workers who may have lost their jobs to new technology or industry restructuring.

The program awarded block grants to communities with populations of 100,000 or larger, or to rural states where populations were more dispersed. As the U.S. economy slumped in the 1970s, presidents Gerald R. Ford and JIMMY CARTER expanded the CETA program, despite mounting criticism that they were training people for jobs that didn't exist. One of the most controversial features was funding for "public-service employment," which critics derided as make-work projects. Though sponsors were required to submit training plans to the U.S. Department of LABOR, government audits later revealed that vague program guidelines and less-than-stringent oversight by some local governments contributed to widespread fraud, with ineligible people receiving government money for questionable projects. The revelations led to passage of the JOB TRAINING PARTNERSHIP ACT of 1982, which consolidated job-training efforts under tougher federal guidelines.

Concord Coalition

The Concord Coalition was formed in 1992 by former Nixon administration secretary of commerce Peter Peterson with former senator Warren Rudman, R-N.H., and the late senator Paul Tsongas, D-Mass., as a lobbying group dedicated to eliminating the federal deficit. Over the years, it has become a vocal advocacy organization, arguing that government overspending could be cured through cutbacks to government programs and reform of MEDICARE and SOCIAL SECURITY. In 1998, the group, with AARP and the Clinton administration, sponsored a nationwide series of forums on the future of Social Security featuring President Bill Clinton, members of Congress, and local lawmakers and policy experts. In 1997, former senator Sam Nunn, D-Ga., replaced Tsongas, who had died of cancer, and joined Rudman as cochairman.

The Concord Coalition has weighed in on the debate over what to do with projected federal budget surpluses, preaching a stern message about a "demographic tidal wave" of aging BABY BOOMERS that threatens to swamp Social Security and Medicare. However, the group seriously underestimated the power of sustained economic growth in correcting the budget imbalance in the 1990s. Only in 1999 did the group acknowledge that economic growth, combined with targeted tax increases and spending cuts, obviated the need to cut Social Security and Medicare in order to erase the budget deficit. Nonetheless, the group has continued to chide the Social Security trustees for not paying enough attention to long-term projections according to which, it says, the program won't be able to pay retirees what has been promised. It also has warned about accounting techniques that make the federal surplus appear larger than it really is, because the figures include Social Security program surpluses that legally shouldn't be counted in budget calculations.

On Medicare, the Concord Coalition opposes creating a proposed new entitlement for PRE-SCRIPTION DRUGS until Congress is certain it can ensure the long-term financial stability of the health-care program. The group favors a kind of "premium support," similar to the plan proposed by the National Bipartisan Commission on the Future of Medicare, that would give recipients a fixed payment to purchase health insurance from competing plans. During the 2000 presidential campaign, the group distributed literature to voters and repeatedly questioned candidates of both parties on entitlement reform, the budget, and related matters. *See also* BIPARTISAN MEDICARE REFORM.)

Congregate housing

Congregate housing is a living alternative for elderly people that is less restrictive than NURSING HOMES or ASSISTED LIVING facilities. It features private homes or apartments located within a larger compound offering communal activities and common areas, such as living rooms and libraries. Usually, one communal meal is served daily, and laundry services, housekeeping, and transportation services are provided. But most of the time, residents live independently, shop on their own, and plan their activities. Some congregate housing communities match up seniors as roommates in a dormitory-type arrangement with private bedrooms. AARP and other senior-advocacy groups warn that such arrangements

aren't for everyone, especially for the elderly who enjoy their privacy.

Congregate housing is primarily directed at individuals over the age of seventy who are in relatively good health and can perform some essential ACTIVITIES OF DAILY LIVING. Because space is limited, waiting lists for the facilities tend to be long, and the cost can exceed $2,000 per month. Congregate housing for low-income seniors is available in many communities and prevents premature or unnecessary institutionalization of those who are frail. The cost of providing meals and other services is covered under SECTION 202 of the U.S. Department of Housing and Urban Development's Section 8 program or through HUD's Rural Housing Service. However, because these HUD programs have been under intense budget pressure in recent years, many elders around the country continue not to have access to this living arrangement.

Congressional Budget Office (CBO)

The Congressional Budget Office (CBO) was created as part of the Congressional Budget and Impoundment Control Act of 1974 and is responsible for estimating the budgetary and economic impact of federal legislation. Its projections are highly influential in political debates, particularly when the CBO "scores" bills and estimates whether the legislation will cost or save the government money over the next five years. The CBO isn't the only government office that serves this function. The White House Office of Management and Budget performs similar analyses for the executive branch—and often disagrees with the CBO. Under budget law, the CBO's estimates prevail in any showdown with the White House. The CBO is nonpartisan and does not make recommendations on policy.

In estimating budgetary impacts, the CBO has to assume the economy will grow a certain amount in the future. But because it's nearly impossible to predict the future, the CBO's estimates can sometimes be dramatically off. Robert Reischauer, a Democrat who was CBO director from 1989 to 1994, has observed that even a modest slowdown in economic growth can turn an estimated $20 billion surplus into a $120 billion deficit. Indeed, the CBO's 1997 estimates of the federal deficit were off by more than $90 billion because the strong economy produced larger-than-expected tax revenues.

The CBO gained prominence during the heated 1994 debate over President Bill Clinton's health-care plan. The CBO said the plan would not save money, but would instead add $74 billion to the federal deficit over the first six years of its existence. The CBO also said that a requirement in the legislation that employers pay for their workers' health insurance should be counted as a tax for budget purposes.

More recently, the CBO has been instrumental in the debate over what to do with the federal surplus. Early in 2000, the CBO dramatically increased its estimates of government revenue, predicting that, over ten years, surpluses of revenues over government spending would range from $800 billion to $1.92 trillion as a result of sustained economic growth. The numbers, based on three different spending models, intensified the election-year debate over what to do with the windfall—cut the federal debt, cut taxes, or increase spending on government programs. But many observers doubt that the high-end estimates are realistic, because they assume lawmak-ers will be willing to freeze government spending for a decade, with no increase for inflation, and make other fiscally prudent but politically unpopular moves.

Consumer Price Index (CPI)

The Consumer Price Index (CPI), calculated by the BUREAU OF LABOR STATISTICS, is one of the most closely watched economic indicators. It represents changes in the prices of goods and services purchased by consumers, including user fees and sales and excise taxes. As the government's benchmark for measuring inflation, it is used to calculate both initial SOCIAL SECURITY benefits and annual COST-OF-LIVING ADJUSTMENTS. There actually are two indexes: one for "all urban consumers," known as CPI-U, which covers approximately 87 percent of the population, and one for urban wage-earners and clerical workers, called CPI-W, which covers about 32 percent of the population and is the index used to calculate Social Security payments.

The practice of tying increases in Social Security payments to inflation was instituted by President Richard M. Nixon in 1972. The increases are automatic and require no vote of Congress. But many seniors contend the system puts them at a disadvantage during times of low inflation, such as most of the 1990s, because prescription-drug costs, medical treatments, and other common expenses rise considerably faster than consumer prices. Indeed, many seniors complain they are giving back their Social Security increases and more in the form of higher MEDICARE premiums and deductibles for drugs and hospital stays.

Economists periodically spar about how to improve the Consumer Price Index. In recent years, some conservative economists, such as Michael Boskin, have advocated adjusting the index so that the automatic cost-of-living adjustments would be lower. Boskin argued the Consumer Price Index was artificially high and costing taxpayers too much. However, liberal economists challenged his figures. This debate is expected to resurface when inflation returns. Meanwhile, the government has developed an experimental Consumer Price Index that more accurately takes into account the goods and services the elderly buy. However, implementing it could cost tens of millions of dollars—a cost Congress shows little willingness to absorb.

Contingent work

Contingent work refers to temporary or part-time jobs—a category of employment that has drawn a growing number of retirees since the mid-1980s. As corporations downsized and reduced the number of full-time employees, they turned to contingent workers to fill out their ranks. The arrangement has appealed to seniors who worked all of their lives but found full-time retirement boring or lonely and missed the purposefulness of a workplace. Senior advocacy groups say this has blurred the definition of what "retired" is, because many people leave their primary line of work around age sixty-five only to quickly return to other jobs for weeks or months each year.

The MacArthur Foundation's 1998 study of aging in America found four out of ten Americans aged fifty-five and older reported working 1,500 hours per year, with about the same num-

ber reporting they worked 500 to 1,499 hours. Many of those surveyed attributed their continued vitality to their jobs. Indeed, part-time employment has taught retirees new skills, such as computer literacy, and provides extra income for cash-strapped seniors. However, there are drawbacks. Working more than a certain number of hours per month can interrupt the pension benefits a retiree receives from his former employer. Some companies have tried to work around these limitations. The Philadelphia health-care and financial services company Cigna Corporation has created programs that invite company retirees to return for a number of hours each month. The Clinton administration and Congress in the spring of 2000 gave Americans between the ages of sixty-five and sixty-nine more of an incentive to continue working by scrapping SOCIAL SECURITY's Depression-era EARNINGS LIMIT, which reduced a retiree's benefits for every dollar he or she earned above a designated threshold.

Continuing-care retirement community (CCRC)

Continuing-care retirement communities (CCRCs) are relatively new, comparatively expensive senior living options that feature multiple levels of care in the same physical complex. The arrangement allows elderly residents to receive what health-care experts call a "continuum of care" as they gradually lose the ability to perform some activities of daily living, without having to move. The communities are ideally suited for seniors with degenerative conditions such as ALZHEIMER'S DISEASE or other forms of DEMENTIA, who may be required to move from an INDE-

PENDENT LIVING arrangement to ASSISTED LIV-ING to a SKILLED NURSING FACILITY or NURSING HOME over the course of a few years. However, the definition of a CCRC remains inconsistent because of the wide variety of services offered and different housing options.

The American Association of Homes and Services for the Aging defines CCRCs as facilities that offer older people a long-term contract for housing, services, and nursing care, often in the same location. The SENATE SPECIAL COMMITTEE ON AGING estimates there are approximately 2,100 such facilities with an estimated 625,000 residents—about 2 percent of the elderly population.

Residents usually enter CCRCs in relatively good health and sign contracts with the facility operator outlining the levels of care they expect to need. The biggest obstacle is cost. Entry fees can total several hundred thousand dollars, depending on whether the person needs round-the-clock nursing, specially appointed rooms, or other considerations. Residents also pay monthly rents ranging from several hundred to several thousand dollars. Many states have laws allowing residents of CCRCs to form tenant councils and negotiate with facility operators on maintenance and other issues. Some CCRCs have the added attraction of being located adjacent to, or near, nursing homes or medical centers. Accommodations vary from stand-alone housing to apartment-like buildings or condominiums. Senior advocates say it is important to understand what services the fees cover and what contingency plans are available should a person suddenly need to move to a higher level of care, if no rooms are available.

Cost-of-living adjustment (COLA)

A cost-of-living adjustment refers to a change in the payments given by entitlement programs to their recipients that is intended to reflect the rate of inflation. SOCIAL SECURITY's COLA is tied to the CONSUMER PRICE INDEX, as calculated by the BUREAU OF LABOR STATISTICS. However, many seniors complain COLAs don't accurately reflect their true costs, because they are geared to overall consumer prices when drug prices and other medical costs tend to rise faster than average. For this reason, the elderly maintain their buying power has steadily eroded during the 1990s. The 2000 Social Security payment adjustment averaged about $19 per month, the biggest increase in three years, bringing the average monthly payment to retirees to $804. The SOCIAL SECURITY ADMINISTRATION said consumer prices rose somewhat more than in previous years, but noted that inflation remained under control.

Crime

The specter of elderly people falling victim to violent crime, abuse or neglect, or various forms of fraud has preoccupied lawmakers in recent years. U.S. Department of Justice statistics indicate overall crime rates are on the decline, and that the elderly make up a smaller proportion of victims than other age groups. The Justice Department's Bureau of Justice Statistics estimated 15.7 percent of the victims of all crimes in the late 1990s were individuals aged fifty to sixty-four, while 4.9 percent were over the age of sixty-five. In contrast, teenagers had a victimization rate for

AARP volunteer "fraud fighters" sort through mail collected as part of AARP's Project Senior Sting, a Boston conference to raise seniors' awareness of mail and telephone fraud. Source: Patricia McDonnell, AP Photo

violent crime, alone, that was more than 20 percent higher.

Still, the elderly are more vulnerable to the effects of certain types of crime. Studies suggest they are more likely to be injured as a result of criminal activity and take longer to heal, both physically and psychologically. They also tend to lose a larger percentage of their income and savings to fraud than younger Americans.

Telemarketing fraud has been a particular concern with the profusion of scams designed to bilk seniors out of their savings. The FBI estimates that individuals aged fifty-five and older lose approximately $40 billion annually to various forms of telemarketing fraud and another $25 billion to scams involving the sale of fake health products. The 105th Congress adopted the Telemarketing Fraud Prevention Act, which was signed into law in 1998 and increased penalties for fraud, provided for forfeiture of property used in committing the crime or gained by the offender, and specified mandatory restitution to victims. After 1996 hearings in the SENATE SPECIAL COMMITTEE ON AGING, the Federal Trade Commission and Congress moved to limit the hours during which telemarketers can operate and imposed tougher

Columbia Care facility warden Bill Davis, left, and Just Care president Tull Gearreald pose in front of the Columbia Care Center in Columbia, South Carolina. The Columbia Care Center is a geriatric prison, targeting prisoners needing frequent attention but not hospitalization. Source: Kim Truett, AP Photo

penalties on unscrupulous operators who specifically targeted older people. A two-and-one-half-year Justice Department sting called Operation Double Barrel focused on telemarketers who offered prizes or products that never arrived in exchange for a fee paid up front, usually with the victims' credit cards. Concerned that some frail elderly victims' credit card numbers can fall into the wrong hands, some banks have begun offering privacy waivers that can be used in a manner similar to ADVANCE DIRECTIVES for health care. The waivers authorize the bank to contact designated

persons if it detects unusual patterns of transactions.

Advocates for the elderly are urging that judges, attorneys, and prosecutors also undergo special training to make the judicial system more sensitive to elderly people. The advocates believe a more sensitive environment would encourage elderly victims to prosecute cases against wrong-doers, without fearing that they would become confused or forget facts during questioning and cross-examination. Some advocates also are pressing states to make their jury systems more senior-friendly, noting that some jurisdictions prohibit individuals over age sixty-five or seventy from serving on juries, while others don't require that older individuals who are summoned actually report for jury duty.

While the effects of crime on the elderly are increasingly discussed, a less-explored topic is how authorities should respond to the increased number of elderly people in state and federal prisons. Statistics show that by the late 1990s, 6.8 percent of the prisoners in federal and state prisons were aged fifty-five and older, a rise from approximately 5 percent in 1990, in part because of tougher sentencing for sex and drug crimes. Officials say special accommodations may be necessary for elderly inmates, particularly repeat offenders who have been in and out of prison and whose health suffers because of persistent smoking, drinking, and drug use.

A number of institutional geriatric wards and prisons for the elderly have been designed or built, with features such as multiple dialysis stations and specially trained attendants who can instruct inmates on how to take proper medications. But lawmakers in some localities have delayed plans to build such facilities because of liability concerns. Criminal justice experts are exploring alternatives for elderly offenders, including community service, less restrictive facilities, or more liberal granting of parole for individuals with chronic health problems.

D

Decision-making capacity

In the context of elder care, *decision-making capacity* refers to a person's ability to make essential health-care decisions and has become an important legal benchmark in connection with ALZHEIMER'S DISEASE and other degenerative conditions that can rob an elderly person of judgment. Individuals in the early stages of these conditions may still be able to make their wishes known. At that point, they may consider drafting an ADVANCE DIRECTIVE, such as a LIVING WILL, that outlines what kind of treatments should be administered in the event of debilitating illness. Such a directive can help loved ones or other CAREGIVERS make choices later for individuals who could die without supplied respiration, tube feeding, or similar medical interventions. The failure to make such decisions in advance can lead to confusion about what level of care the patient may desire when the medical condition turns serious, or who should be deciding for the patient. Even if an elderly patient is partially incapacitated or cannot fully understand his or her medical options, experts say family members and medical personnel should involve the individual in treatment decisions as much as possible, so that he or she retains some semblance of autonomy.

Some individuals alternately choose to designate "medical proxies," essentially appointing a person to make decisions about what care should be administered if the patient no longer can. Federal law has tried to strengthen patients' rights in this area. The 1990 PATIENT SELF-DETERMINATION ACT requires health-care facilities that receive funds under MEDICARE or MEDICAID to inform patients about advance directives and give them the option of executing such documents.

Deductible

A deductible is the out-of-pocket expense that a person pays before insurance coverage is activated. MEDICARE has two important deductibles. The Part A deductible of $776 (in 2000) per "benefit period" covers stays in hospitals for the first sixty days of treatment. For days 61 to 90, a daily co-insurance payment of $194 is required. For hospital stays longer than ninety days, patients can draw upon a sixty-day "lifetime reserve," and pay a co-insurance payment of $388 per day, or pay the full cost of service. A Medicare patient who needs to be hospitalized again more than sixty days after the last admission will have to pay a new deductible.

The Part B deductible of $100 begins January 1 of each year and covers items including diagnostic tests, doctors' office visits, and physical therapy. Medicare Part B pays 80 percent of the approved charges for medical services after the deductible is met.

Defined-contribution plan

A defined-contribution plan is a type of PRI-VATE PENSION largely funded by a company's employees. Such plans now account for more than 60 percent of all employer-sponsored retirement plans. The most popular variety is a 401(K), a type of deferred-compensation plan that allows workers to set aside a portion of their income in such investments as mutual funds, not paying taxes until they begin making withdrawals. In general, defined-contribution plans state a rate at which annual or periodical contributions can be made to an individual's retirement account. The key is that the onus is on the employee: the size of the retirement benefit depends on how much the worker contributes and the performance of the investment portfolio the worker selects.

Defined-contribution plans have surged in popularity since the mid-1980s as employers shift away from more traditional defined-benefit plans, which are funded by company contributions and tend to base their payouts on the employee's length of service or a combination of salary and length of service. To encourage participation in defined-contribution plans, many employers match a small percentage of each employee's contributions. Some large companies have supplemented their traditional defined-benefit plans, such as employee stock ownership plans (ESOPs) or profit sharing, by also offering 401(k)s—a trend that has given many working Americans a stake in the stock market. By 1999, nearly half of the $3 trillion invested in stock mutual funds was held by defined-contribution plan accounts.

Delayed retirement credit

The delayed retirement credit is a form of compensation for SOCIAL SECURITY benefits that are lost if a retiree remains in the work force up to the age of seventy and elects to collect income instead of Social Security benefits. The credit is due to the Social Security earnings test, which decreases benefits for every dollar earned above a threshold. The test was deleted in the spring of 2000 for individuals aged sixty-five to sixty-nine; however, it remains in effect for those aged sixty-two to sixty-four. The test was created during the Great Depression to keep the elderly out of the workforce at a time of high unemployment. A provision creating a 1 percent credit, per year, for delaying collection of benefits past age sixty-five was first enacted as part of the Social Security Amendments of 1972 and has been modified several times since then.

Until recently, an estimated 1.4 million retirees decided to forgo part or all of their Social Security payments because they chose to work instead. At age seventy, these individuals received a future annual credit that is equal to a percentage of what the benefit payment will be, regardless of whether or not they continue working. The credit worked on a sliding scale, depending on the beneficiary's year of birth; for a sixty-five-year-old who lost income before the earnings test was lifted, the delayed retirement credit is scheduled to rise incrementally from the current 6 percent rate to 8 percent annually in 2008. The credit could only be added to a worker's benefit and not to a spousal benefit. AARP and some other advocates of the elderly contended that as long as the delayed retirement credit remains below 8 percent, workers sixty-five and over who elected to remain in the workforce will not be adequately compensated for their decision to forgo benefits.

Dementia

"Dementia" is a general term used to describe mental impairment. It includes, but is not limited to, loss of memory, reduced motor skills and judgment, disorientation, and sometimes significant behavioral changes. ALZHEIMER'S DISEASE is the most prevalent condition associated with dementia. But doctors frequently have to administer a battery of physical and mental tests before making a diagnosis and determining how the degree of impairment may affect a patient's ability to perform ACTIVITIES OF DAILY LIVING.

A variety of other diseases can give rise to dementia. The second-most prevalent in elderly people, after Alzheimer's, is multi-infarct dementia, a vascular disorder characterized by a series of sometimes-miniature strokes that damage brain tissue over time. Those at greatest risk are men between the ages of sixty and seventy-five. High blood pressure, DIABETES, and high blood cholesterol are contributing factors.

Infectious diseases also can lead to dementia. One such condition is Creutzfeldt-Jacob disease, a rare disorder caused by a virus-like organism called a prion that causes Alzheimer's-like lesions in cerebral tissue. The onset typically takes place around age fifty. Some inherited neurological disorders also result in dementia, including Pick's disease, a hard-to-diagnose condition that is usually confined to the frontal lobes of the brain. Environmental factors, such as drug and alcohol abuse or repeated trauma to the head, also can eventually lead to dementia.

Demographics

Demographic studies of the elderly population strongly influence debates on the future of SOCIAL SECURITY, MEDICARE, MEDICAID, and the United States' overall health system. Most efforts to reform or overhaul the ENTITLEMENT PROGRAMS are predicated on the belief that a demographic tidal wave of aging BABY BOOMERS will swamp the programs, creating an imbalance in which recipients will outnumber younger workers who pay taxes to support the payments. The end result in this scenario is depletion of the programs' resources.

While some of the concerns are valid, the demographic picture of aging America is far more complex. Projections by the Bureau of the CENSUS and the SOCIAL SECURITY ADMINISTRATION show an increase, rising by steps, in the population of Americans aged sixty-five and older that won't peak until after 2010. The projections also indicate a surge in the population of what demographers like to call the "OLDEST OLD," namely individuals aged eighty-five and older, who are often depicted as at greatest risk of contracting long-term chronic diseases and in need of the most living assistance.

Using government projections, the ADMINISTRATION ON AGING anticipates only a modest increase in the elderly population until about 2010, with the proportion of elderly in the population remaining at approximately 13 percent, or 39.4 million in 2010. This is because births during the Depression era (defined as between 1925 and 1945) were relatively low compared to the first two decades of the twentieth century. The situation changes dramatically between 2010 to 2030, when the population of individuals aged sixty-five and older is projected to increase by 75 percent to more than sixty-nine million. This is due to the baby boom, commonly defined as births between 1946 and 1964, that was triggered by the wave of post–World War II prosperity. From 2030 to 2050, the number of elderly is again expected to increase more modestly, to about 79 million, with all of the age segments of the population growing more evenly.

While the numbers might indicate that the demographic squeeze is a decade off—and perhaps make lawmakers less inclined to place items like Social Security and Medicare reform at the top of their agendas—they nonetheless show the number of oldest old rising 56 percent between 1995 and 2010, compared to 13 percent for the population aged sixty-five to eighty-four. The Administration on Aging says this is due to the surge of immigration to the United States between 1915 and 1925, the youngest of whom will be eighty-five in 2010. The net result is that a larger percentage of the elderly will be eighty-five or older—a sobering projection for officials dealing with future elder-care needs, particularly housing and health services.

While the figures tend to reflect the aging of whites, government projections show the racial and ethnic composition of elderly America also will change in the coming decades. Hispanics are expected to make up approximately 16 percent of the elderly population in 2050, compared to 4.5 percent in 1995. The jump is due to increased immigration and comparatively high fertility rates. Low mortality rates for Asians, Pacific Islanders, and Hispanics and higher-than-average fertility rates for African Americans also will combine to reduce the proportion of whites in the elderly population from 90 to 82 percent between 1995 and 2050, the Administration on Aging reports.

Demonstration program

Demonstration programs, in the context of aging, are government-funded or private-policy experiments aimed at modifying the way services are delivered under MEDICARE and MEDICAID. The HEALTH CARE FINANCING ADMINISTRATION (HCFA) typically has to approve the experiments by granting the health-care organization, academic center, or other sponsoring agency a waiver from existing rules. If the experiment is judged a success, HCFA and Congress can designate it a permanent alternative program that can be developed anywhere in the country, if local organizations meet program guidelines.

One example of such a demonstration program is the PROGRAM FOR ALL-INCLUSIVE CARE FOR THE ELDERLY (PACE), developed in the early 1970s by On Lok Senior Health Services in San Francisco. The program is targeted at frail seniors aged fifty-five and older in need of nursing home care and allows the individuals to continue to live at home and receive a package of acute and long-term health services at designated PACE centers. Congress enacted legislation in 1997 to significantly increase the number of PACE sites across the country.

Congress in 1999 authorized a demonstration program called "Medicare subvention" aimed at allowing military retirees to use their Medicare benefits at military medical facilities. Current law prohibits Medicare from paying the Department of Defense for health services. The pilot program allows Medicare-eligible military retirees to enroll in a Pentagon-run health-maintenance organization that can collect payments from Medicare, subject to certain conditions.

The Center to Improve Care of the Dying, located at George Washington University in Washington, D.C., is leading another demonstration program aimed at improving care for people suffering from advanced congestive heart failure and other terminal illnesses. The university wants to develop alternatives to HOSPICE care that still meet a Medicare requirement that a person be within six months of death to qualify, or make the requirements more flexible for those with congestive heart failure and other terminal illnesses not as easily timed as cancer within the six-month time limit set by the law.

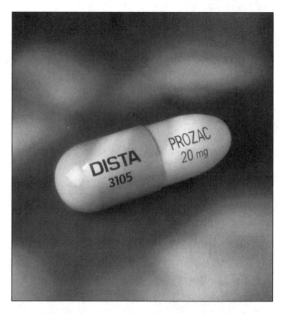

Prozac, a popular antidepressant drug introduced in 1986, increases levels of serotonin, a neurotransmitter. Prozac is effective in treating the entire spectrum of depression, from the milder types to the most severe.
Source: File photo

Depression

Depression is a sometimes-debilitating mental ailment affecting approximately five million Americans aged sixty-five and older. While the condition is often perceived as a normal by-product of aging, health professionals stress it is an abnormality that often has underlying biological causes and should be treated with counseling, antidepressant drugs, or both. However, telltale signs of depression—apathy, a lack of energy, poor sleep habits, the loss of appetite, and difficulty concentrating—are frequently overlooked or mistaken as signs that one is just getting older. Indeed, experts estimate that only 10 percent of the depressed senior citizens in the United States are being treated for their condition.

Depression can intensify as a result of the loss of loved ones or friends, boredom and inactivity linked to retirement, or the realization that one can no longer perform some physical tasks or partake in certain activities. Yet psychologists say that while each of these factors can be emotionally devastating, mentally healthy people usually can recover over time and find new sources of happiness. On the other hand, persistent depression can lead to social isolation or anxiety, which has been linked to serious health conditions, including heart and lung disease and gastrointestinal problems.

Clinical depression, a serious form of the disorder affecting about a million elderly Americans, has been linked to SUICIDE in various studies, though the connections aren't fully understood. Studies by the U.S. Centers for Disease Control and Prevention show that the suicide rate among the elderly began increasing in the 1980s after nearly four decades in decline. It is markedly higher in white males aged eighty-five and older. The National Institute of Mental Health, part of the NATIONAL INSTITUTES OF HEALTH, is trying to improve ways of recognizing depression in the elderly and improve the efficacy of treatments.

Doctors caution that some antidepressant drugs can trigger adverse effects in the elderly. Additionally, various types of DEMENTIA, STROKE, and other conditions can trigger chemical changes in the brain and bring on depression. An increasing number of psychotherapists believe a combination of drug therapy and counseling can help alleviate recurrent depression in senior citizens. However, these professionals note that many managed-care guidelines discourage such combination therapies, with health insurers choosing to pay only for medications or for medications and limited therapy.

Diabetes

Diabetes is a medical condition characterized by abnormally high levels of blood sugar. It is almost always caused by an inadequate amount of insulin, a hormone produced in the pancreas that breaks down glucose. There are two types of diabetes: Type I, or insulin dependent, and Type II, or non–insulin dependent. Type I typically strikes individuals under the age of twenty and is due to the pancreas's inability to produce enough insulin. Type II is by far the most prevalent form in elderly people. This variety of the disease is characterized by the patient's producing enough insulin in the blood but having a lower-than-average number of insulin receptors in the fat cells, usually because the individual is obese or has a diet high in saturated fats and sugars. The disease also may be influenced by genetics.

The American Diabetes Association estimates

half of the diabetes cases in the United States are found in individuals aged fifty-five and older, and that 6.3 million Americans aged sixty-five and older have the condition. If left untreated, diabetes can lead to serious long-term health problems, including heart disease, blindness, and kidney failure. Public health officials say diabetes now is one of the top ten leading causes of death in the United States, with more than 190,000 fatalities annually.

Detecting the disease in older patients isn't always easy. Telltale fatigue and vision problems associated with the disease are sometimes attributed to the normal aging process. Health professionals have begun lowering benchmark measurements of blood-sugar levels to diagnose the condition more quickly. Once a diagnosis is made, doctors often prescribe a diet low in fats and sugars. They may also prescribe medications that kick-start insulin production in the body or that directly break down sugar, assuming the patient has healthy kidney functions. Most of the oral drugs used to treat Type II diabetes are sulfonyl urea compounds. In more extreme cases, patients can take insulin directly by injection. Individuals in need of these medications need to monitor their blood-sugar levels regularly by taking a small blood sample with a pinprick and measuring it in a device called a glucometer.

The NATIONAL INSTITUTE ON AGING and the National Institute of Diabetes and Digestive and Kidney Diseases, both part of the NATIONAL INSTITUTES OF HEALTH in Bethesda, Maryland, are the leading federal institutes conducting research into the causes and treatment of diabetes. Scientists are trying to maintain pancreatic cell function in older animals by cloning genes that appear to control cell regeneration. They also are creating new chemical compounds that can enhance the

Rep. George Nethercutt, R-Wash., second from left, and Deborah K. Willhite of the U.S. Postal Service, right, unveil a new thirty-four-cent stamp during ceremonies at the Joslin Diabetes Center in Boston on March 16, 2001. The stamp is meant to draw attention to the disease. Sen. John Kerry, D-Mass., left, looks on. Source: AP Photo, Steven Senne

ability to receive insulin. Separately, government scientists are investigating the higher-than-average incidence of diabetes in minority groups, particularly African Americans, and new ways to prevent the disease through diet, exercise, and drugs.

Disability Insurance

See SOCIAL SECURITY DISABILITY INSURANCE.

"Do not" order

A "do not" order, a term often used interchangeably with a "do-not-resuscitate" order, is a type of ADVANCE DIRECTIVE that explicitly instructs doctors and other medical personnel not to revive a patient if the patient's heart or breathing stops. This legal order is most applicable in cases where a person is suffering from terminal illness and likely would remain in grave health or extreme pain if revived. Like other such orders, it is designed to outline to medical personnel the patient's wishes if the patient becomes unable to communicate.

Dual eligibles

The term "dual eligibles" refers to the approximately twelve million individuals who are simultaneously eligible for MEDICARE and MEDICAID benefits. This group includes frail elderly people with low incomes (usually below $10,000 per year) who tend to have complex medical problems and, proportionately, use up more healthcare resources than other demographic groups. Policymakers say these individuals are at risk of getting caught in bureaucratic snafus and going without some types of care because Medicare and Medicaid have different rules and eligibility criteria and sometimes are at odds over which program should pay for what service. For example, Medicare, which is heavily weighted to providing acute care, encourages hospitals to rapidly discharge the elderly to NURSING HOMES or HOME HEALTH CARE facilities. Medicaid, which pays for many elderly recipients' LONG-TERM CARE, prefers that nursing homes discharge higher-cost residents and those with more complex medical needs to hospitals, where Medicare is expected to pay the bill.

Medicaid coverage is very important for frail seniors because it covers Medicare's premiums, deductibles, and copayments and additionally provides benefits Medicare does not, such as prescription drugs and long-term care. Not surprisingly, dual eligibles consume higher-than-average amounts of services under the program; in fiscal 1997, they made up about 16 percent of all Medicaid recipients but accounted for 35 percent, or about $58 billion, in program payments.

Washington policymakers have made several attempts to confront both the needs of dual eligibles and the pressures they place on government entitlements. Congress in 1988 enacted the Qualified Medicare Beneficiary (QMB) program to limit Medicaid payments to individuals whose incomes are below the federal poverty threshold and who have few assets (below $4,000 for an individual and $6,000 for a couple) but who still aren't poor enough to qualify for full Medicaid benefits. The program was created as part of the 1988 MEDICARE CATASTROPHIC COVERAGE ACT and left intact when the law was repealed by Congress the following year. QMBs are entitled to have Medicaid pay their Medicare cost-sharing, including the Part B premium, as well as deductibles and copayments.

Besides frail low-income seniors, a second group of dual eligibles, known as Specified Low-Income Medicare Beneficiaries (SLIMB), was targeted in the 1990 Omnibus Budget Reconciliation Act (see OMNIBUS RECONCILIATION BILLS). These individuals have slightly higher incomes—between 100 percent and 120 percent of the federal poverty level—and are eligible for Medicaid to pay the Medicare Part B premiums. However, they must pay deductibles, copayments, and other out-of-pocket cost-sharing expenses.

Federal officials say participation rates in these programs have been lower than expected, in part because the low-income elderly and disabled aren't aware the options exist. The advocacy group Families USA reported in 1998 that nationwide there were between 3.3 million and 3.9 million senior citizens and disabled persons who were eligible for QMB and SLIMB benefits but weren't receiving them. The HEALTH CARE FINANCING ADMINISTRATION (HCFA) has begun publicizing the programs while screening new Medicare beneficiaries to determine whether they may qualify for the QMB program.

E

Early retirement

Early retirement is defined as voluntarily leaving the workforce before reaching the normal retirement age. Once regarded as a luxury, it is increasingly becoming a reality for employees in their forties and fifties who receive lucrative buyout offers from corporations trying to pare their payrolls, or for other workers who have reaped a windfall from 401(k)'s or other defined-contribution plans tied to the stock market and can leave whenever they want, on their own terms. But the phrase "early retirement" is something of a misnomer, because many of the workers who opt out of their jobs change careers and reenter the workforce. Others who remain retired still apparently want to continue to work, at least some of the time. A 1999 Harris Poll showed that 10 percent of the population over age fifty-five—about 3.7 million people—currently is not working but would prefer to have a job.

It is difficult to gauge exactly how many people take early retirement, because retirement age varies from company to company. Still, demographers say the numbers are rising—a potential cause for concern because the number of young workers, aged twenty-five to thirty-four, is projected to decline in the first decade of the twenty-first century. The cumulative effect will be a labor shortage that will promote fierce competition among employers to keep their best workers. Those workers who can't afford to retire will stay

in their jobs as long as possible. However, those with generous retirement plans and other BENEFITS may have the advantage of opting out, collecting their benefits, then returning to work part-time. Some companies, sensing a future labor squeeze, are creating programs that allow workers to "retire," then return to work on a limited basis to retain their expertise.

Early retirement also can create strains on national pension systems because it creates more beneficiaries faster, putting greater pressure on younger workers who must finance the benefits through payroll taxes. The U.S. SOCIAL SECURITY system allows workers who take early retirement to collect benefits as early as age sixty-two. However, the benefits—and, by extension, the incentive to take early retirement—will be less than if the person waits until the regular retirement age. For example, if the retirement age is sixty-five, the reduction in benefits for starting Social Security at sixty-two is about 20 percent. Retiring at sixty-three means benefits will be cut approximately 13-1/3 percent, while retiring at sixty-four will bring an approximately 6-2/3 percent reduction.

Policymakers cited higher labor force participation rates among older workers as one reason they abolished the earnings limits that restrict the amount Social Security recipients can earn in salary while retaining their program benefits. But personal savings may be the most significant determining factor. Individuals who fail to build up a generous nest egg, then take early retirement hoping to live on Social Security and liquid assets often find they can't pay their bills and have to return to work.

Earnings limit (Social Security)

SOCIAL SECURITY's earnings limit emerged in 2000 as one of the most watched features of the national retirement system. The Depression-era provision was designed to keep older workers out of the labor force at a time of high unemployment by reducing their Social Security BENEFITS for every dollar they earned above a designated threshold. At the time of the debate, more than 800,000 seniors between the ages of sixty-five and sixty-nine were losing $1 in Social Security benefits for every $3 they earned beyond $17,000. Seniors aged seventy and older were not affected by the provision.

For years, critics have charged the earnings limit unfairly penalizes older workers who want to remain active and employed. But efforts to repeal the penalty often were characterized as tax cuts that could increase the budget deficit and imperil some government programs—even though repeal, technically, does not alter the U.S. tax code.

Several factors changed the political landscape in 2000. First, an unusually tight labor market, with approximately 96 percent of the labor force holding jobs, increased the demand for qualified workers. Lifting the earnings limit was seen as one way of helping U.S. employers bring in more qualified, experienced workers. Also, the federal budget surplus made it more difficult to argue that repealing the limit would be fiscally irresponsible. And lawmakers from both parties realized the issue could help court senior voters in a very

President Bill Clinton proposed scrapping the Social Security earnings limit in his 1999 State of the Union address. Source: Scott J. Ferrell, Congressional Quarterly

competitive election year. The earnings limit remains in place for individuals between the ages of sixty-two and sixty-four, and is likely to remain that way. Experts say that this should be the case, at least until research shows the extent of the impact of lifting it on the labor force for people in that age range.

Somewhat lost in the debate was the fact that the earnings limit doesn't really give the federal government much added revenue. That is because workers who lose income now get it back after age seventy in the form of delayed retirement credits that are added on to their regular Social Security payments. The annual cost of repealing the penalty would start at $8 billion in fiscal 2001 and cost an estimated $23 billion over ten years. However, the cost would eventually decline to zero, because seniors who continue to work would pay payroll taxes that would offset the cost of repealing the earnings limit.

President Bill Clinton proposed eliminating the earnings limit in his 1999 State of the Union address as part of a broader plan to ensure the solvency of the Social Security system. But even though Republican and Democratic lawmakers endorsed the idea, they differed on the method to lift the limit. Republicans proposed stand-alone legislation, while the Clinton administration opposed addressing Social Security provisions one piece at a time without addressing the broader issue of solvency. In the end, Congress proved eager to win senior votes, passing stand-alone measures by votes of 100–0 in the Senate and 422–0 in the House. "Conventional wisdom says nothing important happens in Washington in an election year," Clinton said at a White House ceremony to sign the legislation on April 7, 2000. "Today we have proved the conventional wisdom wrong."

Echo boomers

The term "echo boomers" refers to the estimated 75 million children of BABY BOOMERS who were born during a mini-population-boom that took place between 1977 and 1994. The surge of births has been partly attributed to the desire of many baby boomer women to focus on their careers and delay starting families until well into their thirties. Echo boomers will be the focus of increased attention, because they will bear the brunt of financing their elderly parents' SOCIAL SECURITY, MEDICARE, and MEDICAID BENEFITS. Demographers project that, by 2025, echo boomers in their thirties and forties will account for approximately 22 percent of the population.

But there is fierce debate over whether their numbers are high enough to sustain the ENTITLEMENT PROGRAMS in their present form. Conservatives generally contend they are not, pointing to Social Security trustee projections that show there will only be enough money funneled into the system by 2034—soon after the last of the baby boomers retire—to pay about 71 percent of promised benefits. However, others believe the fact that this generation was so surprisingly large should be a matter of relief, because more workers will be available to sustain the current system. This camp, which includes liberal-leaning economists, also questions the trustees' conservative growth projections for the U.S. economy (about 1.7 percent annually), noting historic trends over the past half century show it may be more like 3 percent.

Eden Alternative

The Eden Alternative is a concept of elder care that attempts to transform standard NURSING HOME environments into more stimulating places through the presence of pets, collections of indoor plants, and other innovations. The concept stems from a pilot project begun in 1990 in New Berlin, New York, by Harvard University–trained gerontologist William H. Thomas and now is offered in many resident-care facilities across the country. Facilities typically bring in cut flowers, plants, dogs, cats, and birds. Facility staff may be divided into "permanent care teams" that serve "neighborhoods" of residents who are grouped according to special needs.

Advocates of the concept say it alleviates residents' loneliness, helplessness, and boredom by

"Duke," one of the many therapy dogs from Paws'itive Teams, waits to accompany his handlers on visits to patients in hospitals and residents in nursing homes.
Source: Jeremy Lyverse, AP Photo

offering them a chance to give of themselves, either by tending to some of the resident animals or by puttering in the gardens that have been installed in some facilities. Texas facilities embracing the approach, for instance, report reductions in medication needed for anxiety and depression and a lower incidence of bedsores. An Eden Alternative nursing home in Milwaukee also reported lower staff turnover and less need for restraining residents. Adherents of the system offer CERTIFICATION programs and training.

The Eden Alternative has figured into a broader reform movement called the Nursing Home Pi-

oneers Movement, of which Thomas is a leader. The concept is that at a time when nursing homes are increasingly under fire for substandard care, leaders for humane developments in LONG-TERM CARE around the country have joined in an effort for reform. The Pioneers movement has held conferences beginning in the late 1990s and formed groups calling for others to become innovators in humane long-term care.

Elder abuse

"Elder abuse" is a general term referring to various forms of wrongdoing directed at elderly people, particularly physical and psychological abuse, financial exploitation, and neglect. The subject received comparatively little attention in public policy circles until the mid-1980s, when reports by the Institute of Medicine and the U.S. General Accounting Office of substandard care in NURSING HOMES led Congress to pass the Nursing Home Reform Act (PL 100-203), which was incorporated into the Omnibus Budget Reconciliation Act of 1987 (see OMNIBUS RECONCILIATION BILLS). The law strengthened rules that nursing homes must comply with to gain MEDICARE CERTIFICATION, as well as outlining residents' rights, including the right to be free from physical restraints.

It is virtually impossible to measure the extent of elder abuse because many of the victims live alone and are not inclined to report incidents to authorities. A noteworthy 1998 study by the American Public Human Services Association's National Center on Elder Abuse estimated that about 450,000 persons aged sixty and older experienced various forms of abuse in domestic settings in 1996. Most of the victims were believed to be women in the "OLDEST OLD" category—age eighty-five and above. Widely publicized incidents in which elderly people with DEMENTIA have been left in public places with no identification are considered somewhat rare. More common are instances in which people swindle vulnerable seniors out of their savings. Many times, those committing the wrongdoing are the children of the elderly victims.

The ADMINISTRATION ON AGING reports that legislatures in all fifty states have enacted some protections for vulnerable seniors—either through social services departments or agencies for the aging. Many states also have laws requiring doctors, law-enforcement officials, and clergy to report suspected cases. Federal funding for these efforts is provided through the SOCIAL SERVICES BLOCK GRANT and OLDER AMERICANS ACT. In particular, the Social Services Block Grant supports the activities of adult protective services units that are a part of social-services programs in many states.

Nursing homes and other types of LONG-TERM CARE institutions that tend to the frail elderly remain a focus of surveillance to root out elder abuse. Since 1998 the U.S. Department of Health and Human Services inspector general has warned that state efforts to protect nursing home residents from abuse are inconsistent and unreliable. The reports say there is great variety in how states report and investigate suspected abuse, and few assurances that individuals who pose a threat of abusing residents are prohibited from further nursing home employment. At the same time, the inspector general's surveys of various states indicate that nursing home deficiencies have been on the decline in recent years.

Elder Cottage Housing Opportunity

The Elder Cottage Housing Opportunity, also known as ECHO units or "Granny Flats," is an unusual, relatively recent development in senior housing, in which small, free-standing removable houses for elderly individuals are erected next to or near single-family homes. The concept originated in Australia and has been praised for simultaneously giving the elderly independence and peace of mind that family is nearby.

The units are often installed on the property of the elderly person's children, but can also be grouped together on land leased by local housing authorities or by private organizations, zoning laws permitting. The cost of erecting the structures can exceed $100,000, and some communities insist that they meet certain appearance standards and can be easily removed if the resident dies. The structures typically include one or two bedrooms, a bathroom, kitchen, and living room.

The National Affordable Housing Act of 1990 authorized a demonstration program in the United States to test the durability of the units. The Housing and Community Development Act of 1992 reserved Department of Housing and Urban Development (HUD) SECTION 202 funds for the program. However, HUD never completed follow-up studies, and there have been few official evaluations of whether the concept could work on a large scale.

Elderhostel

Elderhostel is a nonprofit organization founded at the University of New Hampshire and now

American seniors enjoy the sights at London's Thames River. There are now more than 100,000 Elderhostel education programs with more than 270,000 participants.
Source: John Ware, Grandtravel

based in Boston that arranges educational experiences for seniors at reasonable cost. In addition to its original offerings of multiday classes and field trips, Elderhostel also sponsors a "service program" allowing participants to do community-service work and an "Institute Network" of classes at local colleges and universities.

The organization was founded in 1975 by a former educator and a university administrator after one of the founders, Marty Knowlton, spent four years in his mid-fifties walking through Europe, using low-cost youth hostels to sleep in. Knowlton was struck by the Scandinavian institutions known as "folk schools," in which older adults would hand down musical, artistic, or dance traditions to younger learners. The concept of late-life learning was still novel in the United States at the time. Knowlton and his cofounder, David Bianco, believed that programs for U.S. seniors modeled on the European programs

Knowlton had seen would be highly beneficial. There are now more than 100,000 Elderhostel programs with more than 270,000 participants. The organization offers activities in seventy countries and has annual revenues of about $120 million.

Employee Benefit Research Institute (EBRI)

The Employee Benefit Research Institute, known as EBRI (pronounced ee-bree), is a nonprofit, nonpartisan THINK TANK based in Washington, D.C., that is exclusively devoted to studying economic security and workers' benefits. Its unique role has made it an important resource in public policy debates over the future of SOCIAL SECURITY, MEDICARE, MEDICAID, health-care reform, and the UNINSURED. Founded in 1978, the organization claims financial support from a broad membership, including labor unions, management consultants, health-care companies, banks and brokerages, law firms, and mutual fund companies.

EBRI's Databook on Employee Benefits and its monthly issue briefs are often cited in debates over ENTITLEMENT PROGRAMS. Recent studies have taken up issues such as how age and tenure affect the amount of money in workers' retirement accounts, trends in employer-provided health coverage, the national savings rate, and the size and characteristics of the population of Americans who are uninsured and lack health coverage.

Employee Retirement Income Security Act of 1974 (ERISA)

This law (PL 93-406), commonly known as ERISA (pronounced er-iss-ah), is a complicated and far-reaching statute affecting millions of Americans' pensions and health BENEFITS. It is notable not only for the significant effect it had on employer-sponsored benefits in the last quarter of the twentieth century but for the numerous legal fights it spawned over federal and state treatment of retirement and health plans. The law's ability to preempt state laws for certain kinds of health plans has in recent years put it at the fulcrum of heated congressional debates over the "patients' bill of rights" and whether individuals can sue their health plans for service denials.

ERISA's main purpose was to establish a general set of rules for employee benefit plans, basically so companies that had operations in many states

could offer one, unified plan. The law established minimum standards for participation in pension plans, required that plan sponsors disclose important information about the plans' financial conditions, and gave participants and retirees the right to sue for benefits denied or breaches in the plan administrators' fiduciary responsibilities. A key feature was legally establishing that the employer is responsible if a pension plan fails—an important development at the time of passage, when many companies were offering defined-benefit plans whose payments could be interrupted if the company experienced financial distress. The new guarantee was accomplished through the creation of an insurance fund known as the PENSION BENEFIT GUARANTY CORPORATION (PBGC), into which companies paid premiums to back workers' benefits.

While ERISA is credited with establishing a nationwide set of rules for retirement plans, it also has had a predictable chilling effect on employers. Faced with new potential liabilities, increased regulation, and added costs in the form of insurance payments, many employers gradually switched from offering defined-benefit plans to DEFINED-CONTRIBUTION PLANS, in which workers make decisions about investments, and the size of the benefit is not guaranteed. This trend accelerated after Congress enacted ERISA reforms in 1994 in response to mounting liabilities of the PBGC brought on by underfunded plans. The reforms increased employers' insurance payments and required more stringent financial disclosure of plans' financial conditions. Today, defined-contribution plans account for more than 60 percent of employer-sponsored retirement plans—a number that is expected to increase in the coming decades.

Advocates for the elderly, such as AARP, complain that ERISA has left some older workers and pensioners helpless because of the way in which it preempts state laws in the name of uniformity. Courts, for instance, have generally ruled that ERISA preempts legal actions against fraud and misrepresentation in connection with retirement plans, leaving workers without recourse if they are persuaded to make inappropriate investment decisions. Additionally, the law permits employers to reduce or cancel retirement plan benefits if the employer clearly states that it reserves the right to do so and communicates that right to its workers.

ERISA is generally less protective of retirees' health benefits than their pensions. ERISA in some way regulates more than 2.5 million private sector employer-sponsored health plans—virtually every plan except MEDICARE, MEDICAID, public employees' health plans, and individually purchased health coverage. The law establishes minimum standards regarding disclosure and financial reporting. However, it blocks most people in employer-sponsored plans from suing the plans if certain health services are denied. ERISA does not prevent employees from filing malpractice suits, or from collecting damages due to actions taken by health-care providers. ERISA also contains language exempting so-called self-insured health plans, in which employers pay for benefits instead of buying insurance, from state laws that may mandate some services be provided or impose some premium taxes. About 40 percent of workers, or some 48 million workers, are in self-insured plans. However, if a company buys insurance, ERISA permits the state to regulate the plan.

Energy assistance

Energy prices have a significant effect on the lives of low-income elderly people, who have been shown to pay three to four times what all households combined pay for residential home energy costs as a percentage of total income. The problem is not simply budgetary; the elderly tend to be more vulnerable to heat exhaustion and heatstroke in the summer and hypothermia in the winter. One study by the Washington-based Center for Environmental Physiology estimated 25,000 elderly people die each year as a result of hypothermia, with the majority succumbing to prolonged cool temperatures indoors, as opposed to exposure outside. The energy crisis of the 1970s—particularly the spike in home heating-oil prices that it spawned—prompted policymakers to respond with a series of temporary relief measures. Gradually, these were to be incorporated into a more comprehensive energy assistance program.

One of the federal government's primary efforts is the Low Income Heating Assistance Program, or LIHEAP (pronounced "lie-heap"), which was authorized by Title XXVI of the Omnibus Budget Reconciliation Act of 1981 (see OMNIBUS RECONCILIATION BILLS). The program operates as a block grant to assist eligible households to pay for heating and cooling bills, inexpensive weatherization assistance, and crisis intervention. Grants are distributed annually by the U.S. Department of Health and Human Services to states, based on a formula that takes into account home energy spending by low-income households (typically defined as those with annual incomes under 150 percent of the federal poverty line). States establish their own eligibility rules and benefit packages and sometimes supplement the federal funding with local funds. While the elderly are not the only beneficiaries of the program, state and federal data suggest that about one-third of the recipient households contain a person aged sixty or older. Most recent estimates indicate the program helped deliver heating assistance payments to about four million households.

Federal budget cuts have taken a toll on LIHEAP. In fiscal 2000, the program was funded at about $1.4 billion, consisting of a base appropriation of about $1.1 billion and $344 million of emergency funding. The program reached a high-water mark for funding in 1985, when it received $2.1 billion. The White House often releases hundreds of millions of dollars in contingency funds to deal with cold- and hot-weather emergencies. However, advocates for the elderly say a significant gap remains between program resources and recipients' needs.

A second federal energy-assistance program is the U.S. Department of Energy's Weatherization Assistance Program, created in the wake of the 1973 oil embargo under Title IV of the Energy Conservation and Production Act (PL 94-385). This formula grant program distributes money from the federal government to states to local nonprofit agencies, which help install energy-conserving materials and insulation in dwellings to cut heating and cooling costs. More than five million homes have been weatherized to date, and program administrators report an average savings on heating bills of 23 percent. Funding comes from a combination of LIHEAP, the Department of Energy budget, and local sources, such as utilities and states.

Entitlement fraud

The intentional defrauding of federal ENTITLEMENT PROGRAMS costs taxpayers billions of dollars each year. The wrongdoing takes many forms, but some common scams involve billing MEDICARE for health services that aren't actually provided, or "upcoding," in which a hospital or doctor charges the program for more expensive or extensive services than those that were administered. The elderly sometimes unwittingly help unscrupulous operators by giving out their Medicare health insurance claim numbers or their Medicare cards to unauthorized individuals, or by accepting some services that are represented as free but actually are charged to the government. Despite efforts to crack down on abuses, the Department of Health and Human Services reported improper Medicare payments rose to $13.5 billion in fiscal 1999, compared to $12.6 billion a year earlier.

Health insurers were the first to mount large-scale anti-fraud efforts in the early 1990s by using their computerized billing systems to ferret out questionable charges. The efforts were saving upward of $200 million per year by the mid-1990s, according to insurance industry groups, who said their vigilance helped hold down overall health-care costs. Bill Clinton's administration in 1995 launched Operation Restore Trust, a pilot program involving federal, state, and private agencies to fight fraud in Medicare and MEDICAID that proved so successful it went national two years later. By focusing in particular on the nursing-home and medical-equipment industries and home health services, the program returned $23 in overpayments for every dollar spent investigating problems and expelled some 2,700 fraudulent providers.

Entitlement fraud remains widespread, however. The U.S. General Accounting Office (GAO) and the SOCIAL SECURITY ADMINISTRATION's inspector general have detailed how some 60,000 prison inmates illegally collect about $500 million in SOCIAL SECURITY benefits each year, simply by not informing the agency when they go to jail. Prison authorities often know these inmates are receiving the payments—usually through electronic-funds transfers—but are prohibited by federal regulations from confiscating them. The GAO has criticized the Social Security Administration for failing to adequately cross-check computerized information on jail populations.

NURSING HOMES continue to be a focus of investigations. In February 2000, the nation's largest nursing-home chain, Beverly Enterprises, agreed to pay $175 million in fines and give up control of ten of its nursing homes after the U.S. Department of Justice found the company's California subsidiary submitted phony billing documents. The wrongdoing was reported by a whistleblower, who received 17 percent of the settlement under federal anti-fraud rules. Outpatient rehabilitation services are another focus of investigators. The Department of Health and Human Service's inspector general has detailed how more than half the Medicare payments for outpatient treatments made in a six-state survey for the twelve months ending June 30, 1998, were questionable in nature. One facility submitted a claim for payments for boating-related expenses and trips to the Caribbean.

Congress has periodically dealt with entitlement fraud by beefing up enforcement. Lawmakers in 1987 passed legislation (PL 100-93) that allowed the secretary of health and human services to ban for five years from Medicare and Medicaid those program-certified physicians or health-care providers who committed crimes delivering services. The measure also gave the secretary the option of banning and fining individuals or organizations that committed fraud, theft, or embezzlement, or who interfered with the investigation of wrongdoing.

Another important anti-fraud measure was the Health Insurance Portability and Accountability Act of 1996 (PL 104-191), which increased penalties for fraud from $2,000 per violation to $10,000 and earmarked more than $100 million for the Departments of Justice and Health and Human Services to fight fraud and to coordinate state and local efforts. Medicare says the program helped return nearly $1 billion to the Medicare TRUST FUND through the collection of fines, settlements, and judgments. The measure for the first time also discouraged the intentional "spending down" of elderly people's assets so they could qualify for Medicaid, the federal program for the poor that offers LONG-TERM CARE benefits.

Congress again took up entitlement fraud in the BALANCED BUDGET ACT OF 1997 (PL 105-33), increasing penalties and including a provision that could permanently bar a health-care provider from federal programs if convicted of health-connected felonies for a third time. This legislation also mandated that doctors and hospitals provide itemized bills on request and make their patients aware of telephone hotlines the government set up to report fraud. Some of the provisions drew fire from groups such as the AMERICAN MEDICAL ASSOCIATION, who contended the government was unfairly singling out health-care professionals who made comparatively simple billing mistakes or did not understand the technicalities of program reimbursements.

Entitlement programs

An entitlement is defined as a government program that pays recipients who are automatically eligible for BENEFITS because they meet certain criteria outlined in federal law. The term is applied both to universal entitlement programs such as SOCIAL SECURITY and MEDICARE, which are available across the widest spectrum of American society, and to means-tested or income-tested programs that are available, at least in theory, to all who meet certain income criteria. This has become a problem when those ideologically opposed to entitlements lump in MEDICAID to pad figures for arguments that the government was spending too much on older Americans.

More than 350 federal entitlement programs exist, but the three biggest—Social Security, Medicare, and Medicaid—dominate public-policy discussions. Other entitlements include veterans' benefits, foster care, and food stamps. One important feature of entitlements is that the spending is "mandatory," meaning Congress does not have to annually budget for the programs in its appropriations bills.

The concept of an entitlement would probably be foreign to the Founding Fathers. Until the early twentieth century, most Americans didn't see the need for big government-sponsored social-welfare programs, choosing to rely on the Jeffersonian philosophy of self-reliance. However, the economic vulnerabilities brought about by rapid industrialization and calamities like the Great Depression led progressive lawmakers to carve out programs such as Social Security.

Despite the recent appearance of federal budget surpluses, Congress continues to spend a great deal of time worrying about the future growth of entitlement spending and how it could deplete the reserves that pay for programs such as Social Security and Medicare. Proposals to slow down the rate of spending include accelerating the twenty-two-year period during which the retirement age is being raised from sixty-five to sixty-seven, "means-testing" recipients and reducing payments to higher-income individuals, or restructuring the programs entirely.

Equal Employment Opportunity Commission (EEOC)

This federal agency fights discrimination based on race, color, religion, sex, or age in all aspects of employment. It is charged with enforcing the Age Discrimination in Employment Act of 1967 (ADEA), which bars discrimination against workers aged forty and older. The commission investigates charges of discrimination, makes its determinations, and in some cases, brokers disputes or files lawsuits. Civil rights experts maintain the EEOC is too short-staffed to enforce the ADEA by itself. (See also AGE DISCRIMINATION.

Estate planning

Estate planning involves creating a wide-ranging financial plan that outlines how and when a person wishes to distribute assets after death. This task is no small matter because failing to develop an adequate plan can expose the individual's heirs to significant taxes. The lack of a plan also means a court likely will step in and distribute the assets according to set formulas, without any regard to the individual's stated wishes.

The most essential component of estate planning is a will, which is an enforceable legal document that details the person's wishes and names an executor to control distribution of the individual's property. In certain situations, the individual may instead opt for a TRUST—a financial arrangement in which the person may transfer assets while still alive. Trusts are sometimes criticized for achieving limited goals and not taking into account all of the person's wishes. Some trusts, like wills, must go through probate, a process in which a court itemizes assets and pays off taxes and debts. Some individuals select a third option: making sizable gifts of money or property to heirs to reduce the size of the estate and the potential tax burden.

The Taxpayer Relief Act of 1997 (PL 105-34) made a number of important changes to estate and gift taxes. The legislation gradually increases the allowable size of an estate exempt from taxes from $675,000 to $1 million in 2006. It also makes special allowances for estates that include family-owned businesses and for land that is subject to conservation easements. The law also reduces the interest rate for installment payments of the estate tax.

Older investors have found innovative arrangements to help their heirs. One increasingly popular tack is converting assets the individual doesn't need into a ROTH IRA, a variety of individual retirement account created by the 1997 tax act, in which taxes are paid before the money is invested. Because the IRA owner isn't required to withdraw the assets, heirs are left free to withdraw the assets at a later date tax-free.

Estrogen

Estrogen is a female sex hormone whose concentrations in the body decrease during MENOPAUSE. This is a cause for concern because research has linked low levels of estrogen to OSTEOPOROSIS and HEART DISEASE. Many women choose to take estrogen supplements to fend off this potential health hazard. However, other studies have shown that estrogen can increase the risk of breast cancer or endometrial cancer. For this reason, the decision whether to undergo hormone replacement therapy must be made very carefully, in consultation with a doctor. Because of the connection to endometrial cancer, estrogen supplements are often taken in tandem with another sex hormone, progesterone. Many health professionals also suggest that patients get a mammogram before they get estrogen treatments, fearing that undetected breast cancer can spread faster in the presence of more of the hormone.

The cost of estrogen replacement therapy has risen steadily—a fact noted by lawmakers arguing that the MEDICARE program should pay for a PRESCRIPTION DRUG BENEFIT because elderly people usually need drugs more often. A study by University of Minnesota researchers for the advocacy group Families USA found the cost of one year's worth of Premarin estrogen replacement tablets rose from $135 to $208 between January 1994 and October 1999.

Estrogen also has surfaced in a heated medical controversy over whether women over seventy should get regular mammograms. A 1999 study in the *Journal of the American Medical Association* said that women over seventy have shorter life expectancies and stand less chance of dying from breast cancer than younger women. It suggested bone mineral density scans could help women decide whether to have a mammogram, reasoning if a woman has dense bones, it is likely she has higher estrogen levels which would increase her risk of breast cancer. Some critics have questioned whether low bone density would be reason enough to forgo mammograms.

Health professionals may get a more complete understanding of estrogen's effects on the body through the Women's Health Initiative, a federally sponsored effort that is examining the effects of hormone replacement on more than 27,000 middle-aged and older women. Results are expected within five years.

Exclusion of gain

Exclusion of gain refers to the amount of profit (for instance, from the sale of one's house) that is tax-free. The Taxpayer Relief Act of 1997 (PL 105-34) made major changes to the tax code regarding real estate sales, eliminating provisions such as a one-time $125,000 exemption and a "rollover" provision that only helped individuals who sold houses and then purchased more expensive properties. Now, on all sales of a principal residence after May 6, 1997, individuals can deduct $250,000 in proceeds from their taxable incomes, while couples can write off $500,000. There are no limits on how often the exclusion is used, so long as the property in the transaction was used as the principal residence for two out of the five years preceding the sale.

The changes were a boon for people nearing retirement age, who could sell their homes and buy or rent smaller dwellings without having to worry about tax consequences. But some believe the lower exemption for singles unfairly discriminates against older people whose spouses have died. However, these individuals may deduct home improvements and real estate commissions in such a way as to adjust the basis price of the property from the date of the spouse's death—a provision that likely would reduce the taxable portion of a profitable sale.

F

Family and Medical Leave Act

The 1993 passage of the long-stymied Family and Medical Leave Act (PL 103-3) signaled the first legislative victory of President Bill Clinton's administration and brought important changes to workplace law with respect to caring for children and the elderly. The law allows twelve weeks of unpaid leave during any twelve-month period because of the birth or adoption of a child, the placement of a foster child, serious illness, or the need to care for an ailing elderly parent or relative. The law applies to any employee who has worked for the employer for at least twelve months and for at least 1,250 hours during that period. Employers can deny leave for certain highly paid workers or others deemed essential to keeping the business running.

Congressional Democrats had pushed family leave legislation for years, but had been thwarted mostly by Republican presidential administrations, who believed it could economically damage businesses. Clinton's election changed the dynamic, partly helped by Vice President Al Gore, who championed the legislation during their first campaign, telling how fortunate he had been to be able to take time off from work when his young son lay critically ill in the hospital after the boy was hit by a car. Because the law only applies to businesses with fifty or more workers, about 95 percent of all employers are exempt. However, the

The Family and Medical Leave Act was the first legislative victory of the Clinton administration, partly due to Vice President Al Gore's championing of the legislation during the first Clinton/Gore campaign. Source: R. Michael Jenkins, Congressional Quarterly

5 percent subject to the law employ some 60 percent of the nation's workers.

The law has provided relief to many workers who have aging spouses or parents suffering from terminal illnesses. However, the public frequently associates the law with child care, and does not recognize its full scope. Not only does it allow someone to tend to a frail, elderly relative, but it permits the CAREGIVER to take time off in increments, not all at once. The law does not apply to cases in which a person needs time off to take an ailing spouse or parent to the doctor, nor to situations in which a frail senior develops less-serious health problems, such as a cold. However, legislatures in such states as California, Minnesota, and Oregon have passed laws extending the reach of the Family and Medical Leave Act to apply to these situations. Typically the state laws require employers to allow workers to take up to half of their paid sick leave to take care of ill family members.

Federal Council on the Aging

The Federal Council on the Aging is an advisory board created through the 1973 amendments to the OLDER AMERICANS ACT and consists of fifteen members appointed by the president and Congress who review, evaluate, and recommend federal policies targeted at elderly people. Members have included former actress June Allyson, who was appointed by President Ronald Reagan. The panel is supposed to sponsor public forums on aging issues and prepare an annual report to the president. However, its existence and relevance has come into question during broader congressional debates over streamlining and reauthorizing the Older Americans Act. The last time the council received federal funding was in fiscal 1995, and the 1999 Omnibus Appropriations Act permanently prohibited spending federal funds for the council. The ADMINISTRATION ON AGING, a branch of the Department of Health and Human Services, long has been recognized as the primary agency advocate for the elderly.

Federal employee retirement

Federal workers are covered by one of two retirement systems. The Civil Service Retirement System, or CSRS, was established in 1920 and remained the pension plan that covered most government workers until 1984. More than two million retirees continue to draw pensions through CSRS, but the program no longer admits new applicants. Virtually every federal worker hired since 1984 belongs to the Federal Employees' Retirement System, or FERS, which was created by Congress in 1986 through PL 99-335 and is modeled on successful PRIVATE PENSION plans run by mid-sized and larger businesses. FERS is a defined-benefit plan, meaning pension payments are determined by a formula that takes into account past salary (the highest three consecutive years of basic pay) and years of service. However, workers proportionately pay only a small amount into the system, and the majority of benefits are covered by taxpayers.

The need for two systems came about due to the 1983 amendments to the SOCIAL SECURITY ACT. To raise revenues for the then financially stressed system, Congress enacted a recommendation of the GREENSPAN COMMISSION and brought the federal civil service system into the SOCIAL SECURITY system. This increased payroll tax collections, but the combined increase of taxation between Social Security and CSRS was so great (more than 13 percent) that policymakers spent two years designing a new system to remove duplication between the two systems, modernize benefits, and charge a more reasonable rate. CSRS will cease to exist when the last employee or survivor in the system dies.

In 2000, federal workers under FERS contributed a tax of 1.2 percent of their pay and those under CSRS 7.4 percent. Covered workers under FERS receive the basic program benefit, Social Security benefits (reduced by $2 for every $3 received under FERS), and benefits under the Thrift Savings Plan, or TPS, a 401(K)-type investment. Federal workers may invest up to 10 percent of their pretax pay in the TPS and receive a government match of 5 percent of their contribution. Unlike workers in private pension systems with tax-deferred retirement savings plans, these workers may not contribute up to the $10,500 limit mandated by law.

The balances in federal workers' retirement systems do not reflect outstanding obligations; by the late 1990s the balance needed to cover all future benefits exceeded the amount in the fund by about $350 billion. Critics of the system say this unfunded liability is inconsistent with the federal law that requires private pension plans to be prefunded. However, private employers that run these plans can go out of business—an event not likely to happen to the U.S. government. In essence, defenders of the federal pension system say it represents an ongoing obligation to future retirees that will not all come due at once. Like the Social Security system, the system's surplus assets are placed in a TRUST FUND in the form of special U.S. Treasury IOUs. The money to pay current retirees comes from general taxes and payroll tax contributions from current workers.

Federal Insurance Contribution Act of 1937 (FICA)

The Federal Insurance Contribution Act, often referred to as FICA (pronounced fai-cah), was enacted two years after the creation of SOCIAL SECURITY and formally established the concept of taxing the working public to support the national retirement system—the basis of the PAY-AS-YOU-GO SYSTEM. Most of the two-year interval was spent waiting to see whether Social Security would survive court challenges; it was unclear whether the Tenth Amendment, or "reserve clause," of the Constitution—which states that powers not specifically granted to the federal government by the Constitution are reserved for the states—gave the federal government the power to expand its responsibilities and establish a national social-insurance system. The U.S. Supreme Court's decisions in HELVERING V. DAVIS and two other cases, all issued in May 1937, affirmed the legality of an old-age insurance system.

Under FICA, workers and their employers fund the system by each paying payroll taxes equivalent to 6.2 percent of covered wages. Self-employed individuals pay 12.4 percent of taxable self-employment income. The INTERNAL REVENUE SERVICE collects the taxes and deposits the money in government-administered accounts known as the OLD-AGE AND SURVIVORS INSURANCE AND DISABILITY INSURANCE TRUST FUNDS (OASDI). Proposals to "PRIVATIZE" Social Security often center on allowing workers to invest a percentage of their FICA taxes in stocks, bonds, bank certificates of deposit, or other financial instruments.

Workers' wages in 2000 were subject to FICA up to a cut-off point of $72,600 (the figure rises from year to year). Individuals who work two jobs

FICA and Self-Employment Contributions Act (SECA) Tax Rates and Maximum Taxable Earnings, Selected Years, 1937–2001 (in percent)

Social Security and Medicare taxes over the years

		Rate paid by employee and employer					
Calendar year	OASI	Disability insurance (DI)	OASDI	Hospital insurance (HI)	Total	Self-employed rate	Maximum taxable earnings
1937	1.0	NA	NA	NA	1.0	NA	$3,000
1950	1.5	NA	NA	NA	3.0	NA	3,000
1960	3.0	0.25	2.75	NA	3.0	4.5	4,800
1970	3.65	0.55	4.20	0.60	4.8	6.9	7,800
1980	4.52	0.56	5.08	1.05	6.13	8.1	25,900
1990	5.60	0.60	6.20	1.45	7.65	15.3	51,300
1995	5.26	0.94	6.20	1.45	7.65	15.3	61,200[1]
1999	5.35	0.85	6.20	1.45	7.65	15.3	72,600[1]
2000	5.30	0.90	6.20	1.45	7.65	15.3	76,200[1]
2001 and later	5.30	0.90	6.20	1.45	7.65	15.3	([2])

[1] OASDI; no limit (HI).
[2] Not yet determined for OASDI; no limit (HI).
NA: Not applicable.
Note: Until 1991 the maximum taxable earnings for HI were the same as for OASDI. In 1991, 1992, and 1993 maximum taxable earnings were $125,000, $130,200, and $135,000 respectively, with no limit after 1993. Only 92.35 percent net self-employment earnings are taxable and half of the SECA taxes so computed is deductible for income tax purposes.
Source: House Ways and Means Committee *Green Book* (2000); Congressional Research Service.

and earn combined incomes above this ceiling often have too much FICA tax withheld by employers, who assume they are only working one job. If proof is presented, the Internal Revenue Service credits individuals for overpayments. Likewise, temporary nonresident aliens who don't participate in the Social Security system and are not subject to FICA withholding taxes often get the appropriate amounts deducted anyway. These individuals can apply to the IRS for refunds.

Flemming v. Nestor

The landmark U.S. Supreme Court case *Flemming v. Nestor* established that individuals have no legal claim to accrued SOCIAL SECURITY con-

tributions or anticipated Social Security payments. Put another way, the payroll taxes workers contribute to Social Security in no way assure that they will receive any benefits from the system, unlike in a private pension system.

The case was brought by Ephram Nestor, a Bulgarian immigrant who arrived in the United States in 1918 and paid Social Security taxes from the inception of the system until 1955, when he retired. One year later, at the height of the Cold War, Nestor was deported for having been a member of the Communist Party in the 1930s. Because Congress in 1954 had passed a law denying Social Security benefits for deportees, Nestor sued, saying his FICA tax payments essentially amounted to a property right.

The high court disagreed, ruling in 1960 that treating Social Security taxes and payments as accrued personal property would rob the system of the flexibility to adjust to changing demographic conditions. The decision tracked with the 1937 decision in *HELVERING V. DAVIS*, in which the majority of justices ruled that Social Security taxes are supposed to be paid into the U.S. Treasury like other forms of internal revenue, and not to be earmarked in any way.

Formulary

A formulary is a list of drugs that are covered by a health insurance plan, a hospital, or a government agency, such as the U.S. Department of Veterans Affairs (VA). Formularies became symbols of cost-conscious health care in the 1990s when HMOs and other health-care providers adopted them in an effort to curb rising drug costs and better focus on their financial bottom lines. But critics contend many insurers restrict their lists to only the cheapest drugs or only approve a limited number of medications for particular medical problems. Critics say this standardized approach causes problems because it does not always address patients' individual needs and can limit access to new drugs because of the time it takes to review their efficacy, or insurers' unwillingness to do so. Defenders counter that formularies, when used properly, ensure that patients have access to only the safest and most effective medications, as determined by health professionals, and improve the overall quality of care.

Many private insurers or government agencies refuse to pay for drugs that are not on their lists. Others impose an added charge for nonformulary prescriptions. Physicians, by law, must be able to supercede a formulary limitation with an applica-

tion to a health insurer stating they feel the patient needs to have a drug that is not listed on the formulary. However, outcomes research has shown that doctors get frustrated with the lengthy application process. While these practices are most commonly associated with the managed-care revolution of the 1980s and 1990s, some organizations like the VA have been using formularies since the 1950s in an effort to standardize drug availability in many different facilities, ensure some continuity of care, and keep costs in line.

Many health insurers contract with companies known as PHARMACY BENEFIT MANAGERS to run their prescription drug programs, negotiate volume discounts with pharmaceutical companies, and in some cases, try to urge doctors and patients to use only selected medications. These benefit managers now control more than one-third of the national market for prescription drugs.

401(k) plan

The popular 401(k) plan, a variety of DEFINED-CONTRIBUTION plan, provides a nest egg for an estimated thirty million Americans by allowing workers to divert a portion of their paychecks into stocks, bonds, mutual funds, or other securities. The money grows tax-free until retirement, when the individual makes withdrawals and is taxed at presumably a lower rate. The plans are often credited with enabling many middle-class workers to invest in the stock market for the first time, though the size of the benefit almost entirely depends on how much the worker decides to contribute to the plan, and to the type of

Theodore Benna, father of the 401(k) plan, peers over his educational 401(k) "komic" book. Launched in November 1999, 401 Komics aims "to take the traditional stuff of retirement planning and bring it to life more powerfully." Source: Michele Mott, AP Photo/Centre Daily Times

investments the worker selects. Surveys of plans suggest the majority of allocated assets in 401(k) plans are in groups of U.S. stocks, followed by individual employers' stocks and "stable value" instruments, such as money-market funds. More than 80 percent of employers who offer the plans match all or a portion of their employees' contributions.

The 401(k) plan came about quite by accident. In the 1970s, the INTERNAL REVENUE SERVICE began to question the propriety of profit-sharing plans some corporations set up for highly paid executives that allowed the recipients to shelter the money from taxes. Congress responded by inserting paragraph "k" into Section 401 of the Revenue Act of 1978, which protected plans that allowed employees to put bonuses in tax-free investment trusts, as long as they didn't discriminate against lower-paid workers.

In 1980, Philadelphia benefits consultant Theodore Benna recognized that the law enabled companies to establish retirement savings plans for all their workers—and even gave employers the option of matching employees' contributions to give them an added incentive to participate. Instead of paying bonuses, Benna argued, the companies could oversee increasingly large pools of money and take advantage of growing securities markets to build up significant investment trusts. But many companies balked, worried about the legality of the practice, and questioning why large corporations had not yet set up such plans. Benna and his associates eventually set up a plan at their own company as a kind of demonstration project for clients, and the idea slowly gained popularity.

The surge of corporate mergers in recent years has caused some concern for owners of 401(k) plans. Individuals who lose their jobs in mergers, or whose 401(k) plans are terminated, receive cash distributions of accumulated assets. Financial advisors suggest the best move in cases such as this is to roll the distribution over into a tax-sheltered INDIVIDUAL RETIREMENT ACCOUNT (IRA) in order to avoid what could be a staggering tax bill and penalties imposed for early withdrawals. In fact, evidence shows that three out of four people cash out of the plans and decide to spend some of the money, though mostly for purposes such as paying for children's college tuition, retraining for themselves, or medical expenses.

Many companies that go through mergers or are acquired by another corporation continue to have some form of 401(k) plan, but may operate it under different conditions. Financial advisors suggest workers who want to continue participating in the plan read the new rules and study the investment options, perhaps requesting a prospectus for new mutual funds.

403(b) plan

The 403(b) tax-deferred DEFINED-CONTRIBUTION PLAN, named for the section of the INTERNAL REVENUE SERVICE code that established it, is often referred to as a 401(k) plan for nonprofit corporations, such as hospitals, schools, and charitable foundations. The similarities are numerous: employees choose the contribution level and investment portfolio, and the plans are "portable," meaning they can be rolled into an IRA or another organization's 403(b).

However, there are some key differences between the two types of plans. Tax-free organizations usually do not have a waiting period before employees are "vested" and can participate in 403(b) plans, unlike many corporations with 401(k)'s. Additionally, employer participation is not required in a 403(b) plan, as opposed to

401(k)'s, where the sponsoring company is responsible for setting up and administering the program and making sure it doesn't discriminate against certain classes of workers. The 403(b) also is subject to regulations in the EMPLOYEE RETIREMENT INCOME SECURITY ACT OF 1974 (ERISA) only if the employer is actively involved in establishing the program, unlike 401(k)'s.

Free radical

A free radical is a highly reactive atom or molecule that has at least one unpaired electron and exists in an agitated state because electrons prefer to exist in pairs. Free radicals have the tendency to attack the body's cells to gain the extra electron and have been linked to CANCER, HEART DISEASE, ALZHEIMER'S DISEASE, cataract formation, and the more generalized breakdown of tissue that accompanies aging. The body produces a class of compounds known as ANTIOXIDANTS that normally can keep free radicals subdued. However, older individuals whose cells are weakened by aging are more vulnerable to free-radical attacks. Hundreds of nutritional supplements are aggressively marketed every year as an effective defense against these cellular predators. However, scientific studies so far have only identified a handful—such as the group of fat-soluble antioxidants known collectively as Vitamin E—that actually appear to have some protective properties, particularly in the case of heart disease. Doctors say maintaining a balanced diet that is low in fats, avoiding excessive sun exposure, and not smoking or drinking also prevents the buildup of free radicals.

Fuller, Ida Mae

Ida Mae Fuller, a retired law clerk from Ludlow, Vermont, became a footnote figure in American history on January 31, 1940, when she was the first person to receive a monthly SOCIAL SECURITY check—for $22.54. At the time, American society was very different from today. There were many more workers than retired people, and the average American was only expected to live to sixty-one, meaning many would never receive a single Social Security check. Additionally, Social Security initially limited who could participate in the program to employees in commerce or industry (the program gradually was expanded over the years, with categories added beginning in the early 1950s to include government workers, employees of nonprofit organizations, individuals in agriculture, and the self-employed). Under the then-new Social Security system, the first retirees like Fuller predictably collected much more in benefits than they had paid into the system. Fuller had paid a lifetime Social Security tax bill of less than $25 because taxes had only been collected since 1937. At the time of her death at age one hundred, in 1975, she had collected $22,000 in benefits.

Ida Mae Fuller was the first person to receive increased benefits under a new Social Security law. Source: AP Photo

Functional impairment

Functional impairment generally is understood to mean the loss of normal physical or mental functions. It is one of the most anxiety-producing aspects of aging because it can prevent elderly people from performing ACTIVITIES OF DAILY LIVING, as well as tasks they have become accustomed to all of their adult lives, such as cooking, gardening, or driving. This can lead to increased isolation, boredom, depression, and physical ailments linked to inactivity. The most common form of functional impairment is the memory loss and cognitive problems arising from ALZHEIMER'S DISEASE or related DEMENTIA. However, some studies suggest that non-disease-linked functional impairment in elderly people can be avoided, or at least delayed.

The 1998 MacArthur Foundation Study of Aging in America suggests cognitive losses are not necessarily an unavoidable part of aging. Though thought processes tend to slow down, and elderly people often get more easily distracted than younger individuals, they can continue to pursue intellectual goals by being more patient and focusing on single tasks, one at a time. Scientific

A Texas funeral director points out a display of compact coffins during the National Funeral Directors Association's trade show in Las Vegas. The fast-changing funeral industry has attracted constant scrutiny recently for a number of reasons, among them misleading customers who were unaware that they could purchase caskets from third parties. Source: Lennox McLendon, AP Photo

studies also suggest that, while the elderly have more trouble recalling specific bits of information, such as a name or phone number on demand, their "working memory"—or ability to recall recognized routines—remains comparatively sharp. Similarly, the MacArthur study and other clinical research suggests that a healthy diet and reasonable amounts of exercise often can forestall physical conditions, such as HEART DISEASE, DIABETES, and hypertension, and sometimes alleviates symptoms of ARTHRITIS and OSTEOPOROSIS.

Funeral arrangements

Planning a funeral can be one of the most emotionally trying experiences in a person's lifetime. Many elderly people try to relieve the burden that would be placed on their families by preplanning funerals, perhaps by purchasing a cemetery plot or buying life insurance to pay for a funeral by naming the funeral home as a beneficiary. However, the $10-billion-per-year funeral industry has come under increased scrutiny over the past two decades because of increased reporting of fraud. In particular, federal officials cite instances in which funeral home operators misled people who weren't aware they could reduce their costs by purchasing caskets from third parties. Some unscrupulous operators also imposed hidden charges for cremation or body refrigeration fees or lied about state regulations governing grave-liners and other items. Prepaid cemetery plots are another source of concern, especially because nearly one-quarter of all funerals now are prepaid. Often depicted as a hedge against inflationary costs, consumer advocates say some prepaid plots are riddled with hidden fees.

The Federal Trade Commission (FTC) maintains oversight of the funeral industry through the so-called Funeral Rule, which went into effect in 1984 and requires funeral operators to itemize prices for services and outline to customers which services are required and which are optional. However, the U.S. General Accounting Office in 1999 reported that enforcement of the rule is spotty and that fines are inconsistent. The SENATE

SPECIAL COMMITTEE ON AGING took an interest in the subject and asked for more investigations. AARP reported that it had conducted spot surveys, in which its anonymous shoppers were lied to by some funeral directors in an effort to boost sales. FTC officials say they are exploring ways to tighten oversight and indicate they will revise major portions of the rule. Some areas likely to be addressed are funeral homes that raise prices excessively, then persuade customers to purchase a supposed discount package that really is not a bargain. Officials also want to make consumers aware that they can purchase caskets from independent vendors.

The problems are a big concern for some longtime family funeral operators, who note their industry has undergone many changes since the 1980s. Large chains have spent heavily to buy out family-run funeral businesses and have asked federal regulators for more uniform rules so they don't have to adapt to regulations in each state. Many cemeteries also have been sold. Sometimes, new owners raise prices while individuals are in the midst of paying for funeral plots via installment plans.

Groups such as the Hinesburg, Vermont–based Funeral Consumers Alliance are lobbying for more information up front. Consumer groups also want subtle changes to wording in the Funeral Rule, which they say now creates a loophole for those who only sell items pertaining to funerals, such as caskets, or who only provide services, such as cremations. In 2000, the FTC contemplated revising the funeral rule, and undertook a review of public comments on how the regulation might be strengthened.

G

Gay and lesbian issues

The plight of older homosexuals is an understudied area of social policy but one that is getting more attention with the greater awareness of the diversity within the elderly population. After decades of hiding their sexual preferences for fear of discrimination, many elderly gays and lesbians are beginning to exert clout through organizations such as Senior Action in a Gay Environment (SAGE) in New York City. They also are giving social scientists a new appreciation of how one minority group accepts the aging process.

Researchers at the University of Minnesota in the early 1990s studied the attitudes of gay and lesbian elderly people and found many shared the same anxieties as "straight" seniors—fears of loneliness, health problems, lack of income, and concerns about discrimination they might encounter in the health-care system. But respondents also said that being gay or lesbian helped them deal with aging. Being part of a sometimes ostracized sexual and social minority group encouraged independence and a certain caution, for instance, in saving money to guard against economic hardship, the researchers reported.

Particular attention has been focused on the local level at housing options for senior citizen gays and lesbians. A number of ASSISTED LIVING communities targeted at gays and lesbians have been established, addressing a need advocates say is critical because many older gays and lesbians lack confidants and support networks. Developers have even talked about creating Sun City–like retirement cities, such as the proposed Our Town, in California's wine country, a collection of five hundred condominiums and homes in a resort-type setting whose population would primarily be gay.

However, not everyone wants to live in such settings. Developers exploring construction of more modestly scaled housing in other areas found many gays do not want to live in a segregated setting, and consider the political interests of neighbors a more important factor than their sexual preferences.

The Lesbian and Gay Information Network (LGAIN) was formed in the early 1990s by the AMERICAN SOCIETY ON AGING in San Francisco to inform practitioners, researchers, and policymakers in aging about the concerns of serving this population of elders. For example, a life partner of someone who has a stroke or develops ALZHEIMER'S DISEASE may be deliberately or inadvertently barred from access to their loved one in a hospital because he or she is not a member of "the immediate family," even though the partner may be the best source of information that providers may need to take care of the patient. LGAIN sponsors conferences, a newsletter, and networking opportunities.

While his wife, Cindy, videotapes the event, Sen. John McCain addresses an MTV reception at the Philadelphia Hard Rock Café on July 31, 2000. Of all the candidates during the 2000 presidential campaign, McCain tried hardest to target Generation X voters. Source: Suzanne Plunkett, AP Photo

Generation X

The people born immediately after the BABY BOOM, from 1964 through the early 1980s (there is no consensus, yet, on which year) are collectively known as Generation X. These individuals are often cast as the political antagonists of elderly people in debates over the future of government ENTITLEMENT PROGRAMS. While Generation Xers contribute payroll taxes to fund the SOCIAL SECURITY, MEDICARE, and MEDICAID benefits of current retirees, polls suggest the majority of these younger Americans don't believe these programs will exist by the time they retire because older people will have depleted the resources. Polling also indicates Generation X members are generally more apathetic toward government than previous generations, and less inclined to believe that politicians have solutions to society's big problems. This translates into lower voter turnout. According to the National Association of Secretaries of State, voter participation among eighteen- to twenty-four-year-olds has declined from 50 percent in 1972—the first presidential election after the minimum voting age was lowered to eighteen—to 32 percent in 1996.

The 2000 election cycle was a significant one for Generation X because it marked the first time that virtually all of its members were eligible to vote. Still, advocacy groups such as THIRD MILLENNIUM complained that most candidates, and the major political parties, didn't target them as a bona fide voting bloc. Sen. John McCain's insurgent Republican campaign came the closest, with McCain's exhortations that young people devote themselves to lofty causes and the campaign's clever use of rock music at some political rallies. Other politicians who have adroitly tried to tap support among this group include President Bill Clinton, who appeared on MTV during his 1992 presidential campaign, and Minnesota governor Jesse Ventura, whose 1998 third-party candidacy featured unconventional advertising aired on rock radio stations.

However, it is still unclear whether Generation

X is overlooked or merely apathetic. A big question for members of this DEMOGRAPHIC group is how active will they be in looming national debates over the future of Social Security and Medicare. While many politicians continue to fret about how reform proposals will affect their standing among SENIOR VOTERS, studies suggest they might tap support among younger workers by advocating proposals such as Social Security PRIVATIZATION plans that reduce payroll taxes and allow the creation of personalized retirement accounts. Yet, to date, support for these proposals has mainly come from middle-aged conservatives and some centrist Democrats. Indeed, a Harris Poll on "Myths and Realities of Aging," sponsored by the NATIONAL COUNCIL ON THE AGING in Washington, D.C., and the International Longevity Center in New York City and released in the spring of 2000, found two-thirds of those surveyed who were under the age of sixty-five rejected the idea that some money spent on Social Security should be used for children instead of elders. The vast majority of this group also believed Medicare should be expanded to include benefits such as LONG-TERM CARE.

Geriatric-care manager

Geriatric-care management, also known in some areas by the more bureaucratic term "case management," is a relatively new profession built around helping elderly people with financial, legal, and LONG-TERM CARE arrangements. These individuals may be registered nurses, trained social workers or psychologists, or gerontologists. But because geriatric-care managers are not certified by federal or state authorities, it is important that the individuals who hire them interview candidates extensively and review their qualifications and the scope of their services. Some professional organizations offer geriatric-care manager certification programs.

Geriatric-care managers are often retained by family members of an elderly person who does not live nearby, or who needs assistance with some ACTIVITIES OF DAILY LIVING. Fees can often run in excess of $100 per hour. One key aspect of the service is that the care manager not only recommends services and solutions but also monitors the quality of whatever assistance is provided. For instance, the care manager should be responsible for assessing the quality of in-home services and paratransit options for a partially disabled elderly person or a senior who is recovering from surgery. Similarly, the care manager should act as a liaison between service providers and the family and mediate disputes that may arise over moving an older person to or from a NURSING HOME, or preserving assets through a particular kind of investment. State and local agencies on aging and the Tucson, Arizona–based National Association of Professional Geriatric Care Managers provide information about practitioners.

Geriatrics

"Geriatrics," or "geriatric medicine," is a somewhat broadly used term describing a medical specialty that focuses exclusively on the needs of elderly people. This field takes up care of chronic illnesses, such as OSTEOPOROSIS, HEART DISEASE, and STROKE, as well as palliative end-of-life care. Only three of the 126 medical schools in the United States have a full department of geriatric medi-

A doctor briefs residents at George Washington University Hospital in Washington, D.C. With only about one-third of U.S. medical schools requiring their students to take courses in geriatrics, and a rapidly expanding aging population, there is a dearth of much-needed geriatric care in the United States. Source: R. Michael Jenkins, Congressional Quarterly

cine that offers formalized programs of study in medical care for the elderly for physicians and nurses. The main one was established by Dr. ROBERT BUTLER at Mount Sinai School of Medicine in New York City. Only about one-third of the other medical schools require their students to take any courses in geriatrics. This is unlike other economically advanced nations, such as England, Germany, or Japan, where almost every medical school has a geriatrics department. Advocates for the elderly say such nationwide approaches assure older people receive a continuum of care for all their medical needs, from acute conditions, such as broken hips or heart attacks, to the care terminally ill people receive in HOSPICES.

Public health officials say the United States faces a shortage of physicians who are adequately trained in geriatric care as the first wave of baby boomers reaches sixty-five. The Health Resources and Services Administration, a branch of the U.S. Department of HEALTH AND HUMAN SERVICES, estimates that some 30,000 primary care internists and family physicians were needed in the year 2000 in geriatrics, though less than one-third of that number were actually practicing. The Health Professions Education Partnerships Act of 1998 amended the Public Health Service Act and authorized grant programs for geriatric residencies and fellowships. The act also provided funding for a network of geriatric education centers at medical schools to develop curricula for the treatment of health problems common to elderly people, provide continuing education to doctors and nurses involved with geriatric care, and offer medical students clinical training in NURSING HOMES, senior centers, and hospitals that specialize in chronic diseases.

Health professionals believe such training may

narrow critical gaps in care that currently exist, particularly for terminally ill elderly patients. For instance, it is widely assumed that older CANCER patients cannot handle aggressive chemotherapy regimens as well as younger patients because they have other health problems, such as failing kidneys, that make it more difficult to excrete toxic drugs. But several studies suggest elderly breast cancer patients respond better than their younger counterparts to aggressive chemotherapy. On the other hand, some surveys of patients and health professionals indicate that doctors sometimes give critically ill patients overly optimistic diagnoses, leading the patients to opt for grueling treatments that can leave them debilitated and in pain. In some cases, a more pragmatic approach might allow patients to spend their final days at home with loved ones, or in other more comfortable surroundings. In either case, advocates for the elderly say better training might make doctors less inclined to make decisions about patient care based on gut instinct.

Geriatrics is related to, but different from, gerontology, which is the aging-related discipline for social researchers, nonmedical health and service practitioners—such as social workers or private care managers—and program managers in aging. Some, but not many, doctors refer to themselves as gerontologists. However, physicians who specialize in aging generally belong to the American Geriatrics Society in New York and call themselves geriatricians.

Geroergonomics

This evolving field centers on adapting technology to help elderly people continue to live independently. Examples of geroergonomic research range from studies of light levels in public spaces to research on reaction times of older workers and their adaptive strategies, to studies on the range of mobility of impaired seniors in moving around their homes and neighborhoods. Many associate it with "assistive devices," such as automated tub chairs that allow frail seniors to get in and out of bathtubs safely. But senior advocates and medical experts say the gadgetry has measurable benefits; a 1999 study in the Archives of Family Medicine reported frail, older adults outfitted with devices and certain safety modifications in their homes required only one-quarter as much in-home care, NURSING HOME care, and hospitalizations. The individuals also were reported to be able to perform more ACTIVITIES OF DAILY LIVING and were in less pain. Despite such findings, most assistive devices aren't covered by MEDICARE or private insurance, unless they are deemed medically necessary and tied to an acute condition.

Some common devices found in homes include adjustable-height counters and toilet seats that can be used by wheelchair-bound individuals, magnifying glasses for reading, and remote controls to adjust temperature and turn lights on and off. The technological focus isn't only on homes. Some geroergonomic efforts are directed at improving lighting in public spaces, particularly restaurants, airports, and libraries, where seniors frequently complain they have trouble seeing.

Foreign nations with rapidly aging populations are even applying the geroergonomic concept to the workplace. Japan, which because of population and longevity trends will be the oldest nation in the world by 2020, has begun formalized programs to restructure workplaces, known as *kaizen*, according to *Aging Today,* the bimonthly newspaper of the AMERICAN SOCIETY ON AGING. Some companies have improved lighting, installed magnifying glasses, and changed aural signals for performing a task to visual ones to accommodate older workers with vision or hearing loss. The Japanese Ministry of Labor also is studying workers' postures to help employers prevent injuries.

Gerontological Society of America

A Washington, D.C.–based professional organization, the Gerontological Society of America is a leading source of information about current aging research and is perhaps the only entity that takes a multidisciplinary approach to the subject, by simultaneously focusing on aspects including psychology, sociology, medicine, biology, and policy. Its approximately five thousand members hold an annual meeting in Washington that has become one of the largest gatherings for educators, researchers, and policymakers active in the field. The rest of the year, the organization is best known for publishing the major peer-reviewed journals in the field—*Journal of Gerontology* and *The Gerontologist*, which are published together each month for the biomedical sciences, social sciences, and psychological sciences.

The Gerontological Society keeps abreast of cutting-edge developments through a series of "formal interest groups" of researchers who target study in subjects such as the economics of aging, mental retardation and developmental disabilities, technology and aging, and the research and evaluation of special-care units. Other areas of interest include nutrition, grandparents as caregivers, religion and aging, health promotion, and disease prevention.

Grandparents' rights

"Grandparents' rights" have become synonymous with the legal issues surrounding what kind of roles grandparents can play in their grandchildren's upbringing. Circumstances include grandparents fighting for more contact with their grandchildren, as well as situations in which grandparents have assumed the responsibility of raising a grandchild—a phenomenon also known as kinship care. Grandparents' rights have become an increasingly discussed social policy topic due to a number of recent high-profile court cases that took up whether grandparents have the right to court-ordered visits with their grandchildren. One such case involved two Washington state grandparents who sued for rights to visit their two granddaughters after their son's suicide, over the objections of the mother. The U.S. Supreme Court in June 2000 ruled, 6–3, in favor of the parents, in effect stating that America's sixty million grandparents did not have special rights to visitations and had to be included with persons outside the immediate family when determining visitation rights. State legislatures from Florida to Arizona, having overcome lawmakers' traditional aversion to delving into personal matters, also debated legislation to address the issue, often upholding visitation rights. However, legal experts say it remains difficult for grandparents to get courts to enforce such rights, unless the grandparents can prove the visits are in the best interests of the child.

While visitation issues get most of the attention, grandparents with custody of their grandchildren must navigate a different thicket of issues. Approximately four million children live in a household headed by a grandparent, according to a 1995 U.S. Census Bureau study, a 40 percent increase over the previous decade. For nearly 1.3 million children, a grandparent—usually the grandmother—is the primary caregiver. The ADMINISTRATION ON AGING says 46 percent of these children are African American, while 42 percent are white and 12 percent are Hispanic.

In many cases, the parents are unable to take care of the children because of physical ailments or other problems, such as drug abuse or teenage pregnancies in which a parent may be emotionally not ready to take care of a child. AARP, nonprofit groups such as the National Coalition of Grandparents, and some local agencies for the aging have begun serving as resource centers to help elderly people in charge of young children cope with financial and legal issues.

Low-income grandparents who are raising their grandchildren often are eligible for forms of federal assistance, such as SUPPLEMENTAL SECURITY INCOME, public housing, and school meals. But the sweeping welfare reform proposal known as the Personal Responsibility and Work Opportunities Act (PL 104-193), passed by Congress and signed into law by President Bill Clinton in 1996, has made the situation more complicated. AARP notes that grandparents have to decide whether to receive public assistance for themselves, which is subject to a lifetime limit of five years, or opt for a "child only" grant that pays less money but isn't subject to a time limit and doesn't require the grandparent to work. Senior advocates suggest individuals facing such choices consult with social services case workers or local legal services organizations.

Gray Panthers

Founded in 1970 by social activist Maggie Kuhn, the Gray Panthers is a left-leaning advocacy group for the elderly that has been among the most vocal organizations calling for universal health care, economic justice for minorities, and the preservation of the SOCIAL SECURITY and MEDICARE programs as they currently exist. The Washington, D.C.–based organization prides itself on challenging the status quo with tactics that sometimes hark back to the 1960s; in 1974 the Gray Panthers picketed the annual meeting of the AMERICAN MEDICAL ASSOCIATION in Chicago, protesting the group's traditional opposition to expanded government-provided health benefits and staging street skits calling for "health care as a human right."

Though overshadowed by the more centrist and establishment AARP, the Gray Panthers continue to influence the political debate. The organization's "wall of shame" and other public displays at its biennial convention highlight the plight of the uninsured, elderly persons without prescription drug coverage, and seniors who must see "gatekeeper" doctors before they are allowed access to medical specialists. The Gray Panthers also have long-standing ties to consumer organizations affiliated with Ralph Nader that have resulted in collaborative efforts to spotlight NURSING HOME abuse and fraud in the hearing aid industry.

Great Britain pension system

Great Britain is one of the many countries that have overhauled their social security systems in recent decades. A PRIVATIZATION plan begun by then prime minister Margaret Thatcher in 1986 established a two-tiered system that includes a traditional PAY-AS-YOU-GO national retirement plan, plus the opportunity for some workers to invest in private retirement accounts.

All British workers and their employers pay into the basic government plan, known as the National Insurance Fund, which pays a defined benefit. Workers and employers also pay a payroll tax into the State Earnings Related Pension Scheme, known as SERPS, which acts as a supplemental government plan. However, workers can opt out of SERPS and redirect a portion of the tax into personal pension plans that operate similarly to IRAS or mutual-fund-type investments and, presumably, generate a higher rate of return. Workers who take this route get a portion of their payroll taxes rebated by the government directly into their accounts.

The restructuring allowed the British to amass more than the equivalent of $1 trillion in retirement savings by the late 1990s while getting better control over entitlement spending. The system has been credited with helping Britain remain economically vibrant and competitive with other European countries by providing plentiful capital for British companies through the financial markets. However, individuals who opted for the privatization option have lost significant sums by succumbing to high-pressure sales tactics from certain financial firms. Some companies are compensating them for losses, but the questionable activities have sparked numerous criminal investigations.

Greenspan Commission

The National Commission on Social Security Reform, commonly known as the Greenspan Commission, was a fifteen-member, bipartisan panel convened by President RONALD REAGAN in late 1981 to address structural reforms to the SOCIAL SECURITY system, and chaired by the current Federal Reserve chairman, Alan M. Greenspan. At the time, Social Security was going through a major financial crisis. The federal budget deficits of the late 1970s combined with "stagflation" that resulted in CONSUMER PRICE INDEX increases of more than 10 percent left the national pension system perilously close to insolvency. The OLD-AGE AND SURVIVORS DISABILITY TRUST FUNDS (OASDI) by 1981 only had enough reserves to pay about one and one-half months' worth of benefits. By November 1982, the OASDI funds had to borrow from other Social Security TRUST FUNDS to finance benefit payments.

The Greenspan Commission made a number of significant changes that were adopted by Congress in the form of the 1983 amendments to the SOCIAL SECURITY ACT (PL 98-21). Combined, they represent the most recent restructuring of the system. The commission recommended a series of increases to Social Security tax rates, as well as an increase in the FICA tax on self-employed workers. The 1983 COST-OF-LIVING ADJUSTMENTS were delayed six months. Beginning in 1984, up to half of the Social Security benefits of wealthier retirees—defined as individuals earning more

Alan Greenspan speaks before a congressional committee in September 1982. In the most recent restructuring of the Social Security system, the Greenspan Commission, convened the year before, recommended a series of increases to Social Security tax rates, as well as an increase in the FICA tax on self-employed workers. Source: Brad Markel, Congressional Quarterly

than $25,000 and couples earning more than $32,000, in addition to Social Security—were made subject to income taxation. Finally, the commission recommended slowly increasing the retirement age from sixty-five to sixty-seven by 2027.

Greenspan predicted these reforms would keep Social Security solvent until at least 2068. However, Social Security's trustees now think the TRUST FUND surplus will be exhausted some three decades sooner. That is because the trustees assume wages will grow more slowly than the Greenspan Commission believed. In addition, there are fewer workers and more retirees than when the commission did its work in the early 1980s.

Guardianship

Guardianship, also called conservatorship, is the status of a person appointed to make important decisions and, in some cases, handle the personal affairs of incapacitated people. Guardians are appointed by state courts and usually are friends or family members of the disabled person. In the case of elderly people, guardianship may become an option if a person is stricken by a debilitating condition like ALZHEIMER'S DISEASE or a related DEMENTIA and has not made a will or TRUST or engaged in other aspects of ESTATE PLANNING. The stricken individual, known as the ward, retains the right to have a say in how his or her affairs are handled, if applicable.

Courts in recent years have been increasingly sensitive to the prospect of unscrupulous individuals using guardianship and the power of attorney powers it confers as a tool to commit fraud. Judges increasingly are defining a guardian's duties very specifically—for instance, limiting the person to making financial decisions. Guardians frequently are required to post a bond equal to the ward's estate and provide to the court an accounting of what steps he or she has taken on the ward's behalf.

Officials say there are few assurances that a frail, elderly person can avoid slipping through the social safety net if a friend or family member is not available to take on the guardian's role. Federal SOCIAL SERVICES BLOCK GRANTS, enacted as part of the Omnibus Budget Reconciliation Act of 1981 (see OMNIBUS RECONCILIATION BILLS), fund local adult protective service units that provide some guardian-type services as part of state social services programs. The federal government also allows for the designation of a "representative payee" who can receive and cash government benefit checks on behalf of the recipient. There are no similar provisions for medical decision-making, however, meaning it usually takes an emergency for important care decisions to be made.

H

Health and Human Services Department (HHS)

The sprawling government agency known as the U.S. Department of Health and Human Services (HHS) came into existence on May 4, 1980. The department was originally known as the Department of Health, Education and Welfare (HEW) but saw its education functions spun off into a separate, cabinet-level agency through the Department of Education Organization Act (PL 96-88) in 1979. The SOCIAL SECURITY ADMINISTRATION also was part of HHS but became a separate stand-alone agency on March 31, 1995. HEW was originally formed during the administration of President Dwight D. Eisenhower, on April 11, 1953, to serve as the executive branch's key agency for social policy.

Today HHS has the largest budget of any federal agency, surpassing even the Department of Defense. With approximately 61,600 employees and a fiscal 2000 appropriation of $395 billion, it administers more than three hundred federal programs, including many important aging-related initiatives. The department serves as the nation's largest health insurer through its administration of MEDICARE, which handles more than 900 million claims each year.

Important divisions of HHS dealing with aging policies include the ADMINISTRATION ON AGING—the government's advocate agency for the elderly—which administers the numerous federal programs created by the OLDER AMERICANS ACT and its amendments. These include supportive services, such as MEALS ON WHEELS, grants for state and community programs on aging, senior-citizen employment programs, and elder rights-protection programs. The Administration on Aging's fiscal 2000 budget was $933 million.

HHS also is the parent of the U.S. Public Health Service, which includes eight research and health agencies. The most prominent are the Food and Drug Administration, which oversees trials and approves all prescription medications, the Centers for Disease Control and Prevention (CDC), and the NATIONAL INSTITUTES OF HEALTH (NIH), the government's premier biomedical research institution. NIH divisions include the NATIONAL INSTITUTE ON AGING, the National Cancer Institute, the National Heart, Lung, and Blood Institute, the National Institute of Neurological Disorders and Stroke, and other institutes that study DIABETES, ARTHRITIS, deafness and other communications disorders, mental health, and drug abuse. NIH's fiscal 2000 appropriation was $17.8 billion.

Another important HHS division is the HEALTH CARE FINANCING ADMINISTRATION (HCFA), which runs the Medicare and MEDICAID programs. Together, these programs serve about one in four Americans. Medicare provides health insurance for elderly and disabled Americans

The U.S. Department of Health and Human Services administers more than three hundred federal programs and serves as the nation's largest health insurer. Source: *Sue Klemens, Congressional Quarterly*

while Medicaid is a joint federal-state effort that provides health coverage for the poor, as well as LONG-TERM CARE for low-income elderly people. HCFA's fiscal 2000 budget was $325.4 billion—about $200 billion of which was directed at Medicare.

Health Care Financing Administration (HCFA)

The Health Care Financing Administration, commonly known as HCFA (pronounced hick-fa), was created by former secretary of Health, Education, and Welfare Joseph Califano in 1977 to administer the MEDICARE and MEDICAID programs. Before then, Medicare was run by the SOCIAL SECURITY ADMINISTRATION, while Medicaid was administered by the Social and Rehabilitation Services Administration. Unlike most federal agencies, HCFA is headquartered outside of Washington, D.C., in Baltimore, Maryland, and has about 4,400 employees and 10 regional offices. In addition to Medicare and Medicaid, the agency also administers the Children's Health Insurance Program, which was created by Congress as part of the BALANCED BUDGET ACT OF 1997 (PL 105-33).

HCFA is a frequent target of criticism from Congress, government auditors, and health-care providers because of its critical role as the buyer of more than $300 billion worth of health care for Americans each year. Doctors and hospitals frequently complain about the thicket of rules and regulations that govern Medicare and about HCFA efforts to restrict the use of Medicare funds in order to reduce the risk of fraud and abuse. But the agency also gets criticized by Congress and its investigative arm, the U.S. General Accounting Office (GAO), for not maintaining sufficiently strong anti-fraud measures. A 1999 GAO audit found contractors HCFA hired to root out fraudulent Medicare billings had themselves paid at least $235 million in civil and criminal penalties for misusing government funds. However, HCFA maintained that tougher oversight on its part had cut fraudulent billings and returned $1.2 billion to the Medicare TRUST FUND between 1997 and 1999.

HCFA was put in the difficult position of implementing measures to cut Medicare spending that were part of the Balanced Budget Act of 1997. Cuts in payments to Medicare HMOs in 1998 led ninety-nine of the managed-care companies to drop out of the program or reduce their coverage areas, forcing more than 400,000 Medicare beneficiaries to find new health-care arrangements. While new HMOs applied to join the program, health insurers complained that region-by-region variations in payments were leading managed-care companies to drop out of marginally profitable areas, restricting patient choice. The Balanced Budget Act also forces HCFA to come up with new payment formulas for HOME HEALTH providers and NURSING HOMES. Defenders of the agency say it will continue to be hard-pressed to simultaneously implement rules, run complicated and massive government programs, and coordinate large-scale anti-fraud efforts.

Hearing loss

An estimated ten million elderly Americans, including one-third of those between the ages of sixty-five and seventy-four and more than half of those over the age of eighty, suffer from some form of hearing loss. Many resist publicly acknowledging the problem because of its association with frailty and the way it makes people appear confused. For this reason, hearing tests have become a standard part of geriatric medical check-ups. However, MEDICARE does not pay for hearing aid evaluations or for the devices themselves. The cost of hearing aids varies widely, from $500 to more than $1,000, and has become a much-discussed consumer issue because of the high markups charged by some sellers.

Hearing loss can be caused by prolonged exposure to loud noise, past ear infections, or simpler problems, such as a buildup of wax in the ear canal. Physicians tend to break hearing loss into several categories. Presbycusis is a condition caused by aging-related changes to the inner ear and can result in difficulty hearing normal conversations or oversensitivity to loud noise. Tinnitus results in telltale ringing, buzzing, or other sounds that come and go. While certain types of drugs can trigger the condition, its cause often cannot be found. Conductive hearing loss is a blockage of sounds that are carried from the ear drums to the inner ear, usually due to wax or fluid. Sensorineural hearing loss often occurs as a result of physical damage to the auditory nerve or inner ear, and can be due to trauma to the head, birth defects, high blood pressure, or STROKE.

The National Institute on Deafness and Other Communication Disorders, a division of the NATIONAL INSTITUTES OF HEALTH, is the federal agency that conducts biomedical and behavioral research on hearing loss, as well as balance, smell, voice, and speech. Individuals who may suffer from hearing loss are usually referred to an otolaryngologist (a head and neck specialist) or to an audiologist, who tests hearing levels. The audiologist can also help suggest varieties of hearing aids that work best for an individual's needs.

Heart disease

Though deaths from heart conditions plummeted 71 percent from 1958 to 1992 and continue to decline due to healthier living, cardiovascular disease continues to be the number one killer of elderly Americans. Approximately sixty million individuals suffer from the condition, which is understood to mean heart failure or the death of heart cells due to lack of blood flow from a heart attack. Heart disease is brought on by a variety of causes, most notably cholesterol in the bloodstream, high blood pressure, and smoking. Women, in general, are at greater risk of dying from heart failure. The Centers for Disease Control and Prevention in February 2000 reported annual rates of mortality in 1997 due to heart disease among women were 401 per 100,000 women—more than all forms of cancer combined. Black women are most at risk of dying from heart disease, but white women from Appalachia and the Mississippi Delta suffered almost identical mortality rates. White women as a group had higher mortality rates than American Indians, Asian and Pacific Islanders, and Hispanic women.

A variety of conditions either give rise to or occur concurrently with heart disease. Angina pectoris refers to the chest pains that occur when the heart does not receive sufficient amounts of blood. Commonly experienced by elderly people—especially after exercise or exertion—the condition is treated with nitroglycerine, which widens the blood vessels and increases the flow of blood to the organ. Arrhythmia is a condition common in middle-aged people as well as in elders and describes situations in which the heart beats irregularly or skips a beat. The condition can be caused by stress, caffeine, or alcohol, though researchers say often there is no recognizable cause.

Atherosclerosis refers to a thickening of the walls of the coronary arteries with cholesterol, narrowing the available space for the blood to flow. Mild cases are treated by changing one's lifestyle habits—quitting smoking, lowering one's blood pressure and cholesterol intake, and losing weight. More serious blockages require coronary bypass surgery, in which a blood vessel is harvested from another part of the body and grafted onto the blocked artery, effectively bypassing the blockage. Hypertension (the general condition of a person with high blood pressure) is another serious condition and a major risk factor for heart failure, kidney disease, and STROKE in elderly people and often occurs without any warning symptoms. It is controlled by maintaining a healthy weight, being physically active, partaking of a diet low in sodium and salt, and drinking alcohol in moderation. More severe cases of hypertension are treated with drugs that block the flow of certain ions in the blood stream.

Federally funded studies of heart disease continue to have a prominent place in the government's research portfolio, though in recent years they have been overshadowed by advances in diagnosing and treating CANCER, HIV/AIDS, ALZHEIMER'S DISEASE, and PARKINSON'S DISEASE. Indeed, society's emphasis on regular exercise, healthy eating, and less smoking and drinking obscures the fact that the projected annual economic cost of heart disease at the end of the 1990s stood at $424 billion.

The National Heart, Lung, and Blood Institute,

part of the NATIONAL INSTITUTES OF HEALTH, is the government's lead agency for research on heart conditions. The institute in 1997 took over administering the Women's Health Initiative, a fifteen-year federal research effort begun in 1991 that is aimed at investigating leading causes of death among postmenopausal women. Recent institute-supported research has determined that most first instances of heart attacks or angina occur after age sixty-five, and that cholesterol-lowering drugs called statins produced the largest reduction in both men and women. The institute recommends that older Americans have their total cholesterol tested at least once every five years and, if problems are found, should turn to lifestyle changes before they consider taking drugs.

Helvering v. Davis

Helvering v. Davis was the pivotal U.S. Supreme Court case that affirmed the constitutionality of the SOCIAL SECURITY system. The case was argued in 1936, at a time when courts were striking down portions of President FRANKLIN D. ROOSEVELT's New Deal, and jurists were questioning whether new, large-scale government programs violated the Tenth Amendment, or "reserve clause," of the Constitution. This provision states that powers not specifically granted to the federal government by the Constitution are reserved for the states or the people.

The case was among three cases decided simultaneously by the high court that paved the way for the enactment of the Social Security system. George P. Davis was a shareholder in the Edison Electric Illuminating Company at a time when the company was preparing to pay the employer's

share of new payroll taxes under the FEDERAL INSURANCE CONTRIBUTION ACT. Davis believed this new spending would dilute his equity in the company and sued Edison to block its compliance with the SOCIAL SECURITY ACT OF 1935. The government, in the person of IRS commissioner Guy T. Helvering, intervened, setting the stage for the dramatic arguments.

Davis relied on definitions of taxes used at the time the Constitution was written, in the 1780s, to prove payroll taxes were not on the document's list of taxes and, hence, were illegal. However, justices ruled by a 7–2 vote that such a strict interpretation was unrealistic and that Congress needed the flexibility to reinterpret the law, when appropriate. Justice Benjamin Cardozo, writing for the majority, said the new national pension system would "save men and women from the rigors of the poor house, as well as from the haunting fear that such a lot awaits them when journey's end is near."

The court decision, interestingly, came soon after Roosevelt made one of the biggest political mistakes of his career and unsuccessfully tried to "pack" the court. Frustrated by decisions against his New Deal programs, particularly the high court's 1936 invalidation of the Agriculture Adjustment Act, Roosevelt tried to persuade Congress to grant him new powers to add additional federal judges when those jurists over the age of seventy refused to retire. The new power would have overturned federal judges' privilege of lifetime tenure and radically changed the makeup of one of the oldest Supreme Courts in U.S. history. It was widely seen as a transparent attempt to allow Roosevelt to add six Supreme Court justices and tip the balance of the court away from older, conservative jurists who voted against him. The gambit resulted in a major political defeat and the heaping of scorn on Roosevelt. Ironically, the same high court soon handed the president one of his greatest social-policy victories.

Henry J. Kaiser Family Foundation

The Henry J. Kaiser Family Foundation, an independent philanthropy named for the family of the late industrialist and pioneer of the HMO, is a leading health-policy THINK TANK that has played a major role in debates over MEDICARE, MEDICAID, women's health, and the changing health-care marketplace. Based in Menlo Park, California, it has no connection with the Kaiser Permanente HMO, except that both entities share the founding family's name.

Higher profile than most foundations, the Kaiser family foundation targets its studies at the media, lawmakers, and the public and has cosponsored reporting projects with major media organizations, including the *Washington Post, U.S. News and World Report,* NBC, and ABC. It is viewed as a reliable, independent source of information on how the health-care sector has made the transition from a market dominated by not-for-profit institutions to one now largely run by big commercial interests.

Heritage Foundation

The Heritage Foundation, a conservative, Washington-based THINK TANK, was founded in 1973 on the principles of free enterprise and limited government. It has long been an influential voice in efforts to reform the SOCIAL SECURITY system. Long before it was fashionable for politicians to challenge the validity of Social Security, Heritage in 1980 issued a paper comparing the national retirement system to an illegal "Ponzi scheme," in which new investors are bilked to pay off old investors who were promised payouts. Another well-publicized analysis, issued in 1997, held that older African Americans and Hispanics fared worse under Social Security because their life expectancies are shorter. Critics responded that minority groups tend to benefit the most from Social Security because its progressive benefits structure favors low-income workers and the widows and offspring of deceased workers. More recently, Heritage scholars have focused on PRIVATIZATION efforts of national retirement systems in foreign countries, and how elements of those reforms might be applied to the United States' system. (See also AUSTRALIAN PRIVATE PENSION PLANS; CHILEAN PENSION SYSTEM; GREAT BRITAIN PENSION SYSTEM.)

HMO

See BALANCED BUDGET ACT OF 1997; MEDICARE + CHOICE.

Home health benefits (Medicare)

MEDICARE's home health benefit is one of the most popular aspects of the federal health-care program—and one of its most troublesome. Home health care has become an important option for the growing number of elderly who need help with certain ACTIVITIES OF DAILY LIVING but are not sick enough to be confined to hospitals or NURSING HOMES. This covers anyone from STROKE patients undergoing long periods of recovery to individuals with kidney disease or DIABETES. But the growing volume of services available and the expanding caseload of patients have driven up program costs. Medicare revised home health guidelines in 1989, increasing the number of allowed visits per week and the duration of program eligibility. The revised guidelines also have attracted more individuals with chronic health problems who might be better served in a LONG-TERM CARE setting than by an acute care program like Medicare.

The government has responded in recent years by sharply curtailing payments to home health providers. Reimbursement changes imposed by the BALANCED BUDGET ACT OF 1997 (PL-105-33) have shaken the home health industry, forcing some home health companies to turn away the sickest elderly patients, who often are the most expensive to care for, and reduce services for others. A CONGRESSIONAL BUDGET OFFICE study found Medicare spending on home health plunged 45 percent from 1997 to 1999, from $17.5 billion to $9.7 billion. The situation loomed as a potential political issue in some parts of the country.

The home health benefit is aimed at homebound individuals under the care of a doctor who are being treated for an acute illness. If these individuals meet eligibility requirements, they are entitled to an unlimited number of visits and not subject to deductibles or copayments. Home health services provided include part-time or occasional skilled nursing care; physical, occupational, and speech therapy; medical supplies and equipment; and medical social services administered under the direction of a physician. Statistics show the benefit has become popular with heavy users of home health services; individuals who received more than one hundred visits per year increased from 4 percent of all users in 1988 to 21 percent by fiscal 1996. While a portion of the surge in visits is attributed to fraud, experts say home health providers also have "fudged" on program restrictions in order to give their patients more of the care they feel is needed. The average annual number of visits per person increased from twenty-three in 1988 to seventy-two by 1997, good for a 14 percent annual increase.

Prior to the Balanced Budget Act, home health providers were paid for whatever they spent on care, a situation critics said encouraged unnecessary treatments. The 1997 law made significant changes, creating a prospective payment system that paid home health companies a predetermined amount based on a sixty-day "episode of care" for each beneficiary, with adjustments to reflect the severity of the person's condition. The changes in federal payment policies were a factor behind total Medicare spending dropping in 1999 for the first time since the program was established in 1965.

However, congressional planners underestimated how the mandated cuts would play out against the rising costs of home care. Home care agencies began adopting stricter criteria for accepting patients—a move observers say cut off services to many of the sickest elderly people with complex health needs and several different kinds of chronic illnesses. Ironically, without home health options, these individuals have been forced to seek care in more expensive institutional settings, checking in and out of nursing homes and hospitals and potentially increasing the government's total bill for their care.

Policymakers in mid-2000 focused on additional home health cuts mandated by the Balanced Budget Act that would reduce payments another 15 percent in 2001. A bipartisan group of lawmakers in the House and Senate sought to postpone the cut and again overhaul the federal payments system, arguing that it should not leave the sickest elderly at the greatest risk. Meanwhile, a federal district court ruling in March 2000 determined that home health agencies could not cut off the benefits of Medicare recipients without giving them ample notice and the opportunity to appeal.

Home health care

Home health care is a general term referring to medical and social services that are provided in a person's home. These can include part-time skilled nursing care, physical, speech, and occupational therapy, and assistance with household chores that are provided to elderly people who are homebound or too frail to leave the house on a regular basis. The services are provided under the MEDICARE Part A home health benefit and MEDICAID. Doctors have to first certify the need for care.

Home health benefits are among the fastest growing segments of federal ENTITLEMENT spending—in 1990, the government spent $3.5 billion on home health services, and the CONGRESSIONAL BUDGET OFFICE estimates that spending will exceed $30 billion by 2002. But home health care also has become the focus of intense scrutiny because of the prevalence of fraud and abuse. Both the U.S. General Accounting Office and the Department of HEALTH AND HUMAN SERVICES's inspector general have repeatedly criticized the HEALTH CARE FINANCING ADMINISTRATION (HCFA) for lax oversight that allowed home

health care providers to bill the government for services that were not provided or authorized by physicians, or that were not medically necessary or reasonable.

HHS's inspector general found that as many as 25 percent of home health care providers in states targeted for audits were "problem providers" who practiced questionable billing and received disproportionately large shares of Medicare home health spending in those states. HCFA, the inspector general added, stood little chance of recovering the money, because many suspect home health providers are closely held companies in interlocking networks of businesses, making the money hard to trace.

Home health agencies tend to blame hospitals and doctors for "double-dipping" into Medicare and driving up program costs. This happens when doctors prescribe or recertify home health treatments to hospital-based or—owned home health agencies when the doctor is employed by the hospital. Independent home health agencies say these self-referrals, also known in industry parlance as "downstreaming," deny patients of their rights to choose health-care providers while enriching large hospital chains. The leading lobbying group for home health providers is the National Association for Home Care in Washington, D.C.

Congress tried to gain some control on home health spending through a provision in the BALANCED BUDGET ACT OF 1997 (PL 105-33). The law called for creation of a PROSPECTIVE PAYMENT SYSTEM that would reimburse agencies based on a patient's diagnosis, similar to the system used to pay hospitals. Under the old system, home health agencies were paid for whatever they actually spent—a situation critics said encouraged UNNECESSARY TREATMENTS. Congress implemented a temporary system until the new system could be put in place. However, HCFA's inability to meet an October 1, 1999, deadline for the new payment system forced Congress to revise the temporary payment schedule, after home health providers complained that disparities in reimbursement rates were driving some agencies out of business. HCFA's prospective payment system went into effect in October 2000.

Hospice

Hospice care is a type of care for terminally ill people that emphasizes pain management and general comfort over active medical treatments that could help the patient live longer. The hospice movement traces its roots to Cicely Saunders, a British physician who opened the first hospice in London in 1967. She believed there was a need to accept death as a part of life. This notion, at times, does not square with today's cutting-edge medical therapies and the tendency of some doctors to prescribe aggressive treatments when patients are in late stages of cancer or other chronic diseases. Advocates say the hospice concept addresses a spiritual need of patients to enjoy the best quality of life for themselves and their families.

Hospices began operating in the United States in the mid-1970s. MEDICARE in 1982 began providing a hospice benefit on the condition that a doctor certifies that the patient is terminally ill—usually defined as having a life expectancy of less than six months. Though patients can receive hospice services for longer periods of time, Medicare caps the total annual payments a hospice can receive, forcing doctors and hospice administrators to work together to ensure that the sickest people can gain admittance. Unlike the rest of the Medicare program, the Medicare hospice benefit does cover the cost of outpatient prescription drugs to manage pain and other symptoms of the patient's illness. It also covers RESPITE CARE, which "spells" family caregivers in need of temporary relief.

Hospital Insurance (HI)

Hospital Insurance (HI) refers to Part A of MEDICARE, which covers inpatient hospital care, treatment at SKILLED NURSING FACILITIES and HOSPICES, and at home through HOME HEALTH agencies. Because hospital and skilled nursing care account for some of the highest costs in the health-care sector, Part A is the largest component of Medicare, and its financial condition is often used as a barometer of Medicare's overall health. Cuts imposed by the BALANCED BUDGET ACT OF 1997 (PL 105-33), more efficient billing practices, and federal and private anti-fraud efforts made payments from the Hospital Insurance fund decline 4 percent in fiscal 1999, to $129 billion from $135 billion in fiscal 1998, according to U.S. Treasury Department statistics. However, the White House and Congress in late 1999 agreed to restore $17 billion in cuts over five years, after strenuous lobbying by health-care providers, who argued the cuts went too far. Another so-called giveback package estimated to cost $35 billion over five years was approved in 2000.

The Hospital Insurance TRUST FUND is financed by a special payroll tax of 1.45 percent of income, paid by both the worker and employer. Self-employed individuals pay both the employer and employee shares. The Hospital Insurance tax is applied to all earnings, regardless how high, unlike the SOCIAL SECURITY payroll tax, which is capped at an income limit. The income taxes that some Social Security recipients must pay also help finance the Hospital Insurance program.

Hospital Insurance makes payments to health-care providers based on a PROSPECTIVE PAYMENT SYSTEM, in which hospitals are paid fixed amounts for procedures, based on the average costs for treating specific conditions. Medicare beneficiaries who are admitted to a hospital are assigned to one of about five hundred diagnosis-related groups, or DRGs. This avoids the old practice of paying based on services provided, a system critics said encouraged UNNECESSARY TREATMENTS. If a hospital can provide treatment for less than the DRG sum, the institution gets to keep the difference. If the treatment costs more, the hospital must pay the difference, not charge the beneficiary. Certain teaching hospitals and those that see a disproportionately large percentage of severely ill patients may receive additional amounts above the DRG rate to reflect their extra costs of providing care.

Critics of the prospective payment system, which uses DRGs as a cost-cutting tool, argue that while the system somewhat slowed medical inflation by shortening patient lengths of stay in costly acute-care settings, it pushed older patients out of the hospital "quicker and sicker." Patients continuing to need convalescence were moved into subacute care in NURSING HOMES with high-tech capability or into special LONG-TERM CARE units newly created by hospitals to compete for subacute-care reimbursements with nursing homes.

House Appropriations Committee

The House Appropriations Committee is one of the most important in Congress; it controls the discretionary spending portion of the federal budget through thirteen subcommittees that write annual spending bills, enabling the government's agencies to continue running. Many aging-related programs are financed through the appropriations committee. However, SOCIAL SECURITY, MEDICARE, and MEDICAID are not, because those programs are entitlements that are funded according to estimates of what they will cost. Any changes to the way these programs operate is handled by authorizing committees, not through spending bills that come through appropriations.

Among the important appropriations bills affecting elderly people are the Labor, Health and Human Services, and Education bill, which funds the U.S. Department of HEALTH AND HUMAN SERVICES and the various programs that fall under the OLDER AMERICANS ACT and its amendments. The Labor-HHS bill, as it is known, also contains funding for the NATIONAL INSTITUTES OF HEALTH and its myriad biomedical research activities directed at aging-related diseases.

Another important spending bill is the VA, HUD, and Independent Agencies bill, which funds programs such as the U.S. Department of Housing and Urban Development's SECTION 202 SUPPORTIVE HOUSING FOR THE ELDERLY and Veterans Administration health care. The Commerce, Justice, State, and Judiciary spending bill funds U.S. Department of Justice efforts to prevent crime against the elderly, while the Treasury, Postal Service, and General Government spending bill provides health insurance for elderly federal government workers.

House Appropriations Committee chairman C. W. "Bill" Young (far right) confers with ranking Democrat David Obey (far left) during a committee meeting. Appropriations controls the discretionary spending portion of the federal budget, which includes spending for many aging-regulated programs. Source: File photo

The spending bills the House committee develops are later harmonized with equivalent measures developed by the Senate Appropriations Committee.

House Commerce Committee

The House Commerce Committee has some of the broadest latitude of any congressional committee, weighing in on a myriad of aging issues, including health-care delivery, ENTITLEMENT FRAUD, the Public Health Service, and the Food and Drug Administration (FDA), as well as the MEDICAID program. It shares jurisdiction over MEDICARE Part B with the HOUSE WAYS AND MEANS COMMITTEE; Medicare Part A is entirely in the province of Ways and Means because it is funded by a payroll tax.

Since Republicans won leadership of the House in 1994, the committee, under the leadership of Chairman Thomas J. Bliley Jr., R-Va., focused on issues such as streamlining the FDA, monitoring the HEALTH CARE FINANCING ADMINISTRATION (HCFA), and assessing HCFA's efforts to root out fraud in the Medicare and Medicaid programs. Under the Democratic leadership of Rep. John Dingell, D-Mich., in the 1980s, the committee was responsible for expanding Medic-

House Ways and Means Committee members confer in the committee's grand meeting room. With the House Appropriations Committee, the House Ways and Means Committee is arguably the most powerful and influential legislative panel in the House. Source: Scott J. Ferrell, Congressional Quarterly

aid and speeding up the FDA's drug-approval process by imposing user fees on drug companies.

The committee's Health and Environment Subcommittee considers the vast majority of aging issues. The Oversight and Investigations Subcommittee has the power to investigate wrongdoing, such as consumer fraud, and emerging issues, such as drug sales on the Internet.

House Education and Workforce Committee

The House Education and Workforce Committee has jurisdiction over retirement security and pension reform, including amendments to the EMPLOYEE RETIREMENT INCOME SECURITY ACT (ERISA) (PL 93-406). It also considers laws governing employee stock ownership plans, stock options, and other benefits, though the tax treatment of each falls to the HOUSE WAYS AND MEANS COMMITTEE, which presides over tax issues in the House.

Typically this committee is one of the more

partisan in the House. Democrats tend to assign more liberal members to this panel to handle legislation affecting labor unions, while Republicans assign conservative lawmakers, who usually focus on efforts to weaken unions and fight efforts to create more federal education standards.

House Ways and Means Committee

With the HOUSE APPROPRIATIONS COMMITTEE, the House Ways and Means Committee is arguably the most powerful and influential legislative panel in the House, controlling virtually all aspects of tax policy and exerting major influence over ENTITLEMENT PROGRAMS.

The committee's Social Security Subcommittee serves as the main conduit for proposals to reform the national retirement system, particularly PRIVATIZATION plans that would allow individuals to defer a portion of their payroll taxes and establish personalized retirement accounts. The subcommittee separately has taken up issues such as

SOCIAL SECURITY's protections for working and nonworking women, disability benefits, and the financial effects of the surge of aging BABY BOOMERS on the program. The subcommittee also oversees operation of the Social Security TRUST FUNDS and receives the much-anticipated annual trustees' reports that size up the general health of the retirement system.

The Ways and Means Health Subcommittee is equally influential, overseeing MEDICARE Part A, sharing jurisdiction with the HOUSE COMMERCE COMMITTEE over Medicare Part B, and presiding over MEDICARE+CHOICE. It also oversees Medicare coverage decisions and beneficiary appeals and issues surrounding uninsured Americans. This panel also was instrumental in making private LONG-TERM-CARE insurance more financially viable, in an effort to reduce reliance on MEDICAID.

Housing programs

Since the 1930s, the federal government has provided assistance so low- and moderate-income individuals have access to decent housing. Though substantial progress has been made, a large percentage of subsidized housing built in the 1990s was targeted at elderly individuals. And several trends have experts worried that indigent older Americans may yet face an unprecedented housing squeeze in the coming decade.

Most assistance is provided through programs administered by the U.S. Department of Housing and Urban Development (HUD). HUD's Section 8 housing program, created in 1974, provides vouchers and certificates to households that rent subsidized units. The individuals renting these units pay 30 percent of their income as rent, while the government pays the remainder based on

An elderly homeless woman eats her meal in a tent city in Houston, Texas. Source: Ravi Arya, Black Star

market-rate rents. The units can either be rented from private developers whose projects are formally enrolled in the Section 8 program, or from other landlords who are willing to negotiate rents in their respective buildings. Renters who choose to negotiate must do so knowing HUD will only agree to pay a fixed amount, and must be willing to pay any extra rent out-of-pocket.

Two developments have housing advocates worried about the supply of available housing for individuals receiving assistance. Thousands of Section 8 contracts the government negotiated with landlords in the late 1970s and early 1980s are expiring, and property owners, encouraged by the robust real-estate market in most parts of the country, are seeking to convert their buildings to market-rate rents. An estimated 2.7 million units will expire in 2002, for instance, requiring Congress to approve a budget authority of $16.2 billion that year just to renew the contracts at prevailing rates. Even if lawmakers approve the money, housing advocates say many landlords already are walking away from the program, convinced they can get more from the private sector. Between 1998 and 2000, an estimated 2,500 subsidized units were lost each month in this way.

At the same time, some other property owners are paying off federally subsidized mortgages that required them to keep rents below market rates. This "prepay" option was allowed under the 1990 Housing Act (PL 101-625) and is expected to further diminish the availability of subsidized units. HUD must allow mortgage prepayments if it cannot give property owners sufficient economic incentives to keep the buildings for low-income use, and if the agency determines that comparable and affordable alternative housing is available to tenants.

The developments could spell trouble for elderly couples who have lived in the same subsidized dwelling for many years and may have to scramble to find new housing arrangements if the building is converted to market-rate rents. Those who remain will find themselves increasingly "cost burdened" in housing-speak, meaning they will be paying more than half of their incomes for rent.

The concerns about Section 8 programs could have a ripple effect on other federal housing efforts specifically targeted at the elderly. One is HUD's SECTION 202 SUPPORTIVE HOUSING PROGRAM for the elderly, established in 1974 and re-

vised in 1990, which provides federal subsidies for constructing rental housing specifically for older people. Rental assistance comes in the form of twenty-year contracts between HUD and project owners, and tenants are required to pay 30 percent of their income. Landlords enrolled in the program agree to provide supportive services, such as meals, housekeeping, transportation, and personal care. But with more money expected to be targeted at the Section 8 program, it is unclear whether this effort will continue to be funded at current levels. Another HUD program that could be affected in this way is the Depression-era Public Housing Program, which works with local public housing authorities to acquire and lease properties suitable for low-income housing.

Despite the impending cash crunch, HUD continues to adapt programs to address the needs of elderly people. The agency is allocating money for a "service coordinator program" that allows seniors-only buildings to hire individuals who help residents better use community services, such as paratransit. HUD also is seeking more flexibility in the Section 8 voucher program by proposing that it allow the elderly to use the vouchers in ASSISTED LIVING facilities. Separately the agency and some in Congress favor giving states federal matching grants to maintain and preserve a certain number of affordable housing units. However, many of these proposals could bump up against the reality of congressional spending caps.(See also CONGREGATE HOUSING.)

HRT

See ESTROGEN.

I

Immigration

The plight of elderly legal immigrants has become a frequently discussed social-policy issue since passage of the 1996 welfare reform legislation (PL 104-193), which restricted the benefits these individuals can collect from the federal government. It also made aliens with permanent resident status who entered the United States after August 22, 1996 (the date the act was signed into law), ineligible for SUPPLEMENTAL SECURITY INCOME disability benefits or entitlements such as food stamps.

Many newly arrived families in the United States bring an elder with them, often to care for the home and children while younger family members work and draw paychecks. The older family members are the most likely to need health and social services, but often have to rely on locally run programs aimed at low-income individuals. Typically, resident immigrants cannot qualify for MEDICAID until they reside in the United States for five years. Organizations such as the U.S. Conference of Mayors and the National League of Cities have complained that current policies unfairly shift the cost of caring for these individuals from the federal government to states and municipalities, and discriminate against immigrants. However, courts have ruled that the federal government does not have to give noncitizens the same ENTITLEMENT benefits available to citizens.

The welfare-reform cuts came at a time of broader budget-cutting aimed at eliminating the budget deficit, and as the Republican-controlled Congress was passing several immigration bills to crack down on illegal aliens. Critics contend both the Congress and the Immigration and Naturalization Service (INS) went too far in tightening eligibility requirements for some federal programs, leaving legal immigrants without access to key components of the social safety net.

Congress in succeeding years passed legislation to restore some benefits. In 1997, Congress gave back disability benefits to those legal immigrants who were residing in the country before passage of welfare reform. The following year, food stamps were restored to some 250,000 children and elderly legal immigrants. However, immigrant advocacy groups complain Congress has been reluctant to deal with those immigrants who arrived after passage of welfare reform, after August 1996.

In 1997, the City of Chicago sued to block the welfare-reform cuts, arguing they would cost the city millions of dollars in expansion of social services for legal immigrants. The city charged that the policies violated the equal protection guarantees in the Constitution, but a federal appeals court in Chicago upheld the law. In March 2000, the U.S. Supreme Court rejected a challenge by the city and let stand the lower-court ruling that concluded the federal government has the right to cut off welfare to noncitizen residents.

An elderly Chinese immigrant pickets U.S. senator Dianne Feinstein's San Francisco office to oppose 1996 immigration legislation passed by Congress. PL 104-193 restricts the benefits elderly legal immigrants can collect from the federal government. Source: Judi Parks, AP Photo

A number of recent federal efforts attempt to better address the needs of elderly immigrants. Legislation has been proposed in Congress that would make it easier for legal immigrants to take U.S. citizenship tests in their native languages. The U.S. Census Bureau also made special outreach efforts during Census 2000 to identify elderly immigrants and reflect their true numbers. Census officials say they believe this group is among the most undercounted in the popula-

tion—a trend that affects the way federal grants are targeted at their needs.

Impotence

Impotence, also known as erectile dysfunction, is defined as the inability of a man to have an erection or maintain an erection in order to have sexual intercourse. The condition affects more than ten million American men, many of whom are aged sixty and older. There are myriad physical and psychological causes for impotence. The most common ailments linked to the condition are DIABETES, cardiovascular disease, multiple sclerosis, spinal injuries, and the side effects from medications, particularly drugs to treat high blood pressure. Treatments include prescription drugs, such as VIAGRA, surgery to correct blockages of blood vessels, or the insertion of pumps and related devices that can enable the patient to have erections.

The shame associated with impotence made mention of the subject almost taboo until former senator Bob Dole, R-Kan., made a highly publicized series of advertisements touting the effects of Pfizer Incorporated's Viagra. Dole was hailed for having the courage to discuss a previously rarely mentioned problem. But Viagra soon became the subject of a heated policy debate. When private health insurers began covering the cost of the drug, some advocates for the elderly began pressing the federal government to make the medication available via MEDICARE and MEDICAID. The government declined, reasoning Viagra was a "lifestyle drug" that was not necessary and did not treat acute medical conditions.

The popularity of Viagra also has spawned numerous instances of consumer fraud. The Federal Trade Commission in 1999 issued an alert advising men to be leery of products with names that sound like Viagra or that claim to treat impotence but do not require a prescription. The agency said one company with a sound-alike product may have cheated 150,000 customers out of as much as $19 million. The agency continues to warn against buying any anti-impotence products that are heavily promoted as scientific breakthroughs, or herbal or "all natural" substances, neither of which has been proven to be effective against the condition.

Indemnity policy

Indemnity policies are a form of health insurance that pays a fixed amount for each day of care that is administered. One common variety is the hospital indemnity policy, which typically pays up to $200 per day for every day one spends in a hospital bed. The policies have proven helpful for elderly individuals with kidney disease, CANCER, DIABETES, or other chronic conditions that can lead to frequent hospitalizations. Indemnity policies also pay for skilled nursing care or medically necessary services at home.

Indemnity policies are a common feature of private LONG-TERM CARE insurance, a slowly growing alternative to the long-term care administered through the MEDICAID program. Because Medicaid requires that a person must be at the poverty level to receive care, some middle-income and wealthier individuals have turned to private long-term insurance as a way of preserving one's estate and protecting oneself against future medical price shocks. However, the policies have been criticized for being limited in scope. Some publications such as *Consumers Digest* have concluded it may be better for individuals under sixty to simply put money aside for future medical contingencies.

Independent living

Independent living has come to be seen as an important part of aging in America, because of many studies that suggest elderly people want to remain in familiar surroundings and keep control of their lives as long as possible. This is reflected in federal spending for MEDICARE home-care services, which surged in the 1990s as recipients opted for HOME HEALTH CARE, rehabilitative services, or less-intensive personal care or homemaker services to help in some ACTIVITIES OF DAILY LIVING. In 1999, there were about 20,000 home-care agencies in the United States, about half of which were Medicare-certified.

MEALS ON WHEELS and other nutrition services provided through the OLDER AMERICANS ACT and the SOCIAL SERVICES BLOCK GRANT assure that homebound elderly people can enjoy an adequate supply of nutritious food and a balanced diet. These services deliver hot, fresh meals, or frozen meals that can be reheated, to elderly individuals who cannot get out regularly to shop for groceries but want to avoid living in institutional settings.

A variety of emerging elderly housing options address many older individuals' desire to live independently but remain close to some form of assistance. One is CONGREGATE HOUSING, which features stand-alone homes or apartments located within a larger compound that has common areas and serves communal meals. The arrangement allows individuals to pursue their own interests and do chores, yet still get some help to perform essential activities of daily living. A more exotic housing alternative is the ELDER COTTAGE HOUSING OPPORTUNITY (ECHO), which features small, one- or two-bedroom homes that are either built in clusters on leased land or on the property of an adult child or relative.

Designers continue to work on innovations that can allow elderly people to live in their homes and reduce the chances of falls or other accidents. Devices such as wheelchair lifts, adjustable counters, automated temperature controls and special railings have been shown in studies to reduce the need for federally subsidized home-care services and NURSING HOME care and lead to fewer hospitalizations. (See also GEROERGONOMICS; "AGING IN PLACE.")

Individual Retirement Account (IRA)

The Individual Retirement Account, or IRA, is a common type of private pension that was created through the EMPLOYEE RETIREMENT INCOME SECURITY ACT OF 1974 (PL 93-406). Traditional IRAs allow working individuals up to age 70-1/2 to make tax-deductible, tax-deferred contributions to personal retirement accounts that are usually invested in mutual fund–type investments, stocks and bonds, or bank accounts. Interest and capital gains grow tax-deferred until the individual begins making withdrawals. The government penalizes withdrawals made before age 59-1/2, except in cases of financial hardship, disability, or a limited number of other extenuating circumstances.

Public participation in IRAs has varied widely due to a series of changes Congress made to the federal tax codes that alternately made the accounts more or less attractive. When IRAs were first conceived, they were aimed at individuals who were not already covered by a company pension plan. Workers with company-sponsored plans were not permitted to open the accounts, keeping national participation minimal. The situation changed dramatically in 1981, when Congress enacted the Economic Recovery Tax Act (PL 99-514), which allowed every worker to contribute up to $2,000 per year to an IRA and allowed nonworking spouses to contribute up to $250. From 1982 through 1986, Americans opened approximately fifty million IRA accounts, and the investments represented about 20 percent of total U.S. savings. While the trend appeared in sync with the supply-side economic theories in vogue at the time, IRAs also helped drive up the federal budget deficit because lawmakers could not find corresponding spending cuts to make up for the lost tax revenue. By 1986, federal officials estimated the annual revenue loss totaled $16.8 billion.

In 1986, Congress again acted, passing the Tax Reform Act, which restricted the tax deductibility of IRAs to lower-income workers or those without company-sponsored pensions. Contributions fell dramatically through the mid-1990s as individuals flocked to other tax-deferred investments, such as 401(K) PLANS. In 1997, lawmakers again passed sweeping legislation affecting IRAs in the form of the Tax Reform Act of 1997 (PL 105-34). This act began gradually raising the income thresholds used to phase out IRA tax deductibility for workers with company plans. It also created a new variety of IRA known as the ROTH IRA, named for its chief architect, Sen. William Roth, R-Del., chairman of the SENATE FINANCE COMMITTEE.

The Roth IRA operates entirely differently

Intergenerational conflicts over federal entitlement programs peaked during mid-1990s debates on reforming Social Security. Source: Scott J. Ferrell, Congressional Quarterly

from conventional, tax-deferred IRAs because it requires that contributions be taxed as income at current rates before they are deposited in the account. However, interest earnings grow tax-deferred and eventually are withdrawn without having to pay any taxes, as long as the accounts have been established for at least five years. The Roth IRA has proven popular with elderly individuals who worry that their tax bill in retirement will be as large as or larger than it was when they were working. The Roth IRA effectively "locks in" one's current tax rate and, additionally, can provide a way of sheltering extra money for one's heirs without paying estate or inheritance taxes. The Roth IRA is available to individuals with incomes of less than $110,000 or couples with incomes of less than $160,000.

Another common IRA is the Simplified Employee Pension Individual Retirement Account, or SEP-IRA. This variety is aimed at self-employed individuals or small business owners and is fund-ed entirely by employer contributions, which can be deducted from taxes as a business expense. SEP-IRAs work in a similar fashion to traditional IRAs, but the amount that can be contributed is limited to 15 percent of an employee's salary up to $160,000, effectively capping contributions at $24,000.

Instrumental activities of daily living

See ACTIVITIES OF DAILY LIVING.

Intergenerational warfare

"Intergenerational warfare" is generally understood to refer to the conflict between elderly people and younger generations over increasingly scarce resources, particularly those covered by SOCIAL SECURITY, MEDICARE, and other federal EN-

TITLEMENT PROGRAMS. It has led to the stereotyping of elderly Americans as an affluent class of "greedy geezers" intent on securing expanded health-care coverage and government pensions at the expense of future generations.

The conflict was most pronounced during the mid-1990s debates on reforming Social Security, during which polls revealed that most members of GENERATION X did not believe the program would be around by the time they retired. Americans in their thirties and forties questioned why seniors were demanding more BENEFITS and expecting current workers to sacrifice their economic self-interest simply to fulfill the promises of a DEPRESSION-era program.

The rhetoric has quieted in recent years as a result of several factors. First, robust economic growth and federal budget surpluses have extended the time period during which the Social Security and Medicare TRUST FUNDS will remain solvent, essentially delaying debate over the future of the system. In addition, increased publicity about rising drug costs and other health-care expenses have drawn more attention to the plight of low-income seniors, who most benefit under a progressive program like Social Security. The increased debate over establishing some kind of Medicare outpatient PRESCRIPTION DRUG BENEFIT, which would have been unheard of just five years ago, reflects the changing nature of this debate.

Intermediate-care facility

Intermediate-care facilities are state-licensed institutions that provide health care and supportive services to individuals whose health problems are not serious enough to require admission to a hospital or SKILLED NURSING FACILITY. Not every state uses this designation. Intermediate-care facilities include public institutions for the mentally retarded, but should not be confused with "rest homes" and other facilities that do not provide health care.

Typically, an intermediate-care facility will provide skilled nursing care on an as-needed basis, instead of round the clock. It also provides custodial care (assistance with dressing, personal hygiene, and other ACTIVITIES OF DAILY LIVING). However, unlike a NURSING HOME, there are no doctors or teams of health professionals on the premises, meaning MEDICARE does not certify or pay for these facilities. Elderly people best suited for intermediate-care facilities are still generally fit but increasingly in need of help performing certain essential tasks. Many such facilities do not accept nonambulatory patients.

Internal Revenue Service (IRS)

The Internal Revenue Service, or IRS, is probably no more beloved by older Americans than younger generations. But the nation's tax-collection agency plays an important role in the daily operations of the SOCIAL SECURITY system by collecting payroll taxes from workers, their employers, and self-employed individuals. The IRS then deposits the money in government-administered accounts known as the OLD-AGE AND SURVIVORS INSURANCE AND DISABILITY INSURANCE TRUST FUNDS (OASDI), which are used to pay BENEFITS to those people currently collecting Social Security pensions. Any excess of taxes over benefit payments is invested in U.S. Treasury bonds, which earn the average rate of return on publicly traded government debt. The taxes also pay for MEDICARE, the national health program for the elderly. The services funded come under Medicare

The Internal Revenue Service, the nation's tax-collection agency, plays an important role in the daily operations of the Social Security system. Source: Sue Klemens, Congressional Quarterly

Part A, including inpatient hospital care and skilled nursing care.

The IRS not only helps pay entitlement benefits to older Americans, but taxes them, too. In 1983, the National Commission on Social Security Reform, also known as the GREENSPAN COMMISSION, recommended that up to half of the Social Security benefits of higher-income individuals be taxed so revenues could be returned to the then cash-strapped Social Security TRUST FUNDS. The Omnibus Budget Reconciliation Act of 1993 (see OMNIBUS BUDGET RECONCILIATION BILLS) expanded taxation by subjecting up to 85 percent of Social Security benefits to taxation for individuals whose other income, plus half of their Social Security benefits exceeded $34,000, or $44,000 for joint filers. Revenues from taxation of benefits continues to increase, and were anticipated to total $9.3 billion in 2000.

International Year of Older Persons

See UNITED NATIONS YEAR OF OLDER PERSONS.

IRA

See INDIVIDUAL RETIREMENT ACCOUNT.

IRS

See INTERNAL REVENUE SERVICE.

J

Job Training Partnership Act; Workforce Investment Act

The Job Training Partnership Act of 1982 (PL 97-300), commonly known as JTPA, was one of the federal government's primary means of helping older workers find employment or obtain new job skills. The law provided for a nationwide adult training effort for lower-income individuals, as well as a separate "dislocated worker" program aimed at middle-aged and older Americans who lost their jobs through an industry restructuring and were not likely to find new employment in the same industry. The JTPA was repealed, effective July 1, 2000, by the Workforce Investment Act of 1998 (PL 105-220), which established new training guidelines and standardized services for adult trainees and dislocated workers. Funding for the two groups continued to be provided separately in the Labor–Health and Human Services–Education Appropriations Bill.

Job training remains a major concern of older American workers. A 1998 U.S. Department of Labor survey of workers who lost jobs from 1995 through the end of 1997 found the majority were victims of plant closings who had insufficient seniority. Older displaced workers also were more likely to permanently leave the labor force than their younger counterparts—the reemployment rate for workers aged twenty and older was 76 percent; for workers aged fifty-five to sixty-four, 60 percent; and for workers aged sixty-five and older, 35 percent.

Funds under the JTPA and the Workforce Investment Act are allocated to states according to unemployment rates and the number of jobless people who have stayed off employment rolls for fifteen weeks or longer. The Workforce Investment Act made some changes in program requirements, including eliminating a mandate that 5 percent of money distributed to states for adult training be reserved for low-income workers aged fifty-five or older.

Joint Commission on the Accreditation of Health Care Organizations

The private, nonprofit Joint Commission on the Accreditation of Health Care Organizations, based in Oakbrook Terrace, Illinois, inspects and accredits the nation's hospitals. In recent years it has expanded its mandate to also evaluate NURSING HOMES, HOME HEALTH CARE providers, and "integrated care networks" that provide a range of services for the elderly. Founded in 1951, the joint commission is the oldest health-care accreditation organization in the country and has evaluated more than 19,500 health-care organizations and programs. Its evaluations sometimes play a role in whether a facility receives CERTIFICATION-to participate in MEDICARE. Favorable reviews also can help health organizations recruit staff and get managed-care contracts.

K

Kaiser Family Foundation.

See Henry J. Kaiser Family Foundation.

Keogh

Named after former representative Eugene James Keogh, D-N.Y. (1907–1989), who originated the idea in the early 1960s, a Keogh plan is a type of personal pension for self-employed individuals. Similar to an INDIVIDUAL RETIREMENT ACCOUNT (IRA) but technically more complicated to set up, it allows qualified individuals to make contributions to investment accounts that grow tax-deferred until the money is withdrawn, after age 59-1/2. The major difference is that the maximum contribution a person can put in per year is $30,000, and the contributions can be deducted from a business's taxable income.

There are two different kinds of Keoghs. A money-purchase Keogh allows one to contribute up to 25 percent of self-employment earnings, up to the $30,000 limit, but requires that the individual contribute the same amount each year or pay penalties. A profit-sharing Keogh allows one to invest less income—up to 15 percent of earnings—or $30,000, but allows the person to change the percentage contributed each year. This second variety gives one more flexibility if income from self-employment fluctuates from year to year. However, the money-purchase is the more gener-

Eugene James Keogh originated a special type of personal pension for self-employed individuals. Source: AP Photo

ous tax shelter, as long as one is assured of a fairly consistent self-employment income.

Congressionally mandated changes to pension rules since the 1974 enactment of the EMPLOYEE RETIREMENT INCOME SECURITY ACT (PL 93-406) have played havoc with many small businesses' Keoghs, leaving some noncompliant with current distribution rules and contribution formulas. The INTERNAL REVENUE SERVICE has granted many businesses amnesty to make necessary corrections. But the IRS requires that businesses that make any changes to plans must produce necessary documentation in the event of an audit.

L

Labor Department

The U.S. Department of Labor plays an important and varied role in the administering of federal programs affecting older Americans. The department's BUREAU OF LABOR STATISTICS tracks key economic indicators and publishes the CONSUMER PRICE INDEX, the government's primary measurement of inflation. The SOCIAL SECURITY ACT Amendments of 1972 automatically indexed SOCIAL SECURITY benefit increases to this benchmark, ensuring that program payments will not be outstripped by cost-of-living increases. The Consumer Price Index also is used to calculate one's initial Social Security benefits.

The Labor Department's role extends beyond statistical measurements to program administration. It runs the Senior Community Service Employment Program, an initiative that receives annual funding in excess of $400 million and places unemployed, low-income people in part-time community-service jobs. Eligible individuals must be deemed to have poor reemployment prospects and have incomes below 125 percent of federal poverty guidelines. The program is authorized by the OLDER AMERICANS ACT.

The Labor Department also oversees federal employment and training assistance for "dislocated workers" and other unemployed adults through the Workforce Investment Act of 1998 (PL 105-22) and the Adult and Dislocated Worker Program. These efforts have received increased attention over the past decade after industry restructurings, particularly in the manufacturing sector, left many older Americans without jobs and with few prospects for finding similar work. Funding for these two initiatives exceeds $2 billion per year. (See also JOB TRAINING PARTNERSHIP ACT.)

Lead or Leave

Lead or Leave, a short-lived GENERATION X advocacy group based in Washington, D.C., emerged prior to the 1992 election cycle, advocating federal deficit reduction and criticizing aspects of SOCIAL SECURITY and other entitlements its members said benefited rich seniors and could bankrupt the country. The group's twenty-something founders, Rob Nelson and Jon Cowan, became minor celebrities by taking their generational warfare message to Congress, appearing on MTV, and even addressing meetings of AARP. Nelson and Cowan promised bigger things for the 1996 elections, saying they were on the cusp of a twenty-something revolution. However, news reports revealed their organization was largely funded by corporate groups, most notably the Blackstone Group headed by CONCORD COALITION cofounder PETE PETERSON. When at least one of the founders tried to make it clear they wanted to assert their organizational independence, Peterson and some of the corporate backers pulled their funding. Lead or Leave folded in 1995. Another Generation X group, THIRD MILLENNIUM, remains in operation and advocates similar positions with respect to budget politics and entitlement reform. However, other members of Generation X defend the existing entitlement system. The 2030 CENTER, formed out of the United States Student Association, counters the idea that all young people think Social Security is a ripoff.

Leadership Council of Aging Organizations

The Leadership Council of Aging Organizations, or LCOA, is a coalition of some forty national organizations that regularly deal with aging issues and provide lawmakers with a sounding board on policy decisions. Membership includes professional organizations, labor unions, political advocacy groups, and consumer groups. The LCOA has weighed in with letters and resolutions to Congress and the White House on issues such as proposed tax credits for CAREGIVERS, MEDICARE reform, and the merits of using federal budget surpluses to shore up the Medicare TRUST FUNDS. The group does not mount lobbying efforts per se, but instead tries to anticipate emerging issues and coordinate efforts among its member organizations. It also provides a valuable resource for the White House and members of Congress who want to make their opinion known on particular aging issues or address one or more of the member organizations.

Legal services

Legal aid for the elderly population has become increasingly important in recent decades as more older people are forced to navigate the thicket of rules for complicated government programs, such as SOCIAL SECURITY and MEDICARE. Elders also routinely need advice on civil legal matters dealing with such issues as PROBATE, GUARDIANSHIP, consumer fraud, personal finance, and housing laws. However, many older Americans cannot afford to retain the services of private attorneys.

Since 1974, the federal government has provided funding for legal assistance for lower-income individuals through the Legal Services Corporation (LSC), a private, nonprofit corporation run by an eleven-member bipartisan board of directors consisting of presidential appointees who are confirmed by the U.S. Senate. The LSC funds state and local support centers that provide counseling for clients embroiled in civil cases, such as disputes over eligibility for subsidized housing or controversies over whether a person qualifies for certain government ENTITLEMENT PROGRAMS. Amendments to the OLDER AMERICANS ACT also mandate that certain percentages of federal funds awarded to local agencies for the aging be directed at legal services. Though the effort is targeted at individuals with incomes less than 125 percent of federal poverty guidelines, government officials say there is no accurate way of establishing eligibility because means testing for such services is prohibited.

The LSC has become embroiled in serious partisan political skirmishing because of the perception largely held by conservatives that its attorneys are more interested in engaging in social activism and promoting liberal causes than simply providing legal aid to low-income individuals. The administration of President RONALD REAGAN called for eliminating the LSC and instead giving states SOCIAL SERVICES BLOCK GRANTS. Supporters of the LSC successfully argued that neither state and local governments, nor private law firms, could assume its role because its lawyers have expertise in poverty law, and that private or government lawyers have less experience and interest in dealing with the problems poor people face.

Debate continues over funding levels for the LSC, and whether law firms and corporate legal departments could be persuaded to devote more time on a pro bono basis to LSC clients to counter the effects of potential funding cuts. One somewhat controversial approach is the growing practice in which lawyers place clients' trust deposits in interest-bearing accounts and use the income generated to fund legal services. The American Bar Association has estimated that doing this, on a nationwide basis, could generate $100 million per year. However, opponents say it constitutes an illegal misuse of the money of a paying client.

Various professional organizations have sprung up since the 1980s to help deal with the special legal needs of elderly people. The Academy of Elder Law Attorneys, established in 1987, helps lawyers who are advising elderly clients and promotes public awareness of legal hurdles facing older Americans. Local bar associations and agencies on aging have teamed up in many states to establish telephone hotlines offering legal advice and to publish brochures on seniors' legal rights. Special training programs have also been established for lawyers advising elderly individuals on financial planning for LONG-TERM CARE.

Life expectancy

Few statistics more starkly display medical and scientific breakthroughs in health care than life expectancies. Consider that in 1900, the average American could expect to live forty-seven years, and leading causes of death included tuberculosis and pneumonia. In 1999, the average life expectancy in the United States was seventy-six years, and most of the common bacterial infections that for centuries contributed to appalling mortality rates had been controlled, if not completely eliminated. Life expectancies remain on the rise. The U.S. Census Bureau in 1999 reported the number of Americans aged one hundred and older doubled during the 1990s, and predicted the trend likely could continue, with the centenarian population reaching 834,000 by 2050. Americans apparently have mixed feelings about reaching such a lofty age; an AARP survey found 63 percent of 2,032 respondents polled wanted to live fewer than one hundred years and expressed concerns about being plagued by poor health and financial problems during their later years. The spring 2000 "Myths and Realities of Aging" survey by Harris Interactive polls, however, found that of all respondents aged eighteen and older, 84 percent said they would like to live to be ninety.

Increased life expectancy has greatly influenced the way the federal government tailors social services for the elderly, evidenced by the creation of classes such as the "oldest old" (individuals aged eighty and older), who are more likely to be in need of certain kinds of health care and financial and LEGAL SERVICES.

Life expectancy also is an important factor in the federal government's rules for retirement income. The required minimum distribution that

Life Expectancy at Birth and at Sixty-Five Years of Age, by Sex and Race, Selected Years, 1950–1997

Remaining life expectancy in years

Year	At birth			At 65 years			At birth	
	Both sexes	Male	Female	Both sexes	Male	Female	White	Black
1950[1]	68.2	65.6	71.1	13.9	12.8	15.0	69.1	60.7
1960[1]	69.7	66.6	73.1	14.3	12.8	15.8	70.6	63.2
1970	70.8	67.1	74.7	15.2	13.1	17.0	71.7	64.1
1980	73.7	70.0	77.4	16.4	14.1	18.3	74.4	68.1
1988	74.9	71.4	78.3	16.9	14.7	18.6	75.6	68.9
1989	75.1	71.7	78.5	17.1	15.0	18.8	75.9	68.8
1990	75.4	71.8	78.8	17.2	15.1	18.9	76.1	69.1
1991	75.5	72.0	78.9	17.4	15.3	19.1	76.3	69.3
1992	75.8	72.3	79.1	17.5	15.4	19.2	76.5	69.6
1993	75.5	72.2	78.8	17.3	15.3	18.9	76.3	69.2
1994	75.7	72.4	79.0	17.4	15.5	19.0	76.5	69.5
1995	75.8	72.5	78.9	17.4	15.6	18.9	76.5	69.6
1996	76.1	73.1	79.1	17.5	15.7	19.0	76.8	70.2
1997	76.5	73.6	79.4	17.7	15.9	19.2	77.1	71.1

[1] Includes deaths of nonresidents of the United States in the 1950 and 1960 data.
Source: House Ways and Means Committee, *Green Book* (2000); National Center for Health Statistics (1999a, Table 28, p. 139).

Death Rates for Leading Causes of Death among Older People, by Age, 1997

Death rates per 100,000 population in age group

Rank	Cause of death	Age			
		65+	65–74	75–84	85+
1	Diseases of the heart	1,781	754	1,944	6,199
2	Malignant neoplasms	1,124	847	1,335	1,805
3	Cerebrovascular diseases	412	135	462	1,585
4	Chronic obstructive pulmonary diseases	277	165	360	562
5	Pneumonia and influenza	228	57	234	1,025
6	Diabetes	139	88	167	294
7	Accidents	92	46	103	276
8	Alzheimer's disease	65	11	73	299
9	Nephritis, nephrotic syndrome, nephrosis	64	26	74	218
10	Septicemia	53	23	60	178
	All other causes	839	358	916	2,904
	All causes	5,074	2,510	5,728	15,345

Source: House Ways and Means Committee, *Green Book* (2000); National Center for Health Statistics (1999b, Table 7, pp. 24–26, and Table 8, p. 28).

owners of an INDIVIDUAL RETIREMENT ACCOUNT (IRA) must withdraw in the year they turn 70-1/2 is based on the life expectancy of the owner and his or her beneficiaries, to ensure that a sufficient amount of the IRA's assets are depleted. If the proper amount is not withdrawn, the INTERNAL REVENUE SERVICE levies a fine of half of the amount that was not withdrawn.

Forecasts of SOCIAL SECURITY's solvency additionally hinge on life-expectancy calculations. In general, longer life expectancies increase the size of projected deficits, all other things being equal, because current workers will have to pay benefits for retirees over a longer period of time. However, factors other than asset-depletion often come into play, including the rate of return the Social Security TRUST FUNDS receive on current surplus revenues.

Jeanne Calment gestures at her nursing home in Arles, southern France, on October 17, 1995. That day, after 120 years and 238 days on the planet, Calment was entered into the Guinness Book of Records as the oldest living person whose date of birth could be authenticated. Source: Georges Gobet, AP Photo

Life span

The concept of life span is different from LIFE EXPECTANCY because it focuses on the body's response to the aging process absent certain external factors, such as disease, environment, and personal habits. Estimates of the average human life span vary greatly, from eighty-five years to more than one hundred years. But recent scientific discoveries are raising the prospect that genetic manipulation may within decades allow individuals to live longer and forestall the telltale breakdown of biological functions that accompanies older age. The prospect of an ever-expanding population of older people poses vexing problems for policymakers; one DEMOGRAPHIC study estimates that for every year added to the average life span, the economy will have to grow 1 percent to pay for additional health and social care.

Science has established that cellular death is partly responsible for aging. Conventional human cells divide about fifty times, then die of old age. But recent discoveries have shed light on a gene that creates an enzyme called telomerase that can lengthen the ends of DNA packaged in chromosomes. The enzyme is critical because it can build up the tips of chromosomes that are lost each time DNA is copied when cells divide. Scientists have already shown how manipulating the telomerase gene can allow cells grown in a test tube to divide ninety or more times without an abnormality. Current research is being directed at rejuvinating certain kinds of human tissue in this way, and learning whether some types of undesired cells—for instance, CANCER cells—can be inactivated by having their telomerase production turned off.

Corporate- and government-sponsored researchers have identified other genes that play roles in the aging process, including ones that protect the stability of DNA and protect against oxidative damage to cellular structures known as mitochondria. While scientists are optimistic about keeping aging in check, they note that, to date, most of the work has been performed with laboratory animals, and the prospects for applying the findings to humans are still uncertain. (See also TELOMERE.)

NATURAL DEATH ACT DECLARATION ("LIVING WILL")

Virginia's Natural Death Act was enacted in 1983 to permit Virginians to record their wishes regarding extraordinary care in the event of terminal illness. The declaration below is the suggested form developed by the state legislators to implement the Act. Fill out this form and give it to your physician and any relatives and friends you would like to have a copy. You must sign in the presence of two witnesses, and both witnesses must sign in your presence. Blood relatives or spouse may not be witnesses.

DECLARATION

In accordance with the Virginia Natural Death Act, this Declaration was made on _____.

Month/Day/Year

I, _____, willfully and voluntarily make known my desire and do hereby declare:

Name of person making declaration

You must choose between the following two paragraphs. PARAGRAPH ONE designates a person to make a decision for you. In PARAGRAPH TWO, you make the decision. Cross through the paragraph you do NOT want.

PARAGRAPH ONE:

If at any time I should have a terminal condition and I am comatose, incompetent or otherwise mentally or physically incapable of communication, I designate _____ to make a decision on my behalf as to whether life-prolonging procedures shall be withheld or withdrawn. In the event that my designee decides that such procedures should be withheld or withdrawn, I wish to be permitted to die naturally with only the administration of medication or the performance of any medical procedure deemed necessary to provide me with comfort care or to alleviate pain. (OPTION: I specifically direct that the following procedures or treatments be provided to me:

OR

PARAGRAPH TWO:

If at any time I should have a terminal condition where the application of life-prolonging procedures would serve only to artificially prolong the dying process, I direct that such procedures be withheld or withdrawn, and that I be permitted to die naturally with only the administration of medication or the performance of any medical procedure deemed necessary to provide me with comfort care or to alleviate pain. (OPTION: I specifically direct that the following procedures or treatments be provided to me:

_____

_____

An example of a living will—Virginia's "Natural Death Act Declaration."

Living benefit

See ACCELERATED DEATH BENEFIT.

Living will

A living will is a common type of ADVANCE DIRECTIVE designed to outline a patient's wishes in the event he or she is medically incapacitated. Guidelines vary from state to state, but the forms, in general, direct doctors and other medical personnel to undertake certain medical procedures in order to save the patient's life. Conversely, the documents also outline how far doctors should go if the patient is suffering from terminal illness, or could die without being supplied respiration or some other form of medical intervention. Some living wills contain a patient's general wishes—say, to avoid pain and unnecessary suffering—because the documents cannot anticipate every medical circumstance that may arise. The forms are recognized by state law. Health-care facilities that receive MEDICARE or MEDICAID funds are required to inform patients about living wills or other forms of advance directives and give them the option to execute one of the documents.

"Lockbox"

As the 106th Congress debated the future of SOCIAL SECURITY and other federal ENTITLEMENT PROGRAMS, Republican lawmakers proposed sequestering surplus Social Security payroll tax revenues in a "lockbox" so the money could not be used to finance any other government programs. This approach, embodied in several different legislative proposals, came in response to Democratic charges that Republicans were more interested in using budget surpluses to hand out tax cuts than to shore up the national retirement system. It also countered President Bill Clinton's proposal that surpluses be used to pay down the national debt and generally help put the country on a more solid financial foundation.

In reality, neither the lockbox proposal nor Clinton's approach would solve the impending financial squeeze surrounding Social Security brought on by the retirement of millions of BABY BOOMERS. Since the 1960s, Social Security's financial numbers have been kept with other federal programs in the government's accounting ledger. The U.S. Treasury borrows from the Social Security surpluses to offset its operating deficit and issues special government securities in return. But when Social Security TRUST FUND assets are exhausted—in 2037, according to 2000 projections—the government will have to redeem the securities and return what it borrowed. Hence, the cross-financing has little impact on the program's future. Indeed, some analysts believe enacting a lockbox plan will only delay more substantial—and politically unpalatable—legislation that they feel is necessary to overhaul and strengthen the program. These critics term the lockbox proposals budget-making reform rather than Social Security reform.

Nonetheless, the lockbox proposal gave Republicans new life on an issue with which they rarely have political success, making proponents appear both fiscally responsible and sensitive to the needs of current and future retirees. Republicans proceeded to run advertisements accusing those Democrats opposed to the lockbox concept of wanting to "raid" the Social Security trust fund. A lockbox proposal passed the House in 1999 before running into a filibuster by Senate Democrats, who wanted MEDICARE trust funds protected in a similar fashion. Some Republicans revived lockbox proposals during the second session of the 106th Congress, saying they were open to extending the concept to surpluses from the separate Medicare tax.

Longitudinal studies

Longitudinal studies are long-running scientific research projects on comparatively large groups of subjects. The studies are designed to produce epidemiological data that can reveal new facts about healthy living and the aging process. A number of government-sponsored efforts have helped scientists better manage the risks of certain diseases, such as HEART DISEASE, DIABETES, and ALZHEIMER'S DISEASE, while offering clues about how to reduce health-care costs and generally promote better health.

One longitudinal study is the Framingham Heart Study, which has been conducted in the Massachusetts town of Framingham since 1948 under the auspices of the National Heart, Lung, and Blood Institute, a division of the NATIONAL INSTITUTES OF HEALTH. More than five thousand local residents were initially recruited, and many of these people and their children have returned every two years to submit to physical exams, lifestyle interviews, and laboratory tests. Researchers looking for common patterns to cardiovascular disease development have identified major risk factors from the study, such as high blood pressure, high blood cholesterol, smoking, obesity, and diabetes. They also have drawn connections between MENOPAUSE and a greater risk of heart disease, and between enlarged ventricles and the risk of STROKE.

Another well-known longitudinal study is the Baltimore Longitudinal Study on Aging, conducted since 1958 by the NATIONAL INSTITUTE ON AGING, also part of the National Institutes of Health. Over forty years, scientists have observed various aspects of aging on a test group of more than two thousand people. One noteworthy finding, reported in 1997, documented the effects of ESTROGEN on the changes in memory of 288 women. Researchers concluded those women on estrogen supplements were significantly better at drawing figures from memory than those who had never had hormone-replacement therapy, raising intriguing questions about whether estrogen can slow the cognitive decline seen in conditions such as Alzheimer's disease. The Baltimore study also has documented how variations in human development increase as people age, and how different organ systems in the body change at different rates.

Long-term care

The term "long-term care" is understood to define the panoply of health and social services aimed at individuals who can no longer completely tend to their own needs. Some common services include daily visits to help an elderly person with personal-hygiene needs, rehabilitative services, and physiotherapy or specialized nursing care, including the administering of drugs. With the costs of NURSING HOMES and other forms of institutionalized care now nearing $100,000 per year in some urban areas, and with HOME HEALTH CARE costs frequently exceeding $100 per day, long-term care can potentially bankrupt even financially secure middle-class families. And with overall costs projected to surge as the nation's BABY BOOMERS get older, federal and state governments have intently focused on finding new alternatives and ways to control expenses. The federal government's estimated cost of paying for long-term care is expected to rise about 2.6 percent annually, from $123 billion in 2000 to $346 billion by 2040.

Selected Reported Chronic Conditions per 1,000 Elderly Persons, by Age and Family Income, 1995

		Age		Family income			
Chronic condition	All elderly	65–74	75 and older	Less than $10,000	$10,000–$19,999	$20,000–$34,999	$35,000 and over
Arthritis	490	448	548	633	503	442	413
Cataracts	159	105	234	250	146	141	177
Hearing impairment	284	236	351	298	310	289	286
Deformity or ortho- pedic impairment	178	166	193	252	196	191	149
Hernia of abdominal cavity	55	54	55	57	55	56	70
Diabetes	126	133	117	212	98	144	94
Heart disease	308	268	364	333	308	335	229
High blood pressure[1]	403	392	420	482	432	381	328
Chronic sinusitis	153	157	149	188	194	156	125
Emphysema	34	36	32	50	36	39	21

[1] As self-reported in the 1995 National Health Interview Survey.
Source: House Ways and Means Committee, *Green Book* (2000); National Center for Health Statistics (1998, Table 57, pp. 77–78, and Table 60, pp. 83–86).

The most common type of long-term care is the nursing home—which provides round-the-clock care for the sickest or frailest elderly—evidenced by the fact that roughly 70 percent of long-term-care spending in the United States still goes to institutional care. Other varieties include home health care, which is aimed at individuals who need help performing certain ACTIVITIES OF DAILY LIVING but are well enough to continue living at home; ASSISTED LIVING services provided in special facilities or COMMUNITY-BASED settings. Long-term care also includes nutritional programs, such as the popular MEALS ON WHEELS program, which provides home-delivered meals to older Americans. These various programs target the estimated 7.3 million elderly needing help with activities of daily living.

Though the government has no comprehensive long-term care program, approximately eighty federal programs provide some form of assistance and also dictate the framework in which services are provided across the nation. The most

prominent is MEDICAID, the federal-state ENTITLEMENT PROGRAM for low-income individuals, which has become the principal source of public funding for nursing home care. Many elderly Americans enter long-term care arrangements with incomes well above poverty levels but gradually see their savings depleted due to the high cost of treatments. Medicaid takes over coverage for long-term custodial care in nursing homes after a person or couple has "spent down" most available assets. Medicaid law has several built-in provisions to prevent situations such as SPOUSAL IMPOVERISHMENT, in which virtually all of a couple's assets are spent tending to one individual, leaving the other with nothing to live on. Medicaid since the 1980s also has extended waivers to localities to move some elderly people out of institutional settings and into assisted living facilities. This has helped some disabled or mentally ill individuals who otherwise would have to be treated in hospitals or nursing homes.

MEDICARE, though primarily targeted at acute

health-care needs, has several long-term care provisions. The program provides a SKILLED NURSING FACILITY benefit through Medicare Part A for individuals who need REHABILITATION after a hospital stay. Beneficiaries are entitled to one hundred days of skilled nursing care per illness. Medicare also provides the fast-growing HOME HEALTH BENEFIT, which provides nursing care in the home on a regular basis to individuals under the care of a doctor. Because of the growing number of services covered under the program, the home health benefit, provided under both Part A and Part B of the program, has experienced average annual growth rates of 10 percent. Congress responded to rising costs with a provision in the BALANCED BUDGET ACT OF 1997 (PL 105-33) that establishes a PROSPECTIVE PAYMENT SYSTEM that sets predetermined fees for services.

The federal government also provides long-term care through SOCIAL SERVICES BLOCK GRANTS, which reimburse states for community-based care, such as ADULT DAY CARE or home-delivered meals. But because of competing demands and limited funds, the program's ability to serve people in need of long-term care is limited.

The financial pressures surrounding long-term care—and the prospect of more elderly turning to the government for help paying bills—have led many policymakers to advocate private long-term care insurance policies, or employer-provided long-term care coverage to avoid a crisis in public health-care financing. Private long-term care policies vary greatly in coverage and can pay for assisted living, skilled nursing, nursing home, and HOSPICE care over predetermined periods of times. Premiums are lower for younger individuals; the average annual cost of a policy with $100-per-day nursing home care and $50-per-day home health care is about $1,000 for a sixty-five-

year-old, versus about $275 for similar coverage if the person is forty, according to the Health Insurance Association of America. Some lawmakers have advocated allowing federal workers and military personnel to buy long-term care insurance at a discount, hoping the buying power of the federal workforce will bring premiums down and prompt private businesses to offer similar benefits. The EMPLOYEE BENEFIT RESEARCH INSTITUTE says company-sponsored long-term care insurance may be the best mechanism for large-scale expansion of coverage, but notes that, to date, that national rate of employer sponsorship is only 0.2 percent. Furthermore, many long-term care policies remain very limited in scope and coverage. Even as employers begin to offer them and group policies become more available, most experts do not expect more than 15 to 20 percent of the population to have these policies, despite insurance industry claims that the figure could reach 30 percent.

Lump-sum buyouts

The phrase "lump-sum buyout" refers to employers' increasingly common practice of terminating overfunded pension plans and paying out benefits due to the participants in one large sum, instead of in many future payments. The practice can leave workers with a sudden windfall. However, the money must quickly be transferred to an INDIVIDUAL RETIREMENT ACCOUNT (IRA), ROTH IRA, or the new company's 401(K) PLAN in the case of a merger, in order to avoid a steep tax bill. Failure to move the money within a sixty-day grace period means the recipient is forced to declare the payout to the IRS as income.

Pension terminations were common in the

1980s, when corporate raiders bought companies and quickly closed down pension programs to lay claim to surplus assets. Congress virtually halted the practice in 1990 by imposing a 50 percent excise tax on pension reversions. But companies can escape the steep tax and only pay a 20 percent bill if they invest a percentage of the surplus in a replacement pension plan.

Pension buyouts began to be rekindled in the 1990s because pension managers began investing more assets in the booming stock market, dramatically increasing the value of their plans' assets. At the same time, many companies scaled back their workforces, effectively reducing pension liabilities. The result is some of these employers now can terminate their plans, pay off

workers, pay the lesser tax bill, and still walk away with hundreds of millions of dollars in assets. The practice works well both for companies that are acquiring a merger partner and can shift a percentage of assets into the new partner's pension plan, and for cash-strapped companies that can set up replacement plans and use what is left over to cover costs, pay off banks, or for other purposes.

Lump-sum buyouts have added an extra measure of unpredictability to an already jittery corporate-pension scene. Many companies have opted to switch from traditional pension plans to so-called CASH-BALANCE PENSION plans that allow retirement benefits to accumulate in a more even fashion over a worker's career—a move that, older workers allege, amounts to AGE DISCRIMINATION.

M

Meals on Wheels

Meals on Wheels, the nationwide program that brings prepared meals to frail, elderly people is one of the most widely recognized senior services funded by the federal government. It is technically known as a congregate- and home-delivered nutrition service and is funded by the OLDER AMERICANS ACT of 1965 (PL 89-73) and its amendments, and the SOCIAL SERVICES BLOCK GRANT. Federal funds are distributed to a network of state and area aging agencies and local service providers, who also pick up a portion of program costs. One 1996 evaluation of the program by the U.S. Department of HEALTH AND HUMAN SERVICES determined that for every federal dollar spent, another $3.35 was spent by states and other entities for home-delivered meals.

The meals themselves are usually delivered hot to the homes of individuals who either are recuperating from illness or are unable to shop or cook for themselves. Providers typically supply two meals per day, with some meals arriving cold or frozen so that they can be reheated later. A number of service providers in outlying areas have tried distributing preprogrammed microwave ovens with the meals, so clients are assured of getting properly prepared and nutritious lunches and dinners. Providers also try to accommodate individuals' special dietary needs resulting from health conditions or religious beliefs.

An elderly woman receives food from Meals on Wheels of San Francisco. Meals on Wheels has provided about 240 million meals to some 3 million elderly people throughout the United States. Source: Meals on Wheels of San Francisco

Proponents say the program not only provides an essential service in a health and nutritional sense, but often represents the only regularly scheduled daily social contact for homebound elderly people. However, some advocates for the elderly say the program's federal budget has not kept up with inflation or with the growing elderly population, pointing to some areas where eligible elderly recipients have to wait months on standby lists before they can receive their first meals.

Overall, the Older Americans Act's nutrition program has provided about 240 million meals to some 3 million elderly people. The vast majority are poor, living alone, and many are members of minority groups. The meals are designed to meet federal nutrition guidelines and often provide recipients with their primary source of daily calories and nutrients. Funding for the Older Americans Act nutrition program stands at about $625 million per year and has generally received bipartisan support in Congress, despite broader concerns on the part of some lawmakers about the way the act authorizes community service efforts. The program also delivers prepared meals to congregate settings, such as local senior centers.

Means testing

Means testing refers in general to the practice of measuring an individual's or family's income and assets to gauge whether the person or family qualifies for a federal program directed at low-income individuals. MEDICAID, the federal-state health program for the indigent, is the most prominent example of a means-tested program. In recent years the term also has been applied to proposals to limit the distribution of SOCIAL SECURITY benefits to middle- or upper-income individuals, and to charge wealthy MEDICARE beneficiaries more for their coverage, especially through their Part B premiums.

Means testing is one of the most politically controversial proposals surrounding ENTITLEMENT PROGRAMS—about as palatable as raising payroll taxes. Congress attempted to charge well-heeled Medicare recipients an extra sum when it passed the MEDICARE CATASTROPHIC COVERAGE ACT (PL 100-360) in 1988, but repealed the law the next year, after a flood of voter complaints about this premium and other provisions. More recently, the idea has gained some currency with

strict fiscal conservatives and some centrist Democrats, in light of forecasts predicting severe financial problems facing the Social Security and Medicare TRUST FUNDS in the coming decades. However, winning passage of any strict income thresholds is considered politically difficult because it would target wealthy elders, an influential voting bloc.

Media and aging

Despite the increased prominence of aging in national politics and policy debates, major media organizations have been slow and somewhat inconsistent in formulating strategies to cover the topic. Part of this is due to the way aging cuts across many dimensions of society. Coverage of senior health issues and the MEDICARE program may be folded into a newspaper, magazine, or network's broader health-care beat. Reporting on the pros and cons of certain eldercare systems may be lumped with consumer journalism. NURSING HOME abuses may be assigned to the investigative team. Apart from a handful of pioneering news organizations—the *Arizona Republic, Atlanta Constitution and Journal, Los Angeles Times, Philadelphia Inquirer, St. Petersburg Times,* and the *Star Tribune* (Minneapolis), to name a few—newsrooms in print and broadcast journalism have been slow to assign a reporter or reporters full-time on the aging beat. Some also have been reluctant to devote substantial resources to examinations of seldom-covered issues, such as end-of-life care, which won the *Philadelphia Inquirer* a Pulitzer Prize in 1997.

The results of giving short shrift to aging issues became clear during the SOCIAL SECURITY debate during the 105th Congress. Surveys showed the majority of Americans rated the news media's coverage of the topic "fair or poor," with many complaining the news outlets had to do a better job of explaining the program and putting a human face on the issue. More broadly, a computer-assisted study of two decades of coverage of ENTITLEMENT PROGRAMS by Lawrence Jacobs of the University of Minnesota and Robert Y. Shapiro of Columbia University revealed that the "crisis and conflict" orientation of major media led to a skewed picture of Social Security and Medicare, portraying the programs in much more dire straits than they actually were. Jacobs and Shapiro found news organizations tended to seek out outspoken conservative experts and Republican critics of the programs.

By the late 1990s, more news organizations are rethinking the aging beat and looking for unique story angles. They also are writing stories aimed at BABY BOOMERS and GENERATION X, two DEMOGRAPHIC segments that are most likely to feel the effects of any major shifts in aging policies. Journalists with expertise in the subject also are banding together. The Journalists' Exchange on Aging was begun in 1993 during an AMERICAN SOCIETY ON AGING conference and consists of a loose confederation of aging-beat reporters who share sources and news tips and generally agitate for more coverage. The collaborative effort, which includes a newsletter called "Age Beat," is coordinated by Paul Kleyman, editor of *Aging Today*, a bimonthly newspaper published by the American Society on Aging. Reporters also are tapping personal experiences to bring home the universal nature of aging topics. One celebrated series on caregiving for the elderly in the *San Francisco Examiner* was inspired by reporter Beth Wintorgen McLeod's caring for two terminally ill parents.

The 1995 project won a number of national awards and was nominated for a Pulitzer Prize.

Medicaid

Medicaid is Title XIX of the SOCIAL SECURITY ACT and became law in 1965 as part of President Lyndon Johnson's War on Poverty. This complicated program is a joint federal-state matching ENTITLEMENT PROGRAM to provide health care to needy individuals. In fiscal 1999, the program spent approximately $190 billion to provide care to 41.4 million Americans. Of that amount, $108 billion was paid by the federal government. While the public generally views Medicaid as a single program, it really is fifty-six different programs because each state, the District of Columbia, and each U.S. territory establishes eligibility standards, determines the type and extent of care it will provide, sets payment rates, and administers its own program. Though programs vary from state to state, they typically are designed for three essential purposes: providing LONG-TERM CARE for sick, disabled, and elderly individuals; offering comprehensive health insurance for low-income children and families; and reimbursing hospitals that treat a disproportionate share of needy patients who cannot pay all their bills.

Though Medicaid was designed primarily as a health-care program, it has become the main source of public funding for NURSING HOME care. This is because the cost of providing long-term care for elderly and disabled people is significantly higher than the cost of providing acute medical care. Though elderly and disabled Americans make up about 31 percent of Medicaid recipients, they account for approximately 64 percent of pro-

Using the pen with which President Lyndon B. Johnson had signed the Medicare law in 1965, President Bill Clinton vetoed the Republican Congress's budget bill on December 6, 1995, saying the legislation would lead to the biggest cuts to the Medicare and Medicaid programs in history. Medicaid is a focal point of social policy debates between Democrats and Republicans. Source: Reuters

gram spending. Worried about even larger disparities due to rising health-care costs and the growing elderly population, states have taken steps to curb spending, such as setting fixed payment schedules for nursing homes and approving waivers to move some Medicaid recipients out of institutions and into less expensive community-based settings, including HOME HEALTH CARE.

Medicaid is subject to MEANS TESTING, meaning it covers target groups of individuals with few savings and assets. These include the elderly, blind, and disabled; families with dependent children; and low-income pregnant women and their children who receive cash payments through the Temporary Assistance for Needy Families program or who qualify by meeting federal poverty thresholds. Because Medicaid is an entitlement program, recipients are eligible for payments from the state for "covered services"—always doctors' and hospital services and nursing home care,

and, depending on the state, optional services such as prescription drugs or treatment of the mentally retarded in INTERMEDIATE-CARE FACILITIES. States receive matching funds from the federal government for the covered services. There are no limits on matching-fund payments, but each state's allowable claims are subject to a formula based on per capita income. The result is states with higher per capita income get a lower percentage of federal matching funds, while low per capita income states get more.

Aspects of Medicaid coverage of particular interest to elderly Americans include the following:

• *Nursing facility services.* In response to rising long-term care expenses, many states have implemented prospective payment systems that pay nursing homes a fixed amount for every day of care that a Medicaid enrollee needs. The payment is designed to cover all costs of care; if the nursing home can provide the services for less, it keeps the difference. If costs exceed the prescribed amounts, the nursing home has to make up the difference. At least thirty states also have instituted prescreening programs or toughened eligibility standards to ensure that only the sickest or most disabled Medicaid enrollees gain admission. The BALANCED BUDGET ACT OF 1997 (PL 105-33) also allowed states the option of offering the most frail, elderly Medicaid recipients the choice of receiving a package of nursing-home-like services in day-care centers or in their homes for a capped monthly payment. Care also would be provided by doctors, hospitals, and nurses on an as-needed basis. This option, known as the PROGRAM FOR ALL-INCLUSIVE CARE FOR THE ELDERLY, or PACE, is an example of a DEMONSTRATION PROGRAM that attempts to change in a fundamental way how some MEDICARE and Medicaid services are delivered. And yet since PACE was approved by

Congress as an option to be made generally available, few states have set up such a program despite mounting research evidence that home- and COMMUNITY-BASED SERVICES save money.

• *Home health services.* These services are a mandatory benefit for Medicaid beneficiaries who would be entitled to nursing home care under a state's plan. Services must be ordered by a physician and include skilled nursing on a part-time or periodic basis, home-health aides, and any necessary medical supplies and equipment. Physical and occupational therapy, and speech pathology or audiology services may also be provided, depending on the state plan.

• *Hospice care.* Medicaid offers HOSPICE care as an optional benefit to individuals who have been certified by a physician as being terminally ill—that is, who are expected to live six months or less. Services provided at home under the care of a hospice or in the hospice itself must be laid out in a plan of care before the services are provided. Medicaid pays at one of four predetermined rates for each day that an individual is under the care of a hospice. Rates vary with levels of care—from routine home care to continuous home care, inpatient RESPITE CARE, and general inpatient care. Payments for inpatient care are subject to certain limits. If a Medicaid hospice patient resides in a nursing home, the state also must pay at least 95 percent of the nursing home rate to the hospice so that the patient's nursing home room and board services are covered.

• *Rehabilitation services.* Medicaid also optionally provides REHABILITATION services, if a physician recommends them. These services are provided in any type of setting and include mental health therapy, psychosocial counseling, physical therapy, and occupational and speech therapy.

• *Personal care services.* This is another form of optional care that is provided to Medicaid recipients not already inpatients in a hospital, nursing home, or intermediate-care facility. These services must be authorized by a physician and include help with ACTIVITIES OF DAILY LIVING, such as eating, bathing, using the toilet, and dressing.

• *Services for people with speech, hearing, or language disorders.* This is another type of service that states may choose to provide. Prescribed by a physician or other licensed practitioner, they can include physical or occupational therapy.

Efforts to enroll Medicaid beneficiaries in health-maintenance organizations go back to the 1980s. The Balanced Budget Act of 1997 tried to promote this on a widespread basis by allowing states to require beneficiaries to enroll in HMOs, instead of having to apply for waivers from rules that gave the beneficiaries a choice of health-care providers. But many health insurers limited enrollment or dropped out of the program, saying Medicaid's reimbursement rates were too low. The insurers complained that it was both difficult and expensive to serve elderly and disabled people with complex health-care needs. Medicaid administrators continue to explore whether managed care can better fit within the program's parameters, perhaps through the establishment of more specialized Medicaid-only HMOs.

The HEALTH CARE FINANCING ADMINISTRATION (HCFA) has adopted a number of Medicaid rules in response to rising nursing home costs, which often exceed $40,000 per year. SPOUSAL IMPOVERISHMENT rules prevent the spending down of the major share of a couple's assets on one spouse requiring nursing home or other long-term care while the other spouse continues to live at home. The rule allows for the transfer of assets and income from the institutionalized spouse to the "community spouse" after an assessment is done on the couple's combined resources. HCFA requires nursing homes to advise individuals purchasing care that resource assessments are available. It also requires that states recognize minimum living allowances for the community spouse, which ranged between $1,383 and $2,049 per month in 1999. The amounts may be increased depending on the community spouse's housing costs and whether he or she is living with dependents. Medicaid also allows nursing home residents to keep a small portion of their income or assets as a personal-needs allowance. The allowance was initially set by Congress in 1972 at $25 per month and has been increased by states to reflect the higher cost of living. Such allowances come in handy if a nursing home patient has to leave the facility for a hospital stay and needs to pay to reserve a bed on his or her return.

The Medicaid program regularly grants waivers to move program beneficiaries to less cost-intensive environments. One example is the "Section 2176 waiver," named for the part of the Omnibus Budget Reconciliation Act of 1981 (PL 97-35) allowing the exemption, which allows some aged, disabled, and mentally retarded Americans who would otherwise need hospital or nursing home care to be shifted to community-based care, such as home health care, ADULT DAY CARE, or personal care assistance.

Medical power of attorney

A common variety of ADVANCE DIRECTIVE, a medical power of attorney designates a surrogate to make health-care decisions in the event that a patient is incapacitated by illness and cannot make his or her wishes known. This written document is somewhat more personal than a LIVING WILL, and is best used when the patient has a loved one or close friend that he or she can count on to be nearby for the duration of the medical treatment. The PATIENT SELF-DETERMINATION ACT requires health-care facilities that receive MEDICARE or MEDICAID funds to tell patients about such documents and give them the option of drawing one up.

Medical savings account

A medical savings account, or MSA, is a controversial type of savings vehicle that would allow people to set aside some of their income tax-free to cover basic health-care costs. First proposed by the insurance industry in the late 1980s and championed mostly by conservative Republicans, MSAs essentially would make consumers responsible for enforcing market discipline in the health-care sector. Individuals would first purchase a catastrophic health insurance policy with a high DEDUCTIBLE to cover costs associated with any serious illness. They then would activate an MSA to cover more routine doctor visits, preventive care, and other basic services. Money in the account could not go toward any other expenses except health care. The theory is that individuals responsible for their own medical expenses will have an extra incentive to seek out only necessary care and obtain the best price.

MSAs have been proposed as part of broader legislation known as the "Patients' Bill of Rights" and were championed by Republican presidential candidate George W. Bush and GOP congressional leaders during the 2000 campaign cycle. However, critics say the proposals have a fundamental flaw, in that MSAs will largely be attractive to younger, healthier people who typically do not run up high medical bills. That will leave older, sicker people making up a larger proportion of the insurance pool, increasing premium costs and likely making health insurance policies less affordable. MSAs also primarily benefit wealthier individuals who would be helped more from the tax-deferred treatment and be more likely to be able to make up any difference between the amount of money saved in an MSA and any large deductibles they might incur.

Congress has authorized several DEMONSTRATION PROGRAMS to test the viability of MSAs. The Health Insurance Portability and Accountability Act of 1996 (PL 104-191) authorized a pilot program aimed at self-employed individuals and companies with fifty or fewer employees. Though the pilot program was authorized to sell as many as 750,000 of the policies, response has been low because many consumers find the MSAs unnecessarily complicated and balk at the high deductibles for catastrophic coverage. INTERNAL REVENUE SERVICE data showed that only 42,477 tax returns for the calendar year 1998 reported an excludable or deductible contribution to an MSA.

The BALANCED BUDGET ACT OF 1997 (PL 105-33) also authorized an MSA demonstration for MEDICARE recipients, initially making the option available to approximately 1 percent of program enrollees. Under the program, Medicare would pay for recipients' catastrophic coverage and give recipients payments for basic medical services that were equivalent to those paid to managed-care providers in the areas where they lived. Beneficiaries also could use money saved in an MSA

for LONG-TERM CARE, and could withdraw a portion of the money for non-health purposes. Again, response has been slow due to the fact that almost no insurers have agreed to set up the plans because they do not deem them as a promising market. Political opponents of MSAs have also criticized rules they say will allow Medicare money to be treated the same way as a tax-deferred retirement account.

Medicare

The giant health insurance program known as Medicare came into being on July 30, 1965, when President Lyndon B. Johnson signed legislation (PL 89-97) that aimed to provide health coverage for all elderly Americans. Politicians since the late 1940s had battled over various proposals for national health insurance, with Democrats and labor unions most strenuously backing the concept, and Republicans and the AMERICAN MEDICAL ASSOCIATION providing much of the opposition. Medicare was established at a time when nearly half of American senior citizens had incomes below federal poverty levels and many had trouble obtaining private insurance. The program provides health-insurance protection to virtually every American who reaches age sixty-five. In fiscal 1999, Medicare insured approximately thirty-nine million elderly and disabled individuals at an estimated cost of $212 billion, making it the second most expensive federal domestic program after SOCIAL SECURITY. However, in its current form Medicare primarily covers hospital and surgical care and the medically necessary REHABILITATION period that follows. That means LONG-TERM CARE, custodial care, outpatient prescription

With former president Harry S. Truman at his side, President Lyndon B. Johnson signs the legislation that would bring Medicare into being on July 30, 1965. Source: Lyndon B. Johnson Library

drugs, and many other health needs go uncovered. Medicare does provide care in SKILLED NURSING FACILITIES, as well as HOME HEALTH CARE and some HOSPICE care.

Medicare's package of BENEFITS consists of several parts. Part A, known as HOSPITAL INSURANCE, is provided free to all Americans currently receiving or eligible to receive Social Security and is financed by a special payroll tax of 1.45 percent of income, paid by both the employer and the worker. It covers inpatient hospital treatment, skilled nursing facility care, and some home health and hospice care. Most hospitals are reimbursed according to a prospective payment system that pays hospitals predetermined amounts based on the average cost of treating a condition. The BALANCED BUDGET ACT OF 1997 (PL 105-33) provided limits for future increases in hospital spending, including reductions to annual adjustments for inflation, known as the Market Basket Index, or MBI.

Medicare Part B is an optional package covering physicians' office visits and outpatient services that is available to individuals aged sixty-five and older who are willing to pay a monthly premium of $45.50, an annual DEDUCTIBLE of $100, and 20 percent copayments. Part B pays for physical or occupational therapists, certain home health services, medical equipment, prosthetics, and doctors' services deemed "medically necessary." It also covers preventive services, such as certain vaccinations, screening for cervical, colorectal, and prostate CANCER, and mammograms. Health-care experts say the Part B package is a significant bargain in the current health-care marketplace because recipients only pay about one-quarter of what the covered services are worth, with the remainder covered by federal taxpayers.

In 1972, Congress expanded the Medicare program by making individuals with end-stage renal disease eligible for coverage. Medicare covers both dialysis treatment and kidney transplantation. Though it was assumed at the time of enactment that enrollment would level out at about 90,000 beneficiaries, the program today treats approximately 320,000 Americans.

Congress added another piece to Medicare with passage of the Balanced Budget Act of 1997, creating Medicare Part C, also known as MEDICARE+CHOICE. This provides expanded options for individuals enrolled in Medicare Parts A and B, including the ability to enroll in managed-care plans and other private forms of insurance. Many managed-care plans try to attract customers by offering services not provided under "traditional" Medicare, such as prescription drugs, eyeglasses, and hearing aids. Medicare recipients who opt for these plans must remain enrolled in Medicare Part B, and have to continue paying the Part B premiums. Lawmakers established protections for Part C enrollees, including assuring beneficiaries access to emergency services, external reviews of participating plans, and the ability to appeal medical treatment decisions. Medicare reimburses the plans under a complicated formula that takes into account prevailing health-care spending in the locality where the plan is located. Administrators are mov-

ing toward a blended national rate to reduce variations in pricing across the country.

One of the most vexing questions facing policymakers is how to control rising Medicare costs while still ensuring that the program delivers quality care at affordable prices. The future solvency of the Medicare TRUST FUNDS has been a major topic of concern because the aging of the population and the growing availability of new medical treatments and technology is making health-care spending grow faster than the overall economy. Current projections show the Hospital Insurance (HI) trust fund, the bellwether used to assess the overall financial health of Medicare, will remain solvent until the year 2025—eight years longer than Medicare trustees predicted in 1999. However, skeptics say the projections may be overly optimistic because home health services—one of the fastest-growing components of the program—were moved from the HI trust fund to Medicare's SUPPLEMENTARY MEDICAL INSURANCE trust fund, thereby reducing the services covered by the Part A dedicated payroll tax and creating a bigger surplus. These skeptics fear Medicare spending by the second decade of the twenty-first century may well eat into general government revenues.

Congress has a number of options, chiefly adding benefits or imposing new price controls. With political momentum behind a proposed Medicare PRESCRIPTION DRUG BENEFIT and pressure building to improve NURSING HOME benefits, lawmakers may have to contend with staggering new expenses. They could respond by restricting other benefits, raising payroll taxes or deductibles paid by beneficiaries, or by restricting payments to doctors, hospitals, and other health-care providers. Some members of the National Bipartisan Commission on Medicare in 1999 recommended a

Use of Inpatient Hospital Services by Medicare Enrollees, by Type of Enrollee and Type of Hospital, Calendar Year 1998[1]

Type of enrollee and type of hospital	Bills[2]		Covered days of care			Reimbursement		
	Number in thousands	Per 1,000 enrollees	Number in thousands	Per bill	Per 1,000 enrollees	Amount in millions	Per bill	Per enrollee
All enrollees								
All hospitals	11,834	308	69,924	5.9	1,819	$74,153	$6,266	$1,929
Short stay	11,335	295	64,454	5.7	1,677	70,813	6,247	1,843
Long stay	499	13	5,470	11.0	142	3,340	6,693	87
Psychiatric	205	5	1,837	9.0	48	712	3,473	19
All other	294	8	3,633	12.4	95	2,628	8,939	68
Aged								
All hospitals	10,021	300	58,849	5.9	1,761	63,372	6,324	1,897
Short stay	9,249	277	55,133	6.0	1,650	60,868	6,581	1,822
Long stay	772	23	3,716	4.8	111	2,504	3,244	75
Psychiatric	52	2	563	10.8	17	242	4,654	7
All other	720	22	2,295	3.2	69	2,262	3,142	68
Disabled								
All hospitals	1,775	353	11,075	6.2	2,205	10,780	6,073	2,146
Short stay	1,553	309	9,322	6.0	1,856	9,945	6,404	1,980
Long stay	222	44	1,753	7.9	349	835	3,761	166
Psychiatric	153	30	1,274	8.3	254	470	3,072	94
All other	69	14	479	6.9	95	365	5,290	73

[1] Preliminary data. Totals may not add due to rounding.

[2] Discharges not available by type of hospital.

Note: Only services rendered by inpatient hospitals are included.

Source: Health Care Financing Administration, Office of Information Services, unpublished data.

PREMIUM SUPPORT system that would give seniors federal dollars to buy private health insurance as one solution to the financial squeeze. However, the suggestion was voted down amid concerns that it would not help the neediest seniors and would amount to a subsidy for the insurance industry.

Specific recommendations to reform the program include the following:

• *Raising the eligibility age from sixty-five to sixty-seven.* Some reform advocates believe Medicare should follow the Social Security program's lead with respect to the retirement age and gradually increase the eligibility age for Part A and B benefits. The CONGRESSIONAL BUDGET OFFICE in 1997 estimated that this proposal would save $10.2 billion in costs between fiscal 2002 and 2007. Moreover, some lawmakers believe raising the age would

more accurately reflect the increased LIFE EXPECTANCIES and the availability of more medical treatments than when Medicare was first enacted. However, opponents argue that raising the eligibility age would put the "near retired," that is, individuals in their early sixties, at risk. About 16 percent of this age group is uninsured, and at least one-quarter of that percentage live in poverty. Raising the eligibility age would make these people wait longer for guaranteed government coverage. It also could prompt some employers to reconsider whether to stop offering health insurance, reasoning that extending their plans another two years is uneconomical.

• *Means testing.* Unlike MEDICAID, Medicare is not a means-tested program. The version of the Balanced Budget Act of 1997 that passed the Senate

Skilled nursing facility caregivers cheer for the cameras at the end of a September 5, 2000, rally urging Congress to reverse Medicare cuts. Source: Scott J. Ferrell, Congressional Quarterly

included a provision that would have imposed a higher Part B premium for well-off beneficiaries. However, the provision was dropped during the House-Senate conference, in part over concerns about how the testing would be administered. Some lawmakers also worried that the move would be interpreted as a new tax.

• *Increased deductibles and copayments.* Various bills have proposed increasing the Part B copayment from 20 percent to 25 percent, or at least doubling the $100 Part B deductible to make it resemble the deductibles in private insurance plans. Having beneficiaries pay more of the cost would make them more careful and prudent in the selection of health services, reform advocates say. How-

ever, opponents fear increased out-of-pocket expenses would weigh heavily on low-income beneficiaries. A key issue is that research throughout the world in advanced economies suggests that copayments and deductibles actually deter people from seeking medical care until their problem becomes more severe or acute, resulting in greater medical costs to the system and opportunity costs, such as the lost on-the-job time by family caregivers.

• *Restructuring the program.* A variety of proposals are built around much more sweeping changes to the Medicare program. These include the "premium support" model advocated by some members of the National Bipartisan Commission on Medicare. Some have suggested Medicare be closely modeled on the Federal Employees Health Benefit Plan, in which the government sets service standards for a wide variety of private health plans to participate. Medicare enrollees could shop and select from plans that offer different services, premiums, and copayments, essentially purchasing one package of health care. The individual would end up paying any difference between the government's contribution and the selected plan's premium. Proponents of such a DEFINED-CONTRIBUTION PLAN say it would give the government more control over Medicare outlays. However, opponents fear that rising health-care costs could exceed COST-OF-LIVING ADJUSTMENTS in the government's payment system, again putting some seniors at risk.

The surest reform proposal in 2000 was one that would again expand the program by adding a Medicare prescription drug benefit, long seen as one of the program's most glaring deficiencies. After years of fighting proposed Medicare coverage of prescription drugs, pharmaceutical companies in early 2000 signaled they would be willing to accept a drug benefit as prelude to broader changes to the program. The drug industry appeared tiring of persistent Democratic attacks on the price of new drugs and contentions that seniors were being gouged. Many Republican lawmakers, sensing the political change, began advocating a type of benefit that would give recipients payments to buy private drug coverage. Implementing such a benefit would present significant management challenges to Medicare administrators because even private health insurers have had trouble keeping pace with annual drug price spending increases of 15 percent or more. Advocates of the drug benefit have been careful to stress that it would not impose price controls on prescription drugs, long the pharmaceuti-

cal industry's biggest concern. (See also BIPARTISAN MEDICARE REFORM.)

Medicare+Choice

Medicare+Choice, also known as Medicare Part C, was established by the BALANCED BUDGET ACT OF 1997 (PL 105-33) as an alternative to the traditional fee-for-service MEDICARE system. It allows recipients to enroll in various types of managed-care plans that have agreements with the Medicare program. In theory, this allows recipients to get a wider range of covered medical services while leaving the managed-care plans, instead of the government, responsible for the difficult task of managing health-care costs. Approximately 17 percent of Medicare beneficiaries had opted for the managed care option in 1999, and Medicare administrators predict that 38 percent of Medicare recipients will be enrolled in the plans by 2008.

Managed-care entities offering services under Medicare+Choice include health maintenance organizations (HMOs), which designate a network of doctors and other health professionals to administer care; point-of-service plans, which have somewhat more liberal rules that allow patients to visit out-of-network providers for an extra fee; preferred provider organizations (PPOs), in which networks of doctors offer discounted health services; and private fee-for-service plans. This latter category was included in the authorizing legislation at the insistence of conservative Republicans and basically operates like a traditional indemnity system. Patients can visit any doctors or health-care providers they wish. The private fee-for-service plan, not Medicare, decides

In spite of negative media coverage, which highlighted the overly restrictive health care delivery policies of some managed care providers, enrollment in managed care programs exploded between 1985 and 1996. Medicare+Choice allows Medicare recipients to enroll in various managed-care plans. Source: Beth Balbierz, KRT

what it will pay for services. Doctors and other providers can bill the Medicare recipients for amounts beyond what the health plan pays, meaning the recipients sometimes have to pay steep out-of-pocket expenses.

Medicare+Choice also authorized a MEDICAL SAVINGS ACCOUNT demonstration project. Up to 390,000 recipients are permitted to open accounts through 2002. The beneficiary typically selects a private insurance plan with a high DEDUCTIBLE of as much as $6,000. Medicare pays the plan's premium and makes a deposit in the individual's medical savings account. The individual uses the money in the account to pay for services until the deductible is reached. Health-care providers can bill for amounts above what is paid by the medical savings account.

Medicare payments to the managed-care plans have been the subject of considerable controversy.

Medicare typically pays an amount based on the prevailing cost of care in the county where the service is provided. The Balanced Budget Act attempted to even out regional differences by creating a minimum payment in low-cost areas and enacting automatic 2 percent increases each year. The law also called for the gradual implementation of a "blended" regional and national payment rate that would help lower-cost areas that were not helped by the minimum payment. However, the Medicare program did not have enough money to achieve all three of these goals. Just setting the minimum payment and paying the 2 percent increases exhausted the program's resources, preventing the blended rate from being immediately implemented. The result was that managed-care companies in lower-cost areas continued to be underpaid, while those in high-cost areas complained the 2 percent increases were not keeping pace with medical inflation. This and other market conditions led to a mass withdrawal of managed-care plans from some areas in 1998 and 1999 and a cutback in services in other regions. In all, more than 700,000 Medicare beneficiaries were forced to change plans or to return to the traditional fee-for-service program by the beginning of 2000.

A number of studies, however, have raised questions about the managed-care plans' enrollment policies, pointing to evidence the plans focus largely on enrolling healthier elderly individuals while rejecting older, frailer Americans. Critics contend this creates instability in the health-care system and effectively rewards managed-care plans for providing less care. This runs counter to Medicare's original goal of providing guaranteed health-care coverage, the critics contend. However, many lawmakers respond that the original Medicare program was poorly designed and inefficient, and that managed-care only now is beginning to impose the fiscal discipline needed to ultimately fix the program.

Medicare Catastrophic Coverage Act of 1988

Congress's most ambitious attempt to date to expand the MEDICARE program, and charge beneficiaries for the extra coverage, demonstrated the political perils of tinkering with ENTITLEMENT PROGRAMS, not to mention the clout of SENIOR VOTERS. The Medicare Catastrophic Coverage Act (PL 100-360) began in February 1987 as an initiative on the part of President RONALD REAGAN's administration to establish ceilings on how much Medicare beneficiaries should pay out-of-pocket

for hospital coverage and for the optional medical care covered under Part B. Medicare pays the first sixty days of hospitalization after DEDUCTIBLES, after which the patient pays an increasingly larger portion of the bill—a situation critics say penalizes the sickest patients.

The proposal, devised by then secretary of HEALTH AND HUMAN SERVICES Otis Brown, was not enough for congressional Democrats, who had recently retaken control of the Senate and wanted to significantly expand the scope of the program to include more NURSING HOME, HOME HEALTH, and HOSPICE care. Before negotiations were over, these provisions were added, as well as first-time coverage of outpatient prescription drugs (80 percent of the cost after beneficiaries paid a $600 annual deductible), RESPITE CARE for family CAREGIVERS, and mammograms. President Ronald Reagan signed the bill in July 1988.

Lawmakers reasoned that they could get the bill passed with the Democratic additions and Republican support of the financing mechanism they had insisted on, because AARP endorsed it. The NATIONAL COUNCIL OF SENIOR CITIZENS and some other smaller groups objected to the financing restriction because it was not universal like Part A. However, AARP led the effort to soften opposition with the promise that catastrophic coverage would be a foot in the door to expansions Republicans would not have agreed to had it not been for the participation of Secretary Brown—a move that was to prove highly damaging to AARP's national clout. The lawmakers agreed on a "seniors-only" financing scheme in which about 37 percent of the cost would be financed by a $4.90 monthly increase in the Part B premium. The remainder would come from a surcharge levied on wealthier Medicare beneficiaries who owed more than $150 of federal income taxes. However, an aggressive lobbying campaign from both liberal and conservative opponents (opposed, respectively, to the idea of senior-only financing, and to new taxes and surcharges) began to swing public sentiment against the changes. A series of staged protests included one memorable incident in which a group of angry senior citizens harangued powerful HOUSE WAYS AND MEANS COMMITTEE chairman Dan Rostenkowski, D-Ill., a supporter of the legislation, outside his Chicago district office.

Faced with mounting opposition from an influential block of voters, Congress did an about-face and repealed the law in November 1989, less than eighteen months after it was signed. The repeal actually increased the federal deficit because extra premiums already were being collected and deposited in federal coffers. However, Congress kept some provisions, including Medicaid "SPOUSAL IMPOVERISHMENT" rules. It also authorized a commission headed by House Rules Committee chairman CLAUDE PEPPER, D-Fla., to look into new ways to cover LONG-TERM CARE and cover America's UNINSURED.

Medicare givebacks

"Medicare givebacks" refers to the packages of spending Congress passed in 1999 and 2000 to offset deeper-than-expected cuts to MEDICARE providers set by the BALANCED BUDGET ACT OF 1997 (PL 105-33). Hospitals, NURSING HOMES, REHABILITATION therapists, managed-care plans, and HOME HEALTH CARE agencies complained for most of the year that congressional budget planners underestimated how quickly health-care

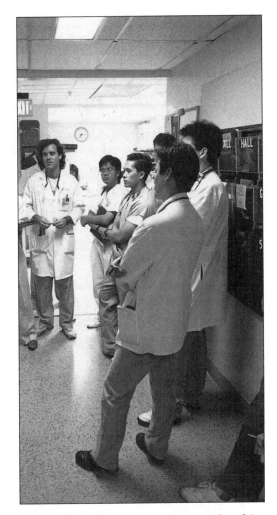

Teaching hospitals were among the groups benefiting from Congress's 1999 and 2000 giveback packages.
Source: R. Michael Jenkins, Congressional Quarterly

costs were rising and, correspondingly, how deeply program cuts would affect the health-care sector. Lawmakers were receptive to the arguments, reasoning that because Medicare spending was lower than expected, they could ante up a relief package. The 1999 legislation gave health-care providers $17 billion over five years. An even larger package, written by Republicans with virtually no Democratic input, in 2000 awarded approximately $35 billion in givebacks over five years. The givebacks did not, however, address broader underlying financial problems surrounding Medicare.

Among the groups helped by the giveback bills were teaching hospitals, which received increases in payments for the indirect costs of teaching and training physicians (such as additional tests new residents might order) and a freeze in proposed cuts in so-called disproportionate-share payments. These payments reimburse facilities that see a larger-than-average share of low-income patients. Also helped were home health agencies, which won a delay in a 15 percent cut scheduled to go into effect in October 2000. SKILLED NURSING FACILITIES received temporary increases in daily payment rates by 20 percent for certain categories of higher-cost patients, while spending caps limiting the cost of physical and speech therapy were lifted at a cost of $600 million.

Managed-care plans received about $4.8 billion over five years in 1999 and another $11 billion in 2000, as well as a more gradual phase-in of a "risk adjustment" system that pays less to plans with proportionately healthier employees. The giveback bills also awarded bonus payments for managed-care firms that agreed to serve counties that were not currently served by a Medicare-participating managed-care provider. About 17 percent of Medicare beneficiaries use managed-care plans instead of the "traditional" Medicare program.

Medicare home health benefit

See HOME HEALTH BENEFITS (MEDICARE).

Medicare Payment Advisory Commission

The Medicare Payment Advisory Commission, informally known as MedPAC, is an independent government agency established by the BALANCED BUDGET ACT OF 1997 (PL 105-33) to advise Congress on MEDICARE issues. The agency was created by merging two other health-care advisory bodies, the Prospective Payment Advisory Commission, which was responsible for monitoring Medicare payments to hospitals, and the Physician Payment Review Commission, which tracked payments to physicians. The seventeen-member MedPAC's main activities include issuing two reports each year, in March and June, that make recommendations on Medicare payment policies, in light of developments in health-care markets. The agency, staffed by approximately thirty economists and analysts, also monitors quality-of-care issues, comments on U.S. Department of HEALTH AND HUMAN SERVICES reports to Congress, briefs congressional staffs, and assists lawmakers in crafting formal regulations.

Medicare prescription drug benefit

See PRESCRIPTION DRUG BENEFIT (MEDICARE).

Medigap insurance

"Medigap" is a term referring to private supplemental insurance policies that MEDICARE beneficiaries purchase to cover the gap between what Medicare pays and what the beneficiaries owe. More than three-quarters of Medicare recipients have such policies, with about half purchased out-of-pocket and the remainder supplied by current or former employers. Congress has regulated the sale of the policies since 1980 after hearings revealed abuses in the marketing of the products. But lawmakers regularly have had to rein in insurers who fail to pay out enough of a percentage of premium dollars in benefits or who charge too much for overhead and administrative costs. Recent surveys show pricing for Medigap plans continues to vary widely, with some companies charging by age and others charging according to how long the policyholder has been a customer.

There are ten different Medigap policies, labeled A to J, the result of provisions Congress inserted in the Omnibus Budget Reconciliation Act of 1990 (PL 101-508; see OMNIBUS BUDGET RECONCILIATION BILLS) that standardized sales and helped consumers better understand levels of coverage. All Medigap policies must cover copayments from hospitalizations longer than sixty days, pay the 20 percent copayment for Medicare Part B, and provide the first three pints of blood needed for medical services in a year. The BALANCED BUDGET ACT OF 1997 (PL 105-33) also required insurers to sell policies to any senior citizens, except disabled Medicare beneficiaries, during the first six months after they turn sixty-five. Following this open enrollment period, insurers can make limited denials of coverage due to pre-existing health conditions or turn down applicants entirely for certain conditions. Seniors who leave traditional Medicare and drop their Medigap coverage to enroll in a MEDICARE+CHOICE but return within one year may enroll in their old Medigap plan, if it is available, or in one of four other designated Medigap plans.

The Medigap Plan A, which is the least expensive option, covers only the basic services for long hospitalizations, Part B copayments, and the three-pints-of-blood allowance. Plan B covers those services and Medicare's annual hospital DEDUCTIBLE ($776 in 2000). Plan C adds the $100 Medicare Part B deductible. Other plans cover options such as co-insurance for skilled nursing care, home health coverage beyond what Medicare already provides, doctors' bills above and beyond Medicare's approved fee up to 115 percent of the charge, additional preventive health benefits, and up to $3,000 per year in PRESCRIPTION DRUG costs. The fully loaded Plan J, created by the Balanced Budget Act, has all of these options. Deductibles for the most expensive plans are high—$1,500 annually in 1999 and to be increased by the CONSUMER PRICE INDEX in subsequent years—and not all plans are available in all states. However, insurers are required to offer the core plan.

Medigap policies may be suitable for individuals who were dropped by or have grown disenchanted with Medicare managed-care plans that are part of the Medicare+Choice program. Medicare plus the Medigap supplement can provide a package of services comparable to an HMO. But the coverage can cost hundreds of dollars each month, meaning seniors must assess their health needs and avoid being talked into buying the most expensive packages, unless it is necessary. Low-income senior citizens should first also check to see whether their income levels are low enough to qualify for MEDICAID.

Melatonin

Melatonin is a hormone produced in the body by the pineal gland at the base of the brain that has attracted attention and comment in recent years due to claims it plays a role in CANCER, aging, and a host of other health problems, including obesity and insomnia. Secreted into the bloodstream at night, it causes people to become drowsy and plays a role in setting the body's biological clock. However, the body's natural production drops in half by age forty-five, making supplements an attractive option for some elderly people.

Unlike most other hormones, melatonin is not classified as a drug but as a food supplement, like vitamins or other naturally occurring substances. That means it does not require U.S. Food and Drug Administration approval or a doctor's prescription. The product has been marketed aggressively at seniors as a nutritional supplement that gives users renewed vigor and sound sleep—not an insignificant claim because many seniors have difficulty sleeping. But the small doses sold often provide 10 to 100 times higher concentrations than the body's natural nighttime production, raising concerns that they could constrict blood vessels and increase the risk of STROKE.

Many physicians advise patients not to take melatonin because there is not enough sound scientific evidence that it helps people with chronic sleep problems. The NATIONAL INSTITUTE ON AGING also has urged caution, saying overuse has been linked to cancer and DEPRESSION. While demand appeared to peak in the late 1990s, demand for melatonin remains high, in part because people continue to look for cures for aging-related ailments.

NASA had hoped to test the effects of melatonin on former senator John Glenn, D-Ohio, during his 1998 space shuttle mission but removed him from the experiment at the last minute, saying Glenn failed one unspecified pre-

flight test criterion. The decision, and Glenn's refusal to talk about it, led to some apprehension about whether the substance was safe to take. Questions continued in late 1999, when a NATIONAL INSTITUTES OF HEALTH-sponsored study found that in a small group of subjects, melatonin levels in a group of elderly people aged sixty-five to eighty-one were the same as those in a group of younger men. The findings raised questions about whether the pineal gland really acts as a kind of aging clock.

Menopause

Menopause is the period in a woman's life during which menstruation ends and production of the hormone ESTROGEN declines—usually between ages forty-five and fifty-five in the United States and western Europe. A major focus of federally funded research, it has been linked to a variety of afflictions, from uterine CANCER to OSTEOPOROSIS and HEART DISEASE. It also marks the entry into middle and older age, which, combined with psychological factors, can contribute to changes in lifestyle and personal health.

Since the 1940s, doctors have treated menopause with forms of hormone replacement therapy, first by administering large doses of estrogen. This has since been deemed to be medically risky because the hormone stimulates growth of the endometrium, the inner lining of the uterus that is eliminated during menstruation. Uncontrolled growth of the lining brought on by heavy doses of estrogen can lead to cancer. Doctors today almost always treat menopausal patients with low doses of estrogen and a synthetic version of the hormone progesterone, which causes the monthly shedding of the endometrium. One unpleasant side effect of this treatment is that it causes women to continue monthly bleeding.

Federally funded researchers are studying how to better combine dosages of estrogen and progesterone to slowly stop bleeding, without triggering irregular episodes. They also are trying to discover the mechanism by which estrogen has been observed to help bones absorb calcium, reducing the chances of osteoporosis. Estrogen also has been shown to reduce the risk of heart disease.

One important federally funded effort in this area is the Women's Health Initiative, a fifteen-year research project inaugurated in 1991 to study some 164,000 women to determine how diet and hormone replacement therapy contributes to or reduces the risk from these various ailments. The study, which also takes up the leading causes of death and disability among postmenopausal women, is being conducted under the auspices of the National Heart, Lung and Blood Institute, a division of the NATIONAL INSTITUTES OF HEALTH.

While chairman of the House Ways and Means Committee, Rep. Wilbur Mills oversaw creation of Medicaid and Medicare. Source: File photo

Mills, Wilbur

Wilbur Mills, veteran Arkansas lawmaker (1909–1992) and longtime chairman of the HOUSE WAYS AND MEANS COMMITTEE, crafted some of the most significant legislative changes to the nation's ENTITLEMENT PROGRAMS. An expert on the details of taxation who got along equally well with Republicans and members of his own Democratic party, Mills during his tenure as chairman (1957–1975) oversaw creation of MEDICAID, the federal-state health-care program for the poor, and MEDICARE, the giant health-insurance program for the elderly and disabled that was carved out under SOCIAL SECURITY. Mills also oversaw major changes to the Social Security program, adding disability benefits, lowering some age requirements, and raising benefits.

Mills's ability to craft Medicare legislation was helped by political momentum arising from the Democratic sweep in the 1964 elections. He effectively combined health-insurance proposals put forth by President Lyndon Johnson's administration and its Republican rivals, then added components to expand services to the poor that became Medicaid. But while Medicare was greeted with wide public approval, Medicaid had a far cooler reception, in part because payments to doctors would be limited.

Mills's legislative power began to dwindle in the 1970s, as Congress began to shift some power away from Ways and Means. But his drinking habits eventually led to scandal and resignation. In October 1974, his car was stopped by U.S. Park Police. Mills, who was not driving, was one of five passengers inside. One of the others was an Argentinian stripper named Fanne Foxe, who proceeded to jump into the Tidal Basin. The incident made front-page news and was highly embarrassing to the lawmaker. After a second, less dramatic but still widely publicized incident, Mills resigned his chairmanship, entered an alcoholism treatment program and served out the rest of his two-year term. He retired to become a tax lawyer and lecturer.

Modern Maturity

One of the largest circulation magazines in the world, *Modern Maturity* is a bimonthly publication of AARP that is distributed to the organization's thirty-four million members free of charge with their membership and is not available on newsstands. It is one of several magazines targeted at the aging; others include the *Reader's Digest's New Choices* and Meredith Publishing's *Mature Outlook,* both of which have audited circulations of about 600,000. But because advertisers have yet to recognize aging as a significant magazine topic—except for frequent but varied features on health, sex, and beauty, and the occasional article on caregiving for aging parents—the main vehicle for this limited market has become a membership publication that comes with many other discount offerings, including a monthly newspaper (the *AARP Bulletin*) and other membership benefits.

Modern Maturity relies on a combination of features, profiles, and essays, as well as practical ad-

In its effort to target aging baby boomers, Modern Maturity *features cover stories on popular figures such as Paul McCartney. Source: Christine Nesbitt, AP Photo*

vice on topics such as computers and consumer issues. In a move reflecting AARP's membership pitch at aging BABY BOOMERS, *Modern Maturity* now publishes two versions of the magazine with different covers, one for younger retirees and a second for more senior Americans. The magazine has attracted recent attention for apparent efforts to avoid being stodgy that include colorful layouts, surveys on topics such as sex, and cover stories on popular figures such as actress Susan Sarandon and ex-Beatle Paul McCartney. The magazine has even indicated it may change its name to better reflect AARP's wider target audience.

Multi-infarct dementia

Multi-infarct dementia is the second most prevalent form of dementia, after ALZHEIMER'S DISEASE, that strikes elderly people. It is characterized by a series of small STROKES that often produce no observable symptoms but over time can cause damage to brain tissue. Gradually victims may display forgetfulness, emotional problems, and unfamiliarity with familiar places. Men are slightly more at risk than women, and most cases are observed in people with high-blood pressure, DIABETES, and high cholesterol levels.

The condition is one of a number of dementias being studied by government researchers at the NATIONAL INSTITUTE ON AGING and National Institute of Mental Health, both divisions of the NATIONAL INSTITUTES OF HEALTH. Public health experts are trying to raise awareness of the condition, fearing that, if left unchecked, the miniature strokes could create the need for LONG-TERM CARE and place new stresses on a health system that remains largely focused on acute care. Anti-hypertension and even the hormone ESTROGEN have been mentioned as effective ways of preventing this condition.

N

National Advisory Council on Aging

The National Advisory Council on Aging is an advisory board of the NATIONAL INSTITUTE ON AGING and deals with various aspects of research, training, dissemination of health information, and other programs related to aging and age-related disorders. The eighteen members of the panel are appointed by the president and serve overlapping four-year terms. Twelve of the members are physicians or scientists, while the remaining members come from other disciplines, such as gerontology, demography, economics, and politics. The board's responsibilities include advising federal officials on the parameters of biomedical, behavioral, and social research dealing with conditions such as ALZHEIMER'S DISEASE and related DEMENTIAS, as well as problems such as DEPRESSION and SUICIDE among the elderly.

National Bipartisan Commission on the Future of Medicare

See BIPARTISAN MEDICARE REFORM

National Committee to Preserve Social Security and Medicare

Often referred to as the nation's second-largest seniors organization (after AARP), this Washington, D.C.–based advocacy group, known as NCPSSM, was founded in 1982 as a direct-mail fundraising organization. In its early years, it was known for sending out oversized envelopes with literature containing exaggerated claims about MEDICARE and SOCIAL SECURITY being threatened. *Changing Times* magazine in 1989 traced the group's roots to a California political consulting firm specializing in initiative campaigns that had hired James Roosevelt, son of FRANKLIN D. ROOSEVELT, as a consultant to speak, and to use his name. In 1984, the U.S. Department of Justice admonished the organization for using the Great Seal of the United States on its mailings, and members of the HOUSE WAYS AND MEANS COMMITTEE publicly criticized the group for its misleading statements and outright inaccuracies in its solicitations.

NCPSSM began to capture attention and clout by leading forces for the repeal of the MEDICARE CATASTROPHIC COVERAGE ACT (PL 100-360) in 1989 and tapping elderly voter anger at AARP. Soon after, it hired Martha McSteen, a former acting Social Security administrator in RONALD REAGAN's administration, who insisted the group break from its somewhat seedy past and transform itself into a grassroots lobbying force to preserve the Social Security and Medicare programs in their present form. In recent years, the national committee has been most vocal fighting for a proposed Medicare outpatient PRESCRIPTION DRUG BENEFIT, calling rising drug costs the "quiet crisis of retirement in America." The organization's network of organizers arranges town meetings and policy briefings across the United States and claims to have five million members and supporters.

NCPSSM attracted controversy in 1999 when it attacked the proposed PREMIUM SUPPORT model to overhaul Medicare that came out of meetings of the NATIONAL BIPARTISAN COMMISSION ON THE FUTURE OF MEDICARE. Alarmed at a proposal that would have the government pay health-insurance premiums and allow Medicare beneficiaries to select coverage from a list of pre-approved insurers, the organization sent a six-page letter to a million senior citizens in an envelope marked "urgent." The letter termed the proposal a "voucher program," implied that it was headed for quick approval in the U.S. Senate, and asked for contributions to fight the effort. Critics chastised the organization for employing scare tactics to raise money and failing to point out that the premium support proposal would offer essentially the same amount of BENEFITS as the present Medicare system. In the end, premium support did not muster enough votes to even win the approval of the bipartisan commission. The NCPSSM did not apologize for its tactics and continues to attack congressional efforts to overhaul and significantly change essential ENTITLEMENT PROGRAMS.

National Council of Senior Citizens

This now-defunct Democratic-leaning organization, supported by labor unions, was founded in 1961 as an outgrowth of the senior citizen voting bloc that backed the Kennedy-Johnson presidential ticket. Its function was to lobby for creation of the MEDICARE program and counter the political efforts of the AMERICAN MEDICAL ASSOCIATION and other program opponents. Headquartered in Silver Spring, Maryland, the NCSC in the 1990s claimed more than 500,000 members in 2,000 clubs and councils across the country. An affiliated organization, the National Senior Citizens Education and Research Center, operated some 145 programs to employ low-income senior citizens as library aides, as literacy tutors, and in other jobs, and received grants from the LABOR DEPARTMENT.

The organization prided itself on having remained scrappy and activist—noting in its literature how its first office was in a tiny hotel room on Washington's Capitol Hill where the mimeograph machine was kept in the bathtub, and telling how it secured President John F. Kennedy as the keynote speaker at one of its early rallies, in 1962. It strenuously opposed congressional efforts to overhaul ENTITLEMENT PROGRAMS and had been among the most vocal of the senior advocacy groups in calling for a PRESCRIPTION DRUG BENEFIT. The group took credit for defeating several Republican members of the House of Representatives in several election cycles in the 1990s by running advertising that contended the lawmakers were intent on overhauling Medicare. The NCSC also received some unwanted attention in the late 1990s when it was linked to an effort by the Teamsters' Union to illegally divert union dues through a number of Democratic-leaning organizations, including the council, in an effort to aid the reelection of then Teamsters' president Ron Carey. The scheme resulted in the indictment and subsequent imprisonment of a Teamsters' Union political director. No officials of the national council were found to have committed any wrongdoing. By 2000, the group was inactive, to be replaced by a new labor-oriented group.

National Council on the Aging

The National Council on the Aging, a non-profit organization based in Washington, D.C., was founded in 1950 to promote the "dignity, self-determination, well-being and contributions of older persons." In addition to lobbying on senior-related issues, such as reauthorization of the OLDER AMERICANS ACT, it helps community organizations around the country develop new programs and services for senior citizens.

The National Council on Aging is perhaps best known for a series of studies on retirement and aging in America. One study of more than three thousand adults conducted with the International Longevity Center in New York City and released in 2000 took issue with myths associated with late life, finding that nearly half of the respondents aged sixty-five and older considered their current years to be the best of their lives. The survey also found older people are less worried about crime, their health, and their financial situations than people of similar age were twenty-five years ago, when the council conducted a similar study. The survey also showed that many younger people tend to exaggerate the financial problems and social isolation of older people. Younger and older people did agree on one thing: more than 70 percent of both groups said a seventy-five-year-old man or woman can be sexy.

National Institute on Aging

The National Institute on Aging is an increasingly prominent division of the NATIONAL INSTITUTES OF HEALTH that is the federal government's focal point for conducting biological, behavioral, and social research on aging. Congress authorized the agency in 1974 by amending the Public Health Service Act, and in recent years has bestowed increasingly large sums on its operations, in part because lawmakers designated the institute the government's lead agency for research on ALZHEIMER'S DISEASE. The NIA, as it is informally known, operates with a budget of more than $700 million per year and has a staff of about 450 employees at its Bethesda, Maryland, headquarters. However, a significant portion of the funds are used to provide grants to researchers around the country. The primary thrust of the research is in delaying the onset of, and providing improved treatments for, diseases of aging, particularly Alzheimer's disease, HEART DISEASE, and CANCER.

One of the NIA's significant projects is its Memory Impairment Study, launched in 1999 to study individuals with mild cognitive impairments who are likely candidates for Alzheimer's or related DEMENTIAS. Studies have focused on preventing a further decline in mental functions with the antioxidant Vitamin E and the drug donapezil, and reversing age-related memory loss through the injection of human nerve-growth factor. Scientists also have conducted imaging studies on the brains of subjects, focusing on the hippocampus region that plays a key role in memory and has been observed to shrink with age. Research also has increasingly concentrated on the role of genes in the onset of Alzheimer's. NIA-supported research also has focused on reducing chronic diseases and disabilities and preventing delirium in hospitalized elderly patients. The NIA also oversees the Baltimore Longitudinal Study of Aging, the longest scientific examination of human aging, which since 1958 has measured changes in biological and behavioral processes in more than two thousand people.

Harold Varmus, former director of the National Institutes of Health, speaks with Sen. Tom Harkin at a Labor, Health and Human Services, and Education Subcommittee hearing on funding allocations for disease research at NIH. Source: Scott J. Ferrell, Congressional Quarterly

National Institutes of Health (NIH)

The sprawling National Institutes of Health in Bethesda, Maryland, widely known as NIH, is the nation's premiere biomedical research institution. It comprises twenty-five institutes that have been credited with numerous scientific breakthroughs and have won successively larger budget increases from Congress. Republican plans to double the NIH budget over five years ending in fiscal 2002 resulted in the institutes receiving more than $19 billion in new budget authority in fiscal 2000. The largest portion of the money is directed at CANCER research, with HIV/AIDS, HEART DISEASE, brain disorders, and kidney and urologic diseases also receiving significant financial support.

At least seventeen NIH institutes deal with aging-related issues, the most prominent being the NATIONAL INSTITUTE ON AGING; the National Heart, Lung, and Blood Institute; the National Cancer Institute; the National Institute of Diabetes and Digestive and Kidney Diseases; and the National Institute of Neurological Disorders and Stroke. While research is done on-site at NIH labs, a significant portion of each institute's funding is directed at supporting academic research projects around the country through a competitive grant process.

NIH evolved out of the Marine Health Service, a predecessor agency of the Public Health Service that in the 1880s was largely responsible for examining passengers on arriving ships for dreaded diseases of the day, such as cholera and yellow fever. The discovery that diseases such as cholera were spread by bacteria led Congress, in 1904, to appropriate $35,000 for construction of a lab to investigate contagious diseases, even though lawmakers were not convinced that such an agency would prove useful. As the study of basic biological and medical problems grew, Congress began targeting specific diseases, such as cancer, and defining the scope of medical research. The Public Health Service Act of 1944 began expanding NIH's budget, widening its grants program, and establishing new

Fiscal Year 1999 Appropriations for NIH (in millions of dollars)

Institute or center	Fiscal year 1999 appropriation	Fiscal year 1999 aging research (estimates)
Aging	$596.5	$596.5
Cancer	2,927.2	46.6
Heart/Lung/Blood	1,793.7	90.8
Dental/Craniofacial Research	234.3	10.3
Diabetes/Digestive/Kidney	994.2	69.0
Neurology/Stroke	903.3	83.6
Allergy/Infectious Diseases	1,570.1	68.5
General Medical Sciences	1,197.8	—
Child Health/Human Development	751.0	9.5
Eye	395.9	77.6
Environmental Health	375.7	6.0
Arthritis	308.2	37.5
Deafness	229.9	9.3
Mental Health	861.2	71.9
Drug Abuse	603.3	1.2
Alcohol Abuse/Alcoholism	259.7	5.0
Nursing Research	69.8	9.7
Human Genome Research	264.9	—
Research Resources	554.8	16.8
Fogarty International Center	35.4	—
Library of Medicine	181.3	—
Office of Director	306.6	—
Buildings and Facilities	197.5	—
Total, NIH	15,612.3	1,209.8

Source: U.S. Senate Special Committee on Aging, *Developments in Aging 1997 and 1998*, Vol. I.

institutes. The act also authorized NIH to conduct clinical research on human subjects, which continues today in a 540-bed hospital on the NIH campus.

NIH accomplishments in the aging field over the past decade include conducting clinical trials that helped reduce the risk of getting endometrial cancer from ESTROGEN replacement therapy, identifying a gene that is a major risk factor for late-onset ALZHEIMER'S DISEASE, and identifying the cause of Werner's syndrome—a rare genetic disorder that allows DNA damage to accumulate and results in premature aging in individuals as young as twenty, who often die before the age of fifty.

While NIH is almost universally hailed as a leading example of U.S. scientific know-how, its leadership and decision-making have periodically come into question. A 1998 Institute of Medicine/National Academy of Sciences report criticized NIH for being excessively political in choosing how to spend research dollars. The report said NIH should be more scientifically rigorous in selecting its research priorities instead of tolerating a system in which various patients'-advocacy groups lobby Congress in an attempt to earmark money for certain diseases. The report echoed criticism from some conservative members of Congress, who contend NIH is spending too much money per death on politically "sexy" diseases, such as HIV/AIDS, which do not have the highest mortality rates. Some anti-abortion members of Congress

The Mark O. Hatfield Clinical Research Center is one of many new buildings under construction on NIH's Bethesda, Maryland, campus. Republican plans to double the NIH budget over five years ending in fiscal 2002 resulted in the institutes receiving more than $19 billion in new budget authority in fiscal 2000. Source: Scott J. Ferrell, Congressional Quarterly

also have criticized NIH for endorsing federally funded research on human embryonic stem cells (a primordial variety of cell that has been shown to evolve into virtually every kind of human tissue), arguing the work could be in violation of a congressional ban on embryo research.

National savings

The often-misunderstood term "national savings" is used in debates over the structure and future of ENTITLEMENT PROGRAMS, particularly SOCIAL SECURITY. It is generally used to mean what is left of individuals' incomes after subtracting all federal and local taxes and interest penalties, and all personal consumption spending (food, housing, clothes, transportation, medical care, and utilities). From this figure, economists can derive a "personal savings rate," which in recent years has hovered near zero, despite unsurpassed economic prosperity and evidence from elsewhere that more people are saving for retirement.

This paradox has fueled a debate over whether the Social Security system is helping or discouraging national savings. Proponents of Social Security reform, led by conservative free-market economists, argue Social Security decreases personal savings because it taxes workers' earnings and takes away money they otherwise would have saved for retirement. Because Social Security is a PAY-AS-YOU-GO SYSTEM, these economists argue, the money from payroll taxes is used to pay benefits with no corresponding increase in national savings to offset the decline in personal savings. This camp also argues that Social Security's promise of future retirement benefits, despite uncertainty over the long-term finances of the system, generally discourages individuals from setting aside more money for their later years. One solution, in the opinion of many reform advocates, is a PRIVATIZATION of the system that would allow individuals to divert a portion of payroll taxes into personal savings accounts and thus boost national savings.

Many defenders of the current system believe Social Security actually promotes greater savings because the system, with its guaranteed benefits, encourages a higher rate of early retirement. Workers who contemplate this option will be motivated to save more because they will want to support their spending habits during the extra retirement years. Social Security defenders also cast doubts on whether the creation of personal savings accounts will really boost national savings, arguing that many individuals are likely to funnel money into the accounts that they otherwise would put in conventional retirement savings instruments, such as IRAS or 401(K) PLANS.

A number of economists and analysts take issue with the way the government calculates personal savings, arguing that the national savings rate is distorted and depicts many Americans as spendthrifts. L. Douglas Lee, chief economist at HSBC Washington Analysis, a private securities firm, has noted that despite the investment boom of recent years, stock earnings—such as those earned through mutual funds—are counted by the U.S. Department of Commerce as spending, not savings. On the one hand, income tax from capital gains is deducted from individuals' incomes as a personal expense. Yet a capital gain is not counted as personal income because it does not represent income from current production. Experts like Lee believe personal savings should be calculated in a more consistent way. Using data from the U.S. Department of Treasury's Office of Tax Analysis to recalculate personal savings to include both capital gains as income and taxes on them as spending, Lee showed how the modest 1997 national savings rate of 2 percent declared by the Commerce Department would rise to 3.6 percent.

Regardless of who is right, recent studies have shown that many Americans are unprepared for retirement. The nonpartisan American Savings Education Council says individuals need 70 to 80 percent of their preretirement income to maintain their personal standards of living in retirement. However, 20 percent of workers in their forties reported in one study that they had not begun saving for retirement, while the median amount saved among those who were building a nest egg was $45,238—well short of what is recommended. The education council says a forty-five-year-old worker who makes $50,000 per year and plans to retire at age sixty-five needs to accumulate $336,000 to maintain the current standard of living.

Some observers believe workers are squandering savings opportunities by cashing out their 401(k) plans when they change jobs and using retirement reserves on household goods and luxury items, thus giving up the power of compounded earnings. Others note that workers may be taking advantage of investment gains made in the stock market and using their increased investment income to make more purchases. However, many experts question how many mature adults really look at their retirement plans as money for a spending spree. This group argues that people use the money mostly, or at least as much, for needs such as college education for their children, job training for themselves, caring for their parents, or setting up small businesses after they have been pushed out of jobs or taken early retirements.

National Senior Citizens Law Center

The Washington, D.C.–based National Senior Citizens Law Center, funded by the Legal Services

Corporation, performs legal work on behalf of poor elderly Americans, particularly in the areas of SOCIAL SECURITY, MEDICARE, MEDICAID, HOME HEALTH CARE, protective services, and pension law. The center's initiatives include monitoring the federal government's enforcement of NURSING HOME reform laws and performing advocacy work on behalf of nursing home residents. The center has weighed in on AGE DISCRIMINATION cases, even suing the Agency for International Development for targeting workers over the age of forty during a federal workforce reduction. The action, the first to challenge federal job cuts on the basis of age discrimination, ended in 2000 when the federal government agreed to settle the case and pay $8.5 million. The center also dispenses consumer-oriented legal information dealing with issues such as the practice of doctors entering into contracts with well-off Medicare beneficiaries to provide services covered under Medicare. The situation, arising from a provision in the BALANCED BUDGET ACT OF 1997 (PL 105-33) has caused confusion over whether Medicare beneficiaries can continue to see their doctors and pay out-of-pocket for uncovered services, such as eye exams.

The National Senior Service Corps provides opportunities for seniors to provide supportive services to children, among others. Source: National Senior Service Corps

National Senior Service Corps

The National Senior Service Corps is part of the Corporation for National and Community Service. It is dedicated to the premise that retired individuals can volunteer in their communities and use their skills and knowledge to help the less fortunate and the elderly. The corps' activities primarily center on three federally authorized initiatives: the Foster Grandparent Program (FGP), the Senior Companion Program (SCP), and the Retired and Senior Volunteer Program (RSVP). Project grants for all three programs are awarded to state or local governments or to nonprofit agencies, who each apply to the federal government for money to recruit, train, and assist the volunteers. All federal funds for the programs are contained in the Labor–Health and Human Services–Education appropriations bill.

The FGP began in 1965 as a DEMONSTRATION PROGRAM run by the ADMINISTRATION ON AGING and the Office of Economic Opportunity to show how low-income individuals aged sixty and older could provide supportive services to children with physical, mental, or emotional disabilities. It was authorized by the OLDER AMERICANS ACT and, in 1973, incorporated under the Domestic Volunteer Service Act (PL 93-113). Volunteers serve twenty hours per week, typically provide care to three or four children, and receive a tax-free stipend of $2.55 per hour. As of mid-1997, there were approximately 25,300 volunteers. Annual congressional appropriations in fiscal 1999 totaled $93.3 million. Foster grandparents must have an income of no more than 125 percent of the federal poverty level.

The SCP was authorized in 1973 under the Domestic Volunteer Service Act and is designed to provide part-time community service work to low-income individuals aged sixty and older. This may include helping homebound or disabled elderly people continue to live at home independently. Women make up 85 percent of the volunteers. Stipends, income requirements, and time commitments are the same as for the FGP program. Congress appropriated $36.6 million for the effort in fiscal 1999.

The RSVP program was authorized in 1969 under the Older Americans Act and later incorporated under the Domestic Volunteer Service Act. One of the largest volunteer efforts in the country, it provides a variety of community service volunteer opportunities to individuals aged fifty-five and older, such as counseling youths, crime prevention, housing rehabilitation, and drug abuse prevention. Unlike the SCP and FGP programs, RSVP does not pay an hourly stipend but reimburses volunteers for personal expenses. In fiscal 1997, 453,300 volunteers participated. Congress's appropriation for the effort totaled $43 million in fiscal 1999.

Nonforfeiture benefit

A nonforfeiture benefit is a feature on private LONG-TERM CARE insurance policies that gives the beneficiary credit for covered services if he or she discontinues premium payments. Many insurers offer the benefit in two forms. "Return of Premium" gives the policyholder credit in the form of cash, typically a percentage of the premiums paid up to the point at which the payment stops. This option could reimburse next-of-kin for some expenses if the covered individual dies. The "Reduced Paid Up" option continues long-term care, but reduces the daily payment for covered services on a schedule that is specified in the policy. Either of these options can add 20 percent to 100 percent to the long-term care insurance policy's cost, according to some industry estimates.

Normal retirement age

The normal retirement age, sometimes known as the NRA, is the age when Americans become eligible for full SOCIAL SECURITY benefits—a figure that is gradually rising from sixty-five to sixty-seven over a twenty-two-year period ending in 2022. The changes were mandated by the Social Security Amendments of 1983 (PL 98-21) as a way of alleviating the financial squeeze facing the national pension system and better reflecting increased life expectancies since the program came into being in 1935. However, retirement age continues to be a point of intense debate, because of the changing nature of the workforce and contentions by some advocates of Social Security reform—particularly conservative Republicans—that the figure should be raised further, to age seventy.

The selection of age sixty-five as the earliest point at which retirement benefits could be collected was a kind of compromise on the part of the original Social Security program administrators, who considered age sixty too low for cost reasons and age seventy unreasonably high, given that the LIFE EXPECTANCY at the time was fifty-nine years for men and sixty-three years for women. Women were given the option of obtaining reduced benefits at age sixty-two in 1956, and the option was extended to men in 1961. For this reason, there is a distinction between "early retirement age" and "normal retirement age." Interestingly, most political proposals to raise the normal retirement age do not include a corresponding provision to raise the early retirement age, perhaps acknowledging that most American workers hope not to have to work longer than they must. The current adjustment in the normal retirement age also keeps the early retirement age at sixty-two.

Various studies show raising the normal retirement age could help Social Security's solvency and also increase national economic output. Increasing the NRA would reduce the amount of benefits paid out at a time when people are living longer, helping extend the projected period of solvency of the Social Security TRUST FUND. Reform advocates say it also could boost national economic activity by keeping workers in the labor force longer and increasing the nation's pool of skilled workers. By continuing to draw paychecks, older workers would maintain their standards of living and purchase more goods and services, expanding overall economic output, according to this line of reasoning. This, of course, assumes that older workers would not displace younger workers—a fair assumption, considering DEMOGRAPHIC projections that show BABY BOOMERS leaving the workforce early in the twenty-first century will outnumber young workers entering it, ending the labor surplus that characterized the U.S. economy for most of the twentieth century.

But not everyone is enamored with this argument. Labor unions, liberal Democrats, and advocates of the working poor maintain that raising the retirement age amounts to an unfair benefit cut, because it will delay an important source of income for the most economically vulnerable members of the population. Opponents of tinkering with the retirement age note that more than 25 percent of African American and Hispanic households whose primary wage earners are aged sixty-five or older live in poverty, and are more likely to suffer from health problems and less likely to receive pension benefits from past employers. Increasing the retirement age will "push the finish line back" for these individuals, according to this argument, and also could affect younger elderly who leave the workforce so they can care for older family members.

Some reform advocates believe one way of addressing these concerns would be to raise the normal retirement age but provide more generous eligibility conditions for SOCIAL SECURITY DISABILITY INSURANCE. Regardless of who is right, the political climate for raising the normal retirement age is more acceptable than it was even as recently as the 1980s. Many observers believe adjusting the NRA is as palatable, if not more so, than increasing payroll taxes or reducing Social Security benefits, though some of all three may be necessary to deal with the program's long-term financing problems. With company pensions more common and more opportunities to save for retirement through IRAs and other instruments, many economists and political analysts say that middle-income workers' abilities to live without Social Security income have improved significantly. Others are worried, though, saying that the change from defined-benefit pensions to DEFINED-CONTRIBUTION PLANS in the past two decades actually is putting far less corporate money into the nation's retirement pool, and that with increased longevity, many middle-class individuals could be scraping for income in their old age.

Nurse practitioner

A nurse practitioner is a REGISTERED NURSE with advanced training in a particular medical specialty, meaning he or she has studied beyond the four years necessary to receive a bachelor's degree in nursing. Some 48,000 nurse practitioners work in NURSING HOMES, clinics, doctors' offices, and hospitals and assume some of the same functions as primary-care physicians. Nurse practitioners can diagnose and monitor infections, treat chronic conditions such as DIABETES or high blood pressure, order x-rays and other diagnostic tests, and prescribe drugs. Elderly people in ASSISTED LIVING facilities may encounter NPs, as they are known, more often than doctors when they experience common health problems. Nurse practitioners are licensed and regulated by the states in which they work, and many also have national certification by professional organizations in their specialty area.

The federal government has gradually eased restrictions on the type of areas and settings in which nurse practitioners can deliver health services and be reimbursed by MEDICARE, acknowledging a general push in the health industry to expand NPs' "scope of practice." This has come over the objections of some physicians' groups, who argue NPs should continue to practice under a doctor's supervision. The BALANCED BUDGET ACT OF 1997 (PL 105-33) permitted nurse practitioners to be reimbursed at 80 percent of the lesser of the actual charge or 85 percent of the fee schedule amount that would be paid to a physician for a procedure. These reimbursements track with allowances already permitted for NPs in rural areas, who often cannot find physicians with whom to practice "on site." Nurse practitioners in 2000 were lobbying Congress for laws ensuring they will be able to participate in MEDICAID managed-care programs, noting that some states excluded them from the provider panels of these programs.

Nursing home

A nursing home represents the most intense form of care for the elderly, providing twenty-four-hour nursing care and an array of medical services for frail individuals who cannot live on their own or perform many ACTIVITIES OF DAILY LIVING. Because of the rising costs of LONG-TERM CARE, many states have explored alternatives to nursing homes and, in some cases, enacted curbs on nursing home construction. States also have adopted stronger pre-admission criteria to ensure that only the sickest elderly people are admitted. The nursing home industry has tried to adapt to this climate, focusing more on REHABILITATION services and other forms of "post-acute" care and helping residents make the transition to other, less involved forms of ASSISTED LIVING whenever possible. In the late 1990s, an estimated 1.6 million people received care in more than 16,000 nursing homes across the country. The federal government was the largest single payer for this care, through the MEDICARE and MEDICAID programs.

Nursing homes have been a near-constant source of interest and concern to Congress since the 1950s. Lawmakers for years heard horror stories about negligent care, in which residents were forced to lie in their wastes, were sedated or restrained, and were robbed of their personal be-

MEASURE OF CARE

Wilhelmina Gladden, state legislative issues specialist for AARP, announces an agenda to monitor legislative proposals to make sure patients are protected and that nursing homes are held accountable for abuses. Source: Harry Cabluck, AP Photo

longings by unscrupulous attendants. There also were concerns about untrained staffers being unable to meet residents' basic health needs. The first federal standards for nursing home care were established with the creation of Medicare and Medicaid in 1965. The government set guidelines for adequate care and safe residential environments, both so residents could be protected and so federal program dollars would not be spent on negligent operators. The government made distinctions between SKILLED-NURSING FACILITIES, which are designed to provide nursing care on a daily basis, and INTERMEDIATE-CARE FACILITIES, which are designed for individuals with fewer medical needs but who are unable to care for themselves, such as the mentally retarded. Yet in the first year of the programs, only 740 out of more than 6,000 homes that applied to participate in Medicare or Medicaid could completely meet the health and safety criteria. At a series of congressional hearings between 1969 and 1973, government officials testified that as many as three-quarters of the nation's nursing homes were operating with deficiencies.

Studies by the U.S. General Accounting Office and the Institute of Medicine, a division of the National Academies of Science, indicated that one reason for persistent problems in the quality of care was that the government lacked a means to levy intermediate sanctions against noncompliant facilities. In many cases, the government's only recourse was to respond to repeated violations by disqualifying a facility from Medicare and Medicaid participation. Such moves hurt residents as much as the facility operators, because the nursing homes usually were forced to shut down, leaving patients with few, if any, alternatives. The situation was further complicated by many states' efforts to restrict the number of nursing home beds in order to reduce Medicaid costs. Congress in 1981 authorized the U.S. Department of HEALTH AND HUMAN SERVICES to deny payments for new admissions to those nursing homes found to have repeat violations—an intermediate enforcement rule that took years to implement and was criticized for being too cumbersome. This situation—combined with numerous reports of serious state-by-state disparities in nursing home regulation and of states occasionally reclassifying nursing homes to avoid strict federal regulation—led Congress to adopt tough new rules for nursing homes participating in Medicare and Medicaid as part of the Omnibus Budget Reconciliation Act of 1987 (PL 100-203; see OMNIBUS BUDGET RECONCILIATION BILLS).

The new reforms eliminated the distinction between skilled-nursing facilities and intermediate-care facilities, outlined a series of residents' rights

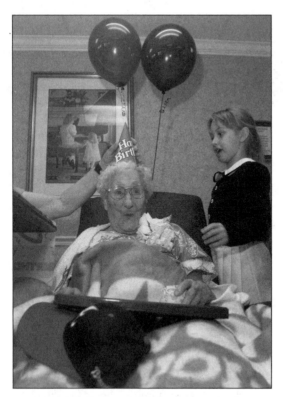

A resident celebrates her 104th birthday at NHC Healthcare nursing home in Knoxville, Tennessee, with her seven-year-old great-granddaughter at her side.
Source: Joe Howell, AP Photo

(including to be free from physical or chemical restraints), required facilities to prepare a plan of care for each patient upon admission, mandated new staffing and training guidelines, and made states responsible for certifying compliance with the new requirements. Perhaps most important, the reforms focused more on "outcomes," that is, what a facility was doing for its residents, instead of whether it was capable of providing care. Advocates for the elderly say the reforms significantly improved the plight of nursing home residents;

one study documented a nearly 50 percent decline in the use of restraints from 1990 to 1994 while a second found there was a 26 percent reduction in hospitalizations of nursing home residents. In general, the reforms are praised for restoring dignity to many residents' lives and for cutting down on some of the most persistent abuses. However, complaints from Republican governors and the nursing home industry that the standards are too burdensome led the GOP-controlled Congress in 1995 to attempt to repeal them. As part of legislation to "block grant" Medicaid, states would be allowed to develop their own standards. The bill was passed by Congress but vetoed by President Bill Clinton.

Congress continues to receive troubling reports about nursing home surveillance. Hearings of the SENATE SPECIAL COMMITTEE ON AGING have revealed that state systems designed to safeguard residents are inconsistent and unreliable—for example, there are no requirements that individuals suspected of abusing residents be permanently banned from nursing home employment. The Department of Health and Human Services' inspector general also has noted that state surveys and CERTIFICATION are predictable, allowing unscrupulous operators to temporarily change their operations and avoid being cited for deficiencies.

Congress additionally continues to consider the financial state of the nursing home industry. Deeper-than-expected cuts in payments to health-care providers mandated by the BALANCED BUDGET ACT OF 1997 severely impacted nursing homes, prompting a bailout in which the facilities received a portion of $16 billion awarded to health-care providers over five years as part of the 2000 omnibus spending measure (PL 106-113).

O

Off Budget

The phrase "off budget" is used frequently in congressional debates and refers to the accounting practice of sequestering funds—and classifying them as untouchable—to prevent lawmakers from tapping them for new spending or to fund a tax cut. Lawmakers from both parties have proposed treating SOCIAL SECURITY and MEDICARE surpluses in this fashion to help shore up the long-term financial condition of both programs, but have disagreed on how to accomplish the task. Republican efforts in the 106th Congress to create a Social Security "LOCKBOX" are one example of off-budget treatment of surpluses. However, experts question whether such proposals would alleviate the impending financial squeeze facing the program because of the large number of retiring BABY BOOMERS. Indeed, some analysts believe sequestering funds could hinder the U.S. Treasury's short-term ability to borrow from the Social Security TRUST FUNDS to pay down the national debt and generally improve the nation's financial foundation. Nonetheless, the off-budget treatment of surpluses remains a politically appealing argument, making proponents appear both fiscally responsible and sensitive to the needs of current and future retirees.

Old-Age and Survivors Insurance

Old-Age and Survivors Insurance, known as OASI, is one component of the core SOCIAL SECURITY program outlined in Title II of the SOCIAL SECURITY ACT OF 1935. It provides replacement income for individuals or families when a worker in covered employment retires or dies. OASI, combined with disability insurance (DI), forms the basic monthly Social Security benefit. The two programs are financed on a combined basis by the OLD-AGE AND SURVIVORS INSURANCE AND DISABILITY INSURANCE TRUST FUNDS, a much-watched barometer of Social Security's financial condition. However, it is important to remember that OASI and DI have separate tax rates, set by law, and separate TRUST FUNDS. The combined financial operations of the trust funds are supervised by a six-member board consisting of two presidential appointees, the Social Security commissioner, and the secretaries of treasury, LABOR, and HEALTH AND HUMAN SERVICES.

The OASI program classifies workers in two ways: fully insured and currently insured. The distinction hinges on a measurement known as "quarters of coverage" that sets the minimum amount of wages a person needs to earn in covered employment during one calendar quarter to be eligible for BENEFITS. The threshold amount of covered wages is indexed for inflation. In 2000, the amount of earnings needed for one quarter of coverage is $750. The figure rises to $780 in 2001 and $810 in 2002. Fully insured workers receive OASI benefits for themselves and their dependents if they earned one quarter of coverage for each year between the time they reached age twenty-one and the time they reached age sixty-two. Hence, a worker with at least forty quarters of coverage is insured for life. Survivors may collect OASI benefits if the worker was currently insured, meaning if the worker had six quarters of coverage during the thirteen calendar quarters ending with the quarter in which the worker died.

Economists project long-term financial strains on the OASDI trust funds because of the difficulties of serving a graying population on a shrinking tax base. However, the OASI's program growth is not projected to fluctuate as dramatically as the DI program. The 2000 annual report of the Social Security trustees estimates the OASI trust fund assets will increase until 2026, then decline until they are exhausted in 2039. The trustees recommended that the long-term deficit should be addressed. Possible legislative solutions include raising the retirement age, "MEANS TEST-ING" benefits, or making more sweeping structural changes to the program, including PRIVATIZATION.

Old-Age and Survivors Insurance and Disability Insurance trust funds

These government-administered accounts, frequently referred to as the OASDI TRUST FUNDS, are used to pay monthly BENEFITS for OLD-AGE AND SURVIVORS INSURANCE and SOCIAL SECURITY DISABILITY INSURANCE, and essentially represent the pool of money available to finance the core SOCIAL SECURITY program. The trust funds are among the most closely watched accounts in the federal government because of projections that the reserves will be depleted within four decades as a result of the DEMOGRAPHIC surge of aging Americans and the shrinking pool of workers who will have to fund the system through payroll taxes. Politicians have proposed a variety of ways of shoring up the trust funds' financial condition, ranging from investing some assets in the stock or bond markets or curtailing some benefits, to enacting a series of incremental adjustments to make up the long-term shortfall of only 1.89 percent of taxable payroll over seventy-five years. However, a lack of political consensus among reform advocates and defenders of the current system has delayed any major action.

Under the current PAY-AS-YOU-GO SYSTEM, federal payroll tax revenues are deposited into the trust funds and used to pay benefits to those people currently collecting Social Security pensions. Any excess of taxes over benefit payments is invested in U.S. Treasury securities, which earn the average rate of return on publicly traded government debt. The securities essentially are future financial claims against the government and earn interest for the trust funds. Social Security checks can continue to be written as long as there is a positive balance in the trust funds.

Recent federal budget surpluses and the robust U.S. economy have brightened the long-term financial outlook for the trust funds. The 2000 annual report of the Social Security trustees stated the trust funds took in $526.6 billion from payroll taxes in 1999 and paid out $385.8 billion in benefits to retired and deceased workers and their families. Administrative costs associated with running the program totaled $3.3 billion. The Social Security system's assets increased by $133.7 billion, to $896.1 billion, and the trust funds earned $55.5 billion on government bond interest.

The 2000 report stated the trust funds are expected to be able to cover Social Security benefits until 2037—three years later than trustees estimated in their 1999 report. However, the trustees noted that benefit payments will begin to exceed income in 2015, and that interest income on the Treasury bonds will be able to keep total income ahead of benefit payments only until 2025. After that, the trust funds will begin to decline until they are exhausted in 2037. At that point, payroll tax revenue will only be able to fund three-quarters of benefit obligations.

The trust funds have been subjected to fluctuations in the economy and budget politics for more than three decades. Until 1970, the trust funds had sufficient reserves to pay a full year of benefit obligations—a safe margin by most estimates. That changed in the early 1970s, when an energy crisis and resulting inflation, combined with lower wage growth, began to play havoc with the system. The problems were compounded by the 1972 amendments to the SOCIAL SECURITY ACT (PL 92-336), which both increased benefits by 20 percent and mandated annual adjustments to reflect the rising cost of living at a time of double-digit inflation. Even though Congress in 1977 raised payroll taxes beginning in 1979 to address the looming crisis, slower-than-expected economic growth and federal budget deficits continued to place major stresses on the Social Security system. By 1982, the OASI trust fund was depleted of reserves and had to borrow $17.5 billion from the Disability Insurance and Hospital Insurance trust funds to continue making payments.

Long-term structural changes came in 1983, when the National Commission on Social Security Reform, also known as the GREENSPAN COMMISSION, made recommendations that were adopted by Congress in the form of 1983 amendments to the Social Security Act (PL 98-21). The commission recommended a series of increases to Social Security tax rates and an increase in the tax on self-employed workers, as well as a six-month delay in COST-OF-LIVING ADJUSTMENTS. A portion of the Social Security benefits of wealthier retirees began to be taxed in 1984. Most notably, the commission recommended, and Congress approved, gradually raising the retirement age from sixty-five to sixty-seven by 2027. Commission chairman Alan M. Greenspan predicted the measures would keep the trust funds solvent until 2068. But his prediction was about three decades longer than current estimates, because Greenspan based his assumption on faster wage growth, fewer retirees, and more workers than are currently expected.

Legislative proposals to improve the long-term solvency of the OASDI trust funds include increasing the retirement age to seventy (and in some cases, raising the early retirement age from sixty-two to sixty-five) or to accelerate the previously agreed-to phase-in of the increase to age sixty-seven. Both measures would delay the period during which future retirees can collect Social Security benefits, though it is unclear whether anticipated increases in longevity would not offset some of the savings. Other, more controversial proposals center on restricting the eligibility of some Social Security benefits based on a recipient's wealth. The most-discussed one to "MEANS-TEST" Social Security benefits was a 1994 plan by the CONCORD COALITION that proposed reducing Social Security benefits on a sliding scale for families with incomes above $40,000. While proponents argued such a move would dramatically cut program costs, many believe it to be politically unfeasible because of the widespread perception that Social Security is an "earned right."

A number of proposals have been made under the broad rubric of "privatizing" the Social Security system to help bolster the trust funds. These include raising payroll taxes, making modest benefit cuts, and investing some trust fund assets in the stock market, whose returns in recent years have well exceeded those on government bonds. Some lawmakers have proposed cutting Social Security benefits, creating new personal savings accounts for workers and forcing employers to make mandatory contributions to them. A more sweeping approach would substitute most Social Security retirement benefits with private savings accounts. To date, none of these has gained sufficient political support to win passage.

Older Americans Act

The Older Americans Act of 1965 (PL 89-73) is perhaps the most wide-ranging law affecting the elderly in the United States, funding efforts such as MEALS ON WHEELS, senior centers, transportation services, and other popular programs. The law nonetheless has been the object of persistent squabbling between congressional Republicans and Democrats and only was reauthorized near the end of the 106th Congress, in a bipartisan deal seen by many as an effort by both parties to appeal to SENIOR VOTERS. Funding for the act's myriad programs has generally remained flat and is provided through Congress's annual appropriations bills.

The Older Americans Act was one of the so-called Great Society initiatives launched by the administration of President Lyndon B. Johnson to help the nation's poor. At the time, many elderly Americans lived in poverty, and lawmakers believed the federal government needed to play a more prominent role in the delivery of essential services. While a variety of federal programs already existed to help aging Americans, the Older Americans Act was the first to lay out policy goals to meet the needs of seniors and organize locally based social services for the elderly population.

The act is notable for establishing the ADMINISTRATION ON AGING, or AOA, within the U.S. Department of HEALTH AND HUMAN SERVICES. The AOA administers all but one of the act's programs (the exception is an employment program that is administered by the U.S. Department of Labor) and in fiscal 2000 spent approximately $933 million on efforts mandated by the act. The act also set up a state grant program for senior services and community planning. Hundreds of millions of dollars are transferred each year from the AOA to 57 state agencies on aging located in each state or territory, as well as more than 200 tribal and Native American organizations that use the funds to address the needs of older American Indians. The state agencies on aging, in turn, transfer the funds to approximately 660 area agencies on aging that coordinate services in specific localities. For every federal dollar spent on activities mandated by the Older Americans Act, it is estimated that state and local governments and private sources spend three dollars.

Congress has amended the act thirteen times since passing the original legislation, expanding services in the 1970s to include a national nutrition program and a NURSING HOME ombudsman program. The 1980s saw the development of in-home services for the frail elderly and efforts to halt ELDER ABUSE. Amendments passed in 1992 dealt with strengthening elder-rights protection, including protection of institutionalized seniors.

The Older Americans Act is divided into seven titles. Title I lays out broad policy goals and outlines how seniors' lives can be improved through expanded job opportunities, improved health programs, and better housing. Title II established the AOA, as well as the FEDERAL COUNCIL ON THE AGING. Title III contains the largest programs, directing funding for supportive services and nutrition programs, such as Meals on Wheels. While the services are available to all individuals aged sixty and older, they are primarily directed at the poorest individuals and minority groups. Senior advocates complain that the static funding for Title III programs and past political debates over reauthorizing the act have put a severe financial squeeze on local service providers, as more people age and a growing number of poor elderly people live alone.

Title IV of the act authorizes funding for research and training in the field of aging. Title V covers a senior community-service program that provides part-time jobs for unemployed, lower-income individuals. Title VI authorizes services for Native Americans while Title VII authorizes five different elder-rights protection programs. Funding for the Title VII activities is apportioned according to CENSUS data showing the percentage of each state's population that is aged sixty or older.

During each session of Congress, lawmakers introduce bills to reauthorize the Older Americans Act and express bipartisan support for its programs. However, there have been sharp partisan battles in recent years over proposals to restructure the community-service program, change requirements for supportive and nutrition services, and transfer certain act-mandated activities into block grants that leave states with broader discretion over how to spend the money. Another controversial issue is whether older people should be asked to contribute to the costs of Title III services. Republicans also frequently complain that the act helps fund the activities of left-leaning groups such as the NATIONAL COUNCIL OF SE-

NIOR CITIZENS and contains language giving priority status to poor minority seniors, which some in the GOP view as affirmative action.

After debate that lasted for most of the year, the 106th Congress in October 2000 cleared a compromise reauthorization bill. The bill, among other things, funds the seniors' jobs program in Title V of the bill that is run by nonprofit groups but had been a target of GOP lawmakers, who wanted to turn administration over to states. The reauthorization bill creates new performance measures the groups must meet to continue to receive federal funding. The legislation also creates a new $125 million National Family Caregiver Support Program to help families care for elders at home by subsidizing such services as RESPITE CARE, counseling and support groups, and information on where to get other services. Program funds would be distributed on the basis of a state's relative share of the total U.S. population of people over the age of seventy. The legislation also contains language allowing states more flexibility to move funding from group-meal programs to home-delivered meals, if they apply for a waiver.

Older Workers Benefit Protection Act

Congress passed the Older Workers Benefit Protection Act (PL 101-433) in 1990 in response to the 1989 U.S. Supreme Court decision in *Public Employees Retirement System of Ohio v. Betts,* in which the court ruled the federal Age Discrimination in Employment Act (ADEA) did not specifically bar discrimination with regard to employee benefits. The case was brought by a former Ohio state employee, who was forced to retire at age sixty-one due to an Alzheimer's-related illness. Under the state pension system, the benefits paid were less than half of what she would have received had she retired under the age of sixty. Justices, in a 7–2 ruling, said the only legal way to challenge a benefits plan was to show it discriminated on the basis of age in a non-benefit-related way, such as hiring or firing.

Some members of Congress contended the court misinterpreted the ADEA and responded with proposals that expressly protected workers' benefits from AGE DISCRIMINATION. Senior-citizens and civil-rights groups supported the effort, but business groups and some labor unions opposed it, saying it could invalidate many common benefit practices, particularly EARLY RETIREMENT buyouts for younger workers. In response, lawmakers clarified legislative language, stating that early-retirement programs were voluntary and would remain legal. The revised bill also provided that workers who retired before they were entitled to a full pension could still receive a subsidized pension, even though workers who remained on the job until the NORMAL RETIREMENT AGE of sixty-five would not receive such adjustments.

Democrats and Republicans engaged in some heated debates over key aspects of the legislation, such as protecting employers from lawsuits, but eventually settled on a compromise that extended the ADEA to employee benefits and also wrote into law the EQUAL EMPLOYMENT OPPORTUNITY COMMISSION's "equal cost or equal benefit" provisions that essentially were invalidated by the high court decision. The compromise gave employers some protection in the awarding of early-retirement incentives, stating that employees could only sue for age discrimination if they claimed their participation in the buyout programs was somehow coerced. Employees still could sue for other forms of benefits-related age discrimination if the employer's plan was not consistent with the "relevant purposes" of the ADEA. The compromise placed the burden of proof in employee-benefit claims on workers and did not require that employers pay workers' legal fees. Despite some lingering reservations from the administration of then-president George Bush, the bill was signed into law on October 16, 1990.

Oldest Old

The term "oldest old," coined by the late pioneering gerontologist Bernice Neugarten in a 1975 essay in *The Gerontologist,* is frequently used by economists and demographers to refer to the population of people aged eighty-five and older. Neugarten differentiated between the young-old (sixty-five to seventy-four years), old (seventy-four to eighty-five), and old-old in order to prompt professionals in the field to begin realizing it was not enough to study elderly people, since that group lumps together three distinct groups with very different qualities, needs, and problems. Because of improved medical care and healthier habits, experts say the oldest old segment is projected to be the fastest-growing age group in the first half of the century. The U.S. Census Bureau estimates the population of oldest old will double by 2020 to seven million, and that their proportion of the population will rise from the current 1.5 percent to 4.6 percent.

Some public policy experts believe this trend is a cause for concern, arguing that the oldest members of society consume more costly health-care services and account for a disproportionate share of the nation's medical bill. In reality, the picture is more complex. Studies show MEDICARE spending on the oldest old has shifted since the mid-1980s away from acute-care services and toward SKILLED

A resident in a Gloucester, Massachusetts, nursing home displays a photograph of herself as a young woman. At 103, she is among the oldest old, the fastest-growing age group in the first half of the century. Source: Lisa Poole, AP Photo

NURSING, HOME HEALTH CARE, and REHABILITA-TION services. One Harvard University study concluded that, from 1985 to 1995, real per capita spending on seniors over age eighty-five rose 53 percent, compared to 22 percent for Americans aged sixty-five to sixty-nine. But this may not necessarily be all due to the individuals' health-care needs. Government regulations on "post acute" health-care services were relaxed substantially over that period, and some hospitals shifted primary care to clinics and other settings to boost their revenues. Fraudulent billing for excessive services or services not rendered may also have driven up the cost, the Harvard study concluded.

The financial status of the oldest old will continue to be a focus for policymakers, because many of these individuals live on modest incomes and will suffer from chronic conditions, such as ARTHRITIS, hypertension, and ALZHEIMER'S DISEASE. On one level, an important question is whether enough of these Americans possess privately purchased or employer-sponsored health insurance to supplement their Medicare coverage.

More broadly, politicians and health-care finance experts will have to consider how these individuals can find more affordable LONG-TERM CARE and personal assistance with ACTIVITIES OF DAILY LIVING to assure a decent quality of life, as medical technology continues to increase their longevity.

Omnibus budget reconciliation bills

Since 1980, some of the most important changes to the MEDICARE, MEDICAID, and SOCIAL SECURITY programs have been enacted through budget-reconciliation bills. These giant pieces of legislation are designed to reconcile Congress's annual budget resolutions that set parameters for federal spending with the existing laws for permanently authorized government programs. Frequently, the numbers do not fit, forcing lawmakers to make changes to the programs to cut costs. Critics say this bottom-line-oriented approach can compromise important programs, because the goal of meeting budget targets and making the math work takes precedence over the underlying policy objectives. Conversely, it can force lawmakers to make fiscally sound but politically unpalatable decisions, such as cutting benefit payments to certain groups of health-care providers that are major contributors to political campaigns. Omnibus budget reconciliation bills also are among the highest priority legislation, meaning they usually are protected from filibusters, excessive amendments, and other legislative tactics that can delay passage. They often are signed into law by the president, though President Bill Clinton vetoed a 1995 budget bill over to Republican-supported changes to Medicare and Medicaid, prompting a partial government shutdown.

Following are some of the most notable omnibus reconciliation bills and important changes they brought for elderly Americans (the summaries are in no way a complete recitation of all of the provisions in a particular bill):

• *Tax Equity and Fiscal Responsibility Act of 1982 (TEFRA; PL 97-248).* One of two budget reconciliation bills passed in 1982, this legislation delivered $13.3 billion in Medicare savings over three years and made significant changes to the health-care program. It most notably authorized contracting between Medicare and health-maintenance organizations (HMOs) to enroll beneficiaries in managed-care plans and allowed first-time Medicare payments for HOSPICE services for the terminally ill. This bill also was the first to require that Medicare Part B premiums cover 25 percent of program costs, a provision that was made permanent in 1997.

• *Deficit Reduction Act of 1984 (DEFRA; PL 98-369).* This legislation was notable for creating Medicare's participating-physician program, which encouraged doctors to accept Medicare's approved fee for all services covered by the program.

• *Consolidated Omnibus Budget Reconciliation Act of 1986 (COBRA; PL 99-272).* This bill is remembered for banning the practice of "patient dumping" by forbidding hospitals in the Medicare program from withholding emergency care for elderly patients without the means to pay. Violating institutions were to be thrown out of the program.

• *Omnibus Budget Reconciliation Act of 1987 (OBRA 87; PL 100-203).* This bill included major provisions that overhauled federal regulation of NURSING HOMES that participate in the Medicare and Medicaid programs. In general, the bill shifted regulatory emphasis from a nursing home's ability to provide care to the quality of care that was actually provided. Nursing homes were required to develop plans of care for each resident, safeguards were enacted to prevent resident abuse, and the legislation defined a set of rights to apply to each nursing home resident, including the right to be free of restraints. OBRA 1987 also required nursing homes to provide a set of basic services, including nursing, dietary, physician, rehabilitative, and pharmacy services.

• *Omnibus Budget Reconciliation Act of 1989 (OBRA 89; PL 101-239).* This legislation completely changed the way Medicare pays physicians for covered services, shifting from a system based on the fees doctors historically charged to one based more on the time and training needed to provide certain services.

• *Omnibus Budget Reconciliation Act of 1990 (OBRA 90; PL 101-508).* This bill was the product of the 1990 budget summit between then-president George Bush and Congress that prompted Bush to reverse his "no new taxes" pledge. The bill cut $44.2 billion over five years from the fast-growing Medicare program, in what was then the largest-ever Medicare reduction. However, the bill for the first time extended Medicare coverage for a preventive service by offering to pay for mammography screening for breast cancer. The bill also simplified MEDIGAP coverage to supplement Medicare policies by requiring that insurers offer a basic group of benefits in their policies. Optional benefits could be sold in up to nine other packages of coverage, for a total of ten different policies. This bill also required Medicare and Medicaid providers to inform patients of their rights to draft LIVING WILLS or other types of ADVANCE DIRECTIVES in the event they become incapacitated and cannot express their health-care choices. In the area of Social Security, the bill created new budget rules known as "firewall" provisions that make it more difficult to tap Social Security reserves for purposes other than financing the program. The provisions also would make it more difficult to raise payroll taxes or make benefit changes.

• *Omnibus Budget Reconciliation Act of 1993 (OBRA 93; PL 103-66).* This politically contentious bill passed without a single Republican vote in the first year of Bill Clinton's administration and relied heavily on tax increases to reduce the federal deficit by some $500 billion over five years. The bill taxed 85 percent of Social Security benefits for higher-income elderly persons (couples earning more than $32,000 and individuals earning more than $25,000) instead of the then-existing 50 percent. It also eliminated the cap on wages subject to the Medicare tax, which stood at $135,000 at the time. The legislation imposed $55.8 billion in Medicare cuts over five years, chiefly in payments to hospitals and physicians. It also included language that made it more difficult for elderly persons to divest their assets in order to qualify for Medicaid-provided LONG-TERM CARE.

• *Balanced Budget Act of 1997* (BBA; PL 105-33). This sweeping legislation was the first budget reconciliation bill to anticipate a balanced federal budget, and it ordered major changes to the Medicare and Medicaid programs. The bill cut Medicare spending $115 billion over five years, primarily by reducing payments to hospitals and other health-care providers. In targeting some of the fastest-growing health-care costs, Congress ordered the HEALTH CARE FINANCING ADMINISTRATION to create new payment systems for HOME HEALTH CARE, hospital OUTPATIENT SERVICES, and nursing home care. In an effort to push more program beneficiaries into managed care, the bill also created a new section of Medicare called Part C, or MEDICARE+CHOICE, that encouraged participants to join HMOs and other private insurance plans. The bill provided for Medicare to cover a range of preventive tests, such as PROSTATE screenings, bone-density tests, and diet counseling. The bill also reduced projected spending on Medicaid by $10.4 billion over five years, mainly from cutting payments to states for hospitals that served a disproportionate share of low-income patients. The bill generally gave states more flexibility in setting Medicaid provider payment levels and repealed a provision that required hospitals and nursing homes receive a "reasonable and adequate" payment rate.

Osteoarthritis

Osteoarthrisis is the most common degenerative joint disease, affecting an estimated forty million Americans, including at least 70 percent of individuals over the age of sixty-five. While the exact causes are unclear, the condition attacks cartilage between joints, making normally smooth surfaces rough and occasionally causing bony spurs or nodes to develop. The condition most frequently manifests itself in weight-bearing

The twisted and gnarled hand of a sixty-nine-year-old osteoarthritis sufferer illustrates the ravages of the disease. Source: Dan Loh, AP Photo

parts of the body, such as the hips and knees, though it also can cause deterioration of the discs that separate the bones in the spine. The result is increased joint irritation and stiffness. Individuals at greatest risk are women over the age of forty-five, those with malformed joints or damaged cartilage due to injuries, and obese people.

Osteoarthritis is not to be confused with rheumatoid ARTHRITIS, a more debilitating condition that is believed to be caused by a breakdown in the body's immune system and causes more swelling than osteoarthritis. Osteoarthritis is treated with anti-inflammatory drugs, nonprescription pain relievers, heat and cold therapy, massage, and, sometimes, splints or braces to protect affected joints. Public-health officials urge sufferers to seek medical help and be skeptical about creams, lotions, and dietary supplements that in recent years have been aggressively marketed as potential cures. Health officials say that most alternative therapies are harmless, but that there is no research definitively showing that they help.

The National Institute of Arthritis and Musculoskeletal and Skin Diseases at the NATIONAL INSTITUTES OF HEALTH is conducting research on how

cartilage cells die and on developing improved imaging techniques to better understand the cause and treatment of the condition. The institute's funding has risen steadily over the past decade and totaled $309.9 million in fiscal 2000.

Osteoporosis

Osteoporosis is a condition characterized by low bone mass and a deterioration of bone tissue that strikes a disproportionate number of post-menopausal women. Government officials consider it a significant public-health threat, noting that an estimated ten million Americans already have the condition and that another eighteen million have low bone mass, putting them at increased risk of developing osteoporosis. Of this population of twenty-eight million, 80 percent are women. The most common result of osteoporosis is bone fractures. The NATIONAL INSTITUTES OF HEALTH estimates the condition is responsible for 1.5 million fractures each year—mostly hip, vertebral, and wrist—and accounts for $14 billion in annual health-care spending.

Osteoporosis is caused by the way the body naturally adds new bone tissue and removes old tissue from the skeleton. Bone formation occurs at a faster pace than removal, or resorption, until peak bone mass is reached around age thirty. After that, resorption begins to outpace formation, particularly in the first few years after menopause. While age, gender, and family health history all factor into whether someone will develop the condition, people also are more likely to develop osteoporosis if they have a diet low in calcium and vitamin D, do not reach peak bone mass during their younger years, have an inactive lifestyle, and smoke or drink. The condition has a tendency to silently manifest itself, and sufferers frequently do not become aware they have it until they suffer a bump or fall that causes a fracture. The diagnostic procedure known as bone-mass density screening now is frequently used to measure bone loss and bone quality and identify potential cases. Medicare in 1998 began covering the procedure for certain individuals at high risk of contracting the condition.

The Food and Drug Administration has approved five different types of medication for preventing or treating osteoporosis, including ESTROGEN replacement therapy for postmenopausal women, particularly over the age of seventy. The hormone is administered via a pill or skin patch and has been shown to block resorption and increase bone density, particularly in the spine and hip. However, the procedure is somewhat controversial because estrogen taken alone can increase a woman's chances of developing endometrial CANCER. For this reason, doctors prescribe the hormone progestin in tandem with estrogen for women who have not had a hysterectomy. Experts generally recommend estrogen treatment only for those women at high risk of osteoporosis. Other types of medication for women and men with osteoporosis include a class of drugs called biphosphonates that have been shown to slow or stop bone loss. Health professionals recommend older people with osteoporosis should use canes or walkers, wear rubber-soled shoes, and take other safety measures to avoid the risk of falls.

The National Institute of Arthritis and Musculoskeletal and Skin Diseases, part of the National Institutes of Health, is the federal government's center for research into the cause and treatment of osteoporosis. An NIH-convened panel on osteoporosis prevention in March 2000 concluded that environmental and lifestyle factors, such as good nutritional habits and more physical activity in early life, can significantly cut the risk of the disease, though genetic factors still play a major role in determining peak bone mass. The panel also said more research needs to be performed on the role and mechanism of estrogen, noting that plant-derived estrogen has not been shown to reduce fractures.

Outcomes research

This increasingly common component of health-care and gerontology studies different treatments for particular conditions or illnesses, in order to document what works best, to develop guidelines for care, and in some cases, study how insurers' reimbursement policies or a patient's insurance status affects the success or failure of medical intervention.

Outcomes research is increasingly studied by so-called third-party payers such as the MEDICARE program, managed-care companies, and hospitals, in the hopes of reducing health-care costs and improving efficiencies. But studies vary significantly. Some very specifically study complications suffered by patients who undergo a procedure at a particular hospital. Others are more general and might study health trends in an entire metropolitan area or nation. One example is a study at the University of Illinois at Chicago, that examines what kinds of occupational therapy practices are most effective in areas such as gerontology, ARTHRITIS, and neurological disorders. The study comes at a time when government and private insurers are placing "THERAPY CAPS" on how much they will pay for occupational therapy services.

Outpatient services

Medical advances over the past twenty years, combined with financial pressures in the health-care sector, have prompted physicians and hospitals to offer a wide array of treatments outside of a traditional acute-care setting—that is, without actually confining the patient to a hospital bed. Ambulatory surgery for procedures such as gallstone removal, diagnostic services such as radiology, and various forms of physical therapy are routinely provided on an "outpatient" basis in hospital outpatient departments (known as OPDs), stand-alone clinics, or in other settings. While this has fulfilled one essential goal of managed care in reducing the number of days patients spend in hospitals, it also has shifted a significant portion of costs to the outpatient arena and presented difficult financial dilemmas to policymakers.

Unlike acute care, which is covered under MEDICARE Part A, outpatient services are covered under Medicare's Part B. Until recently, Medicare reimbursed health-care providers on a "reasonable cost" basis, meaning they were paid for actual charges, less deductibles and copayments. The BALANCED BUDGET ACT OF 1997 (PL 105-33) changed that to a PROSPECTIVE PAYMENT SYSTEM, which went into effect in July 2000 and codes diagnoses into groups of similar kinds of treatment on the theory that they require similar interventions and uses of hospital resources. However, the prospective payment system for OPDs differs from most Part B cost-sharing arrangements in that the beneficiary must pay 20 percent of the actual charges, instead of 20 percent of the Medicare-approved payment, which usually is less. The Balanced Budget Act contains language that will bring outpatient services in line with other Part B services over twenty years by lowering the liability individuals face and shifting the burden back to the federal government.

The policy changes will have a major impact on health-care economics. Gradually, Medicare beneficiaries can expect to pay the same amounts for procedures at any hospital, irrespective of the hospital's charges. Many hospitals are expected to absorb significant financial losses as a result. However, those with comparatively low charges can expect to gain revenues. Medicare beneficiaries also will pay less in the form of copayments because the changes include basing copayment rates on median, instead of mean, charges for procedures. This, too, will result in a reduction of payments to hospitals. Congress is monitoring the changes and may consider shifting course to lessen the financial burden on health-care providers. However, the HEALTH CARE FINANCING ADMINISTRATION is not expected to reverse its decision to use a prospective payment system for outpatient services.

P

Paratransit

Paratransit services are an alternate form of public transportation for people with disabilities or elderly persons who cannot independently use regular mass-transit services. The services came into vogue with passage of the AMERICANS WITH DISABILITIES ACT of 1990 (ADA; PL 101-336), which required that public entities that operate fixed-route transportation services also provide complementary paratransit services by January 1992, and that the services be fully implemented by January 1997. The services often take the form of vans or buses equipped with wheelchair lifts, and have also proven helpful to individuals with vision problems or those who cannot stand for long periods of time. The U.S. Department of Transportation outlines conditions for eligibility, but leaves it to localities to develop and run the process for selecting who can ride. Fares vary, depending on the locality.

Legally, paratransit services are treated as a kind of "property right," because users who depend on them for access to medical care or a job could lose either if the service is not provided. However, the availability of paratransit continues to vary by location. Large cities with coordinated mass-transit systems find it easier to provide such services than municipalities in sprawling suburban areas. Some suburban governments have contracted with private taxi companies to accomplish the task. However, there is practically no federal financial sup-

A bus driver helps an elderly voter to the polls on Election Day. Special transportation for the elderly or people with disabilities has become standard since passage of the Americans with Disabilities Act of 1990. Source: National Archives

port for private transit systems designed especially for elderly suburban citizens. The situation continues to merit study as more elderly Americans disperse to suburban communities that are designed for younger, more mobile residents.

Parkinson's disease

Parkinson's disease is a degenerative disease of the nervous system most commonly seen in people over the age of fifty. It causes rhythmic tremors and rigidity of the hands and other parts of the body, spastic motion of the eyelids, and a bent-over posture. Sufferers have trouble walking and take slow, shuffling footsteps. The disease is named for British physician James Parkinson, who formally described its symptoms in an 1817 article titled "An Essay on the Shaking Palsy." Health officials believe the disease has been around for thousands of years, noting descriptions of Parkinson's-like conditions in India as early as 5000 B.C. More than half a million Americans have the condition, and an estimated fifty thousand new cases are diagnosed each year. The disease has no cure, but standard treatment usually involves the drug levodopa, or L-dopa. This medication often loses its effectiveness over time, bringing on a return of the symptoms.

The cause of Parkinson's disease is unknown. Though a defective gene has been implicated in some families with a high incidence of the condition, researchers believe Parkinson's is triggered by a combination of a genetic predisposition and environmental factors. Researchers also do not know whether the aging process directly influences the onset of Parkinson's, noting that individuals over the age of seventy-five actually have a lower chance of developing the condition.

Once the disease manifests itself, it causes degeneration of an area of the brain known as the substantia nigra, which produces dopamine, a nerve-signaling chemical (neurotransmitter) that influences many parts of the brain, including those that control movement. The administering of L-dopa (a chemical precursor of dopamine) attempts to make up for the deficit of the neurotransmitter. Researchers are studying a variety of other interventions, including drugs that increase the natural production of dopamine, decrease the action of a complimentary nerve-signaling chemical called acetylcholine, or artificially activate dopamine receptors in the body. Scientists also have attempted surgical procedures with mixed success, including transplanting genetically engineered cells that produce dopamine.

Parkinson's is not fatal, but it does cut life short by incapacitating its victims. The disease is often misdiagnosed or confused with parkinsonism, a medical condition also characterized by shaking and rigidity of limbs and impaired movement that can be brought on by a variety of factors, including stroke and head injuries. A definitive diagnosis of early-stage Parkinson's can only be achieved with sophisticated medical imaging techniques involving radioisotopes.

Parkinson's disease has become a federal funding priority of Congress, partly because of the rising caseload and also because of well-known victims, such as former Arizona Democratic representative Morris K. Udall, who died of complications of the disease in 1998, and actor Michael J. Fox. Congress in 1997 passed the Morris K. Udall Parkinson's Research and Education Act, which directed the National Institute of Neurological Diseases and Stroke at the NATIONAL INSTITUTES OF HEALTH (NIH) to develop a wide-ranging research agenda. NIH responded in March 2000 by

Actor Michael J. Fox, a Parkinson's victim and chair of the Michael J. Fox Foundation for Parkinson's Research, testifies at the Capitol on September 14, 2000, on the benefits stem cell research could bring to sufferers of the disease. Source: Kamenko Pajic, AP Photo

submitting to Congress a five-year plan to spend nearly $1 billion in new funding to study and fight the disease.

NIH studies of twins in 1999 concluded that heredity does not significantly contribute to the most common type of Parkinson's, affecting people over the age of fifty. More recently researchers at the University of Colorado and Columbia-Presbyterian Medical Center in New York found mixed success when they transplanted dopamine-producing fetal cells into the portions of the brain most affected by the disease. The researchers in April 1999 reported

the implants improved the motor skills of Parkinson's patients under the age of sixty, but caused no significant improvements in those over sixty. Current research includes studies of environmental toxins that could contribute to the condition, as well as research on altered motor skills and neurochemistry in patients.

Partial reserve

The phrase "partial reserve" is used in discussions about SOCIAL SECURITY financing to refer to the practice of having the system take in more than it has to pay out, in order to build up large reserve funds needed to pay the benefits of an increasing number of retired workers. Social Security essentially has operated under this principle since the GREENSPAN COMMISSION in 1983 took major steps to address Social Security's deficit, including raising payroll taxes, delaying cost-of-living increases, and gradually raising the NORMAL RETIREMENT AGE from sixty-five to sixty-seven.

Social Security reserves that are not used for paying BENEFITS or program expenses are invested in U.S. government securities, usually special Treasury obligations issued specifically for the Social Security TRUST FUNDS. The bonds pay interest equivalent to the average rate of return on publicly traded government debt. The Social Security Board of Trustees reported that, in 1999, the trust funds took in a total of $526.6 billion and spent $392.9 billion, thus increasing reserves by $133.7 billion, to $896.1 billion. However, the trustees also warned that expenditures will begin to exceed tax revenues in 2015, and that the reserves will begin to be drawn down in 2025 until they are exhausted in 2037.

Patient Self-Determination Act of 1990

The Patient Self-Determination Act refers to language inserted in the Omnibus Budget Reconciliation Act of 1990 (PL 101-508; see OMNIBUS BUDGET RECONCILIATION BILLS) that requires hospitals, nursing facilities, HOSPICES, and other health-care providers participating in MEDICARE and MEDICAID to inform patients of their rights to execute ADVANCE DIRECTIVES in case they become incapacitated. The BALANCED BUDGET ACT OF 1997 (PL 105-33) required that these advance directives—most commonly LIVING WILLS and MEDICAL POWER OF ATTORNEY—be placed in the patient's permanent medical record.

Congress passed the Patient Self-Determination Act in the wake of the 1990 U.S. Supreme Court case *Cruzan by Cruzan v. Director, Missouri Department of Health,* in which the high court upheld a Missouri decision that refused the request of parents of a woman left in a persistent vegetative state as the result of an automobile accident to cut off medical care that kept their daughter alive. While the act has been credited with strengthening patients' rights and solving painful decisions about keeping certain individuals alive by artificial means, some medical ethics experts and health-care professionals have questioned whether it forces some older patients with cognitive or physical problems to make critical decisions about their care during a crisis situation when they are entering a hospital. These individuals believe advanced directives may better be executed while individuals are in familiar settings, perhaps with the help of family physicians or area agencies on aging.

Pay-as-you-go system

"Pay-as-you-go" describes the manner in which SOCIAL SECURITY and many other national pension systems are financed: payroll taxes paid into the system by today's workers are used to finance the BENEFITS of current program beneficiaries. The opposite would be a "prefunded" or "fully funded" system similar to PRIVATE PENSIONS, in which the money paid in is saved to pay for future benefits. The pay-as-you-go nature of Social Security is at the crux of many political debates over PRIVATIZATION of the system, with political conservatives and other reform advocates claiming it makes Social Security akin to a crooked Ponzi scheme at a time when the financial future of the program may be imperiled. A more objective analogy might be a pipeline, into which taxes from workers flow at one end while payments for beneficiaries flow out of the other end.

Many economists and social policy analysts argue pay-as-you-go has fundamental advantages, such as a built-in protection against inflation, because the amounts paid in and paid out are both in current dollars. Additionally, this camp argues that pay-as-you-go does not subject retirees' incomes to the volatility of the financial markets, or raise false expectations about how much may be saved in investments to pay future benefits. However, for a pay-as-you-go system to work, one needs a reasonable ratio of workers to retirees. Defenders of the current system believe this can be maintained, despite the projected surge of aging BABY BOOMERS, by raising the retirement age or decreasing incentives to retire early.

Pension and Welfare Benefits Administration

The Pension and Welfare Benefits Administration, known as the PWBA, is the branch of the LABOR DEPARTMENT responsible for enforcing portions of the EMPLOYEE RETIREMENT INCOME SECURITY ACT OF 1974 (ERISA; PL 93-406) dealing with the mismanagement and abuse of PRIVATE PENSION plans. It continues a line of federal regulation that dates to the early 1920s, when the INTERNAL REVENUE SERVICE began regulating private pension plans. The Department of Labor became involved in 1959, when the Welfare and Pension Plans Disclosure Act required employers, labor unions, and other plan sponsors to file descriptions of the plans and financial reports with the federal government.

ERISA requires plan sponsors to give beneficiaries adequate information about the operation of the plans and also to hire qualified individuals to manage plan assets. The PWBA oversees these requirements and also assures that plan funds are protected and that qualified participants receive their benefits. The department's job has become more complex with amendments to the original ERISA legislation and health-care reform. Federal legislation has granted exemptions making it easier for certain employees to participate in private pensions. Moreover, legislation such as the Health Insurance Portability and Accountability Act of 1996 (PL 104-191) expanded health-care coverage provisions under ERISA, giving the PWBA more jurisdiction over private health insurance plans.

Pension Benefit Guaranty Corporation

This branch of the LABOR DEPARTMENT, known as the PBGC, was established in 1974 by Title IV of the EMPLOYEE RETIREMENT INCOME SECURITY ACT (PL 93-406) to insure PRIVATE PENSIONS and pay the benefits of company-sponsored plans that fail. Often this requires the agency to sort through the tangled finances of companies that went bankrupt. However, the agency also has repeatedly had to contend with financially healthy corporations that deliberately terminate underfunded pension plans and shift liability to the PBGC. Not only has the agency been unable to prevent the transfer of liability, it also has been limited in collecting assets to help pay for the underfunded portion. Employers who terminate underfunded plans are liable to the PBGC for up to 30 percent of their net worth.

The PBGC, which guarantees the benefits of approximately forty-two million workers participating in more than forty-four thousand DEFINED-CONTRIBUTION PLANS, has come under periodic criticism from government auditors and members of Congress for mismanagement and delays in settling cases and paying benefits. The General Accounting Office in 1992 rated the PBGC a "high-risk" agency, citing its $2.9 billion accumulated deficit and poor management practices. Congress has responded with a series of laws to discourage pension underfunding and help chip away at the PBGC's deficit. These included provisions in the Omnibus Budget Reconciliation Act of 1987 (PL 100-203; see OMNIBUS BUDGET RECONCILIATION BILLS) that raised the annual premiums paid to the PBGC, and the Retirement Protection Act of 1994, which attempted to close the gap between assets and benefit liabilities in

Rep. Claude Pepper gestures to reporters in his Capitol Hill office in November 1981; behind him is a copy of Time *magazine, featuring the Florida congressman on the cover. Pepper was instrumental in crafting the Older Americans Act, among other things, and winning passage for Medicare legislation.*
Source: Jim Wells Photographers

underfunded plans. In 2000, the PBGC set the maximum benefit it will guarantee at $3,221.59 per month, or $38,659.08 per year for retirees in underfunded single-employer pension funds that terminate. The guarantee applies to workers who retire at age sixty-five or later. Guarantees are lower for individuals who take EARLY RETIREMENT.

Pension plans

See AUSTRALIAN PRIVATE PENSION PLANS; CASH-BALANCE PENSION; CHILEAN PENSION SYSTEM; GREAT BRITAIN PENSION SYSTEM; PENSION AND WELFARE BENEFITS ADMINISTRATION; PENSION BENEFIT GUARANTY CORPORATION.

Pepper, Claude

Through fourteen years in the U.S. Senate and twenty-seven in the House of Representatives, Florida Democrat Claude Pepper (1900–1989) championed proposals for a bigger federal role in helping elderly Americans, the disabled, and the poor. Unabashedly liberal, even in the last decade of his life, he antagonized the Ronald Reagan administration and even his more centrist Democratic colleagues by advocating expanded health care for older persons and tirelessly defending their SOCIAL SECURITY benefits in the face of a federal deficit crisis. Pepper became such a powerful symbol to the elderly, many of whom lived in his Miami congressional district, that his endorsement was viewed as mandatory for any proposed legislation to rescue the Social Security legislation. Appointed to the National Commission on Social Security Reform in 1981, he vigorously fought back attempts to cut benefits and helped shape a final compromise that struck a balance between delaying BENEFITS for current retirees and increasing workers' payroll taxes.

Born in rural Alabama, Pepper worked his way through the University of Alabama, served a short stint in the Army, then attended Harvard University Law School on a disability grant. He moved to Florida in the late 1920s and became known as a powerful speaker and advocate of racial tolerance in the Florida legislature. His first piece of legislation was a bill to eliminate fishing-license fees for the elderly. His narrow primary loss to incumbent senator Park Trammel, D-Fla., in 1934 paved the way for his special election in 1936 to complete the term of Sen. Duncan U. Fletcher, D-Fla., who died in office.

Pepper became a staunch defender of President FRANKLIN D. ROOSEVELT's New Deal programs and in 1937 helped draft the first federal legislation that set a minimum hourly wage and maximum workday. He also cosponsored legislation to establish the National Cancer Institute at the NATIONAL INSTITUTES OF HEALTH. Later, weighing in on foreign affairs after a 1938 trip to Nazi Germany, he introduced a resolution that became the Lend-Lease Act, through which the U.S. provided the Allies with U.S. military equipment to fight World War II. However, favorable comments he made about Soviet leader Josef Stalin after the war led opponents to depict him as a communist sympathizer, leading to his loss in a 1950 Senate primary to Rep. George A. Smathers. Pepper became one of the few defeated senators to return to Washington as a member of the House in 1962, representing a new district for Dade County. As an ally of both John F. Kennedy's and Lyndon B. Johnson's administrations, Pepper was instrumental in crafting the OLDER AMERICANS ACT (PL 89-73) and winning passage for MEDICARE legislation. As chairman of the new House committee on aging, Pepper drafted legislation in the 1970s removing the mandatory retirement age for federal employees and raising it from sixty-five to seventy for more workers in the private sector. He also was the prime advocate of a 1986 measure to eliminate mandatory retirement for most workers. The next year, he helped shape a catastrophic health-insurance law that included a provision for the first Medicare coverage of outpatient drug costs.

Pepper died of stomach cancer, but not before President George Bush presented him with the nation's highest civilian award, the Medal of Freedom. Pepper became only the fourth member of Congress to receive the award.

Pepper Commission

This fifteen-member panel of lawmakers from the House of Representatives and the Senate, officially known as the Bipartisan Commission on Comprehensive Health Care, was created in 1987 to study ways to provide LONG-TERM CARE for MEDICARE beneficiaries and comprehensive health care for the UNINSURED. The commission was named for its first chairman and creator, Rep. CLAUDE PEPPER, D-Fla., who died in 1989, before the panel could issue its final recommendations. Pepper used his power as chairman of the House Rules Committee to force Congress into creating the commission by threatening to add a long-term care program to Medicare catastrophic-coverage legislation then moving through the House. Pepper, who agreed to drop the provision in exchange for creation of the panel, envisioned the commission taking six months to develop a long-term care program for Medicare and another half year to deal with problems of the uninsured. However, members soon found themselves divided along partisan lines and unsure of how to finance various initiatives. Most of the recommendations they subsequently developed were never enacted into law.

Among the proposals members agreed on was one to create a new federal health program to replace MEDICAID for providing basic health care, including hospital stays, doctors' bills, and preventive care. The program was to be financed primarily by the federal government, which would pay health-care providers under the rules used for Medicare. Individuals not enrolled through their employers would have to pay premiums based on income, and coverage would have DEDUCTIBLES and copayments. One of the most controversial aspects was a requirement that large employers with more than one hundred workers had to provide their employees with private health insurance or would be forced to contribute to the public plan on the workers' behalf. Smaller businesses would be encouraged to provide coverage through tax breaks and subsidies. Another notable recommendation was a prohibition blocking private insurers from refusing to cover people with preexisting medical conditions—a provision that eventually was written into law as part of the Health Insurance Portability and Accountability Act of 1996 (PL 104-191).

On long-term care, the panel called for guaranteed federal coverage of up to three months of NURSING HOME care, regardless of an individual's age or ability to pay. Individuals with incomes double the federal poverty level would be required to pay a 20 percent copayment. Additionally, the commission called for the creation of a federal-state program to help prevent individuals who had to stay longer than three months from having to deplete all of their assets. The panel also recommended federal coverage of home and community-based care for the disabled, regardless of age.

The total price tag for both proposals was $66.2 billion per year. However, the commission made no recommendations on how to cover the cost. That uncertainty, plus political opposition from Republicans and some Democrats to the provision requiring employers to provide workers with health insurance or pay into a special fund, doomed the plan. The commission, headed after Pepper's death by Sen. John D. Rockefeller IV, D-W.Va., disbanded with members agreeing that Congress needed White House support to enact any significant changes dealing with health-care financing. One legacy of the Pepper Commission was creation of the bipartisan Alliance for Health Reform, based in Washington, D.C., and directed by Ed Howard, who was chief counsel of the commission. The alliance's cochairmen are Rockefeller and Sen. Bill Frist, R-Tenn.

Peterson, Peter G.

Peter G. Peterson, former secretary of commerce in Richard Nixon's administration, has written extensively for two decades about the impending bankruptcy of the SOCIAL SECURITY and MEDICARE programs. As president of the Blackstone Group, an international investment firm, and head of the CONCORD COALITION, Peterson is one of the most prominent advocates of overhauling and privatizing the traditional Social Security system—steps he believes will both keep the systems solvent and raise Americans' rate of personal savings. However, he also has been criticized as an economic Cassandra who is all too willing to depict older Americans as greedy people who use their political influence to secure their financial futures at the expense of future generations. Some economic analysts have questioned whether Peterson should change his message now that higher economic growth and some policy changes have returned Social Security and its TRUST FUNDS to full solvency.

Peterson has promoted his views in articles in

Atlantic Monthly and in books, such as *Will America Grow Up Before It Grows Old?* and, most recently, *Gray Dawn: How the Coming Age Wave Will Transform America,* in which he also argues for raising the NORMAL RETIREMENT AGE and paying BENEFITS only to those seniors who need financial assistance. He also has provided significant financial backing to the Concord Coalition and GENERATION X groups, such as LEAD OR LEAVE, whose founders complained after they disbanded the group that Peterson withdrew his support when they insisted on setting its agenda. (See also PRIVATIZATION.)

Pharmacy benefit manager

A pharmacy benefit manager, or PBM, is a company that specializes in running prescription-drug benefit programs for health insurers. By negotiating discounts with drugmakers, operating mail-order pharmacies, and adopting other strategies, PBMs have been credited with controlling fast-growing drug costs. However, they also have been criticized for encouraging doctors and patients to use only certain drugs and avoid others, based on studies of cost and effectiveness. A number of large drug companies, including Merck and Eli Lilly, in the early 1990s began purchasing PBMs, prompting conflict-of-interest charges from some lawmakers and patient advocates, who said the arrangements could lead the PBMs to recommend drugs made by their parent companies, regardless of their merits. PBMs remain major players in the health-care industry, controlling approximately one-third of the market for prescription drugs. Some lawmakers have advocated using PBMs when devising an envisioned pre-scription drug benefit for MEDICARE, pointing to the savings the companies delivered to the Federal Employees Health Benefits Program. However, the concept has not picked up appreciable support to date from either the political left or right.

Poverty thresholds

Since 1964, the U.S. CENSUS Bureau has used a series of economic measurements known as poverty thresholds to determine precisely who is poor. If a person's or family's income is lower than the corresponding threshold, they may be eligible for various forms of federal assistance. Poverty thresholds do not vary with geography, but are updated annually using the CONSUMER PRICE INDEX. The official definition of poverty counts income before taxes and does not include capital gains or assistance, such as MEDICAID or food stamps. The measurement does not apply to military personnel living on bases, disabled people living in group homes, or unrelated individuals under the age of fifteen, such as foster children.

Many programs that offer assistance to elderly Americans rely on poverty thresholds to determine eligibility. These include certain job programs for low-income older people and QUALIFIED MEDICARE BENEFICIARY cost-sharing under Medicaid, in which Medicaid pays the MEDICARE Part B premiums of the poor elderly.

One important distinction in poverty thresholds is that people are essentially divided into two groups: those under sixty-five and those over sixty-five. Older Americans have a lower poverty threshold and, as a result, in order to count as "poor," they need to be poorer than poor people under sixty-five by 7 to 8 percent, depending on whether they

The seventy-seven-year-old Penn Alto Hotel, once the finest hotel in Altoona, Pennsylvania, is now a HUD-subsidized residence for the elderly and other low-income people. Many programs that offer assistance to elderly Americans rely on poverty thresholds to determine eligibility. Source: Scott J. Ferrell, Congressional Quarterly

are individuals or couples. For instance, the average poverty threshold in 1999 for a two-person family in which the householder was under sixty-five was $11,214, compared to $10,080 for cases in which the householder was over sixty-five. For a person living alone, the threshold was $8,667 for those under sixty-five and $7,991 for those over sixty-five. This aspect of poverty measurements has aroused controversy and discussion because older Americans have been criticized in media reports and in political discussions for having a lower poverty rate than the rest of the population (in fact, the Census Bureau says the poverty rate for persons sixty-five and over is 10.5 percent, about the same as those aged eighteen to sixty-four).

Some observers, such as economist Molly Orshansky, one of those who developed the thresholds, believe they should be revised upward for elderly Americans, because they were based on "market baskets" for different family types and did not take into account older people's special needs. For instance, it was believed that food and household necessities would cost less for older people because they eat less. However, older people need a higher proportion of protein in their diets. Moreover, the thresholds did not take into account the higher costs of medicines for chronic ailments. Conservative commentators have responded that the thresholds may have to be set even lower, because they should include as income Medicare payments and the market cost of related ENTITLEMENT benefits.

Premium support

This health-care financing system was taken up as a proposal for reforming MEDICARE by the National Bipartisan Commission on the Future of Medicare in March 1999. The seventeen-member board fell one vote short of formally recommending a premium support plan to Congress, but the idea has been revived several times in bills offered by proponents such as Sen. John Breaux, D-La., and Rep. Bill Thomas, R-Calif.

Premium support essentially would give seniors a government contribution to help them pay insurance premiums for a menu of basic health services

Rep. Bill Thomas, left, and Sen. John Breaux listen to opening statements at the first meeting of the National Commission on the Future of Medicare on March 6, 1998.
Source: Douglas Graham, Congressional Quarterly

offered by private health plans. Medicare beneficiaries could opt for more extensive coverage if they are willing to pick up the extra cost. Similarly, those who buy into less expensive health plans would keep the savings. The premium support program would likely be managed by the federal government on a regional basis, giving the government the power to negotiate the premiums and benefits of plans. The theory is this would encourage competitive bidding between private health insurers and bring down costs. Premium support also envisions the federal government paying a portion of Medicare's traditional fee-for-service program, thus helping it compete against private health insurance plans.

The original premium support plan offered by Breaux to the bipartisan commission would have gradually raised the eligible age of participants from sixty-five to sixty-seven over twenty-four years and combined Medicare's Part B monthly premium for doctors' visits and the Part A hospital deductible into one payment. The idea provoked widespread interest. However, some commission members, such as former HEALTH CARE FINANCING ADMINISTRATION administrator Bruce Vladeck, were concerned that premiums could rise over

time because they would be adjusted annually. More broadly, Vladeck and other critics of the proposal believed it amounted to little more than a subsidy for the insurance industry that would leave many poorer seniors unable to cover all of their health-care costs.

Prescription drug benefit (Medicare)

Efforts to add prescription drug coverage to MEDICARE have been around since the program was inaugurated in 1965. However, the subject has acquired significant political currency in recent years as costs of many drugs have soared and reports surfaced of elderly Americans going without essential medications, cutting their pills in half, or hopping the border to Canada or Mexico to buy the same medications for a fraction of the U.S. price. Advocates of the proposed drug benefit also have chafed at the discrepancies between the price drug companies charge consumers and the significantly lower price at which bulk purchasers such as the U.S. government can purchase many medicines.

Medicare provides coverage for drugs used as part of a hospital stay, but generally does not cover outpatient prescriptions. Exceptions are granted for certain medications used to treat end-stage renal disease, a number of CANCER drugs, medicines used in immunosuppressive therapy after organ transplants, and drugs that cannot be self-administered and are incidental to a visit to a doctor's office. Medicare beneficiaries can obtain prescription drug coverage if they opt to join a managed-care plan that offers drug coverage as part of its standard package. Beneficiaries also can obtain drug coverage through certain employer-sponsored plans or by purchasing one of the MEDIGAP policies that offer partial drug coverage. Healthcare experts tend to agree that if the core Medicare program were created today, there likely would be drug coverage for its forty million elderly and disabled beneficiaries, because of the myriad medications that can cure illness and reduce medical costs.

Drug companies and trade groups, such as the Pharmaceutical Research and Manufacturers Association, argue that costs are necessarily high to recoup the huge investment needed to push a promising medicine through the Food and Drug Administration's lengthy series of clinical trials. Much of the profit is reinvested in research and development to create new agents to fight dread diseases, the industry groups say. However, some of those statements were challenged in hearings in the U.S. SENATE SPECIAL COMMITTEE ON AGING and in a 1999 series of articles in the *New York Times* that concluded that a large percentage of money identified as research expenses really goes toward marketing, including paying doctors fees to try new drugs in the hope of making product claims more meaningful. Additionally, many of the new designer drugs are being created by small biotechnology firms, not the largest pharmaceutical companies.

The prescription drug debate neared a crescendo during the summer of 2000, as Republicans and Democrats sought to position themselves on the issue in advance of the November elections, aware that it could help them win the support of SENIOR VOTERS. Polls suggesting that Democrats continued to be seen as the party most capable of implementing a drug benefit prompted Republicans in the House of Representatives in June 2000 to draft a plan to rival a prescription drug proposal by Bill Clinton's administration. Both plans would expand the Medicare program and help low-income seniors pay for drug coverage. With little likelihood of any of the proposals being enacted due to significant policy differences, lawmakers were laying the groundwork for possible action when the 107th Congress and the new president took office—a post-election period when lawmakers might be able to find more common ground. A number of other proposals were contemplated or offered, such as a plan U.S. Senate Democrats offered as an amendment to an appropriations bill funding the departments of LABOR and HEALTH AND HUMAN SERVICES.

While most of the debate over prescription drug benefits was political, the policy implications were huge. Though both the Democratic and Republican plans address drug coverage in the near term, passage of either plan likely would mean that drug coverage would become a permanent part of Medicare. Lawmakers would be reluctant to scale back such a BENEFIT, even if current budget surpluses disappear. However, adding a drug benefit could be potentially risky, because of the anticipated surge in the elderly population and the difficulty calculating long-term costs. Some lawmakers and policy experts have used this argument to advocate government price controls for drugs. However, the drug industry has applied constant lobbying pressure to quash this idea, arguing that capping drug costs will discourage further research and development of new medicines.

Both the House Republican plan passed in mid-2000 and the Clinton plan would, at first, pay half of Medicare beneficiaries' drug expenses, up to $2,100 and $2,000, respectively, and increase the amount over the life of each plan. The House Republican plan would begin catastrophic coverage in 2003 when beneficiaries' expenses reached $6,000. Clinton proposed setting aside $35 billion of the current federal budget surplus to begin catastrophic coverage in 2006. The House Republican plan would cost an estimated $40 billion over five years, including catastrophic coverage. The Clinton plan would cost about $38 billion over five years, not including catastrophic coverage.

The plans joined a long list of proposed legislation to address prescription drug coverage. A limited prescription drug benefit was included in the MEDICARE CATASTROPHIC COVERAGE ACT of 1988, but the act was repealed the following year. The debate was rekindled during consideration of the Health Security Act of 1994, but various sides failed to settle on a compromise.

Soon after taking office, in January 2001, President George W. Bush said crafting Medicare prescription drug coverage was among his top priorities.

Private pensions

Private pensions are employer-sponsored benefit plans that help retirees supplement the income they receive from SOCIAL SECURITY. Though they were first offered on a limited basis in the late nineteenth century by companies such as the American Express Company, most older American workers did not have pension plans until the 1950s. Since the mid-1980s, the share of workers covered by pension plans of any type has fallen, partly because employers are offering benefit packages that require employee contributions. This phenomenon, combined with the fact that less than half of large employers offer health coverage for retirees, has led to what some commentators refer to as an "erosion of benefits" for elderly Americans, making them more reliant on MEDICARE and other ENTITLEMENT PROGRAMS and making it more difficult for them to maintain significant retirement savings.

There are two major varieties of private pensions. Defined-benefit plans are traditional retirement plans that promise a specified monthly payout at retirement or calculate a benefit based on a formula that takes into account such factors as years of service or the beneficiary's salary. Increasingly, these plans are being replaced by DEFINED-CONTRIBUTION PLANS, in which workers and employers both contribute to an individual's account that is then invested on the worker's behalf. The payout from these plans is not guaranteed, making them less costly to employers. However, financial gains from defined-contribution plans could be substantial if the accounts are invested wisely. Examples of defined-contribution plans are 401(K) PLANS and employee stock-ownership plans, also known as ESOPs. Defined-contribution plans now account for more than 60 percent of all employer-sponsored pension plans.

Since the 1920s, Congress has created special tax incentives to encourage employers to offer private pensions. The Revenue Act of 1921, for instance, exempted interest income for stock bonus or profit-sharing plans from taxation. The Revenue Act of 1928 allowed employers to take tax deductions for certain sums paid into retirement plans beyond what was needed to fund existing liabilities. The Tax Reform Act of 1969 allowed for the establishment of pensions plans that could be jointly administered by a company and a labor union. However, retirement security still was not a certain thing because employers could go bankrupt or simply decide to terminate a plan, thereby interrupting benefit payments.

Congress set national standards for pensions with passage of the EMPLOYEE RETIREMENT INCOME SECURITY ACT OF 1974 (ERISA) (PL 93-406), which created rules for participation, vesting, and funding of plans. The act created the PENSION BENEFIT GUARANTY CORPORATION, which insures private defined-benefit pensions. The Tax Reform Act of 1986 and Retirement Protection Act of 1994 both further increased oversight of pension funding and administration through steps such as increasing insurance premiums for underfunded plans. However, some believe the complexity of pension rules brought on by the many laws, plus increased administrative costs and the possibility of legal penalties for failure to comply, have discouraged some employers from offering pensions.

Privatization

Privatization refers to the concept of redirecting some payroll taxes from retirees' SOCIAL SECURITY benefits to individual savings plans tied to stocks and bonds. One oft-suggested figure is 2 percentage points of the 12.4 percent now levied for payroll tax on employers and employees combined. Once viewed as a politically unrealistic product of conservative and libertarian thinking, the idea gained currency during the 105th Congress, buoyed by projections that Social Security's TRUST FUNDS may face a financial squeeze later this century as tens of millions of BABY BOOMERS retire. Even some longtime defenders of the existing PAY-AS-YOU-GO SYSTEM, such as former senator Daniel Patrick Moynihan, D-N.Y., began advocating privatization plans. More than thirty legislative proposals were introduced during the 105th Congress. More recently, sustained economic growth and projections of increasing surpluses in the trust funds have cooled talk of major privatization reforms, though the topic surfaced during the 2000 presidential elections, with Republican George W. Bush advocating a form of privatization.

The 1994–1996 federal Advisory Council on Social Security studied privatization as a way of solving the program's anticipated long-term financing problems, but could not settle on a single approach. Instead, the council outlined three broad privatization schemes that serve as a handy way of evaluating most of the existing political proposals. One approach, called "maintain benefits," would keep Social Security's present benefit structure intact into the future by raising payroll taxes and cutting some BENEFITS. The remainder of the projected financing gap would be made up by investing Social Security's trust funds in the stock market, whose historical returns have outperformed the government bonds the trust funds currently hold. A second proposal advocates the creation of individual savings accounts by making some benefit cuts and forcing workers to contribute to INDIVIDUAL RETIREMENT ACCOUNTS. There would be several options for structuring the accounts, including mutual funds tied to stocks. A third privatization approach would involve a more significant

George W. Bush advocated a form of privatization during the 2000 presidential election campaign. Source: Scott J. Ferrell, Congressional Quarterly

overhaul of the Social Security system and replacing a major portion of the existing Social Security benefit with individual savings accounts.

Expectations of a windfall for future retirees under privatization are tempered by the realization that the presumed higher rate of return from private accounts would be offset by reduced guaranteed Social Security benefits. A number of plans, such as one proposed by the centrist Washington-based Center for Strategic and International Studies, are designed to be more even-handed and politically palatable by designing benefit cuts to hit the wealthy more than people with lower incomes. Such plans also would create a minimum guaranteed benefit on a sliding scale that is tied to how long a person works.

One critical question surrounding privatization concerns how government would finance the transition from the traditional system. Privatization critics, most notably labor unions, contend the first working generation at the time of the changeover would have to save and invest in the newly privatized system while still paying for existing Social Security benefits, effectively paying for two retirements. Privatization proponents dismiss the argument, saying the only transition cost is increased savings in the new system. Those who forgo current consumption will recoup the amount later in more available savings at the time of retirement, according to this argument. Another cause for concern is volatility in the financial markets. Privatization critics maintain it is wrong to put a significant portion of retirees' savings at risk by subjecting the money to the whims of the financial markets. Others are wary of the government's investing Social Security trust fund surpluses in the financial markets and effectively becoming the largest single investor. Some in this camp question whether government officials would have adequate financial acumen, while others worry about market reaction if the officials suddenly decide to purchase or sell significant sums of a particular investment.

One interesting corollary to the privatization discussion is how such plans would benefit women. Proponents say the current Social Security system needs to be changed because it cheats working women by using an outdated "model family" with a stay-at-home mom. When the program was designed, few women worked outside the home. If benefits were to be calculated based on one's own work history, millions of widows would have been left with nothing when their husbands died. To address this, Congress in 1939 introduced spousal benefits that automatically entitled a woman to half of her husband's benefits, regardless of whether she paid payroll taxes. Thus a woman who worked all of her life and paid a significant amount of taxes into the system could receive a smaller retirement benefit than a woman who never was employed, even if their household incomes were identical. Privatization could address this imbalance. Yet defenders of the current system respond that privatization could penalize professional women and dependent spouses. First, working women typically earn less than men and would have less to invest in individual savings accounts. Dependent spouses, who now are entitled to half of their husband's benefits, would lose the subsidy in a system based on private accounts. Some private savings accounts may also be set up to expire at the time of death, leaving the survivor without benefits, privatization foes argue. Whoever is right, gender equity will continue to be a topic of debate if the privatization debate pushes forward.

Probate

Probate is the legal process through which a court identifies a deceased person's property, pays off remaining debts, verifies heirs, and distributes designated assets to them. Probate is both praised and derided. On one hand, it provides certainty that a deceased person's belongings are accounted for, and that his or her wishes regarding inheritance are executed. Probate also provides safety from legal claims against a person's estate after a brief claims period expires. However, the probate process frequently is criticized as cumbersome and time consuming. Many cases take one year to complete and can drag on longer if the deceased had complicated investments, structured assets in an unusual way, or has heirs or beneficiaries with competing claims. Probate also can be expensive, because the process involves hiring attorneys, accountants, and appraisers. And while the court acts as a convenient and helpful "referee," much of

the actual work of identifying and disposing of assets falls to the executor of the estate. In some states, such as California, the probate court serves a double function by also administering GUARDI-ANSHIPS or conservatorships in the event that a person becomes incapacitated.

Individuals seeking to avoid probate often set up living TRUSTS with their heirs. Property in a trust is not subject to the probate process, and "revocable" trusts allow the owner of the assets to maintain control over them and back out of the arrangement at any time. Alternately, the person may specify a beneficiary for life insurance policies, bank accounts, and certain valuable assets such as cars, assuring that the property passes on to the designated person without the need for court verification. Probate law is a constantly evolving process; decisions from the Supreme Court down to local courts clarify how personal property may be disposed and rule on the validity of claims, including tax liens.

Program of All-Inclusive Care for the Elderly (PACE)

The Program of All-Inclusive Care for the Elderly (PACE) provides both acute and LONG-TERM CARE. It was originally developed in the early 1970s by On Lok Senior Health Services in San Francisco, in an effort to allow frail seniors aged fifty-five and older who meet their state's standards for NURSING HOME care to continue to live at home and avoid being institutionalized. The PACE program provides a comprehensive package of nursing-home-type services, usually in an ADULT DAY CARE or health center, with additional services provided at home or on a referral basis, depending on the individual client's needs. A team of health-care professionals assesses each patient's needs and develops a health-care plan. Eligible participants must live in a PACE service area and voluntarily enroll in the program.

Because PACE providers receive fixed monthly payments from MEDICARE and MEDICAID for each eligible beneficiary, they can deliver all the services a patient needs instead of being limited only to those services that are reimbursable under Medicare and Medicaid fee-for-service systems. PACE providers are responsible for all the care required by program participants, twenty-four hours a day and seven days a week. Medicare-eligible PACE participants who are not eligible for Medicaid pay a monthly premium, but do not pay DEDUCTIBLES or co-insurance or participate in other forms of cost-sharing. Such innovative approaches to providing and financing elder care are being studied more as the costs of providing long-term care in institutions rise and consume an increasingly large portion of the nation's health-care bill.

THE HEALTH CARE FINANCING ADMINISTRATION approved testing the PACE model on a nationwide basis as part of a DEMONSTRATION PROGRAM beginning in the mid-1980s. The approach proved so successful that Congress included language in the BALANCED BUDGET ACT OF 1997 (PL 105-33) to significantly increase the number of PACE sites across the country. However, there only were about twenty-five PACE sites in operation as of mid-2000. The option is only available in those states that choose to offer PACE under Medicaid.

Prospective payment system (PPS)

Responding to a severe financial squeeze surrounding the SOCIAL SECURITY trust funds, Congress in 1983 passed legislation (PL 98-21) that changed the way the government paid hospitals under MEDICARE Part A. The prospective payment system, or PPS, paid hospitals a predetermined fee for each patient based on the patient's diagnosis. This ended the practice of paying hospitals for all services delivered and, predictably, sent shock waves through the health-care industry. The system was based on a partially completed DEMONSTRATION PROGRAM being tested by the state of New Jersey that grouped medical conditions into clusters requiring similar kinds of treatment. Initially, 467 of these diagnosis-related groups, or DRGs, were created in an effort to encourage the most efficient use of hospital resources; the number has since increased to 487. The groupings were based on evidence that certain types of diagnoses, such as cardiovascular conditions, require quite similar intervention and use of hospital resources. However, follow-up studies by the Rand Corporation and others suggested the PPS payments also could encourage more rapid discharges of patients—"sicker and quicker," in the words of PPS critics—and that very frail or ill patients could suffer higher mortality rates as a result. Congress has attempted to address this concern by allowing Medicare patients who believe they are being discharged too early to appeal the decision to a Medicare Peer Review Organization and stay at the hospital an extra day at no cost to them.

Under the PPS, each Medicare beneficiary admitted to a hospital is assigned a DRG. If the hospital provides the necessary care for less than the DRG payment, it gets to keep the difference. On the other hand, if the care costs more than the DRG payment, the hospital has to absorb the extra cost. Prospective payment system payments are updated annually according to a measurement of the costs of goods and services used by hospitals that is known as the Market Basket Index.

Evidence suggests the PPS method has delivered significant savings. In 1980, hospitals' share of total health-care spending stood at 41.5 percent and was growing rapidly. By 1990, the hospitals' share was 36.6 percent and continued to decrease during most of the 1990s. While hospitals initially grappled with the reduced payments, the industry adjusted, partly by reducing the number of inpatient admissions and offering more types of care as OUTPATIENT SERVICES, for which reimbursements continued to be cost-based. The PPS system also set in motion the trend of moving patients sicker and quicker into less costly settings known as post-acute or sub-acute care. Because the system had to begin reimbursing more for those patients, it created a kind of sub-industry, with hospitals and NURSING HOMES competing for this business. The industry also was made possible by new medical technology, allowing for intravenous care and medical monitoring that used to be done only in acute-care settings to be done now at lower levels of care.

Hospitals that could not provide certain services efficiently under the new reimbursement system began increasing referrals to those institutions that could. The government, in an effort to lessen the blow to certain institutions, offered special payment adjustments to teaching hospitals, which tend to use more diagnostic tests, and to teaching hospitals and other health-care centers that see a disproportionately large share of very sick patients.

The PPS system so impressed lawmakers that Congress in the BALANCED BUDGET ACT OF 1997 (PL 105-33) ordered PPS systems to be developed for HOME HEALTH CARE agencies, nursing homes, and outpatient hospital care. However, the less

precise nature of providing LONG-TERM CARE has caused difficulties. Home health providers, in particular, have complained that disparities in reimbursement rates under a temporary diagnosis-based system is driving some agencies out of business. The HEALTH CARE FINANCING ADMINISTRATION missed an October 1999 deadline for implementing a PPS for home health care, but had a new system in place by late 2000.

Prostate

The prostate is a walnut-sized male sex gland that produces fluid that is mixed with sperm from the testes and ejaculated through the penis during sex. The gland is a significant source of health problems for males over the age of fifty, in part because of its tendency to enlarge and obstruct the flow of urine from the bladder. The most significant health problem is prostate CANCER, which was expected to account for 180,000 new cases and 32,000 deaths in 2000, according to the American Cancer Society. Despite the grim prognosis, disease advocacy groups such as the National Prostate Cancer Coalition note that prostate cancer deaths have dropped in recent years as a result of improved testing that can catch the disease in its early stages of development. Public health officials urge men over the age of forty to include prostate screening (digital rectal exams) in their annual physicals.

Approximately half of the men over the age of fifty, and up to 90 percent of men over eighty, have enlarged prostates—a condition known as benign prostatic hyperplasia, or BPH. The condition is not cancerous but can cause significant health problems. Blockage of urine flow due to an enlarged prostate can result in infections and kidney damage. Sufferers experience increased urinary urgency, straining, a burning sensation, and sometimes, impotence. The precise cause of the condition is unknown, but scientists suspect it may be triggered by aging-related changes in the body's hormones. Approximately 10 percent of individuals with BPH will also have prostate cancer, while another 10 to 20 percent will need medical treatment. Among the commonly administered drugs are finasteride, which slows the effects of testosterone, the male hormone believed to play a role in enlargement. Another type of medication is the alpha-adrenergic blockers, originally designed to treat hypertension. If the drugs do not work, surgery may be needed to remove the prostate section blocking urine flow.

Public awareness of prostate cancer increased in the 1990s with the deaths of some high-profile victims, such as singer-songwriter Frank Zappa and Nobel laureate Linus Pauling, and the increasingly vocal advocacy of survivors, such as Gen. H. Norman Schwartzkopf. One diagnostic tool that has received particular attention is a test that tracks levels in the blood of prostate specific antigen (PSA), a substance that can indicate the presence of cancer when it is found in abnormally high levels. Doctors are capable of testing both PSA that is bound to blood cells and "free PSA" that floats unbound. This enables them to rule out cancer in patients who may exhibit slightly higher PSA from other causes. The PSA test can give false readings from noncancerous conditions, such as BPH, and some medical experts say there is no correlation between increased PSA screening and a reduction in prostate cancer cases. Many physicians use other diagnostic tools in tandem with the PSA, such as ultrasound, to determine the nature of the cancer and whether it has spread to other parts of the body.

Gen. H. Norman Schwartzkopf, one of the more famous U.S. prostate cancer victims, greatly increased public awareness of the disease. Source: File photo

If there is evidence of cancer, doctors usually order a biopsy. If that test confirms the diagnosis, patients have several treatment options. Those with early stage, or slow-spreading, prostate cancer who are not expected to live more than ten years may opt for no treatment, because the cancer probably will not claim their lives. At the other extreme, some patients undergo a complete removal of the gland, which could completely reduce the risk of cancer if the disease is confined to the gland. In the middle are radiation treatments, which is less radical but can result in impotence, and cryotherapy, in which prostate tumors are removed by freezing them. MEDICARE covers the cost of an annual prostate screening that may include a digital rectal exam or a PSA test.

Psychiatric services

Psychiatric services are an important part of elder care and a source of some concern for policymakers because they can be more expensive than other medical treatments covered by MEDICARE. Services range from the diagnosis and treatment of DEPRESSION, an affliction that affects an estimated five million Americans over the age of sixty-five, to more intensive institutional care for patients suffering from ALZHEIMER'S DISEASE and related DEMENTIAS. Psychiatric problems tend to be overlooked and underdiagnosed. This is partly because general physicians and other health-care professionals who regularly deal with the elderly do not have the expertise, and also because the stigma many older people attach to mental illness may prevent them from complaining about anxiety or depression-like symptoms. The most common psychiatric diagnoses among Medicare beneficiaries admitted to hospitals tend to be depression, followed by dementia or other "organic disorders," followed by substance abuse. The majority of hospitalizations of the "OLDEST OLD"—individuals aged 85 and older—are for organic disorders.

Diagnosing Alzheimer's disease is one psychiatric service that is receiving increased attention due to the anticipated surge in new cases as the BABY BOOMER generation ages. It is impossible to completely confirm that a person has Alzheimer's without a biopsy of brain tissue, and HEALTH CARE FINANCING ADMINISTRATION (HCFA) guidelines prohibit diagnoses termed "probable" or "suspected." However, Public Health Service guidelines published in 1996 allow for the diagnosis of Alzheimer's on clinical grounds without the need for a biopsy if the medical verdict can be backed up with test results, symptoms, or patient complaints. Medicare pays 80 percent of the HCFA-approved amount for psychiatric services if the visit was to diagnose Alzheimer's. The agency only pays 50 percent of the approved amount if the visit was to treat ongoing mental-health problems, such as depression.

The creation of a PROSPECTIVE PAYMENT SYSTEM for Medicare in the early 1980s was expected to change the provision of psychiatric services for the elderly by shortening expensive hospital stays. But studies by the federal Agency for Health Care Policy and Research suggest the system has not always reduced costs per admission. Some health-care providers responded to prospective payment's capped payments based on diagnoses by providing more intense clinical services, such as more lab tests, in an effort to quickly stabilize patients. Hospitals also tended to shift some patients to special psychiatric units that were not under such strict cost restrictions but typically required longer patient stays. A 1998 Harvard University Medical School study of the provision of mental-health services concluded that an increased focus on an elderly patient's mental health should not come at the expense of general medical and surgical care, because the problems can come hand in hand.

Q

Qualified Medicare beneficiary

A qualified Medicare beneficiary, or QMB, is a MEDICARE recipient whose income and assets fall below federal poverty thresholds but are still too high for the person to qualify for MEDICAID. These individuals, sometimes referred to as "quimbees," could fall into a no-man's-land vis-à-vis entitlement payments and face potential hardships, because Medicare requires recipients to pay some cost-sharing for Part A acute health-care services, as well as monthly premiums for enrollment in Part B. Most of the time, these individuals have not purchased supplemental protection in the form of a MEDIGAP policy. To address this group, Congress in 1988 created the Qualified Medicare Beneficiary Program as part of the MEDICARE CATASTROPHIC COVERAGE ACT (PL 100-360), which has the federal-state Medicaid program pay the Medicare DEDUCTIBLES, copayments, and premiums.

Participation in the program has lagged behind expectations—only about three-fourths of those eligible are currently enrolled—in part because many low-income elderly and disabled "DUAL ELIGIBLES" are not aware the options exist. QMBs have been the subject of renewed focus since passage of the BALANCED BUDGET ACT OF 1997 (PL 105-33) because the law allowed states to pay health-care providers at Medicaid rates, instead of the higher Medicare rates. Although providers are prohibited from passing the differ-ence on to patients, some advocates for the poor believe health-care providers may stop serving people in the QMB program because there is little economic incentive, much as many providers have refused to see Medicaid patients.

Quality assurance

Quality assurance is an oft-discussed concept in elder care, especially pertaining to LONG-TERM CARE in NURSING HOMES. Sociologists and gerontologists such as Robert Applebaum of Miami University of Ohio have argued that governments and health-care providers must take steps to measure the quality of long-term care from the patient's perspective, instead of defining quality in terms of standardized health and safety measurements. However, states and federal regulators have been slow to endorse new forms of testing client services, including random tests of whether a particular treatment is working.

The focus on quality assurance can be directly traced to the sweeping set of nursing home reforms included in the 1987 Omnibus Budget Reconciliation Act (PL 100-203; see OMNIBUS BUDGET RECONCILIATION BILLS). Prior to the act's passage, nursing home quality measurements were highly randomized, and usually consisted of teams of inspectors spending several days in a facility without interviewing clients. Emphasis was placed on meeting minimum safety measures and on basic performance measurements, such as whether a patient with anxiety, for instance, was receiving a recommended drug. The act mandated that nursing homes ensure that residents must meet "maximum practicable functioning" standards, requiring health-care providers to take steps such as measuring the rate of decline or improvement in individual patients. The rising costs of long-term care have since prompted more thorough examinations, including studies of whether clients with specific conditions respond better in home-health environments. Quality assurance will continue to be a focus for state administrators of MEDICAID as they will have to contend with tight budgets and an expected rise in the need for long-term care.

R

Railroad retirement program

The railroad retirement program is unique for being the only PRIVATE PENSION system administered by the federal government. Run by the Chicago-based federal Railroad Retirement Board, the program hands out approximately $8 billion in retirement and survivor benefits annually to more than 700,000 annuitants, in addition to providing compensation to unemployed workers and disability benefits. The program delivers two tiers of benefits: Tier 1 is based on SOCIAL SECURITY benefits and delivers approximately the same amount a worker would have received had his or her employment been covered by the Social Security program. Tier 2 benefits are based entirely on a worker's employment in the railroad industry; the size of the benefit is calculated through a formula that takes into account the employee's average monthly earnings in the sixty months of highest earnings. Benefits are indexed annually to account for inflation.

The roots of the railroad retirement program extend to the late nineteenth century, when railroads were among the largest industrial employers and some of the first to offer pension plans. By the 1930s, though, many plans were in financial distress, usually because they were underfunded, or because the sponsoring companies were suffering from the effects of the Great Depression. Many railroads terminated their pension plans without having to account to regulators. The gen-

eral chaos, combined with a desire to clear the labor market of a surplus of elderly railroad workers, led Congress to enact the 1937 Railroad Retirement Act, which established a plan to provide annuities to retirees that was financed by a payroll tax imposed on both employers and workers. In 1951, Congress brought the pension plan into conformity with Social Security by establishing a financial swap, in which the plan transferred to Social Security an amount equal to what Social Security would have collected in payroll taxes if railroad workers were covered by the federal program. In return, Social Security transferred to the private system an amount equal to all of the benefits due to retired workers, their spouses and survivors, had the workers been covered by Social Security. Some government observers later concluded the railroad system was shortchanged, because it transferred an amount equal to Social Security benefits paid to railroad workers who had other jobs that qualified them for Social Security BENEFITS, without receiving a corresponding higher amount from the Social Security system.

Downsizing in the railroad industry, nationwide inflation, and an increase in the number of beneficiaries put new and dramatic financial stresses on the railroad retirement program in the 1970s. In response, Congress reorganized the program by passing the Railroad Retirement Act of 1974 (PL 93-445), which set up the present two-tiered system. The practice of paying dual benefits for both Social Security and railroad retirement was phased out after 1974, except for some individuals with twenty-five or more years of service. Congress has made important changes to the system since then. The Railroad Retirement Solvency Act of 1983 (PL 98-76) increased payroll taxes and deferred cost-of-living increases to alleviate further stresses on the system. The Omnibus Budget Reconciliation Act of 1987 (PL 100-203; see OMNIBUS BUDGET RECONCILIATION BILLS) increased payroll tax rates for Tier 2 benefits. While the industry's financial condition has brightened somewhat, employment continues to decline, meaning lawmakers may be forced to make more adjustments. Railroad companies and unions representing workers regularly discuss and negotiate each side's share of payroll taxes and benefit rates. Congress regularly reviews the agreements and can step in when necessary to decide if the amounts are adequate.

Rand

This Santa Monica, California–based nonprofit THINK TANK, sometimes called Rand Corporation, evolved out of World War II research at Douglas Aircraft Company and became independent in May 1948. In its early years it dealt with a Cold War–era blending of military planning with research and development. Gradually, its mission was enlarged to include social policy planning, including aging-related issues. In recent years, Rand has studied subjects such as the economic costs of poor health, available resources for the elderly, and aging in developing countries. Rand studies have quantified how SOCIAL SECURITY is the single biggest source of assets in low-income retirees' households. Rand also has studied how nations that lack a social security system, such as Malaysia, can develop family-based support systems for the elderly.

Rationing of health care

As the financial strains on the nation's health-care system became more widely discussed in the 1970s and 1980s, a number of politicians and commentators began advancing the controversial notion that lifesaving medical resources ought to be rationed on the basis of age, though exactly what age remained a point of debate. Noted medical ethicist Daniel Callahan of the Hastings Center, in his 1987 book *Setting Limits: Medical Goals in an Aging Society,* argued that such procedures as artificial resuscitation and mechanical ventilation should be withheld from the very old, in order to curb runaway medical inflation. Similar policies were advocated by former Colorado Democratic governor Richard D. Lamm, a 1996 Reform Party presidential candidate, who ignited a firestorm of controversy in the 1980s, when he first suggested that all Americans have a "duty to die," in order to more evenly distribute medical resources across society.

Proponents of health-care rationing frequently argue that limiting the expensive medical interventions that are available to individuals who have lived seventy or eighty years will deliver more benefits to the largest number of people. They point to statistics showing that elderly people consume a disproportionate share of the nation's health-care bill and cite examples in which expensive treatments for terminal diseases—such as certain forms of CANCER—deliver few real benefits for patients or society, and may

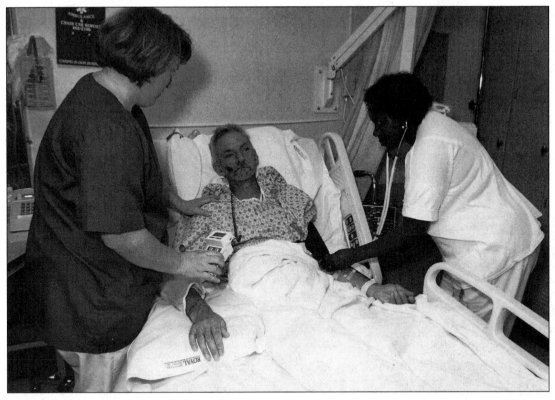

As the financial strains on the nation's health-care system became more widely discussed in the past three decades, a number of politicians and commentators began advancing the notion that lifesaving medical resources ought to be rationed on the basis of age. Source: ©1998 Earl Dotter, Impact Visuals/American Nurses Association

only prolong unnecessary suffering. Moreover, advocates note that the development of new medical technologies has made it more difficult than ever to assess what an ailing elderly person's true health-care needs are, because it is increasingly possible to extend a person's life span for many years with new drugs and cutting-edge therapies.

Such arguments have aroused intense debate among physicians, ethicists, and sociologists. Opponents in the medical community have argued that age is a superficial criteria, because it often does not yield clues about how a person will respond to a treatment, or how well he or she will live after discharge from a hospital or clinic. Instead, physicians tend to judge each case for its therapeutic value, and many high-tech procedures have proved very successful with older patients. Policy analysts additionally argue that the current political system, with its emphasis on fiscal responsibility, does not ensure that any money saved from withholding treatments for the elderly will be transferred for the medical needs of the younger population.

Many social scientists criticize rationing proposals because they contend the theories promote INTERGENERATIONAL WARFARE and set a danger-

Former president Ronald Reagan and his wife, Nancy, share a kiss at a recent birthday party. Reagan's battle with Alzheimer's disease brought a new public awareness of the condition. Source: Office of Ronald Reagan

ous precedent by forcing society to decide what is a sufficient natural LIFE SPAN. Sociologist Amitai Etzioni has argued it is almost pointless to try to define when a person is "old," in light of advancing medical technologies. Additionally, Etzioni argues that the concept of withholding medical interventions that do not deliver tangible benefits puts society on a "slippery slope," because it also could apply to psychotherapy, cosmetic surgery, and other services that frequently are used by younger generations. Opponents also note it is not unusual for some governmental policies to favor certain age groups, noting federal education spending tends to favor children over adults. In that context, they argue, it is not inappropriate to spend more on the elderly's health-care needs, so long as everyone gets equal access to the same treatments. While calls for health-care rationing subsided during the economic boom of the 1990s, they are likely to return to the political arena if the economy slows and budget deficits force politicians to make difficult decisions about the nation's health-care needs.

Reagan, Ronald

Ronald Reagan (born 1911), the fortieth president of the United States, is closely associated with aging politics and policies in a number of ways. The oldest man ever to serve as president by the time he left office in 1988, Reagan dashed some preconceived notions about the elderly by surviving an assassination attempt in 1981 and undergoing successful surgery for colon CANCER in 1985. His administration's policies on SOCIAL SECURITY also illustrated the high-voltage politics surrounding the national pension system.

Faced with bulging budget deficits, and intent on achieving a fiscal surplus by the mid-1980s, Reagan in 1981 proposed cutting Social Security BENEFITS by more than $40 billion over five years. Reagan's plan called for cutting EARLY RETIREMENT benefits and making a 50 percent reduction in COST-OF-LIVING ADJUSTMENTS. The proposal was quickly attacked by congressional Democrats and the seniors lobby and, within one week, rejected by the U.S. Senate by a vote of 92–0. In order to find a long-lasting solution to Social Security's financial problems, Reagan, with the help of House and Senate leaders, later appointed the bipartisan GREENSPAN COMMISSION, which crafted the last significant reforms made to the system. Reagan never could shake the image that he was against Social Security, however, and was hammered on the issue by Democratic presidential candidate Walter Mondale in the 1984 presidential elections. It was not until GOP nominee George W. Bush proposed a PRIVATIZATION plan for Social Security in the 2000 elections that Republicans again dared to touch the issue in a national election.

Reagan in his later years became associated with another, far different aspect of aging—ALZHEIMER'S DISEASE. His public disclosure that he had the condition, in a poignant 1994 letter, brought new awareness of a condition that affects an estimated four million Americans, but the origins of which are still little understood. (See page 12.) In 1995, Reagan and his wife, Nancy, announced they were joining forces with the ALZHEIMER'S ASSOCIATION to form the Ronald and Nancy Reagan Research Institute, which provides grants for Alzheimer's research and fosters cooperation among scientists, drug companies, medical centers, and private foundations.

Recognition bond

A recognition bond is a component of proposals advanced by political conservatives to privatize SOCIAL SECURITY. The bond would act as a refund for those workers who pay payroll taxes for many years under the traditional system, but opt out when Social Security becomes privatized. The size of the refund would be determined by calculating taxes paid and anticipated lifetime benefits. Some proposals would pay the refund in government bonds that could be deposited into personal retirement accounts. The bonds would accumulate interest, but account holders could cash a portion each year to augment their retirement BENEFITS. Recognition bonds were a component of the CHILEAN PENSION SYSTEM and also have been tried in Peru and Colombia. (See also PRIVATIZATION.)

Registered nurse

A registered nurse is a health-care professional who has completed three years of nursing school or graduated college with a degree in nursing, and has passed a state licensing test. These individuals increasingly are used to provide everyday care in NURSING HOMES, ASSISTED-LIVING FACILITIES, and other settings for elder care. Registered nurses can take blood samples, inject medications, and administer fluids intravenously. Some registered nurses also have specialized training in REHABILITATION to deal with patients who have suffered STROKES or heart attacks. Registered nurses are more specialized than licensed practical nurses, who usually work under the direction of doctors and do more routine tasks, such as changing bandages and checking blood pressure.

Rehabilitation

Rehabilitation services are vital for elderly patients recovering from injuries such as hip frac-

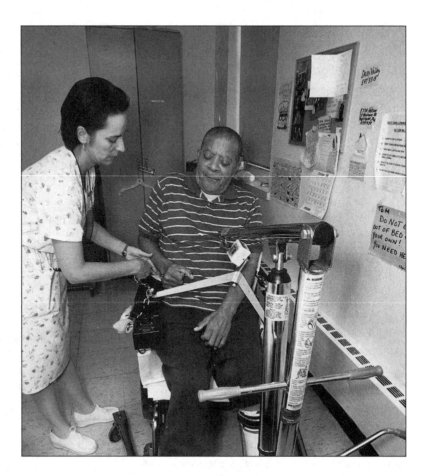

Medicare tends to subject rehabilitation care, such as for the broken foot of this elderly patient, to restrictions tied to an individual's "spell of illness." Source: ©1998 Earl Dotter, Impact Visuals/American Nurses Association

tures, surgery, or illness such as STROKE or heart failure. MEDICARE beneficiaries tend to receive rehabilitation in inpatient rehabilitation hospitals or in SKILLED NURSING FACILITIES (SNFs) or NURSING HOMES. But because Medicare is oriented toward acute care and never was designed to provide ongoing care, the health system pays grudgingly for rehabilitation, and long-term rehabilitation services can be hard to come by. Stroke victims, once stabilized, may be left to their own devices to find occupational, cognitive, or communications therapy that could make the difference between dependency and the ability to function freely. The problem is compounded by

soaring health-care costs—institutionalized care can cost in excess of $60,000 per year, and HOME HEALTH CARE more than $100 per day. MEDICAID is only available if beneficiaries exhaust their personal savings and fall below poverty levels.

Medicare tends to subject rehabilitation care to restrictions tied to an individual's "spell of illness." The program's skilled nursing facility BENEFIT, financed under Part A, will provide rehabilitation services if a person has been an inpatient for at least three consecutive days and was then transferred to an SNF within thirty days of hospital discharge. The beneficiary is entitled to one hundred days of SNF care per spell of illness, with days twenty-one to one hundred subject to a co-insurance charge equal to a percentage of the hospital DEDUCTIBLE. Because SNF costs are among the fastest-growing in the Medicare program, Congress, through the BALANCED BUDGET ACT OF 1997, implemented a PROSPECTIVE PAYMENT SYSTEM to control costs. The home health benefit, covered under both Part A and B, also offers rehabilitation services, subject to similar cost controls.

Health-care experts believe some of the problems associated with rehabilitation can be addressed through improved case management. The HEALTH CARE FINANCING ADMINISTRATION has commissioned studies to determine whether certain patients fare better in rehabilitation hospitals or SNFs, which tend to be favored by HMOs. A 1998 University of Colorado Health Sciences Center study of 1,055 elderly patients—with a variety of ailments and in need of rehabilitation—found insurers and health-care providers do not have enough information to help decide the optimal intensity of rehabilitation services in many cases. The researchers, in general, found stroke patients treated in rehabilitation hospitals tended to recover more function and were less likely to become incapacitated and be placed in nursing homes. However, the study found outcomes for hip fractures were comparable in SNFs and rehabilitation hospitals.

Respite care

Respite care is the practice of providing periodic relief to the CAREGIVERS of frail elderly people. Though not universally available, respite care has received increased attention in debates over LONG-TERM CARE, particularly due to ac-counts of the hardships faced by family caregivers of individuals with ALZHEIMER'S DISEASE and other debilitating conditions. A number of novel arrangements have sprung up to help these individuals, including providing care for the loved one in the individual's home, arranging temporary lodging for caregivers together with the patient in ASSISTED LIVING FACILITIES or NURSING HOMES, or having groups of family caregivers pool their resources to provide voluntary services and help "spell" individuals.

Respite care is not covered as a regular BENEFIT by MEDICAID, because it is not classed as a medical expense. However, states can obtain Medicaid waivers to use federal Medicaid money for respite services. Generally, it is only provided on an occasional basis and cannot be reimbursed for more than five days at a time. One common way states provide respite care is by obtaining "1115 waivers" that allow states to implement managed-care delivery systems or take other flexible approaches to providing services outside of standard Medicaid policies. MEDICARE covers respite care only as part of its HOSPICE benefit for the terminally ill. The MEDICARE CATASTROPHIC COVERAGE ACT of 1988 (PL 100-360) included a more general Medicare respite care benefit that authorized up to eighty hours per year for unpaid family members or friends who cared for "chronically dependent" Medicare beneficiaries. However, the act and the respite care benefit were repealed in 1989, before they ever took effect.

Retirement Equity Act of 1984

The Retirement Equity Act of 1984 (PL 98-397) was an election-year piece of legislation designed to address problems women experienced collecting retirement benefits from PRIVATE PENSION plans. The law expanded coverage for workers who left the labor force for less than five years, then returned to their jobs, and strengthened the pension rights of widows whose working spouses died before they reached NORMAL RETIREMENT AGE. The Retirement Equity Act was part of a broader package of legislation designed to address economic bias against women. Though the law technically applies to both men and women, it clearly was an attempt to lower barriers for women who interrupted their careers to have children or for homemakers who depended on their husbands' pensions. Both then-president RONALD REAGAN and Congress hoped to score political points with passage of the act at a time when Democratic vice presidential nominee Geraldine A. Ferraro of New York was making economic bias a campaign issue.

The act made a series of changes to the EMPLOYEE RETIREMENT INCOME SECURITY ACT OF 1974 (ERISA) (PL 93-406) and the Internal Revenue Code. Lawmakers addressed many private plans' practice of requiring a ten-year "vesting" period before workers could participate. The statutory changes allowed employees to leave and return to their jobs without giving up pension credits earned, except if the break in service was for more than five years, or longer than the period the person worked before leaving the job, whichever was greater. The law also prohibited plans from counting one-year maternity or paternity leaves as a break in service. The law additionally required plans to provide survivor benefits to spouses of workers who died after being vested, regardless of their age when they died. This reversed a provision in the law that allowed plans to deny benefits if workers died young. Another provision required spouses' consent if workers chose to give up joint and survivor pension benefits, changing language in the law that allowed workers to decline such coverage without their spouse's knowledge. The law also allowed state courts to divide pension benefits in divorce cases.

Reverse mortgage

The reverse mortgage is an increasingly popular type of lending instrument that allows elderly people who are short on cash to borrow on the equity in their homes while they still live in them. The mortgage behaves like a home-equity loan with one important difference: the borrowed amount does not have to be repaid until the borrower moves out of the house or sells it. Then, proceeds from the sale are used to pay off the lender. The remainder goes to the homeowner or his or her survivors. If there is a shortfall, the U.S. Department of Housing and Urban Development (HUD) pays the difference.

Reverse mortgages have proven popular with older people who are "house-rich but cash-poor," especially elderly women living alone. A 2000 HUD study found the median age of those using reverse mortgages was seventy-five, three years older than the average elderly American homeowner. Typically, individuals who qualify have lived in their homes for many years and are too wealthy to qualify for government aid but not rich enough to pay for various senior-housing alternatives. Though HUD has closed nearly forty thousand of the loans since the early 1990s, it is not the only federal entity offering the products. A Fannie Mae product called the "HomeKeeper" has a higher loan limit.

While the first reverse mortgages were offered

by private banks in the 1960s, a federal program did not get established until 1991, when HUD published regulations making reverse mortgages available to Federal Housing Administration-approved lenders. The program is open to homeowners aged sixty-two and older who have paid off their mortgages or only have a small balance outstanding. Homeowners can receive the amount they borrow all at once or in increments, and there is no income limitations on who can borrow. Borrowers must pay a premium of 2 percent of the home's value up front, plus one-half of a percent on the loan balance annually. Because most applicants lack the cash for the up-front payment, the lender usually pays the amount and adds it to the homeowners' outstanding balance. The size of the mortgage depends on the applicant's age, the home's value, and prevailing interest rates. But the amount that can be borrowed depends on Federal Housing Administration mortgage caps for a particular area, which are based on local housing costs and cannot exceed $155,250. For this reason, owners of very expensive homes cannot borrow more than people who own residences that are valued at the limit.

Though reverse mortgages are praised as innovative, advocates of the elderly warn they do not work for everyone. Because the mortgages usually exhaust most or all of a homeowner's equity, there may be little left for heirs. Elderly people considering reverse mortgages may also be eligible for other government aid they are not collecting, such as SUPPLEMENTAL SECURITY INCOME. Other affordable housing options may also be available in the area. Individuals can obtain more information about reverse mortgages from the National Center for Home Equity Conversion in Madison, Wisconsin, created in 1981 to discuss the merits, and potential pitfalls, of the products.

Robert Wood Johnson Foundation

The Robert Wood Johnson Foundation, a philanthropic foundation based in Princeton, New Jersey, is the largest organization of its kind in the United States devoted exclusively to health and health care. Since its establishment in 1972, it has awarded more than $2 billion in grants for research aimed at providing basic health care to all segments of society, improving care for people with chronic conditions, and reducing substance abuse. It is named for the industrialist who built the Johnson and Johnson pharmaceutical empire and lobbied throughout the second third of the twentieth century for an ambitious social agenda that stressed corporate responsibility to workers and the community. When Johnson died, in 1968, he left nearly his entire fortune of more than $1 billion to the foundation in the hope of furthering some of his goals.

The foundation is noted in aging circles for its involvement in end-of-life issues. A ten-year study on how Americans die called SUPPORT, for Study to Understand Prognosis and Preferences for Outcomes and Risks of Treatment, was among the first to question society's discomfort with the notion of death and to ask whether measures to ease pain and suffering might be preferable to aggressive medical treatments that may prolong some patients' suffering. The study continues to examine topics such as the care of dying patients in managed-care settings, and whether hospitals can measure the quality of care they provide patients at the end of their lives. Other foundation-supported research has studied how well home- and COMMUNITY-BASED SERVICES tend to the needs of the chronically disabled. Another program supported by the foundation developed

ADULT DAY CARE programs in thirty-one states for individuals with ALZHEIMER'S DISEASE or other mental illnesses.

Roosevelt, Franklin D.

Franklin Delano Roosevelt (1882–1945), the thirty-second president of the United States, regarded the creation of the SOCIAL SECURITY system as the cornerstone of his presidency and a means to shelter the elderly from poverty while allowing them to maintain their dignity. But to create the program, Roosevelt had to overcome the Jeffersonian philosophy of self-reliance and minimal government that prevailed in the United States during the first decades of the twentieth century, as well as fierce opposition from political conservatives and some in his own Democratic party. Roosevelt's victory was in part due to the effects of the Great Depression, which wiped out seniors' savings in bank collapses and ravaged industrial and trade unions' pension plans.

Roosevelt set out designing the system by convening the Cabinet-level Committee on Economic Security in 1934. A hands-on president, Roosevelt insisted that authorizing language in the SOCIAL SECURITY ACT ensure that the system be financed by a dedicated stream of revenues from payroll taxes (2 percent shared equally by workers and employers on the first $3,000 of wages) instead of relying on general revenues. In selling the controversial payroll tax, Roosevelt shrewdly depicted the system as an insurance program financed out of "premiums" workers paid for coverage in their old age. In reality, there were no individual accounts where workers' contributions were stored for their own retirement. Instead, So-

The Franklin Delano Roosevelt Memorial in Washington, D.C., depicts the thirty-second president in his wheelchair. Roosevelt regarded the creation of the Social Security System as the cornerstone of his presidency.
Source: Scott J. Ferrell, Congressional Quarterly

cial Security was a PAY-AS-YOU-GO SYSTEM in which the existing workforce subsidized the benefits of current retirees. Asked about the discrepancy by an aide, Roosevelt responded, "That account is there so those sons of bitches up on the Hill [Congress] can't ever abandon this system after I'm gone."

Once the program won approval from Congress, Roosevelt designated his labor secretary,

Frances Perkins, to run the system with an independent three-member Social Security Board. The system quickly became an issue in the 1936 presidential campaign, with Republican nominee Alfred M. Landon criticizing it as unworkable and financially wasteful. Responding to continuing criticism about Social Security's scope and purpose, Roosevelt in 1939 made changes, reducing the amount of money in the program's reserve funds and expanding benefits for dependents and survivors of deceased workers.

Former Social Security Commissioner Robert Ball, a staunch defender of the system, has noted that Social Security was exceptional: Roosevelt created many experimental and temporary programs—the Works Progress Administration and National Recovery Administration, to name two—to address the crisis of the Depression, many of which disappeared with the emergency that prompted them, while Social Security endured, a permanent institution capable of making life more secure for future generations.

Roth IRA

The Roth IRA—named for its primary sponsor, then Senate Finance Committee chairman William V. Roth, R-Del.—was created as part of the 1997 Taxpayer Relief Act (PL 105-34) as a "backloaded" INDIVIDUAL RETIREMENT ACCOUNT. Investors can stash up to $2,000 per year in the investment vehicles, as with conventional IRAs, but cannot deduct the amount on their income tax forms. While the contribution is taxed as income at current rates before it is deposited into the account, both the interest and principal can be withdrawn tax-free if the account has been open for five years and the account holder is at least 59-1/2 years old. Withdrawals can be made even sooner for certain situations, such as if the money is being used for higher-education expenses or for the first-time purchase of a home. Withdrawals prior to age 59-1/2 otherwise are subject to a 10 percent early-withdrawal penalty. Unlike traditional IRAs, which require their owners to begin withdrawing money at age 70-1/2, the Roth IRA has no mandatory withdrawal age.

The advantages of a Roth IRA are twofold. The investments behave like a tax-free bond, with no taxes imposed on earnings. They also "lock in" one's current tax rate, making them popular with elderly individuals who worry that their tax bill in retirement will be significant, perhaps even larger than it was when they were working. Roth IRAs can provide a convenient way of sheltering extra money for one's heirs without paying estate or inheritance taxes. However, because of these tax advantages, only individuals with adjusted gross incomes of less than $110,000, or couples with incomes of less than $160,000, can open an account.

Roth IRAs proved popular with investors of all ages in the year after they were first made available. Since then, interest in the products has slipped somewhat, due to investor reluctance to pay taxes up front and the products' sometimes confusing eligibility rules. As a result, the extra tax revenues Congress hoped the products would generate did not immediately materialize. Some of the confusion surrounding Roth IRAs centers on "conversions" of conventional IRAs into the newer products. Individuals with traditional IRAs can roll over the investments into a Roth IRA, but have to treat the rolled-over amount as adjusted gross income. This could effectively bump some account holders into higher tax brackets. To ad-

The Roth IRA, named for its primary sponsor, William V. Roth, was created as part of the 1997 Taxpayer Relief Act as a "backloaded" individual retirement account. Source: *Scott J. Ferrell, Congressional Quarterly*

dress those concerns, Congress allowed converters to extend their tax payments out over four years. Individuals who convert, then decide to "recharacterize" their investments as traditional IRAs could be subject to penalties and restrictions, depending on when the transactions take place.

Congress has made further attempts to boost interest in Roth IRAs, either by spreading out the allowable time for conversions or by raising contribution limits. In 2000, Congress considered a proposal to increase the annual allowable limit for both traditional IRAs and Roth IRAs from $2,000 to $5,000—a move that was estimated to cost the U.S. Treasury $18 billion over five years. The proposal also would have increased the annual limit each year to account for inflation. The proposal died in end-of-session wrangling. Some investment executives and IRA holders believe Congress may eventually change its position on Roth IRAs and lift their tax-exempt status, especially if the economy slows and budget deficits reemerge.

However, no such proposals have been made to date, and such moves would likely be opposed by middle-class voters and BABY BOOMERS nearing retirement who now have 401(K) PLANS, Roth IRAs, and other savings products.

Though supporters of Roth IRAs suggest the products' tax incentives help boost savings, conventional economic analysis is more ambiguous. Some economists believe the Roth IRAs higher rate of return will allow individuals to actually save less and still reap significant investment income. Moreover, some believe the money invested in Roth IRAs comes from other investments or assets. Yet supporters cite empirical evidence that the products spur savings, arguing that investors realize the initial tax is offset by reduced future tax liability. Whoever is right, most experts suggest that individuals should consult with an accountant before opening an account, to ensure that the products fit their personal circumstances.

S

"Sandwich generation"

The informal term "sandwich generation" refers to middle-aged Americans who serve as unpaid CAREGIVERS to older parents or relatives while simultaneously taking care of their own children and frequently having to tend to their careers. The twofold obligation has received the attention of politicians, who in recent years have proposed relief in the form of tax breaks or subsidies to help defray the costs of some LONG-TERM CARE. One approach that has been suggested is modifying rules for MEDICAID, the federal-state program that is the largest payer for long-term care, to expand coverage for home- and COMMUNITY-BASED SERVICES.

The sandwich generation was targeted by Democrats in the months preceding the 2000 presidential elections. President Bill Clinton proposed a $1,000 annual tax credit for family caregivers with long-term care needs, and also called for distributing $625 million to local agencies on aging to set up information and referral services. Democratic candidate Al Gore also proposed a more ambitious $30 billion, ten-year program, consisting of tax credits, Medicaid coverage, and other assistance for family caregivers. Republicans and Democrats in the 106th Congress fashioned several alternative approaches, such as giving individuals and families in need of long-term care government subsidies to help purchase private long-term care insurance.

Savings Incentive Match Plan for Employees (SIMPLE)

This retirement vehicle, authorized by the Small Business Job Protection Act of 1996 (PL 104-188), is a scaled-down version of a DEFINED-CONTRIBUTION PLAN for employers who have fewer than one hundred workers and do not already sponsor another retirement plan, such as a 401(K). The plans allow workers to defer up to $6,000 of pre-tax income into an INDIVIDUAL RETIREMENT ACCOUNT (IRA). Employers can choose to match dollar-for-dollar workers' contributions up to 3 percent of a worker's wages, or can opt to contribute up to 2 percent of an employee's compensation into his or her IRA. The plans work particularly well for sole proprietorships, partnerships, tax-exempt organizations, and governmental entities.

One advantage of a SIMPLE plan is that all of the contributions of the worker and employer are immediately vested. However, the worker has to keep the money in a SIMPLE IRA for at least two years or face a 25 percent tax penalty. As with other IRAs, earnings on SIMPLE plans accumulate tax-free until they are withdrawn. There usually is a 10 percent tax penalty if funds are withdrawn before age 59-1/2. The plans tend to be less flexible for workers than 401(k)'s. Employer-sponsors also cannot control the timing of workers' investments or withdrawals.

Section 202 Supportive Housing for the Elderly

Section 202 Supportive Housing for the Elderly, named for and originally authorized by Section 202 of the Housing Act of 1959, is the federal government's primary means of building subsidized rental housing units for elderly people. Since its inception, it has funded construction of more than 260,000 units nationwide—most sponsored by community-based or religious organizations. Since 1992, organizations that provide housing under the program also must provide supportive services for tenants, such as meals, housekeeping, personal care, and transportation.

The Section 202 program has become a focus of policymakers because of the inadequate supply of subsidized housing for older people. One U.S. Department of Housing and Urban Development (HUD) study in 1999 estimated there are more than 1.2 million households headed by an older individual who have "worst-case" housing needs and do not receive federal housing aid. However, policymakers in recent years have opted to use vouchers, instead of new construction, to satisfy the unmet need. The vouchers make up the difference between fair-market rent and a percentage of the qualified tenant's household income and are intended to allow the tenant to compete for units in the unsubsidized housing market, assuming there are a sufficient number of units. For this reason, federal funding for the Section 202 program has dropped off; while the number of newly constructed units hovered around 7,000 per year during the mid-1990s, they fell to an estimated 1,500 per year in fiscal 1999, according to AARP and the American Association of Homes and Services for the Aging.

Significant controversy also surrounds the way landlords can remove their properties from the program and take advantage of the current real estate boom by seeking higher rents on the open market. From 1995 to 1998, nearly 100,000 housing units for low-income elderly people have been lost in this way because property owners either do not renew their contracts when they come due, prepay mortgages to get out of the program, or exercise the option to drop out after twenty years. This has forced thousands of elders in the Section 202 program to move to cheaper communities if their buildings or housing complexes get privatized. Advocates for the poor and senior citizen groups have pressured Congress to respond, noting that by 2004, Department of Housing and Urban Development contracts for one million units of housing are due to expire. But lawmakers have found it difficult to raise subsidies to the level where they approximate market rates and still comply with congressionally mandated spending caps. The matter remains a top priority for senior citizen groups and advocates of the poor.

Eligibility for the Section 202 program is restricted to individuals aged sixty-two and older with incomes that are less than half of the median income of the area in which they live. Studies by the U.S. SENATE SPECIAL COMMITTEE ON AGING have found the typical resident is a frail, elderly woman, living alone, whose income is less than $10,000 per year. Some studies have shown there are more than eight eligible older persons on waiting list for every Section 202 unit.

Until fiscal 1991, the Section 202 program provided subsidies in the form of direct loans that covered all the costs of developing the units. The government provided Section 8 rental assistance (named from Section 8 of U.S. Housing Act of 1937) to residents, and debt service on the federal

Senate Appropriations rankings member Robert Byrd, left, and chairman Ted Stevens, right, confer before markup with colleague Patrick Leahy, center. The committee controls the discretionary spending portion of the federal budget, including small portions of Medicare.
Source: Scott J. Ferrell, Congressional Quarterly

loans were paid using the Section 8 subsidies and with extra rent paid by tenants. The system has been overhauled and now pays capital advances to developers that do not have to be repaid. Rental assistance no longer has to be used to cover debt service and is provided through twenty-year contracts between HUD and project owners. The tenants' portion of rent payments is 30 percent of their income, or the shelter rent payment determined by welfare assistance. HUD currently is exploring using Section 202 money to convert existing rental units into ASSISTED-LIVING facilities to better meet the elderly's needs.

Senate Appropriations Committee

The Senate Appropriations Committee is a powerful congressional panel that controls the discretionary spending portion of the federal budget; it consists of thirteen subcommittees that write annual spending bills. SOCIAL SECURITY, MEDICARE, and MEDICAID are generally out of the committee's purview, because they are ENTITLE-

MENT PROGRAMS that are funded according to estimates of how much they will cost. However, the appropriations panel does have some control over small portions of Medicare, such as how much to spend on Medicare contractors that process claims for the health-care program. Policy changes to any of the big three entitlement programs are initiated by authorizing committees, not the appropriators.

The appropriations panel still exerts significant control over the government's aging-related programs. The Labor, Health and Human Services, and Education spending bill funds the HEALTH AND HUMAN SERVICES DEPARTMENT and the programs that come under the OLDER AMERICANS ACT and its amendments. The Labor-HHS appropriations bill also contains funding for the NATIONAL INSTITUTES OF HEALTH and its biomedical research activities aimed at aging-related diseases. The VA-HUD spending bill (the Veterans Affairs, Housing and Urban Development, and Independent Agencies bill) funds various elderly housing programs, as well as Veterans Affairs health care.

Other spending bills of note include the Commerce, Justice, State, and Judiciary bill, which funds U.S. Department of Justice programs to protect the elderly from CRIME, and the Treasury, Postal Service, and General Government bill, which provides health insurance for elderly federal government workers. The Senate Appropriations Committee traditionally took up these bills after the HOUSE APPROPRIATIONS COMMITTEE finished its drafts of each spending plan, in a ceremonial bow to the lower chamber of Congress. However, in recent years the Senate panel has begun work on some bills ahead of the House, and it now is not uncommon to have both appropriations committees working on the same bill simultaneously. Differences in the two versions are ironed out in a House-Senate conference once the bills are debated, amended and passed by their respective chambers.

Senate Finance Committee

This committee has some of the most far-reaching jurisdiction of any congressional panel, holding authority over all programs in the SOCIAL SECURITY ACT, including MEDICARE and MEDICAID. The committee also writes the federal tax rules affecting pensions and other savings instruments. Under former chairman William V. Roth, R-Del., it developed the ROTH IRA and crafted regulations for conventional IRAS, 401(K) PLANS, and pension portability. It also took up a proposed PRESCRIPTION DRUG BENEFIT for the Medicare program. In 1999, the panel began a comprehensive review of the Medicare program that took up such issues as financing the MEDICARE+CHOICE program, the operations of the HEALTH CARE FI-

NANCING ADMINISTRATION, and government opportunities to support Medicare modernization.

The panel is one of the most closely divided between Republicans and Democrats (in the 106th Congress, the split was eleven Republicans to nine Democrats), meaning it has to work in a more bipartisan fashion than some congressional committees. Because just one defector could produce a tie vote, the bills the committee does report out tend to be carefully crafted and carry enormous influence in both the Senate and House. While the Finance Committee's work and turf resemble the HOUSE WAYS AND MEANS COMMITTEE in some ways, the House panel has to share oversight of health issues with the HOUSE COMMERCE COMMITTEE, while Senate Finance has unquestioned authority over the health-care portfolio.

Senate Health, Education, Labor, and Pensions Committee

The Senate Health, Education, Labor, and Pensions Committee, sometimes referred to by its acronym HELP, was formerly known as the Labor and Human Resources Committee prior to the 106th Congress. It has jurisdiction over most of the programs run by the U.S. Department of HEALTH AND HUMAN SERVICES, except MEDICARE and MEDICAID, and has direct oversight over the programs that come under the OLDER AMERICANS ACT. In the summer of 2000, the panel tried to break years of gridlock surrounding the act by passing legislation that would reauthorize the act for the first time since it expired at the end of fiscal 1995.

The panel also oversees biomedical research at the NATIONAL INSTITUTES OF HEALTH, the activi-

GOP staff director Mark Powden consults with Senate Health, Education, Labor, and Pensions chairman James M. Jeffords, center, while ranking Democrat Edward M. Kennedy consults with staff in the background. HELP has jurisdiction over most of the programs run by Health and Human Services, except Medicare and Medicaid, and has direct oversight over the programs that come under the Older Americans Act. Source: Scott J. Ferrell, Congressional Quarterly

ties of the Food and Drug Administration, labor standards, disability laws, PRIVATE PENSION plans and the RAILROAD RETIREMENT PROGRAM. It has amended the EMPLOYEE RETIREMENT INCOME SECURITY ACT OF 1974 (ERISA) (PL 93-406) to address such issues as the treatment of consumers in managed-care and other health plans. The panel has a reputation for being more politically liberal than the Senate as a whole, evidenced in the 106th Congress by its chairman, James M. Jeffords, R-Vt., who has compiled one of the more liberal voting records among GOP lawmakers.

Senate Special Committee on Aging

This twenty-member congressional panel was established as a temporary committee in 1961 and granted permanent status in 1977 to explore the myriad health, societal, and policy issues surrounding aging. Because special committees cannot draft bills or have other legislative authority, it mainly functions as a platform for members to air

their views or draw attention to special concerns. That is not to say that the committee does not have influence; a series of hearings chaired by then-chairman Frank E. Moss, D-Utah, between 1969 and 1973 drew attention to inadequate care and regulatory problems in the nation's nursing homes and ultimately led to a sweeping series of reforms to NURSING HOME regulations incorporated in the Omnibus Budget Reconciliation Act of 1987 (PL 100-203; see OMNIBUS BUDGET RECONCILIATION BILLS).

The committee investigated health-insurance coverage of older Americans before the enactment of MEDICARE, in 1965, and has reviewed the performance of the program on a nearly annual basis since then. It also has functioned in an advocacy role for seniors, investigating fraud targeting the elderly and the pricing of prescription drugs. During the 106th Congress, the panel, under Chairman Charles E. Grassley, R-Iowa, examined issues including proposed SOCIAL SECURITY reforms, the increasingly important role of geriatric medicine, and pension and health-care challenges posed by the impending retirement of the BABY BOOMER generation. The committee publishes a biannual report, *Developments in Aging,* that provides an overview of aging issues and congressional responses.

Senior voters

Elderly voters are among the most heavily courted segments of the American electorate because their high turnout rates in national elections make up more than one-quarter of actual voters. However, the notion that seniors are a monolithic voting bloc has been disproved since 1994 by polling data suggesting more seniors are turning to the political right. This trend has major implications at a time when control of either house of Congress hinges on a handful of seats and issues such as the future of SOCIAL SECURITY and MEDICARE play prominent roles in presidential campaigns.

Since the New Deal, older voters have been viewed as a reliable Democratic constituency. As recently as 1990, 52 percent of voters aged sixty and older voted for Democratic candidates for the House of Representatives, compared to 42 percent that backed the GOP. However, the trend began to shift in the 1994 midterm elections, and in 1998, 44 percent of voters aged sixty and older supported Democrats, while 54 percent backed Republicans, according to exit polling by Voter News Service. The 1998 race was notable for another reason: it was the first time in modern polling that a majority of older women (52 to 48 percent) supported Republican candidates. Men over sixty chose the GOP over Democrats 57 to 43 percent. However, analysts caution against reading too much into this trend, noting that while se-

niors were casting more ballots for Republican candidates in Congress, they still were giving their votes to the Democratic Party for president.

Both major parties sought to respond to this shift as the 2000 campaign approached, to curry favor with the elderly. Republicans and Democrats in the 106th Congress sparred over rival plans to enact prescription drug programs for Medicare's thirty-nine million beneficiaries. Republicans called for a plan that would subsidize private drug-insurance plans, while Democrats insisted on making a PRESCRIPTION DRUG BENEFIT part of the Medicare program. Both sides, predictably, called each other's plans unworkable and sought to depict themselves as the most sensitive to seniors' concerns about rising drug prices. The Republican majority in Congress also sought to enact tax breaks specifically targeted at seniors, promoting legislation that would repeal a tax on high-income Social Security beneficiaries that was a key part of President Bill Clinton's controversial 1993 budget deal. And Republicans touted their "LOCKBOX" proposal that would protect the Social Security TRUST FUND from being raided to finance other federal programs. Both Republicans and Democrats also explored some ignored aspects of aging legislation, for instance, working together on a bipartisan reauthorization of the OLDER AMERICANS ACT.

There was some peril in taking such a targeted approach. By vowing not to touch Social Security, Republicans ran the risk of running short of billions of dollars of funds to pass annual appropriations bills. That would force them to make politically unpopular cuts to other domestic programs—something Democrats likely would seize on. Neither party has dared to suggest cutting Social Security BENEFITS or raising payroll taxes to shore up the system. But Republican presidential

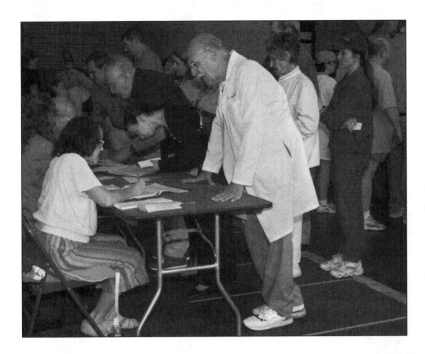

A Florida doctor attempts to get his voting ballot to cast his vote in Miami Beach on Election Day, 2000. Senior voters were the focus of the 2000 presidential election when confusing ballots caused many to inadvertently vote for the wrong candidates.
Source: Marta Lavandier, AP Photo

nominee George W. Bush did endorse the PRIVA-TIZATION of portions of Social Security while Democrat Al Gore defended keeping the program as is—moves both candidates believed would win seniors' support. Bush's move was viewed as bold, in light of the fact that Democrats since the 1980s had hammered Republicans for trying to dismantle the system and help the rich. Polling suggested seniors had misgivings about diverting a portion of payroll taxes to personal retirement plans.

The shift in senior voting has been attributed to a number of factors. Some political scientists believe that economic prosperity has given the voters a greater sense of personal freedom and made them feel less dependent on big governmental programs. While tens of millions of older Americans still live in poverty, statistics indicate the elderly, in general, have seen their financial situation improve faster than other age groups. One analysis by the Center for Budget and Policy

Priorities in Washington, D.C., found that, between 1979 and 1998, median income rose 7 percent, but increased 23 percent for senior citizens. The new wealth has made many of these individuals particularly sensitive to tax issues.

The passing of time also may be a factor. Tens of millions of people who grew up during the New Deal and had a special connection to the FRANKLIN D. ROOSEVELT administration and the traditional policies of the Democratic party are dying. The "new" seniors grew up during the prosperous 1950s and during their middle age were among the voters that elected RONALD REAGAN president. Some of the older voters also have expressed concern about declining cultural values and reacted negatively to the scandals of Bill Clinton's administration.

The outcome of the 2000 elections will provide more fodder for analysts. Senior voters became the immediate focus of the disputed presidential election results in Florida when many elders in Democratic-leaning south Florida counties complained that the design of ballots that were used led them to inadvertently vote for Reform Party nominee Patrick Buchanan instead of the Democratic nominee, Vice President Al Gore.

It is likely that the major parties will continue to tailor large portions of their agendas to older voters. After the election, it also is likely the parties will be more willing to collaborate on aging-related issues, from Medicare financing to aging research and social services directed at the elderly.

SEP-IRA

The Simplified Employee Pension, or SEP-IRA, was authorized by Congress in the Revenue Act of 1978 (PL 95-600) to give owners of small businesses the chance to have a tax-deferred retirement plan without having to set up more complicated instruments, such as KEOGHS. Employers can make contributions of up to 15 percent of each worker's salary, up to $24,000 per year. For self-employed individuals, the limit is 13.04 percent of adjusted net income (calculated by subtracting business expenses from business income, then reducing the amount by one-half of one's self-employed tax). Like conventional INDIVIDUAL RETIREMENT ACCOUNTS (IRAs), the money in a SEP-IRA accumulates tax-free until it is withdrawn, most withdrawals before age 59-1/2 are subject to a 10 percent tax penalty, and withdrawals must begin at age 70-1/2.

SEP-IRAs are unique in that only employers may make contributions, giving workers virtually no control over how much is in the accounts. However, the law allows workers with SEP-IRAs to also open conventional IRAs, giving them one more option to invest for retirement. The advantages for businesses are that SEP-IRAs are easy to set up and require virtually no administrative costs or government reporting. Businesses also can deduct the amount they contribute from their taxes. There are generally fewer restrictions than with other retirement plans—any individual with full- or part-time self-employment income can have a SEP-IRA, and there is no limit on how many employees in a business can participate.

Skilled nursing facility

A skilled nursing facility, or SNF (pronounced snif), provides the kind of intensive medical services that can only be administered by a doctor or licensed nurse. It often is the first stop for elderly patients who have been discharged from a hospital after a STROKE, heart attack, or other serious medical problem, but are not well enough to go home. SNFs are sometimes located within hospitals, but also can be stand-alone units. The push within the health-care industry to reduce the number of days patients spend in hospital beds has made the facilities increasingly used; the number of persons receiving SNF care annually increased from 384,000 in 1988 to more than 1.6 million by 1998, and government reimbursements for covered care rose from $87 per day to $262 per day over the same period.

MEDICARE covers treatment in a SNF under Part A. However, to qualify for the BENEFIT a beneficiary must have been an inpatient in a hospital for at least three consecutive days, and must be transferred to a SNF usually within thirty days of discharge. Medicare covers the skilled care for one

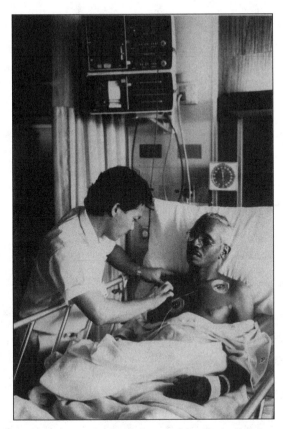

A skilled nursing facility, often the first stop for elderly patients who have been discharged from a hospital, provides the kind of intensive medical services that can only be administered by a doctor or licensed nurse.
Source: Providence Hospital

tem, which was to be phased in over three years ending July 2001, classifies patients in forty-four groups and covers routine services, nursing, room and board, and administrative costs, as well as physical, occupational, and speech therapy, laboratory services, and drugs. It also allows for "consolidated billing," in which a SNF can charge the government for covered Part B services for beneficiaries who reside in the facility but who are no longer eligible for coverage under Part A.

The new payment system has prompted strong protests from the SNF industry, which complains the spending limits are preventing facilities from providing all the care that elderly and disabled patients require. The issue received increased attention after a leading provider, Vencor Incorporated, declared bankruptcy in 1999. Responding to the complaints, Congress in 2000 laid out plans to smooth out the transition to the new system by creating special payment categories to account for the sickest patients who require the most expensive care. The HEALTH CARE FINANCING ADMINISTRATION (HCFA) further said it would increase Medicare payments to SNFs by more than 20 percent in fiscal 2001 to reflect increased costs of care and other factors. For certain Medicare patients with complex medical needs, HCFA said it would pay more than $500 per day for skilled nursing care.

hundred days per "spell of illness," after which the patient must pay for care out of pocket. Days twenty-one to one hundred also are subject to a co-insurance charge.

The government used to reimburse SNFs for costs they incurred after treatments were provided. Passage of the BALANCED BUDGET ACT OF 1997 (PL 105-33) dramatically changed that by implementing a PROSPECTIVE PAYMENT SYSTEM that set a predetermined daily rate for covered services before the services were provided. The new sys-

Social Security

Social Security was created by the SOCIAL SECURITY ACT OF 1935 and is regarded as one of America's greatest domestic-policy programs—a swift response to the Great Depression and the sweeping economic forces that devastated many Americans' financial security. For decades after,

Number of Workers per Old-Age and Survivors Insurance and Disability Insurance Beneficiary

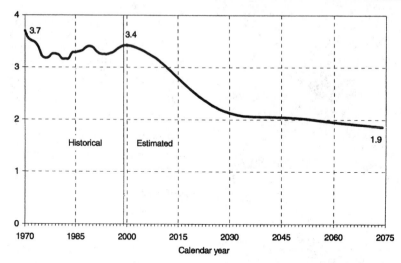

Source: Social Security and Medicare Boards of Trustees, summary of 2000 annual reports.

lawmakers who considered changing the system risked incurring the wrath of seniors, labor unions, and other politically influential program defenders. So few tried that Social Security became known as the "third rail" of American politics; touching it, like touching the electrified linkage on a railroad, meant instant death. Over the past two decades, forecasts of a looming financial crisis for the PAY-AS-YOU-GO SYSTEM brought on by the impending retirement of BABY BOOMERS has led to a reassessment of Social Security's merits. Conservative and libertarian politicians have proposed a variety of methods of overhauling the system to deal with the surge of new retirees, including PRIVATIZATION. While sustained economic prosperity and forecasts of growing surpluses in Social Security's TRUST FUNDS have dimmed some of this talk, debates over the future of Social Security are expected to dominate domestic politics in the first decade of the twenty-first century.

Social Security has its roots in a number of European social-insurance programs developed in the late nineteenth century. Germany's "Iron Chancellor," OTTO VON BISMARCK, established the first social security system in 1889 to ease the pain of unemployment in his rapidly industrializing nation. The pension plan was also created as a small gesture aimed at counteracting the growth of socialism in the wake of Marxism. Britain, France, Russia, and Japan, among other nations, soon established similar national old-age pension programs. Each provided the elderly with defined benefits that were financed by current workers, their employers, or both. The concept was slow to catch on in the United States, because American society in the first decades of the twentieth century remained largely agrarian, and because many in the country viewed social security as a vaguely socialistic European import, hardly in sync with the prevailing ethos of self-reliance. In addition, social historians Carole Haber and Brian Gratton note in their 1994 book *Old Age and the Search for Security: An American Social History,* one major reason Americans were slow to support the program was rising prosperity, mainly from urban industrialism and the rise of the merchant class. This allowed traditional extended families to break away into more congenial separate households, eliminating competition for the same resources between different generations living under the same roof.

The Depression changed everything. Bank failures wiped out many people's savings, and the broader financial crash devastated many industrial and trade union pensions, leaving workers without accumulated savings. Families found themselves consolidating households again to make ends meet, creating a greater impetus for cross-generational support of a national pension plan. Faced with a worsening economic calamity, President FRANKLIN D. ROOSEVELT in 1934 convened top advisors and began to assemble a political proposal that for the first time would put millions of retirees aged sixty-five and older under a retirement plan. At the time of Social Security's passage, in 1935, American society had many more workers than retirees, and the average American was only expected to live to age sixty-one, meaning many would never receive a single Social Security check. The result was a windfall for the first retirees: IDA MAE FULLER, a retired law clerk from Ludlow, Vermont, received the first Social Security check for $22.54 on Jan. 31, 1940. She had contributed only $22 to the system. By the time she died thirty-five years later, her BENE-FITS totaled $22,000.

Congress gradually expanded the scope of Social Security between 1935 and 1980, covering more people and paying out larger BENEFITS. The 1939 amendments to the Social Security Act added benefits for dependents and survivors of a deceased worker. In 1950, the program was expanded to cover agricultural workers, self-em-

Protesters concerned about the future of Social Security join a September 24, 1998, rally against tax cuts. Source: Scott J. Ferrell, Congressional Quarterly

ployed people, members of the armed forces, and disabled individuals aged fifty and older. In 1961, President John F. Kennedy successfully won congressional approval for a 20 percent increase in benefits, as well as an EARLY RETIREMENT provision that offered payouts and survivor benefits to men at age sixty-two.

By the 1970s, Social Security was confronting

its first financial problems. After decades of strong economic growth and low inflation, economic circumstances reversed themselves, and wage growth slowed while prices rose. The energy crisis added further instability, putting pressure on the program because of the many layoffs it spurred and the increase in people leaving the workforce and claiming benefits. DEMOGRAPHICS also shifted, as the number of workers for every retiree fell from 16 in 1950 to about 3.7. Adding to the difficulties were automatic COST-OF-LIVING ADJUSTMENTS, introduced in 1972, that indexed Social Security benefits to inflation. The result was the system could no longer pay for all the benefits it promised. In 1977, President JIMMY CARTER and Congress acted by passing a then-record $227 billion tax increase and slowing down the growth of future benefits. The legislation also shifted a portion of the Medicare HOSPITAL INSURANCE trust fund to Social Security's TRUST FUNDS. The changes at first appeared to work, but when the U.S. economy took another downturn in the early 1980s, workers' wages fell and the system faced a renewed crisis. By the end of 1981, Social Security trust fund reserves declined to $24.5 billion, an amount that was enough to pay benefits for only 1-1/2 months. In 1982 and 1983, Social Security actually had to borrow money from MEDICARE trust funds to finance benefit payments.

Faced with serious and imminent financial problems, President RONALD REAGAN in 1982 convened the bipartisan GREENSPAN COMMISSION, which recommended delaying cost-of-living increases, taxing the benefits of higher-income retirees, and gradually increasing the retirement age from sixty-five to sixty-seven by 2027. The changes were adopted by Congress in 1983, in what was to become the last significant congres-

sionally approved set of reforms to the system. However, the commission overestimated how quickly wages would grow, and did not address the temporary build-up of Social Security trust fund surpluses that the system would experience in the years before the first BABY BOOMERS retire, from 1999 to 2012. When it became apparent that surpluses were occurring in the late 1980s as a result of an expanding workforce, higher wages, and somewhat fewer retirees, Congress used the sums to finance the government's operating budget, in effect disguising the true size of the federal deficit. The Omnibus Budget Reconciliation Act of 1990 (PL 101-508; see OMNIBUS BUDGET RECONCILIATION BILLS) addressed this by enacting "firewalls" that made it more difficult to cut Social Security reserves, for instance, through legislation that calls for a reduction in the program's reserves.

During Bill Clinton's administration, much political debate centered on whether federal budget surpluses that arose from a balanced budget should be used to deal with Social Security's long-term problems or spent for other purposes. Clinton depicted himself as a protector of the system, arguing in his 1998 State of the Union address that Congress should address Social Security's long-term future first before addressing other budget priorities. Republican leaders in the House and Senate alternately proposed using some of the budget surpluses to finance tax cuts, and creating a "LOCKBOX" to sequester surplus payroll tax collections from being used for government programs other than Social Security. Republicans have remained confident that they can protect the viability of Social Security while enacting some targeted, middle-class tax cuts.

To appreciate the semantics of such debates—and to realize the issue is far more complicated than either side depicts—one has to understand the accounting sleight-of-hand surrounding the Social Security program. The money from payroll taxes and interest income is invested in Social Security's trust funds. The OLD-AGE AND SURVIVORS INSURANCE (OASI) trust fund pays retirement and survivors benefits, while the Disability Insurance (DI) trust fund pays disability benefits. But the government really borrows the money in the trust funds to cover its year-to-year operations, issuing the Social Security system U.S. Treasury IOU's. When Social Security needs to redeem the claims plus interest, the Treasury will have to borrow from the public or levy taxes. As a result, many economists say there really is no difference between applying budget surpluses to pay down the national debt or using it specifically for Social Security. Various sides have used the "save Social Security first" argument to appear fiscally prudent. Democrats, in particular, have also used the message to pressure Republicans not to pass election-year tax cuts. Opinion polls continually show the public prefers to see the government attend to the national debt and keep Social Security and other ENTITLEMENT PROGRAMS strong.

The economic boom of the 1990s and the low unemployment and higher wages it spawned have temporarily put off the urgency of the debate over Social Security's long-term future, though politicians still are too willing to use the topic to score political points. The 2000 Social Security Board of Trustees' annual report revealed that the system's trust fund assets will not be depleted until 2037, three years later than was estimated in the 1999 trustees' report. The trustees also projected that the program's deficit will only amount to 1.89 percent of taxable payroll over the next seventy-five years. While there remains a cause for concern, program defenders say a relatively minor payroll tax increase could solve the problem with-

out having to take more dramatic steps, such as raising the retirement age or making steep reductions in benefits.

As of March 1999, there were approximately 30.8 million retired workers and dependents and another 7 million survivors receiving Social Security benefits. The average monthly benefit for a retired worker or dependent was approximately $780, and for a survivor $672. Retired workers and their dependents accounted for 70 percent of total benefits paid, and the SOCIAL SECURITY ADMINISTRATION reported that Social Security benefits represented approximately 40 percent of the income of the elderly.

In the 106th Congress, lawmakers made several adjustments to the program, taking advantage of favorable economic conditions and an election-year desire to deliver savings to elderly voters. In the spring of 2000, Congress scrapped the Social Security earnings limit, a provision in the original legislation that reduces Social Security payments to seniors aged sixty-five to sixty-nine whose annual earnings exceed an annual threshold. At the time of the repeal, about 800,000 seniors were losing $1 in benefits for every $3 they earned beyond $17,000. The penalty did not apply to recipients aged seventy and older. The House of Representatives in July 2000 tried to cut the taxable portion of Social Security benefits of seniors earning more than $34,000 annually ($44,000 for married couples) from 85 percent to 50 percent. The move would have accomplished a long-term Republican goal of reversing an increase enacted in 1993 as part of the budget reconciliation process. Half the benefits would be subject to taxation for seniors earning more than $25,000 and married couples earning above $32,000. Social Security benefits are tax-free for those with less income. However, Democrats contended the move was an attempt to make a few well-heeled seniors richer, there was little enthusiasm for enacting corresponding legislation in the Senate, and Clinton threatened to veto any bill that passed.

The most enduring legacy of the Social Security debate may be a change in the way Americans view personal savings. For decades, retirement income was likened to a three-legged stool—with one leg consisting of a pension; a second, personal savings; and the third, Social Security. But the popularity of employer-sponsored 401(K) retirement plans, fueled by the bull market of the 1990s, has placed more emphasis on personal savings and made some younger workers receptive to a retirement system based on accumulated wealth. The irony is, while many younger Americans believe they will be well off when they retire, they actually are saving comparatively little in their prime earning years. A key question for policymakers is whether sustaining Social Security in its present form will encourage or discourage private saving. Likewise, privatization advocates will have to consider whether setting up personal retirement accounts will automatically increase savings or simply divert contributions from existing IRAs and 401(k)s.

Social Security Act of 1935

The Social Security Act of 1935, enacted by the Seventy-fourth Congress and signed by President FRANKLIN D. ROOSEVELT on Aug. 14, 1935, authorized the original national pension system. The act contained recommendations Roosevelt's Committee on Economic Security developed over slightly more than six months in 1934 and consisted of two titles: grants for state old-age pensions and compulsory old-age insurance, referred to as "federal old-age benefits." Lawmakers in the House and Senate quickly focused on the much more far-reaching second title and engaged in intense debate over whether the federal government should expand its reach and have a hand in individuals' savings and retirement planning. Another heated point of contention was the proposed payroll tax that would fund the system. Advocates of the system, such as bill sponsors Sen. Robert Wagner, D-N.Y., and Reps. Robert Doughton, D-N.C., and David Lewis, D-Md., argued that the program would work like private insurance, with individuals paying "premiums" that would give them a right to future BENEFITS. In reality, this was inaccurate, because the existing work force would be taxed to subsidize current retirees' benefits. However, the insurance analogy proved politically popular and helped win broad support for the legislation. An attempt by Sen. Bennett Clark, D-Mo., to allow private employers with generous retirement programs to opt out of the system passed the Senate, but was dropped in a House-Senate conference in July 1935 under strong pressure from Roosevelt.

In the House, the bill was initially referred to the HOUSE WAYS AND MEANS COMMITTEE, which held debate in March and April 1935. The bill was introduced in the full House on April 4 and passed April 19, by a vote of 372–33, with two members voting present, and twenty-five not voting. Debate in the Senate began in the SENATE FINANCE COMMITTEE in January and February 1935. The bill was introduced in the full Senate June 12 and passed on June 19, 77–6, with twelve senators not voting. The conference report, reconciling differences in the House and Senate versions of the legislation, passed, by voice vote, in the House August 8 and in the Senate August 9.

President Franklin D. Roosevelt signs the Social Security Act of 1935 on August 14, 1935. To his left stands Frances Perkins, the secretary of Labor and first female cabinet member. The act authorized the original national pension system. Source: Franklin D. Roosevelt Library

In the end, the legislation created a dedicated revenue stream for financing the system, as Roosevelt had wished, instead of relying on general government revenues. It imposed a 2 percent payroll tax, to be split evenly by employers and workers, on the first $3,000 of wages. In return, workers who reached age sixty-five would receive monthly benefits calculated through a formula based on taxable wages and payable until death, unless they continued to work. The law applied to all workers, except those in agriculture, government workers, domestic servants, and a number of other excluded categories, such as merchant seamen. The formula was weighted to provide a more generous benefit to low-wage earners.

Despite the overwhelmingly favorable votes for passage, not everyone was pleased with the system. Some politicians on the left believed the government should provide a more generous benefit, backing a proposal by FRANCIS E. TOWNSEND that would have provided a $200 monthly pension to every American aged sixty and older. Politicians on the right bitterly criticized the system on several points, in particular assailing payroll taxes for cutting wages and possibly reducing jobs. In 1937, the constitutionality of the Social Security Act came under question in *HELVERING V. DAVIS*, a case in which the U.S. Supreme Court took up whether Social Security violated the Tenth amendment, or "reserve clause," of the Constitution. The provision states that powers not specifically granted to the federal government by the Constitution are reserved for the states or the people. The justices ruled, 7–2, that such a strict interpretation was unrealistic, and that Congress needed the flexibility to reinterpret the law, when appropriate.

Key components of the Social Security Act include Old-Age, Survivors, and Disability Insurance (Title II), unemployment insurance (Title III), SUPPLEMENTAL SECURITY INCOME (Title XVI), and the SOCIAL SERVICES BLOCK GRANT (Title XX). Few realize that MEDICARE actually is Title XVIII of the Social Security Act, and that MEDICAID is Title XIX.

Social Security Administration (SSA)

The Social Security Administration, known as the SSA, is an independent governmental agency headquartered in Baltimore, Maryland. It administers the federal Old-Age, Survivors, and Disability Insurance (OASDI) program authorized by Title II of the SOCIAL SECURITY ACT OF 1935 that is at the heart of the SOCIAL SECURITY system. It also runs the SUPPLEMENTAL SECURITY INCOME (SSI) program for poor, elderly, blind, and disabled people and, with the U.S. LABOR DEPARTMENT, shares responsibility for the Federal Coal Mine Health and Safety Act, which pays benefits to miners and the families of miners who suffer from the occupational disease known as "black lung." The agency's approximately sixty thousand employees are distributed throughout its headquarters, ten regional offices, and 1,343 field offices. SSA operates on an annual budget of approximately $450 billion.

In 1999, the SSA distributed approximately $385.8 billion in BENEFITS to 44.6 million Social Security beneficiaries. SSA accounted for $3.3 billion of administrative expenses, or approximately 0.9 percent of benefits for the year. The agency often is one of the first points of contact in the federal government for elderly persons whose benefit checks have gone missing or who require an explanation of benefits. It also mounts public education campaigns on various aspects of the Social Security system, such as the gradual raising of the retirement age from sixty-five to sixty-seven. In 1999, SSA also began mailing annual, individualized statements to 125 million covered workers aged twenty-five and older who do not receive Social Security benefits containing estimates of the monthly retirement benefit the worker would receive at age sixty-two, at the normal retirement age, and at age seventy. The statements also included projections of disability benefits should the worker become disabled, and an estimate of the monthly benefit that the worker's family could receive should the worker die. The statements were mandated by the Omnibus Budget Reconciliation Act of 1989 (see OMNIBUS BUDGET RECONCILIATION BILLS).

SSA was an outgrowth of the original Social Security Board, which was created at the same time as the Social Security system. In 1939, the board became part of the Federal Security Agency, the cabinet-level predecessor of the Department of Health, Education, and Welfare (now the Department of HEALTH AND HUMAN SERVICES). The Social Security Board was renamed the Social Security Administration in 1946, and Arthur Altmeyer, who had been chairman of the board, became the first Social Security commissioner. SSA remained a part of the Department of Health and Human Services until 1994, when President Bill Clinton restored its independent status.

Social Security and working women

An important aspect of political debates over whether to privatize the SOCIAL SECURITY system is whether older women would gain or lose if a portion of payroll taxes is diverted into personal savings accounts. Both the U.S. General Accounting Office (GAO) and the EMPLOYEE BENEFIT RESEARCH INSTITUTE have concluded that women as a group could face particular challenges under PRIVATIZATION, because they generally earn less than men, have longer life expectancies, tend to move in and out of the workforce more frequently to tend to family members, and are more dependent on Social Security as a primary source of retirement income. However, many analysts believe lawmakers eventually will have to address inequities in the current system, which was designed when few women worked and, in the view of some, discriminates against certain professional women.

The image of an elderly widow living off her monthly Social Security check is frequently evoked in debates over the system. In 1939, Congress introduced spousal benefits, automatically entitling women to half of their husbands' benefits, regardless of whether they had paid payroll taxes. The net effect is that a couple receives combined benefits equal to 150 percent of the benefits earned by the main income-earner. But privatization advocates say the system's reliance on a "family model" with a stay-at-home mom discriminates against working women, who have been paying payroll taxes into the system without receiving any additional benefits.

An American Society of Actuaries estimate illustrates the dilemma. For a family making $68,400 in preretirement income, a stay-at-home spouse would be entitled to a widow's benefit of $1,354 per month, while a wife who brought home half of the household income would draw a $1,082 monthly benefit check. The difference is even more pronounced for couples who earn less. For a couple making a combined $34,200, the stay-at-home spouse would receive a monthly check of $1,082 on being widowed, while a wife who earned half of the income would receive only $674.

Privatization advocates say women usually qualify for smaller payouts because they often leave the workforce for extended periods during peak earning years to raise children. The Cato Institute, a libertarian THINK TANK, has proposed an alternative in which a husband and wife split contributions to and ownership of personal retirement accounts. If both spouses contribute 10 percent of earnings to the accounts, the think tank calculates that all categories of women would be better off than under Social Security as it now exists.

However, a move to private accounts also could weaken protections for survivors and divorced people, who now get special treatment under Social Security. Most privatization plans envision dropping the 50 percent automatic entitlement for dependent spouses, and some private savings plans may be set up to expire at death, leaving the survivor without benefits. Privatization also could penalize professional women, because working women earn less than men (about 70 cents to the men's dollar) and therefore have fewer funds to invest in individual savings accounts. Additionally, studies by the GAO and others suggest women tend to be more risk-averse when making investment choices and less likely to opt for high-risk investments, such as stocks. That means that even a booming stock market would not ensure that women with private accounts would do appreciably better. Gender equity will continue to be a focus of the broader Social Security debate, as lawmakers decide what shape the retirement system will have in the twenty-first century.

Social Security Disability Insurance (SSDI)

Social Security Disability Insurance is the component of the SOCIAL SECURITY system that pays monthly cash BENEFITS to covered workers and their dependents to replace lost wages if the worker cannot make a living because of a physical or mental impairment. Disability insurance comprises the "DI" of Social Security's core OASDI program (the "OAS" stands for Old-Age and Survivors).

This part of the Social Security program often is overlooked because of the frequent emphasis on retirement benefits in political debates. However, experts say it represents a vital component of the social welfare system because only a small percentage of workers have employer-sponsored long-term disability coverage. SSDI is frequently confused with SUPPLEMENTAL SECURITY INCOME (SSI), a sister program also run by the SOCIAL SE-CURITY ADMINISTRATION that makes cash assistance payments to poor, disabled Americans and is financed out of general tax revenues.

Congress authorized SSDI in July 1956 to help individuals who left the workforce after age fifty but before the NORMAL RETIREMENT AGE of sixty-five because of disabilities. The program was later expanded to cover younger workers.

At the time SSDI was set up, the diagnosis of a serious case of heart disease or other chronic health condition usually meant a worker had to take EARLY RETIREMENT from the workforce. But medical advances over the past three decades have led some to question whether the SSDI is capable of changing with the times. Specifically, members of Congress have criticized the Social Security Administration for failing to adequately monitor whether disabled workers are reentering the work force and continuing to collect benefits. The 1980 Social Security amendments required the Social Security Administration to review the eligibility of nonpermanently disabled individuals at least once every three years to identify recipients who were back on the job, and to terminate their benefits. However, budget cuts have limited the Social Security Administration's ability to conduct these so-called continuing disability reviews.

Lawmakers since the 1930s had debated whether workers with disabilities should receive rehabilitation, instead of a pension that essentially allowed them to retire for good. Historian Edward Berkowitz of George Washington University notes that, because eligibility in the program was initially confined to older workers who tended to be the worst candidates for rehabilitation and who had chronic conditions, such as HEART DIS-EASE and ARTHRITIS, SSDI was destined to become a retirement program unto itself. This was not of great concern to policymakers at the time, Berkowitz notes, because they believed younger disabled individuals who tended to be affected by conditions such as mental disorders could find help in state mental health hospitals, and because mental disabilities were difficult to diagnose.

To qualify for SSDI, an individual has to have worked and paid Social Security taxes for a set period of time (usually twenty quarters, unless the person is blind or under the age of thirty-one) and must have an impairment severe enough to prevent them from performing their previous job or any other "substantial gainful activity." The program defines a disability as a condition that is expected to result in death or can be expected to last for at least twelve continuous months. Those SSDI recipients who are certified as permanently disabled after two years of receiving benefits and a five-month waiting period also are eligible for MEDICARE coverage.

As of March 1999, there were approximately 6.4 million SSDI beneficiaries and dependents receiving $3.8 billion in benefits, accounting for approximately 14 percent of total Social Security benefits paid. The average monthly benefit was approximately $733. While the majority of beneficiaries were older males who had permanent disabilities, officials reported they were seeing a growing number of younger workers suffering from psychological problems. The Social Security Administration estimates that SSDI provides an average young worker with two children the equivalent of a private disability insurance policy worth about $200,000.

The DI trust has been the focus of policymakers' attention since the early 1990s, when rapidly increasing enrollment in the program and flat revenues from a stagnant economy led to predic-

tions the trust fund would be depleted by 1995. Congress in late 1994 reallocated a small percentage of the OASI trust fund to the SSDI trust fund. The total OASDI tax rates were not changed. The reallocation provided a much-needed boost. However, the 2000 Social Security Trustees' report states the DI trust fund assets will begin to fall below 100 percent of estimated annual expenditures at the beginning of 2009.

When Republicans took control of Congress in 1994, GOP lawmakers expressed concern about the manner in which drug addicts and alcoholics could receive SSDI benefits. The lawmakers and the U.S. General Accounting Office faulted the Social Security Administration for failing to monitor whether recipients were getting necessary treatment to wean them from their habits. The Social Security Independence and Program Improvement Act (PL 103-296), passed in 1994, required that any recipients whose drug addiction or alcoholism contributed to their disability receive benefits through a third party. In 1996, Congress enacted, and President Bill Clinton signed, a sweeping welfare reform measure (PL 104-121) that eliminated drug addiction and alcoholism as a basis for disability in both the SSDI and SSI programs. The budgetary savings were used to help offset a measure in the same legislation to increase the earnings limit for receipt of Social Security benefits to $30,000 by 2002. Critics have said the move resulted in fewer people in treatment programs and the potential for more abuse of benefits.

In recent years, lawmakers from both parties have focused on the relatively small number of SSDI recipients who leave the benefit rolls to return to work. Part of this centers on the formulas the Social Security Administration uses to determine how much a person can earn while retaining disability benefits. Many recipients have complained of being caught in a bureaucratic trap because the earnings-limits effectively discourage them from working, even if they are able, because of fears of losing monthly benefits. Congress and the Clinton administration began to address this in the BALANCED BUDGET ACT OF 1997 (PL 105-33), including a provision that allows states to permit SSDI recipients to go back to work and retain coverage under MEDICAID. However, only a small number of states so far have lifted restrictions. In 1999, Congress passed and Clinton signed the Work Incentives Improvement Act (PL 106-170), more popularly known as the "TICKET TO WORK" program, which extends Medicare coverage for four and one-half years for SSDI recipients who return to work, and creates other incentives.

Social Security "notch"

The Social Security "notch" usually refers to the difference between BENEFITS paid to individuals born before 1916 and those born in the following five years. The political controversy, which reached its peak in the 1980s and early 1990s, had its roots in Congress's 1972 decision to create COST-OF-LIVING ADJUSTMENTS to index SOCIAL SECURITY payments to inflation. The move was seen as a way around the time-consuming practice of seeking legislation each time benefits had to be indexed. However, Congress created a flawed formula that indexed the first benefits twice, for wages and prices. This was based on the mistaken belief that the economy would behave as it did for most of the 1950s and 1960s, when wage increases outpaced prices, and inflation re-

mained low. However, in the era of rapid inflation that followed, the formula created such a fast buildup in benefits promised relative to taxes paid into the system, that benefits eventually would have exceeded many recipients' preretirement income.

Concern over the effects on Social Security's long-term solvency led Congress to pass the 1977 amendments to the SOCIAL SECURITY ACT, which changed the benefit calculation for recipients born after 1916. To create a smooth transition, lawmakers devised a "transitional computation method" that scaled down the projected benefit increase for beneficiaries born between 1917 and 1921, then financed the remaining increase with a series of tax increases. Lawmakers hoped they had harmonized differences between those retiring under the old and new systems. However, continued inflation in the late 1970s and early 1980s caused an exaggerated difference in benefit levels, leading the so-called notch babies to call for a correction. More than one hundred notch-related bills were proposed during the 1980s, but lawmakers did not pass any measure mandating a correction.

The 102d Congress tried to put the matter to rest by passing legislation (PL 102-393) creating a twelve-member bipartisan Notch Study Commission that would make recommendations on a course of action by the end of 1994. The commission noted the disparities, represented on a graph by a sharp V-shaped notch between 1917 and 1921. However, the commission concluded that notch babies still were receiving a greater return relative to what they paid into the system than future generations would receive, even though the return was not as generous as for those people born before 1916. The decision not to raise benefits for Americans aged seventy-eight to eighty-four at the time largely put the matter to rest.

Social Services Block Grant

The Omnibus Budget Reconciliation Act of 1981 (PL 97-35; see OMNIBUS BUDGET RECONCILIATION BILLS) amended Title XX of the SOCIAL SECURITY ACT to establish the Social Services Block Grant, which distributes grants to states for a variety of social services programs. States receive funds based on their population and have the latitude to select what services are provided, craft eligibility rules, and decide how the money is distributed among available programs. The thinking behind the grants is that states are best equipped to assess the needs of their residents. One overriding goal is to help beneficiaries achieve self-sufficiency and to reduce the need for institutional care, except when necessary.

Despite the worthy goals of the program, it is unclear just how much the grants help the elderly on a nationwide basis. Because the program provides a variety of social services to diverse populations, community services for the elderly have to compete for funding with child protective services, special programs for the disabled, and other initiatives. Yet many states have used the money to help fund important aging-related initiatives, such as MEALS ON WHEELS, ADULT DAY CARE, transportation services, in-home care for the elderly and disabled, and investigations of ELDER ABUSE.

Annual congressional funding for Social Services Block Grants has declined from peak levels of $2.8 billion, which were held constant from fiscal 1989 to 1995. Beginning in fiscal 2001, the annual amount will be set at $1.7 billion under provisions of the Transportation Equity Act of 1998 (PL 105-178). However, groups such as the National Governors' Association have strenuously protested the cuts, saying they weaken the state-federal partnership to serve needy Americans. The governors are pressing for increased funding, as well as extension of a provision enacted by the 105th Congress that would allow them to transfer up to 10 percent of aid received from the federal Temporary Assistance for Needy Families program to the block grants.

Spousal impoverishment

With the cost of LONG-TERM CARE in the tens of thousands of dollars per year, there has long been concern that admission to a NURSING HOME could rapidly deplete an elderly couple's life savings. Congress addressed this issue in the MEDICARE CATASTROPHIC COVERAGE ACT of 1988 (PL 199-360) by enacting spousal impoverishment rules designed to leave the spouse who was still living at home (sometimes called the "community spouse") sufficient income and resources. The rules allowed the spouse receiving institutional care to transfer some assets and income to the community spouse. No income of the community spouse was to be considered available to the institutionalized spouse, and income paid in both names was to be considered available in equal portions to both individuals. Though most of the 1988 act was repealed in 1989, the spousal impoverishment provisions survived.

The rules require states under the MEDICAID program to use special counting rules in their initial determinations for program eligibility. The rules apply when a member of the couple is in a nursing facility or hospital for at least thirty days. When the couple applies for Medicaid, the couple's financial assets are combined and program administrators exclude the home, household

Paul and Mary Onesi, honored for being the longest-married couple in the United States, have been married for eighty years. Should one of a couple become institutionalized, spousal impoverishment rules allow states to set parameters for how much of his or her income or assets may be applied to the cost of care.
Source: Bill Sikes, AP Photo

goods, personal effects such as a car, and burial-related expenses from the countable resources. From the remaining combined resources, states reserve an amount called the spousal resource amount or minimum resource standard for the community spouse. At the beginning of 1999, this amount could be no lower than $16,392 and no greater than $81,960, with the amounts adjusted annually to track with inflation. If the community spouse's resources fall below the threshold, the institutionalized spouse can transfer sufficient assets to bring the spouse up to the standard. If the community spouse's assets exceed the top end of the limit, he or she may be required to contribute more to the cost of the institutionalized spouse's care.

Spousal impoverishment rules also allow states to set parameters for how much of an institutionalized spouse's income or assets may be applied to the cost of care. At the beginning of 1999, the amount, called the minimum maintenance needs allowance, could be no less than $1,383 per month but no higher than $2,049 per month. The amounts could change, depending on the community spouse's cost of housing and whether he or she had dependent adult children. The minimums also are adjusted annually for inflation.

Stroke

Stroke is the third leading cause of death in the United States, behind HEART DISEASE and CANCER, and kills approximately 160,000 mostly elderly Americans every year. About 730,000 people have new or recurrent strokes every year. Government studies estimate that, for each decade beyond age fifty-five, the risk of stroke doubles, and that individuals over the age of sixty-five have seven times the risk of dying from stroke as the general population. The National Stroke Association in Englewood, Colorado, says strokes cost the nation about $17 billion per year in hospital, doctor, and REHABILITATION costs, plus another $13 billion in lost worker productivity.

Simply defined, a stroke occurs when blood flow to the brain is interrupted. Some doctors re-

fer to this as a "brain attack." There are two primary types of stroke: ischemic, when the blood supply to a portion of the brain is blocked, and hemorrhagic, when a blood vessel in the brain actually bursts and spills blood into the neighboring cerebral tissue. The result in both cases is that brain cells die when the supply of blood is interrupted. Depending on which portion of the brain the stroke occurs, the victim may experience loss of speech, motor functions, or memory. Timely intervention is critical to minimizing damage; if medical personnel respond within a narrow window of time following the stroke—usually six hours—they may be able to save some of the damaged cells and restore certain functions. The symptoms of stroke are easy to recognize and include slurred speech, sudden numbness or weakness, particularly on one side of the body, and difficulty seeing, walking, or understanding conversations. Following a stroke, patients may have to undergo lengthy and painful periods of rehabilitation therapy in order to walk again or restore vocational skills.

While scientific research shows that strokes run in some families and there may be a genetic predisposition to the condition, the National Institute of Neurological Disorders and Stroke (NINDS) says the most common risk factors are hypertension, heart disease, DIABETES, and cigarette smoking, all of which contribute to the formation of plaque or clots in blood vessels. Other factors include high alcohol consumption, elevated blood cholesterol, and drug use. Women seem to be disproportionately affected, accounting for more than 60 percent of stroke deaths, though this is in part due to the fact that they live longer and, thus, are at greater risk. African Americans also are at particularly high risk, and are twice as likely to have a stroke than whites. This is attributed to higher-than-average incidence of hypertension, diabetes, obesity, and smoking among black populations.

Many physicians believe stroke can be as preventable as heart attacks by adjusting one's lifestyle—for instance, drinking in moderation, quitting smoking, and exercising frequently. The federal Agency for Health Care Policy and Research also notes there are medical interventions for individuals with medical conditions that put them at especially high risk. Individuals with atrial fibrillation, a condition in which the upper left chamber of the heart beats irregularly and can tend to form clots, can be treated with the blood thinner warfarin or similar medications. Another high-risk condition is blockage of the carotid artery in the neck, which can cut off the supply of blood to the brain. A surgical procedure called a carotid endarterectomy can remove the fatty deposits called plaque that can build up in the arteries, though there is some risk that portions of plaque can break away and cause further blockages.

The NINDS, part of the NATIONAL INSTITUTES OF HEALTH, is the federal government's focal point for research into stroke and other neurological conditions, though agencies such as the NATIONAL INSTITUTE ON AGING also contribute to the body of federal research. Scientists are attempting to better understand the toxic reaction brain tissue experiences after the flow of blood is interrupted, hoping they can develop improved protective agents. One class of drugs already in use is vasodilators, which expand the blood vessels and can improve the flow of blood. Scientists also are studying why decreased blood flow in hibernating animals does not affect their brain function when it would kill a nonhibernating animal. One relatively new and promising area of research is gene therapy, in which scientists could transplant healthy brain tissue into damaged parts of the organ and restore some critical functions. While the technique has shown some promise in laboratory animals, it has not yet been extensively tested in human subjects because of the risks involved.

Federal researchers also are urging health-care providers to work to reduce stroke-related deaths and disabilities. A group of professional, volunteer, and government researchers called the Brain Attack Coalition in 2000 issued new recommendations for hospital trauma centers to swiftly triage and treat stroke victims with clot-busting therapies.

Suicide

Suicide rates among the elderly have been on the rise since 1980 and are a growing concern of public-health officials, who study risk factors and are trying to develop preventive strategies. The U.S. Centers for Disease Control and Prevention (CDC) found that, from 1980 to 1997, the largest relative increases in suicide rates occurred among individuals aged eighty to eighty-four, particularly those who were divorced or widowed. The rate for men in this group rose 8 percent over the period, to 43.5 per 100,000 people, compared to 11.4 per 100,000 for all age groups combined. Statistics also show disparities between men and women who take their own lives. Suicide in women tends to peak in middle age, while it increases markedly in men as they age. The CDC noted that men accounted for 83 percent of suicides among people aged sixty-five and older in 1997, and that white men above the age of eighty can be as much as six times as likely to commit suicide as the general population. Overall, CDC said suicide took the lives of 30,535 Americans in 1997, making it the eighth leading cause of death in the nation.

Health officials believe DEPRESSION arising from social isolation and mental decline is a leading cause of suicide in older people. Some individuals also suffer from painful and debilitating diseases, or from alcoholism or other substance abuse. The problems are compounded, in many cases, by a reluctance to turn to younger family members as caregivers, because of the elderly person's desire not to be a burden. Some mental-health experts believe this is particularly true among men of the Depression and World War II generations, who are most apt to have been self-reliant for their entire lives and only come to be dependent on others in their later years. Government researchers are studying these and other factors, such as whether moving within the elder care system prevents opportunities to develop social networks that may lessen the sense of being alone.

While suicide committed alone is viewed as a public-health concern, the related matter of assisted suicide has become a heated topic of debate in legal and political circles. Assisted suicide is generally defined as helping a person with a terminal illness take his or her life. It is most commonly associated with Dr. Jack Kevorkian, a Michigan pathologist who claimed to have helped more than 130 people kill themselves between 1990 and 1998. Kevorkian was tried and acquitted three times on assisted-suicide charges, and a fourth trial ended in a mistrial. In March 1999, Kevorkian was found guilty of second-degree murder after appearing on a broadcast of the news program 60 Minutes delivering a fatal injection of potassium chloride to Thomas Youk, fifty-two, a Michigan patient suffering from Lou Gehrig's disease.

Defenders of assisted suicide believe it is a form of compassion toward people who otherwise would live out their lives in pain and suffering with no hope of getting better. Religious and right-to-life groups, and medical bodies such as the AMERICAN MEDICAL ASSOCIATION, strenuously oppose the practice, saying it is unethical and immoral for physicians to help patients kill themselves. In attempting to parse the issue, the government has made important legal distinctions between actively helping someone take his or her life, for instance with a lethal injection, and withholding critical medical care or nourishment. The Republican-led Congress in 1997 addressed the practice by enacting PL 105-12, which was signed by President Bill Clinton and barred the use of federal money to provide a health-care item or service for the purpose of helping cause the death of an individual. However, the law made some apparent allowances by exempting the withholding of medical care, food, or water, and administering pain relief, even if it could increase the risk of death.

The U.S. Supreme Court that same year ruled in two cases that there was no constitutional right to assisted suicide. In June 1997 rulings in *Vacco v. Quill* and *Washington v. Glucksberg,* the high court upheld assisted-suicide bans in New York and Washington state, but also found the law did not expressly bar states from allowing assisted suicide.

Oregon so far is the only state to allow assisted suicide. A 1994 "Death with Dignity Act" was approved by voters, survived a court challenge that led to the Supreme Court, and was reaffirmed in October 1997 by 60 percent of the electorate. In 1999, twenty-seven terminally ill patients used the law to commit suicide with lethal prescriptions obtained from their doctors. Lawmakers in Congress, most notably Senate Judiciary Committee chairman Orrin G. Hatch, R-Utah, and House Judiciary Committee chairman Henry J. Hyde, R-

Surgeon general David Satcher discusses his report Call to Action to Prevent Suicide, in which he declared, for the first time, that suicide is a serious public threat. Suicide rates among the elderly have been on the rise since 1980. Source: Ron Edmonds, AP Photo

Ill., have periodically attempted to overturn the Oregon law. In 1997, lawmakers attempted to get the federal Drug Enforcement Administration (DEA) to state that the federal Controlled Substances Act forbids doctors from prescribing lethal doses of drugs. In June 1998, Attorney General Janet Reno ruled federal law does not prevent physician-assisted suicide in the state, despite an earlier DEA determination that doctors that do engage in the practice may violate language in the law stating that they only can prescribe drugs for "legitimate medical purposes." The House in 1999 passed, 271–156, legislation that would bar doctors from prescribing drugs on a federal list of controlled substances for the purpose of causing suicide. The Senate was considering companion legislation in 2000, but some patient groups warned that the bill, as written, could affect the way doctors administer pain-killers for terminally ill patients.

Supplemental Security Income (SSI)

This federal ENTITLEMENT PROGRAM, known as SSI, was created in 1972 by Title XVI of the SO-CIAL SECURITY ACT (PL 92-603) and began in 1974 to provide financial aid to low-income elderly Americans, the blind, and the disabled. It was designed to replace the Aid to the Old-Aged and Blind component of the original Social Security Act, as well as the federal Aid to the Permanently and Totally Disabled program that Congress enacted in 1950 and similar state programs. Often confused with SOCIAL SECURITY DISABILITY IN-SURANCE (SSDI), SSI is designed to provide income to people who do not qualify for SOCIAL SE-CURITY benefits, or who only qualify for minimal payments that are not enough to make ends meet. Unlike Social Security, the program is financed out of general tax revenues. SSI is one of the programs administered by the SOCIAL SECURITY AD-MINISTRATION.

In recent years, SSI has delivered payments to approximately 6.5 million recipients annually (approximately 5 million of these are disabled, while about 1.4 million are elderly). BENEFIT payments in fiscal 2000 were estimated at $29.2 billion. In 2000, the maximum monthly SSI payment was $512 for individuals and $769 for couples.

Eligibility for SSI is determined through a complicated formula that takes into account an applicant's living situation, citizenship status, and monthly income. In general, the individual has to be earning less than $512 per month ($769 for a couple) and have "countable resources" of less than $2,000 ($3,000 for a couple) to qualify for payments. The countable resources do not include household goods, personal effects, an automobile, life insurance, the individual's home, and burial funds up to $1,500 each for the applicant and his or her spouse. Items that are counted include other real estate, bank accounts, cash, and stocks. If an applicant is living in another person's house and receiving support from that individual, the assistance is counted as an in-kind asset, and payments are reduced by one-third.

While the program has escaped serious congressional budget cuts, it has not been able to significantly eliminate poverty in the elderly population, because payments are too small and do not keep up with the pace of inflation. Moreover, only one-half to two-thirds of individuals who qualify for the program actually receive benefits. Being declared eligible for SSI also automatically qualifies the beneficiary to be enrolled in MEDICAID. Indeed, many elderly in NURSING HOMES get Medicaid coverage for LONG-TERM CARE by qualifying for SSI after depleting their personal assets.

Congress for the better part of the 1990s focused on eliminating abuses in the management of SSI. The sweeping 1996 welfare reform bill (PL 104-193) cut off SSI benefits for people considered disabled because of alcoholism or drug addiction. It also prevented legal aliens who entered the country after the date of enactment (August 22, 1996) from receiving SSI benefits and Medicaid unless they had worked ten years in the United States or were veterans or active-duty personnel. Congress restored the eligibility of some of these individuals as part of the BALANCED BUD-

GET ACT OF 1997 (PL 105-33), allowing SSI benefits for those noncitizens who already were receiving SSI benefits as of August 22, 1996, and those who were in the country as of that date and later became disabled. However, those legal aliens who entered the country after that date would remain ineligible for SSI or Medicaid for five years after entry. Congress and the Social Security Administration have worked in recent years to speed up the process by which disabled individuals are determined eligible or ineligible for the program.

Supplementary Medical Insurance

Supplementary Medical Insurance is another name for MEDICARE Part B, the optional program that provides doctors' care, outpatient services, x-rays and other diagnostic tests, physical therapy, and durable medical equipment and supplies. Individuals over the age of sixty-five, and those under sixty-five who are eligible for Medicare Part A, can obtain Part B coverage by paying a monthly premium that totaled $45.50 in 2000. Beneficiaries also are usually subject to a $100 DEDUCTIBLE and 20 percent co-insurance.

The financing scheme of Part B has changed with the times, as medical costs have risen. Monthly premiums were originally envisioned to cover half of the program's costs. To insulate beneficiaries against health-care inflation, Congress used the BALANCED BUDGET ACT OF 1997 (PL 105-33) to permanently set the amount premiums were to finance Part B services at 25 percent of total program costs. The remainder comes from general funds paid into the U.S. Treasury.

In 1999, Supplementary Medical Insurance covered approximately thirty-two million elderly and five million disabled persons. Benefit payments totaled $80.7 billion, a 6 percent increase over 1998, with average benefits per enrollee increasing 5.2 percent, to $2,178. Fifty-six percent of benefits paid were for physician and other professional services. Actuarial projections show Medicare Part B spending is expected to grow about 8 percent annually through the first decade of the twenty-first century. Part B continues to be a focus of debate as Congress and the White House consider adding a PRESCRIPTION DRUG BENEFIT for Medicare recipients. Democrats argue the benefit should be made a part of Part B, while most Republicans believe the government should subsidize private drug-insurance coverage.

Swing bed

A swing bed is a hospital bed that is designated to be used either for acute care or for less intense medical services, such as skilled nursing care. Swing beds are especially popular in hospitals in outlying areas with fewer than one hundred total beds because they offer the flexibility to care for partially recovered elderly patients without having to transfer them over long distances to NURSING HOMES or other extended-care facilities. Hospitals must be certified as MEDICARE swing-bed providers. MEDICAID reimburses the facilities for skilled nursing services at a rate equivalent to area nursing homes.

Swing beds have helped some rural hospitals get around funding constraints imposed by the BALANCED BUDGET ACT OF 1997 (PL 105-33). Isolated public or not-for-profit hospitals were able to escape serious cuts in payments mandated by the act by declaring themselves a "critical access" facility—essentially the only significant primary care facility in their region. However, the designation meant they would have to turn away patients who likely will need more than ninety-six hours of care, in order to focus on acute care. The swing bed enables the patient to remain in the same facility after his or her condition is stabilized without having to be moved.

T

Tau

Tau is a protein produced in the brain that scientists since the 1980s have implicated in the development of ALZHEIMER'S DISEASE and related DEMENTIAS. Tau is the main component of the neurofibrillary tangles that are a hallmark of Alzheimer's, and contribute to the death of brain cells. However, researchers do not know for sure whether the tangles, or the abnormal buildup of another protein called beta amyloid into plaques, actually trigger the disease—or whether they simply are byproducts of the condition. Researchers at the NATIONAL INSTITUTE ON AGING have succeeded in creating tau-containing lesions for a number of brain disorders in laboratory animals in an effort to find answers.

In normal brain cells, tau acts like a set of railroad ties. It helps bind and stabilize cell components called microtubules that run in parallel tracks and carry nutrients over the length of the cells. In Alzheimer's, however, tau is chemically altered and twists like threads wound around one another. This causes the microtubule transport system to fall apart and likely disrupts communications between brain cells. Later, the cells die.

National Institute on Aging scientists in 1999 created a new strain of genetically engineered mice that contain the human gene coding for tau. While the mice do not develop Alzheimer's per se, their conditions mimic other human brain diseases that involve loss of memory and reasoning.

The researchers hope to learn how and why tau deposits accumulate, and how to prevent the formation of tangles.

Tax credit for the elderly and certain disabled individuals

Individuals aged sixty-five and older, or who retired on permanent and total disability, are entitled to a tax credit, enacted as part of the 1983 amendments to the SOCIAL SECURITY ACT (PL 98-21). Seniors may claim a credit of up to 15 percent of taxable income up to a base amount that is calculated by a formula that takes into account the person's adjusted gross income (AGI) and nontaxable income from pensions, annuities, SOCIAL SECURITY, RAILROAD RETIREMENT PROGRAM, or veterans' non-service-related disability benefits. The credit has existed in several different forms since Congress first enacted it in the Internal Revenue Code of 1954 to correct inequities from the taxation of different kinds of retirement income.

The credit is designed for people who only receive taxable retirement or disability income, or those who receive both taxable retirement or disability income and Social Security. The average credit claimed per return has remained fairly stable, at about $200, since the mid-1970s.

The maximum base amount for the credit is $5,000 for unmarried elderly or disabled persons,

$7,500 for married couples filing a joint tax return in which both spouses are eligible for the credit, and $3,750 each for married couples filing separate returns. The base amount is reduced by how much nontaxable income the individual receives, plus by one-half of the taxpayers' AGI beyond certain benchmarks ($7,500 for a single person, $10,000 for married taxpayers filing jointly, and $5,000 each for married taxpayers filing separately).

Taxation and the elderly

Congress's numerous revisions to the federal tax code in recent decades have caused anxiety among the senior population, because of the way in which each piece of legislation can dramatically change the treatment of BENEFITS from SOCIAL SECURITY, PRIVATE PENSIONS, estates, and distributions from MEDICARE and other vital federal programs. The most important bills are OMNIBUS BUDGET RECONCILIATION BILLS, which set parameters for federal spending that often necessitate major policy changes to the government's largest ENTITLEMENT PROGRAMS. Not all the tax changes have been negative; liberalized rules for INDIVIDUAL RETIREMENT ACCOUNTS (IRAs) and other investment vehicles are credited with helping seniors and near-retirees save more.

Some of the most-watched tax policies concern Social Security benefits. When Congress created the system in 1935, lawmakers did not exclude benefits from being taxed, but also did not include any provisions mandating a tax. Essentially benefits were treated like a gift from the government instead of like an annuity that effectively replaced earnings. That changed in the early 1980s, when the system faced a major financial crisis brought on by a combination of inflation, low wage growth, and automatic cost-of-living increases. The GREENSPAN COMMISSION recommended that, beginning in 1984, wealthier individuals with incomes above $25,000 and married couples with incomes above $32,000 include up to 50 percent of their benefits in their taxable income. The additional revenue was used to shore up the OLD-AGE AND SURVIVORS INSURANCE AND DISABILITY INSURANCE TRUST FUNDS. The Omnibus Budget Reconciliation Act of 1993 (PL 103-66) further subjected up to 85 percent of Social Security benefits to tax for individual recipients who earned more than $34,000 and couples who earned in excess of $44,000. Republicans in Congress, who opposed the provision as part of Bill Clinton's administration's 1993 budget package, attempted to roll back the extra tax during the second half of the 106th Congress.

Another aspect of taxation that is of interest to the elderly is the deductibility of medical and dental expenses. Medicare Part A and B benefits are excluded from the gross income of recipients, though this policy was never actually established by law. Instead, a series of INTERNAL REVENUE SERVICE rulings concluded that Part A benefits should not be subject to tax because they are made to further the government's social welfare objectives while Part B benefits amount to accident and health insurance. Beyond Medicare payments, the elderly spend a greater proportion of their income on health care than the nonelderly, especially in recent years due to rising prescription drug costs. The government has allowed a tax deduction for unreimbursed medical expenses above a specified base amount. However, the "floor" has risen since the 1980s. From 1954 to 1982, a taxpayer could deduct medical expenses above 3 percent of his or her gross income and separately deduct the cost of drugs if they exceeded 1 percent of gross income. The Tax Equity and Fiscal Responsibility Act of 1982 (PL 97-35) raised the floor to 5 percent, effective in 1983, and applied it to all medical expenses, thereby eliminating the separate floor for drug costs. The law also made nonprescription drugs ineligible for tax deductions. The Tax Reform Act of 1986 raised the floor again, to 7.5 percent of gross income, beginning in 1987.

Tax rules for individual retirement plans also have undergone major changes since 1981, when the Economic Recovery Tax Act first allowed workers to make tax-deductible $2,000 contributions to IRAs. The Tax Reform Act of 1986 (PL 99-514) prohibited certain high-income individuals from taking the full IRA deduction, while the Small Business Job Protection Act of 1996 (PL 104-188) expanded contributions that can be made to the IRA of a nonworking spouse. The Taxpayer Relief Act of 1997 (PL 105-34) made more significant adjustments, placing new income limits on deductible IRA contributions to individuals already in employer-sponsored plans and creating the new ROTH IRA, a backloaded variant of a conventional IRA whose contributions are not deductible, but whose earnings are not taxed upon withdrawal, as long as the account holder is at least 59-1/2 years old and the account has been open for five years.

The Taxpayer Relief Act also made changes to estate and gift taxes, gradually increasing the size of a qualified estate that can be exempt from tax from $600,000 to $1 million by 2006. Another provision gave additional exemptions to family farms and closely held family businesses, which would not be subject to tax until their estates exceeded $1.3 million. Other provisions in the act included reducing estate tax on land subject to conservation easements and reducing the interest rate on installment payments of estate tax. The 1997 act had the combined effect of complicating the tax code and generating tax incentives for wealthy and middle-class individuals in the hope of creating more incentives for saving and investment. The 106th Congress took an even bolder step by attempting to entirely do away with the federal tax on estate and gifts over a ten-year period but also change capital-gains laws to require heirs to pay more tax on the appreciated value if they sold family assets. Mostly Democratic opponents termed the effort a tax break for the nation's richest families. However, a number of fiscally conservative Democrats and groups such as the National Black Chamber of Commerce joined Republican sponsors of the effort. The black chamber said the estate tax is a barrier to building wealth in their communities. Despite some growing momentum, the measure could not achieve the two-thirds approval needed in the U.S. Senate to override an anticipated veto by Clinton.

LONG-TERM CARE costs, another source of concern to elderly Americans, are dealt with through several provisions in the Health Insurance Portability and Accountability Act of 1996 (PL 104-191). The act exempts most private and employer-sponsored long-term care insurance payments from taxes and exempts ACCELERATED DEATH BENEFITS from income tax in the case of terminally ill patients. Also excluded is income from VIATICAL AGREEMENTS involving the sale of a life-insurance contract. A number of pending proposals in Congress would address the financial burden long-term care places on families of frail elderly patients, either by providing these CARE-GIVERS tax credits or subsidies to purchase private long-term-care insurance.

While many of the recently proposed tax cuts are politically appealing and cater to well-defined segments of the electorate, policy analysts question what the ultimate cost of such proposals would be. Critics contend that, if most of the tax cuts proposed in the 106th Congress were passed, the reduced revenue to the U.S. Treasury would effectively wipe out projected federal budget surpluses. In addition, moves such as lifting the 85 percent tax on wealthy Social Security beneficiaries would only deliver tax relief to wealthy and middle-class seniors, leaving little for seniors at or near the poverty line who must struggle to pay their bills. President Clinton additionally pointed out that repealing the 1993 Social Security tax increase would rob Medicare of an estimated $2.4 trillion over the next seventy-five years, because the extra revenues are directed to the program's TRUST FUNDS. That could shorten the projected solvency of the Medicare trust fund and force lawmakers to enact benefit cuts or tax increases to keep the program afloat. Similar arguments about the rich getting richer have been made against the proposed estate tax repeal, because only about 2 percent of the population are estimated to have multimillion-dollar estates that would be subject to a tax bill under the existing tax. Despite such arguments, Republicans learned from the 2000 campaign cycle that narrowly written tax bills can gain favor with important segments of the elderly electorate. In comparison to broad tax packages, the narrow bills appear more fiscally responsible and make it harder for Democrats to oppose them, for fear of alienating key constituencies.

Telomere

A telomere is a small piece of DNA on the tip of a chromosome that scientists are studying in order to better understand the human aging process and to better treat CANCER and other diseases that involve the rapid growth of cells. Telomeres serve as a kind of molecular clock, ticking off units when DNA is copied as part of the process in which cells divide. When the telomere runs out, the cell is incapable of dividing again. Conventional human cells typically divide about fifty times, then die of old age. However, researchers at Menlo Park, California–based Geron Corporation and the University of Texas Southwestern Medical Center in 1998 reported they may have found a "fountain of youth" in the form of a rarely expressed gene that creates telomerase, an enzyme that repairs damaged telomeres and lengthens the ends of the DNA so the cells can divide many more times. The researchers were able to insert the telomerase gene into human cells so they could divide up to ninety times without an abnormality. This effectively rewound the molecular clock to a more youthful state.

Scientists hope they can harness this discovery to create new antiaging products. But they note the development only applies to those cells that divide in adulthood, such as blood, skin, and other tissues and body fluids. Other cells, such as heart muscle, do not divide in adulthood, and the way that they age is still largely unknown. Scientists refer to the reengineered cells as "rejuvenated," but stress that does not mean they will be able to rejuvenate human tissue. Instead, they hope to harness the technology to revive telomeres on specific cells—for instance, manufacturing blood

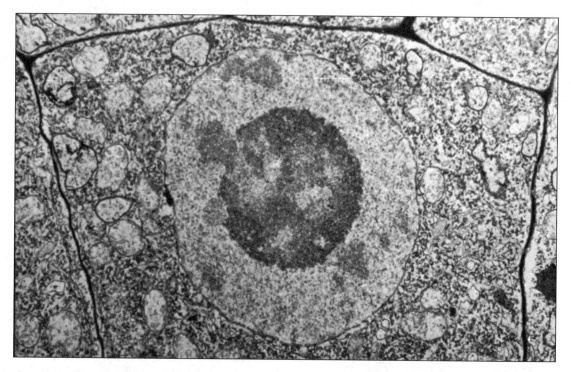

Conventional human cells, like this one, typically divide about fifty times, then die of old age. However, scientists have discovered an enzyme that lengthens the ends of the DNA so that the cells can divide many more times.
Source: National Cancer Institute

vessels for elderly patients suffering from macular degeneration, a disease of the retina.

The telomerase research may also yield promising cancer treatments. Though telomerase is dormant in most cells, it has been found to be active in about 85 percent of cancer cells. Some scientists have speculated it may be possible to develop drugs to turn off telomerase production in cancer cells, causing them to switch back to normal activity. Another school of thought is that the cell-division mechanism is the body's evolutionary response to the spread of dangerous cells like cancer. Researchers who subscribe to this view believe telomerase may actually do harm, by overriding the cell-division limit and making the body

more susceptible to tumors. Molecular biologists at the NATIONAL INSTITUTES OF HEALTH, at universities, and at biotechnology companies such as Geron continue to study telomeres and the role they play in basic cellular functions.

Therapy cap

A therapy cap is a spending limit set by the government for particular kinds of health services that are covered by ENTITLEMENT PROGRAMS. The imposition of caps is a common response to rising medical costs in certain categories of care. But adopting the policy runs the risk of causing great

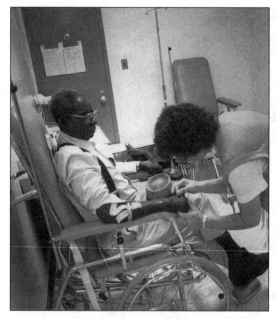

A therapy cap is a spending limit set by the government for particular kinds of health services that are covered by entitlement programs—a cause of hardship for lower-income beneficiaries. Source: D.C. General Hospital

ject to spending restrictions, or could simply switch providers to avoid having caps curtail services.

However, senior advocates complained the policies put a significant burden on STROKE victims, individuals with neurological conditions like Parkinson's disease, and some of the other sickest Medicare recipients, who frequently need OUTPATIENT SERVICES that quickly exceed the $1,500 caps. The rules, as written, put some stroke victims in the position of choosing whether it was more important to get speech or physical therapy. The move also sent shockwaves through the REHABILITATION industry, resulting in layoffs for therapists and general cutbacks in large healthcare providers' rehabilitation divisions. Opponents of the caps disputed the notion that outpatients could automatically go to hospital rehabilitation units, saying a doctor first had to certify to Medicare that the patient would benefit from the therapy, meaning some treatments would not be approved.

Faced with protests, Congress did a turnabout. SENATE SPECIAL COMMITTEE ON AGING chairman Charles Grassley, R-Iowa, inserted language in 1999 Balanced Budget Act adjustment legislation that would place a two-year moratorium on making the caps law, effective January 1, 2000. The language also directed the secretary of health and human services to study how appropriate rehabilitation services could be provided, and to recommend the best way to pay.

hardship to lower-income program beneficiaries, who often are used to obtaining fully covered services and may not have the savings to cover the added expense out-of-pocket.

Therapy caps became a particular focus of seniors after a provision in the BALANCED BUDGET ACT OF 1997 (PL 105-33) established an annual $1,500 per beneficiary limit on payments for outpatient physical and speech therapy and a separate $1,500 cap on occupational therapy. Defenders of the move said it was a legitimate response to lax government oversight of rehabilitative services that resulted in significant MEDICARE payments to therapy companies. The U.S. General Accounting Office in 1999 defended the move, saying most outpatient therapy users likely had access to hospital outpatient departments that were not sub-

Think tanks

Washington's numerous think tanks play a significant role in shaping social policy on issues affecting the elderly, frequently providing ammunition in the rhetorical wars over SOCIAL SECURITY PRIVATIZATION, MEDICARE, and MEDICAID, and in the broader debate over the budget and federal ENTITLEMENT PROGRAMS. Think tanks are often privately funded, nonprofit organizations that represent a kind of ideological "brain trust." Their staffs usually feature prominent scholars and former administration officials, who testify before congressional committees, write books and articles, present their viewpoints to the media, and participate in public forums. The most successful develop an expertise or perspective on an issue before it becomes front-page news, then help frame—and sometimes tilt—the subsequent debate. One good example is the conservative HERITAGE FOUNDATION, which in 1980 issued a paper that compared Social Security to a crooked Ponzi scheme, in which assets are taken from one investor to pay off another. The moniker stuck, and eventually helped drive a push by the Republican majority in the 105th Congress to privatize the system.

Heritage continues to be active in the Social Security debate, putting forth the position that the system faces an impending financial crisis that is impossible to ignore. The longer the wait, the higher the price of the bill to bail out the pension system, argue Heritage's scholars. Heritage in 1997 also put out a highly publicized paper claiming that African American and Hispanic seniors fare poorly under the current system, because they have lower LIFE EXPECTANCIES. Another prominent player on the political right is the libertarian Cato Institute, which has published more than forty books and articles since 1979 outlining various problems with the national pension system. Cato's Project on Social Security Privatization, launched in 1995, has produced studies backing a market-based retirement alternative

that allows workers to reinvest a portion of their payroll taxes into privately owned accounts, similar to 401(K)'s or INDIVIDUAL RETIREMENT ACCOUNTS (IRAs). Cato tends to argue that any Social Security reform should raise the rate of return for future retirees, not just ensure the solvency of the system.

Another group leaning to the right is the pro-business CONCORD COALITION, which maintains the current debate over Social Security and other entitlements should focus on long-term fiscal and economic sustainability of the programs, not only whether they remain solvent. The Concord Coalition argues that because Social Security and Medicare TRUST FUNDS only consist of IOUs from the U.S. Treasury, the moment their operating surplus turns into an operating deficit, Congress will have to take drastic measures, such as raising taxes or cutting program spending. Yet another prominent conservative think tank is the American Enterprise Institute, another proponent of privatization. AEI scholar Carolyn Weaver has also cautioned against having the government directly invest trust fund assets in private financial markets, saying such a move and any financial instability it causes could pose grave dangers to the economy.

There is no shortage of strong views on the political left. One prominent liberal think tank is the Center for Economic and Policy Research, which has challenged privatization advocates to provide reliable details of future stock returns if workers are allowed to set up individual retirement accounts. The center's liberal economists, Mark Weisbrot and Dean Baker, argue investing in the market in the future may not generate returns that outpace inflation, because of slower economic growth. That could destroy an entitlement system that has kept millions of elderly people out of poverty, the two argue. Also on the political left is AARP's Public Policy Institute, a prominent defender of the existing Social Security system. AARP argues that personal savings accounts under privatization will result in the government saving less, and make it harder to fulfill the program's long-term obligations. The organization also has raised concerns about how women would fare under a privatized system, and cautioned against raising the retirement age further as a way of shoring up the program's finances.

A number of think tanks could best be termed "middle of the road" politically. The Urban Institute features conservative scholars such as Eugene Steuerle and liberals such as Joshua Wiener offering their perspectives on Social Security, LONG-TERM CARE, and Medicare finances. The venerable Brookings Institution, often mistakenly characterized as liberal, has urged Congress to act quickly to solve Social Security's financial problems and has discussed both the merits and pitfalls associated with privatization. Perhaps the most balanced think tank is the National Academy for Social Insurance, an elected-member organization, whose scholars have generated studies on the economic status of the elderly, the way people of color fare under Social Security, and related topics.

"Third age"

The term "third age," coined by social scientists, usually refers to the period middle-aged individuals enter when they decide to leave their primary lines of work to actively pursue a second career, go back to school, or take on volunteer tasks in the community. In essence, it is the time

(sometimes decades) between midlife and the years society traditionally associates with sitting on porches in rocking chairs. Though some of these individuals technically may be retired, they remain active, usually by pursuing goals and interests they may not have had time for in their youths. Others try to apply their skills in the community. Thousands of retired business executives, for example, have volunteered to serve as mentors and advisors to small, start-up businesses through the Service Corps of Retired Executives Association (SCORE), a Washington, D.C.–based group that coordinates some of its efforts with the federal Small Business Administration. Experience Corps, a relatively new initiative that is drawing attention with the help of AARP, draws retirees from inner-city neighborhoods to tutor and otherwise assist children in struggling urban schools.

Trends indicate more BABY BOOMERS may choose this path—if they can afford to. Studies by the EMPLOYEE BENEFIT RESEARCH INSTITUTE indicate that about two-thirds of older Americans want to leave their full-time jobs before turning sixty-five, but that the vast majority expect to continue working in some capacity. Though some will have to do this out of economic necessity, many others will do it out of a sense of personal purpose, maintaining an active level of functioning to be engaged with life. One question for lawmakers is whether they should develop policies to build a national infrastructure for older people to enter and apply their talents. This could include federal grants to assist local projects or increased educational funding to retrain individuals for second careers in critical areas. Author Marc Freedman has suggested expanding MEDICARE benefits for "third agers" between ages fifty-five and sixty-five who are involved in part-time service. However, the fates of such proposals would almost cer-

An elderly volunteer tutors students in an urban school. Source: National Senior Service Corps

tainly hinge on the federal budget and spending priorities of Congress, which in recent years has been leery about awarding financial incentives for volunteerism.

Third Millennium

The Third Millennium, a New York City–based GENERATION X advocacy group created in 1993, has been widely quoted in media and policy discussions about the future of federal ENTITLEMENT PROGRAMS. Essentially, the group and its leader, Richard Thau, take the position that young adults will bear a disproportionate share of the load of funding the SOCIAL SECURITY and MEDICARE sys-

tems for the BABY BOOMER generation, but will not be able to count on the programs when their turn comes to collect. The group made waves in 1994, when it released a much-cited poll showing that more young adults believed in the existence of UFOs than believed Social Security would still exist when they retire. Polling by the group also has indicated the vast majority of young Americans want the freedom to invest a portion of their payroll taxes in private retirement accounts. More recently, Third Millennium released a study showing that individuals in their twenties and thirties face lifetime tax rates 40 percent larger than middle-aged Americans unless Congress reforms Medicare and Social Security and places the programs "on a fiscally sustainable path."

While the group depicts itself as generally representative of Generation X views, it has counterparts on the political left, such as the 2030 CENTER in Washington, D.C.

Though recent forecasts of growing TRUST FUND surpluses have taken some of the steam out of the group's arguments, Third Millennium continues to fight to be heard. During the 2000 presidential elections, it tracked how each of the candidates was trying to appeal to Generation X voters and also produced studies of Generation X voting patterns. Third Millennium has argued that the younger generation's apparent apathy to the national political process is at least in part due to politicians' tailoring their pitches and policy agendas to other, older generations, including senior citizens. In making such assertions, Third Millennium frequently triggers criticism that it is fostering INTERGENERATIONAL WARFARE. Moreover, critics of the group contend it does not speak for an entire generation, because younger Americans are more apt to organize along religious, ethnic, and other societal lines. However, Third Millennium and its media-savvy and youthful spokespeople remain influential voices in social-policy debates.

TIAA-CREF

TIAA-CREF, formally known as the Teachers Insurance and Annuity Association–College Retirement Equities Fund, is the largest private pension system in the world, with nearly $300 billion in assets and 2.3 million participants. Begun in 1918 with a $1 million grant from steel magnate Andrew Carnegie, the TIAA component of the company was designed to run the retirement accounts of university professors and individuals at academic research institutions, who tended to move from job to job and were at risk of losing pension contributions. The system allowed educational institutions to pay into a common insurance pool, essentially making participants' pensions portable. CREF was added in 1952 as the nation's first variable annuity, and now serves as the investment arm of the combined company. It offers participants eight variable-annuity options, including the CREF Stock Account, the largest equity fund in the world, with managed assets totaling $133 billion.

Because it operated as a not-for-profit entity, TIAA-CREF sometimes drew the ire of for-profit investment companies, who complained its tax status gave it an unfair advantage. The concerns eventually convinced Congress to include language in the Taxpayer Relief Act of 1997 (PL 105-34) to take away TIAA-CREF's tax-exempt status. The move prompted the company to begin offering mutual funds and other investments to the general public. Today TIAA-CREF offers 11 mutual funds, individual annuities and trust services. The company has earned praise for keeping administrative expenses low by forgoing much of the advertising and marketing its larger rivals embrace.

"Ticket to work" and the Work Incentives Improvement Act

The Work Incentives Improvement Act, more popularly known as the "TICKET TO WORK" program, (PL 106-170) was enacted by Congress and signed into law by President Bill Clinton in 1999 to help some of the approximately eight million individuals on federal disability rolls get jobs without losing their benefits. The legislation clears up a "Catch 22" in federal law under which individuals receiving SOCIAL SECURITY DISABILITY INSURANCE (SSDI) or SUPPLEMENTAL SECURITY INCOME (SSI) risked losing MEDICARE and MEDICAID health-insurance coverage if they returned to work. The law expanded Medicare coverage, allowing individuals receiving SSDI to work up to 8-1/2 years and still be guaranteed Medicare. It also expanded Medicaid coverage for low-income elderly people and the disabled by allowing states to offer Medicaid to individuals whose incomes would otherwise disqualify them from SSI payments. States also could continue to cover disabled workers whose conditions improved. The cost of the bill would be offset by changes in payments to the federal school-lunch program, as well as modifications to earned-income tax credit rules that apply to payments for foster children.

Policymakers developed the program partly because of concerns about the growth of the SSI program and the low number of people who leave the rolls through REHABILITATION (in 1997, only 297,000 individuals out of 7 million federal disability beneficiaries were referred to a state vocational rehabilitation agency). Two U.S. General Accounting Office studies found federal work incentives were not strong enough to encourage people with the potential to work to get rehabilitation training or apply for jobs. Advocates of the legislation say it could prompt millions to take advantage of the measure, including low-income or disabled individuals nearing retirement age. However, some budget forecasts believe participation will be much lower.

The legislation would provide grants to states to conduct outreach for the disabled, including attendant care to help some perform ACTIVITIES OF DAILY LIVING. Grants were to be funded at $20 million in fiscal 2001. The bill also contains a pilot program costing $250 million over six years that would allow states to provide Medicaid to individuals with degenerative conditions who do not yet meet the program's definition of disabled. States hope they can use some of the money to more quickly provide prescription drugs and keep these people in the workforce. The "ticket to work" portion of the legislation allows disabled individuals to buy rehabilitation and employment services through state agencies or private vendors. It explicitly states that taking a job would not prompt a review of the person's disability status.

Tobacco settlement

The $246 billion legal settlement between the tobacco industry and the states over smoking-related claims in November 1998 gave legislators and governors a financial windfall with which to address public-health and other social issues. Many state officials said their tobacco suits were aimed at protecting children from becoming addicted and vowed to spend some of the money on teen smoking-prevention programs. A somewhat less explored option was using the money for programs for the elderly. Groups such as the National Center for Tobacco-Free Older Persons, part of the Center for Social Gerontology in Ann Arbor, Michigan, have argued that an estimated 70 percent of the 416,000 fatalities attributed to smoking each year are among people aged sixty-five and older, and that settlement money should be applied to in-state health programs targeted at older populations.

Anecdotal evidence suggests some states are heeding the advice. A preliminary analysis compiled by the center suggested that, of the nineteen states that appropriated some tobacco settlement money in fiscal 2000, eleven used some of the money for programs for older persons. The center estimated that approximately $160 million would be spent that year, mostly on prescription-drug programs for poor seniors, and in-home care to enable the frail elderly to remain in their homes and avoid having to move to NURSING HOMES. The prescription-drug programs address the effects of rising drug prices on the elderly, an issue at the center of the federal debate over whether to expand the MEDICARE program to cover outpatient pharmaceuticals (see PRESCRIPTION DRUG BENEFIT [MEDICARE]). The issue is expected to gain political traction in the coming years, as more states decide how to spend their portions of the settlement.

Mississippi attorney general Michael Moore testifies before the House subcommittee on Health and Environment hearing on the tobacco settlement relating to Medicaid and the allocation of settlement funds. Source: *Douglas Graham, Congressional Quarterly*

Townsend, Francis E.

Before President FRANKLIN D. ROOSEVELT proposed a national pension system to deal with the effects of the Depression, California physician Francis E. Townsend (1867–1960) was advocating government pensions for the elderly as a way of ensuring economic security. Born in Illinois and a graduate of the University of Nebraska Medical School, Townsend proposed what would become the "Townsend Plan" in a 1933 letter in a Long Beach, California, newspaper. Townsend advocated giving citizens aged sixty and older a $200 monthly pension, on the condition the money be spent within thirty days of receipt, in the United States. The plan was to be financed by a 2 percent sales tax. The plan struck a chord during times of great economic uncertainty, when bank failures made many people's lifetime savings disappear and large companies were dropping their pension programs. The proposal earned the zealous

California physician Francis E. Townsend advocated government pensions for the elderly as a way of ensuring economic security. Source: AP Photo

Townsend a loyal following of "Townsendites," who exerted political pressure on policymakers. Like-minded reformers included novelist Upton Sinclair, who called for $50-per-month state pensions for everyone over sixty-five during his 1932 gubernatorial campaign in California. Most economists, however, viewed Townsend's plan as unworkable and fiscally irresponsible—a view shared by Roosevelt, who never endorsed it.

Townsend was not the only public figure calling for a national pension system. Sen. Huey "Kingfish" Long, D-La., proposed giving every American a $5,000 house and $2,000 in income and other benefits. In Congress, Sen. Charles Dill, D-Wash., and Rep. William Connery, D-Mass., introduced legislation that would provide federal assistance to those states that enacted pension laws for the elderly. The groundswell of support for such plans is believed to have gradually shifted Roosevelt's focus from developing public-works projects that would employ younger people to the design of the SOCIAL SECURITY system in 1934. Townsend expressed disappointment in Social Security, because its payments were far less than the $200 per month he had proposed, because it did not ensure immediate benefit payments, and because recipients had to work as a precondition to receiving a payment. Townsend modified his plan in the 1940s, and bills to establish the plan were regularly defeated in Congress, even as the national economy began to rebound and the effects of Social Security became widespread. Townsend also slipped into disrepute, seeking to revive his fame by appearing on the podium of bigoted radio priest Father Charles Coughlin. In 1956, he wrote President Dwight D. Eisenhower, imploring him to "emancipate" white citizens from poverty, much as Abraham Lincoln emancipated the slaves. Despite sometimes-outlandish behavior toward the end of his life, Townsend wielded significant political influence during the formative years of Social Security and left an enormous mark on Depression-era politics.

Transition costs

The term "transition costs" refers to the billions of dollars in extra costs many say the government would incur if it implements a privatized SOCIAL SECURITY system. Transition costs are due to the fact that the government, in the short term, would continue to pay existing benefits to current retirees, but would be collecting less revenue from younger workers, who presumably would be investing a portion of payroll taxes in private retirement accounts. The Washington-based Center on Budget and Policy Priorities has estimated the shortfall of funds necessary to maintain current benefit levels could total $900 billion over ten years for the most commonly discussed PRIVATIZATION scenario, in which workers would be allowed to invest 2 percent of payroll taxes. The SOCIAL SECURITY ADMINISTRATION has gone further, estimating that costs could total as much as $8.9 trillion over several decades, especially if payroll taxes are diverted at a time of rising wages.

Critics of privatization say the situation amounts to "paying for two retirements," because individuals would have to save and invest in the private system, yet still have to cover the outstanding obligations of the traditional system. The added steep transition costs could well negate any increase in net savings or other positive economic benefits of privatization. Some Democratic critics of privatization have gone as far as saying transition costs, combined with targeted tax cuts also championed by Republicans, could force the government back into a cycle of deficit spending.

Defenders of privatization, however, say the fears are grossly exaggerated. The extra "cost," in the view of advocates such as Peter Ferrara of Americans for Tax Reform and Michael Tanner of the Cato Institute, is increased savings under the new system, which would be recouped at a later date along with the return on the investment. Hence, privatization would not involve sacrificing anything or consuming more resources—traditional definitions of cost. Instead, it would generate new assets through savings and investment that would gradually pay off the program's liabilities.

While some of their argument appears to hinge on semantics, privatization advocates have suggested a number of ways of financing outstanding benefits while workers change over to the new privatized system. First, they note, workers who opt for private accounts will receive fewer BENEFITS from the "old" Social Security system, reducing the transition financing deficit in the long term. Under some privatization schemes, workers and employers would continue to pay full payroll taxes, even though workers will be allowed to divert a percentage of wages into personal retirement accounts. Short-term Social Security TRUST FUND surpluses could also provide a buffer during the transition period. And privatization advocates say levying taxes on a portion of the new savings and investment in private accounts will generate a new source of additional taxes to the government, while still ensuring that workers receive a greater payout than they would have under the old system. This, of course, assumes that stock and bond markets, and the broad indices that the investments would be tied to, would perform according to historical trends.

Trust funds

The trust funds that finance SOCIAL SECURITY and MEDICARE are government accounts that, contrary to popular belief, do not receive and hold the payroll taxes that finance the ENTITLEMENT PROGRAMS, or pay the benefit checks. Instead, the accounts contain the IOUs the U.S. Treasury issues the programs when it borrows the taxes to finance the government's day-to-day operations. When the system collects more in taxes

OASI, DI, HI, and SMI Cost as a Percentage of GDP

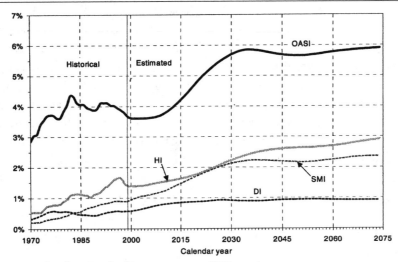

Source: Social Security and Medicare Boards of Trustees, summary of 2000 annual reports.
Note: OASI=Old-Age and Survivors Insurance; DI=Disability Insurance; HI=Hospital Insurance; and SMI=Supplementary Medical Insurance.

than it pays out in benefits, as is currently the case, the surplus is reflected in an increased balance of Treasury securities posted to the trust funds. The balances essentially serve as future claims that, should money be needed to pay program benefits, the Treasury will find the resources to cover the amounts. Like government bonds sold to the public, the securities also generate interest—equivalent to the interest on a Treasury security with a maturity of four years or longer—that is posted to the accounts. It is the Treasury that cuts the benefit checks for the programs, and deducts securities of an equivalent value from the trust funds.

The trust funds include the Social Security Old-Age and Survivors Insurance Trust Fund, created in 1940 to finance the core Social Security benefit, and the Federal Disability Insurance Trust Fund, created in 1956 to fund disability insurance. Medicare trust funds include the Federal Hospital Insurance Trust Fund, created in 1956 to pay the inpatient hospital expenses under Part A, and the Federal Supplementary Medical Insurance Trust Fund, created in 1965 to pay for physician and OUTPATIENT SERVICES under Part B.

The reason that separate Social Security and Medicare trust funds exist is that as long as the trust funds have a positive balance, the Treasury has the legal authority to keep writing benefit checks. In this sense, the government has a long-term budgetary obligation to keep running the program. This is part of the reason that proponents of the programs as well as those who call for overhauling the entitlements both fixate on keeping the trust funds solvent, that is, to have money in the bank, and not to incur even short-term deficits. Unlike most trust funds, the government does not need annual congressional approval to tap the Social Security and Medicare trust funds. Because they are entitlement programs, the Treasury can automatically spend funds on their behalf, as long as the funds have a positive balance.

Trusts

Trusts are estate-planning arrangements that increasingly are being used instead of wills, because of legal and tax advantages, by wealthy individuals or by families that face special circumstances. A trust is set up to establish ownership of assets in a person's estate and usually is run by the individual who sets up the trust, called the grantor. In a revocable, or living, trust, terms of the arrangement can be changed while the grantor is alive. When the grantor dies, the terms become permanent and assets are transferred to beneficiaries by a trustee, who acts like an executor of a will.

One advantage of trusts is they can be used as a way to get around lengthy and sometimes expensive probate proceedings, because transfers are made directly to beneficiaries. Another advantage is that some families can effectively double the estate-tax exemption, which stood at $675,000 in 2000 and gradually is rising to $1 million by 2006. When an individual dies and leaves everything to his or her spouse, there is an automatic tax exemption on unlimited amounts of assets. But when the spouse dies, the estate-tax exemption kicks in, and amounts over the threshold are taxed. Putting all the assets in a trust preserves both spouses' tax exemptions for the heirs, allowing them to inherit up to $1.35 million (two times $675,000) tax free. In addition to these advantages, trusts can help sort out complicated estate issues arising from two or more marriages, the disposition of property in different states, and other considerations.

Congress recognized the growing popularity of trusts, and the fact they perform the same functions as probate estates, by enacting a series of legislative changes in the Taxpayer Relief Act of 1997 (PL 105-34). The technical changes reduced the differences in tax treatments between trusts and estates, allowing trustees to elect to treat and tax the trust as part of the deceased person's estate for up to two years after death. The changes also allowed trustees to elect to designate distribution of assets during the first sixty-five days of the estate's tax year as made in the previous tax year.

But the growth in popularity of living trusts has also prompted a rise in consumer fraud. AARP and other senior advocates report a rise in unscrupulous operators selling living trusts to moderate- to low-income elderly people, who have no need for such complicated instruments. Some marketers are reported to have illegally represented themselves as representing AARP. The operators typically charge large sums to draft documents that in no way take into account the buyers' needs, and often contain boilerplate legal language that does not conform to the particular laws in the state where a senior lives. Some have used high-pressure sales pitches to gather personal financial information about seniors or to sell them other investment products. AARP representatives told a July 2000 hearing of the SENATE SPECIAL COMMITTEE ON AGING that 18 percent of people over the age of fifty with incomes under $25,000 had living trusts, a 125 percent increase over the number that had the legal instruments in 1991. In addition to the potential for outright fraud, financial planners and senior groups warn that opting for a trust could make it more difficult for elderly with modest means to apply for MEDICAID if they have LONG-TERM CARE needs, because income and resources from a trust may be counted in determining eligibility for the program. Experts recommend individuals contemplating setting up a trust first consult with an accountant or estate planner.

2030 Center

This Washington-based GENERATION X advocacy group was founded in 1997 and provides a political counterpoint to the better-known THIRD MILLENNIUM and the now-defunct LEAD OR LEAVE on social-insurance principles. An outgrowth of the three-million-member United States Student Association, the 2030 Center defends the traditional SOCIAL SECURITY system, arguing it is more important to provide a guaranteed benefit for retirement than to increase the program's rate of return. The group (whose name reflects both the target age group of members and the demographically significant year in which many will near retirement age) was started by Christopher Cuomo and Hans Riemer, who have commissioned polls showing a majority of young adults want to use federal budget surpluses to strengthen Social Security.

The 2030 Center also has argued that it is important to provide a social safety net for the growing number of temporary workers in the American workforce, who typically earn lower wages, do not enjoy full benefits, may not be covered under certain labor and employment laws, and generally face more economic insecurity than permanent workers. The group's leaders say many young adults fall into this category because of CONTINGENT WORK in high-tech, telecommunications, finance, and other sectors of the economy.

209(b) states

While being declared eligible for SUPPLEMENTAL SECURITY INCOME (SSI) technically also qualifies a beneficiary to be enrolled in MEDICAID, state governments have several options for ultimately deciding whether the person is admitted into their program. The majority of states enter into agreements with the SOCIAL SECURITY ADMINISTRATION to automatically cover all SSI recipients with Medicaid eligibility, without additional applications or screening. However, eleven states as of 1998 used an option called 209(b), named for the corresponding section of Medicaid law, that allows them to impose Medicaid eligibility criteria that is more restrictive than that used by SSI. This may include tougher definitions of blindness or disability, or different income eligibility tests. The criteria are judged to be valid as long as they are not more restrictive than the state's approved Medicaid plan as of January 1972. These 209(b) states still must allow aged, blind, and disabled persons to spend down their assets in order to qualify for LONG-TERM CARE under Medicaid. States using the more restrictive option are Connecticut, Hawaii, Illinois, Indiana, Minnesota, Missouri, New Hampshire, North Dakota, Ohio, Oklahoma, and Virginia. Approximately 20 percent of SSI recipients nationwide live in these states.

U

Underinsured

Within the context of aging policy, the term "underinsured" often refers to the approximately forty million MEDICARE recipients who lack outpatient prescription-drug coverage. These individuals were at the center of an increasingly heated debate in the 106th Congress, as Republican and Democratic lawmakers prescribed solutions to the problem of soaring drug prices, particularly for low-income elderly people. Democrats unveiled pricing surveys in various cities that showed large discrepancies between what bulk purchasers of drugs—such as HMOs or employers with private health plans—paid for medications, and the prices charged to ordinary consumers with no drug coverage. One U.S. Department of HEALTH AND HUMAN SERVICES study in 2000 concluded the uninsured elderly paid an average of 15 percent more than large purchasers, who typically can negotiate volume discounts with drugmakers.

President Bill Clinton, and the majority of congressional Democrats, argued for adding a PRESCRIPTION DRUG BENEFIT to the Medicare program, while Republicans called for government subsidies so Medicare recipients could buy private drug coverage. Both plans called for special provisions to aid the elderly poor. However, election-year politics and the significant differences in approaches assured that the matter

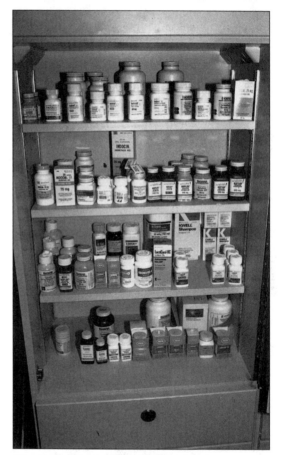

The approximately forty million Medicare recipients who lack coverage for prescription drugs are collectively referred to as "underinsured." Source: R. Michael Jenkins, *Congressional Quarterly*

will not be solved until the 107th Congress, at earliest.

Underinsured Americans should not be confused with the "uninsured," a separate category of approximately three million Americans between the ages of fifty-five and sixty-four who have no medical insurance and whom the Clinton administration recommended offering coverage under Medicare.

Uniform Health Care-Decisions Act

The Uniform Health-Care Decisions Act is a set of procedures developed in 1993 by the National Conference of Commissioners on Uniform State Laws to help state legislatures draft standards dealing with health-care decision making when a patient is incapacitated and cannot express his or her wishes. The effort was prompted by the 1990 U.S. Supreme Court case *Cruzan by Cruzan v. Director, Missouri Department of Health,* in which the high court upheld a Missouri decision refusing the request of the parents of a comatose woman to cut off the medical care that prolonged their daughter's life. Fallout from the case led many legal experts and legislators to conclude something should be done about the fragmented, often inconsistent state-by-state rules regarding ADVANCE DIRECTIVES, powers of attorney for health care, and surrogate decision making. Since the procedures were drafted, at least a half dozen states—Alabama, Delaware, Hawaii, Maine, Mississippi, and New Mexico—have adopted them. AARP and the American Bar Association have endorsed the effort, which has a direct bearing on cases in which a patient is in a coma or being kept alive by artificial means.

The act first recognizes a competent person's right to decide all aspects of his or her care. It authorizes that decisions be made by a surrogate (usually a family member or close friend), who can speak for the individual when he or she cannot, or chooses not to. The act attempts to simplify the drafting of advance directives by stipulating that the instructions can be written or oral, and that MEDICAL POWERS OF ATTORNEY, while required to be in writing, need not be witnessed to be legally binding.

The act also tries to accommodate the ailing patient's desires by stipulating that the agent must make decisions based on the patient's wishes, to the extent they are known, or on what is in the patient's best interests, taking into account his or her personal values. It bars guardians from revoking a ward's advance-care directions without court approval. The act requires health-care providers to comply with the instructions, but allows them to opt out if the directives require medically inadequate care or care that runs counter to acceptable medical standards. Finally, the act authorizes courts to step in when necessary and specifies who can petition the court. The state laws that arise from adoption of the act complement the federal PATIENT SELF-DETERMINATION ACT (PL 101-508) which was enacted in 1990 and requires that health-care providers that participate in MEDICARE and MEDICAID inform patients about advance directives and, in cases where they have not already done so, give them the means to execute one.

United Nations Year of Older Persons

In 1992, the United Nations General Assembly designated 1999 as the International Year of Older Persons, hoping to focus the attention of member

In developing nations, where most of the world's older people live, the United Nations Year of Older Persons helped governments organize and identify agencies that could assess the needs of the elderly and improve their lives. Source: Library of Congress

nations on the needs of the elderly and help them tailor laws, programs, and policies in that direction. A U.N. resolution drafted at the time of the designation noted "humanity's demographic coming of age," and said it should inspire "maturing attitudes and capabilities in social, economic, cultural, and spiritual undertakings." The U.N. adopted eighteen principles that included calls to give older people access to basic services and care; more opportunities to work; better access to health, social, and legal services, as well as access to educational, cultural, recreational, and spiritual resources. The principles also endorsed efforts to fight senior exploitation, as well as physical and mental abuse. Depending on how one looked at

it, some of the broadly worded principles were already being addressed in existing U.S. laws, but nonetheless served to spur more public awareness. The U.S. Department of HEALTH AND HUMAN SERVICES' ADMINISTRATION ON AGING, for example, organized a conference of more than two dozen federal agencies to discuss issues affecting the elderly, while private groups undertook a series of projects to publicize the international year and its goals. In developing nations, where most of the world's older people live, the year of older persons helped governments organize and identify agencies that could assess the needs of the elderly and improve their lives.

Universal coverage

"Universal coverage" refers to a system in which the government guarantees health insurance to all its citizens. The most commonly cited examples are Canada's, in which the government pays private doctors and hospitals, and the system in Great Britain, where the health-care providers work on a government salary. Advocates say importing such a system to the United States would prevent situations in which employers decline to provide insurance for their workers, leaving them uncovered as they approach their retirement years. However, Congress has failed to reach anything close to a consensus on how to implement such a system.

President Bill Clinton called for a universal coverage scheme in his failed 1993–1994 health-care reform proposal. Clinton hoped to prompt employers to insure their workers and have the government provide subsidized health coverage for the remainder of the population. But a large number of Democrats broke with the president and called for a "single-payer" system like Canada's, that would have the government pay private health-care providers. Some Republicans, meanwhile, pushed a third approach that would have required every person to purchase health insurance and also would have provided government assistance for individuals with low incomes. Universal coverage is sometimes confused with universal access, a policy under which insurance companies are required to sell policies to everyone who applies for coverage, regardless of their medical conditions.

Unnecessary treatment

When policymakers discuss the financial state of MEDICARE, they often bring up the issue of unnecessary treatments—understood to mean expensive medical procedures that are billed to the government and deliver questionable, if any, benefit to the patient. Exactly what constitutes an unnecessary treatment, and who should decide, has been a perpetual point of contention between doctors and bottom-line-oriented health insurers in the debate over managed care. But government auditors, by simply confining the definition to suspicious and even fraudulent billings, have shown they are costing Medicare billions of dollars. When Bill Clinton's administration launched a widespread crackdown on Medicare fraud in 1996, one government study discovered $23.2 billion in overpayments, which constituted about 14 percent of the program's fee-for-service spending. By 1999, the figure had fallen to $13.5 billion, or about 8 percent.

Unnecessary treatments can take many forms. They can involve hospitals discharging and readmitting elderly patients suffering from chronic illnesses on a near-weekly basis, in an effort to circumvent Medicare spending caps. Another often-cited tactic is repeatedly ordering expensive diagnostic tests, such as CAT scans and x-rays, for a diagnosis that already is known. Government auditors report that, in many cases, there is inadequate documentation to back up even legitimate medical decisions, leaving the validity of the treatment in doubt. And certain medical treatments that result in inconclusive results also can straddle the line between necessary and unnecessary care. One example is whether to order aggressive and risky treatments for certain small

PROSTATE cancer tumors in elderly men when it is not clear which are latent and which could become life-threatening. Many private insurers, faced with the prospect of patients suing them for denied care, have adopted a strategy of "defensive medicine," and approved many of these questionable charges. The matter is more difficult for government health programs, which often are under severe cost constraints and facing rapid inflation in areas such as HOME HEALTH CARE, medical equipment, and supplies. In the area of diagnostic care, Medicare has been skeptical about a blood test for a protein called prostate-specific antigen (PSA), noting an elevated reading is not necessarily proof that the patient has cancer.

Managed-care companies that participate in Medicare are developing new criteria to gauge what is an unnecessary treatment—much to the chagrin of doctors, who long have complained that their decisions are being questioned. Some Medicare HMOs have developed a payment system called "case-rate capitation" that pays medical specialists a flat fee based on the patient's diagnosis and the severity of the condition. Some health-care experts believe this approach could reduce the wide variation in the way doctors treat patients that some link to unnecessary treatments. However, doctors believe any type of capped rate encourages providing the least care, and could endanger patients.

V

Veterans' benefits

The federal government provides veterans guaranteed health care and a variety of other services through the cabinet-level Department of Veterans Affairs (VA), the second-largest of the fourteen cabinet agencies. In fiscal 2000, the VA was expected to provide care to 3.6 million veterans and dependents through a network directly run by the government that consists of 172 medical centers, 600 ambulatory care and outpatient facilities, 132 NURSING HOMES, 40 domiciliaries (facilities that provide non-skilled nursing care), and 73 home-care programs. The VA's fiscal 2000 appropriation stood at $44.3 billion, up from $43.7 billion in fiscal 1999.

Prior to 1996, the government maintained rigid criteria for which veterans could receive which health services. Priority was given to those with service-related injuries or illnesses, or those low-income veterans who could not afford to get care anywhere else. The system was heavily weighted to providing inpatient care in VA hospitals. The criteria changed dramatically when Congress revised eligibility rules (PL 104-262) to move more care to less expensive outpatient settings and allow the VA to give all veterans as much access to the full range of VA services as the agency's budget allows. The shift in policy was significant; previously many veterans with less-serious ailments had to have already been admitted to a VA hospital or meet a complicated set of legal

requirements to get outpatient care. Previous efforts to change the rules failed because of fears that expanded access to OUTPATIENT SERVICES would prompt many more veterans to seek such care, costing taxpayers billions of more dollars. To address the concern, lawmakers capped spending on medical programs ($19.4 billion in fiscal 2000) and required the VA to set up a new priority system to ensure that the department remains within its budget. One of the ways the department is trying to treat more patients within the parameters is by setting up integrated health networks in certain areas that can provide multiple levels of care and pool resources to save money.

The VA also has a broad array of medical and scientific research programs. VA physicians pioneered treatment of conditions such as post-traumatic stress disorder, and were the first to perform kidney transplants and administer successful drug treatments for schizophrenia and high blood pressure. The department also has been a leader in developing prosthetic devices and in treating exposure to Agent Orange, a defoliant used during the Vietnam War that later was found to cause health problems.

Medical care is but the largest benefit the government provides veterans. Education is another. Since the first GI Bill became law in 1944, more than 20.7 million beneficiaries have received college tuition or vocational training benefits. The VA also provides education subsidies for dependents of veterans whose deaths or permanent or total dis-

Philadelphia veterans protest cuts in veterans benefits when lawmakers capped spending on medical programs.
Source: File photo

abilities were service-related. The total cost of the education benefits has been more than $73 billion.

The VA additionally operates one of the largest life insurance programs in the world, administering six separate programs that had 2.2 million policies in force at the end of fiscal 1998 with a face value of $24.1 billion. The programs include the Serviceman's Group Life Insurance and Veterans' Group Life Insurance programs, which together provide approximately $480 billion in insurance coverage to some 3 million veterans, active-duty personnel, reservists, and national guardsmen. The agency is expected to return nearly $751 million to 1.9 million veterans holding in-force life insurance policies.

Separate from the VA, the military also maintains a retirement system for active-duty personnel that pays benefits based on a percentage of the individual's base pay while on active duty. The system is noncontributory, meaning all benefits are paid by the employing branch of the armed services, without contributions from beneficiaries. Benefits for the approximately 2 million retired officers, enlisted personnel, and their survivors were expected to total $33.7 billion in 2000. Military personnel also have received full SOCIAL SECURITY coverage since 1957. Because many retire from the armed forces after twenty years of service while still in their forties, it is not uncommon to find them retiring from a second career with a private pension from their employer, the military pension, and full Social Security BENE-FITS. Congress in 1986 changed the calculation for future benefits as part of the Military Retirement Reform Act (PL 99-348), in part to award more generous benefits to those personnel who remain on active duty longer.

Viagra

Pfizer Incorporated's anti-impotence drug, Viagra, chemically known as sildenafil citrate, burst onto the market in 1998 and immediately created a social and medical phenomenon. Millions of older men turned to the blue pills to restore lost vitality, making the once-taboo topic of "erectile dysfunction" a common subject in doctors' offices. Public knowledge of the drug was boosted by former senator and Republican presidential candidate Robert Dole of Kansas, who made a series of widely aired television commercials, tastefully touting its effectiveness. As of the first quarter of 2000, there had been more than nineteen million Viagra prescriptions written in the United States for six million patients, and the drug had been approved for use in more than one hundred countries. While the drug was approved by the Food and Drug Administration for use in a relatively small number of cases in which impotence results from a medical condition or treatment (such as men who become impotent as a result of PROSTATE surgery) most of the use of the drug actually is for non-approved reasons. This is legal, as long as the doctor makes this clear to patients.

Many experts lump Viagra with a class of so-called lifestyle drugs that also include medications for weight loss, baldness, and smoking ad-

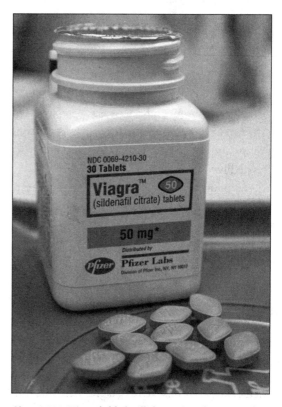

Since 1998, Viagra's blue pills have given hope to millions of older men. Source: Toby Talbot, AP Photo

diction that increasingly are targeted at aging BABY BOOMERS. To maximize sales, drugmakers have spent billions of dollars marketing the products directly to consumers, hoping print advertisements and TV commercials will prompt patient inquiries and pressure doctors to write more prescriptions. The popularity of Viagra also has helped fuel the rise of Internet pharmacies—an increased focus of concern for Congress and federal regulators, because some on-line operators dispense drugs without requiring prescriptions and may be illegally shipping unapproved drugs from abroad.

While its benefits are widely praised, Viagra does not work for everyone. The drug can lower blood pressure to dangerous levels when taken with certain heart medications, and does not work for individuals with heart conditions and other circulatory problems. Its long-term health effects also are largely unknown. However, physicians say the product otherwise is far preferable to other sexual potency treatments, such as vacuum pumps and drugs that have to be inserted or injected directly into the penis.

The popularity of Viagra has created interesting policy considerations for private health plans and the federal-state MEDICAID program. Because of its relatively high cost (usually $7 to 10 per pill), some HMOs like Kaiser-Permanente declined to cover Viagra on economic grounds, arguing that even limiting use to ten pills per month could result in hundreds of millions of dollars of new costs every year. Other HMOs approved rules that limited Viagra coverage to a limited number of pills per month. About half of the state-run Medicaid programs have Viagra benefits, but some states have argued that program dollars should be better spent on medications to treat serious illnesses. MEDICARE does not cover Viagra, because the program does not pay for self-administered drugs. However, some HMOs that participate in Medicare may extend Viagra benefits.

Viatical agreement

Viatical agreements are a controversial type of financial arrangement in which an individual sells a whole, universal, or term life insurance policy to a company and receives a portion of the face value in return. The company then assumes the role of paying premiums, and collects the full amount of the policy when the original holder dies. The amount the holder receives depends on his or her age and health status, the size of the death benefit, and the number of years the policy has been in force. Contract holders typically receive about half the face value of the policy.

Viatical agreements first came into vogue in the late 1980s for people dying of AIDS, who sought new sources of income to pay for experimental drugs and therapies. In recent years, they have become popular among some elderly persons suffering from terminal illnesses, such as CANCER or advanced-stage kidney disease. The companies that purchase the policies often depict the transactions as a compassionate way of helping dying people obtain needed cash during their final days. However, consumer advocates and federal law-enforcement officials say the viatical market has become rife with fraud. Some companies have been accused of using high-pressure sales tactics to convince seniors to close out their life insurance policies without explaining the risks involved. Others have attracted comment and concern about the common practice of packaging the various insurance policies they purchase and selling shares to investors. The "investment" essentially consists of waiting for the original owners to die and betting that the payouts on the face values of the policies exceed the premiums paid in. Some consumer advocates say this unregulated practice should come under governmental scrutiny, because the companies are essentially creating a product that resembles a security. Federal agents in 2000 raided the offices of viatical settlement dealers in four states as part of a fraud investigation.

Viatical companies are often thought to seek out people with shorter LIFE EXPECTANCIES, reasoning that it would take less time to collect on their policies. However, the companies increasingly are buying policies from relatively healthy, well-heeled individuals in their seventies, who no longer think they need their life insurance policies. These transactions, known as "senior settlements," may take longer to generate profits for investors, but also are viewed as somewhat more savory than deals targeting the very ill.

One alternative to viatical agreements is to purchase a life insurance policy with an ACCELERATED DEATH BENEFIT, or living benefit, provision. This allows the insured person to collect a portion of the death benefit before he or she actually dies. This option usually provides a bigger payment than a viatical agreement, but is most often available only to those persons with life expectancies of twelve months or less. Individuals who do consider a viatical agreement should obtain several bids to get a better sense of what their insurance policy is worth, and should check to make sure the company they deal with is licensed in the state where they live, if the state has such a requirement.

Vision loss

Aging-related physiological changes in the eye have placed vision loss only behind ARTHRITIS and rheumatism as a cause of disability among the elderly. Common problems in individuals aged sixty-five and over include macular degeneration in the retina, the thickening and clouding of the lens, DIABETES-related damage to blood vessels in the retina, and glaucoma. An estimated 6.6 million older Americans have trouble seeing, even with corrective glasses, according to the advocacy group Lighthouse International. The ALLIANCE FOR AGING RESEARCH estimates eye diseases account for $26 billion per year in LONG-TERM CARE COSTS, in part because studies have shown vision impairment increases the risk of falls and injuries,

such as hip fractures. MEDICARE does not currently cover rehabilitative services for the visually impaired—a situation some policymakers believe is inconsistent, because the program offers some REHABILITATION coverage to individuals who suffer heart attacks, STROKES, and other types of ailments. Advocates for such coverage note vision loss is a leading cause of loss of independence in the elderly, a situation that can lead to institutionalization, DEPRESSION, and other ill effects. Efforts to expand coverage have been proposed in recent Congresses.

Age-related macular degeneration, or AMD, is the leading cause of blindness in seniors and is characterized by a breakdown of cells in the macula, the light-sensitive tissue at the center of the retina. In most cases, individuals begin to lose central vision in one eye, a condition that cannot be reversed. The disease may or may not spread to the other eye. In about 10 percent of cases, fragile new blood vessels in the retina begin to grow toward the macula and can leak blood and fluid under the tissue, a condition known as "wet AMD" that accounts for 90 percent of the serious vision loss from the disease. While the precise cause of the condition is unknown, researchers say nearly 30 percent of individuals aged seventy-five and older have a chance of getting AMD. Women, smokers, and individuals with high cholesterol seem to be at greater risk of contracting the disease. The National Eye Institute, a division of the NATIONAL INSTITUTES OF HEALTH, is studying how sealing some blood vessels with argon lasers could prevent vision loss for those at highest risk.

Cataracts, or the clouding of the lens, are another common vision problem due to aging. More than half of all Americans over the age of sixty-five have cataracts, but the severity varies. The condition is caused by a clumping of proteins

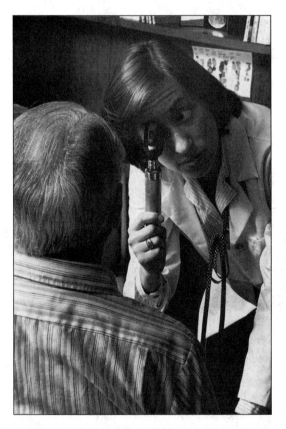

An elderly patient gets scanned for cataracts at a Boston eye clinic. More than half of all Americans over the age of sixty-five have cataracts. Source: USDA Photo

in the lens due to age, congenital conditions, or other diseases. Surgery using ultrasound to break up the cloudy part of the lens, or to simply remove the hard center of the lens, has proven highly effective, with success rates of 90 percent or better.

Older individuals with either Type I or Type II DIABETES also run the risk of developing diabetic retinopathy, a degenerative condition in which small blood vessels in the retina begin to leak, causing swelling and damage to the tissue. Laser surgery or removal of some of the clear vitreous gel that fills the inside of the eye can often correct this problem.

"Glaucoma" is a term describing several conditions characterized by the buildup of pressure inside the eye. If left untreated, the condition can damage the optic nerve at the rear of the organ and cause blindness. More than three million Americans are affected, half of whom do not know they have it because the disease causes no pain and only gradually begins to erode side vision. African Americans are three to four times as likely as whites to have the condition, and all individuals over the age of sixty are at risk of contracting the disease. Eye drops, laser treatments, and conventional surgery to make a new drain to relieve the pressure are all treatment options, depending on severity. National Eye Institute studies have shown that blacks and whites with advanced glaucoma respond better to different treatments.

Vitamins and supplements

Each year, elderly people buy billions of dollars' worth of vitamins, nutritional supplements, and herbal remedies to cure conditions ranging from ARTHRITIS and poor circulation to feeble-mindedness. Some of the products have demonstrable health effects: calcium and vitamin D supplements can reduce bone loss and the risk of fractures. But while most multivitamins approved by the U.S. Food and Drug Administration (FDA) are safe, many other supplements and remedies fall into a regulatory gray zone and have come under increased scrutiny for their safety and efficacy. Consumer advocates and the NATIONAL INSTITUTE ON AGING have issued warnings about certain classes of products, saying they could have unintended side effects or trigger adverse reactions with prescription medications that an elderly person may be taking. Exactly what the government can do in response is the subject of intense debate between the FDA and product manufacturers.

The vitamin and supplement industry has evolved into a business with annual sales in excess of $10 billion. Unlike prescription drugs, which have to pass clinical trials, the products come under the Dietary Supplement Health and Education Act of 1994 (PL 103-417), which permits firms to claim their products have beneficial health effects, as long as they do not claim they cure disease. Companies give the FDA advance warning before they make any product claims, and the agency reserves the right to challenge them. However, regulators have the burden of proving that a product is unsafe before they can request that it be pulled from the market.

Consumer advocates and seniors groups such as AARP worry that products targeted at seniors that claim to improve memory, promote PROSTATE health, and reverse the aging process may persuade a person to forgo proven treatments, but may wind up being unreliable or even dangerous. For instance, St. John's wort, an herbal remedy promoted as a possible remedy for DE-PRESSION in the late 1990s, has been found in some cases to interfere with liver proteins that metabolize drugs, meaning that prescription medications may have their strength and efficacy altered. Questions also have been raised about supplements that have active ingredients that are chemically akin to what is found in some prescription drugs. One such supplement, Cholestin, is a pulverized rice extract touted to improve blood flow. Supplement makers say the 1994 act prohibits them from chemically mimicking an approved drug, adding the FDA should continue to regulate their products as they do food, and only step in when there is a demonstrated safety concern.

Public health officials say the elderly should consult with doctors before taking any supplements, vitamins, or other remedies. Seniors usually obtain enough of these items if they maintain a balanced diet. However, in some cases, the products may prove effective. Vitamin D supplements, for instance, can help postmenopausal women recover more quickly from bone injuries, such as hip fractures. Vitamins C and E have been shown to have anti-oxidative properties that can fight free radicals that damage proteins and nucleic acids, such as DNA in mitochondria, the cellular components that produce energy.

W

Wage base (maximum taxable wage)

The wage base, also known as the maximum taxable wage, refers to the maximum amount of wages that are subject to SOCIAL SECURITY taxes. In 2000, the amount was $76,200, up from $72,600 in 1999. Anything above the wage base is not subject to the 12.4 percent payroll tax that is used to fund current Social Security BENEFITS. However, such excess earnings also are not used to calculate future program benefits. The wage base is adjusted annually based on the growth in average annual wages.

The wage base has fluctuated since Social Security's inception, when Congress in 1939 capped taxable income at $3,000. From 1945 to 1965, the proportion of wages subject to the payroll tax declined. But from 1965 to the mid-1980s, the proportion covered by the tax increased, in part to pay for MEDICARE, COST-OF-LIVING ADJUSTMENTS to Social Security benefits, and other expansions to the system. Since 1983, the proportion has declined slowly and is projected to continue falling until at least 2004. It is important to remember that each time the wage base increases, a higher percentage of workers' income is subject to taxation, though most workers are simultaneously enjoying higher income.

Over the years, some defenders of the Social Security system have suggested eliminating the wage base and subjecting all income to Social Security taxes to extend the system's solvency. The reasoning is that such a move might appear more politically palatable than raising the payroll tax and could raise enough new revenues to deal with any funding shortfalls created by the retirement of the BABY BOOMER generation. However, conservatives say scrapping the wage base would amount to a huge tax increase—$425.2 billion over five years, according to one 1998 HERITAGE FOUNDATION estimate—and damage the economy while removing incentives to work. Indeed, opponents of such a move predict workers would find ways around the tax—perhaps by taking some income in the form of nontaxable fringe benefits. Given the political sensitivity surrounding Social Security, and projections of sustained financial viability, it is unlikely that such a move will be contemplated in the near term.

Waiver of premium

A waiver of premium is a type of rider one can purchase for life insurance or long-term insurance policies. It outlines conditions under which the contract can be kept in force without the payment of premiums. The rider is most advantageous for individuals who suffer serious disabilities that prevent them from working and earning income. Language can be crafted that stipulates that when proof of the disability is furnished to the insurer, all further premium payments are suspended during the disability. While many insurers stipulate that the insured person must have suffered from the disability for a period of time—say six months—most riders are retroactive in nature and will refund premiums that have been paid from the onset of the condition. Such riders may be important for frail individuals who buy private long-term insurance policies for NURSING HOME and HOME HEALTH CARE. However, these individuals must consider questions, such as how long must the insured be receiving treatment before the premium is waived?

Webb, Del

Del Webb, a Phoenix, Arizona, developer (1899–1974), helped establish the modern concept of retirement in 1960 when he opened Sun City, the first large-scale, privately developed retirement community, on a former cotton ranch near Phoenix. Until that time, many gerontologists and other aging experts were skeptical about the idea of segregating senior citizens in specially designed developments, fearing they would become depressed due to the separation from their families. Webb, however, heeded market research showing that precisely that separation and a feeling of independence was what many elderly Americans expected out of retirement. His $2 million initial investment paid off hugely; 100,000 people toured the property over a three-day opening weekend and Webb sold 400 homes in the first month. By 1980, Sun City was Arizona's seventh-largest city, with more than 25,000 homes. Webb eventually built a 31,000-home sister development, Sun City West, nearby, as well as other big retirement communities in Henderson, Nevada, outside of Las Vegas.

Del Webb, the Phoenix developer and owner of the New York Yankees, watches an April 1945 game. Webb helped establish the modern concept of retirement in 1960 when he opened Sun City, the first large-scale, privately developed retirement community. Source: AP Photo

Webb was a colorful figure: a former minor-league baseball player who helped build the modern Las Vegas, a business partner of mobster Benjamin "Bugsy" Siegel, a friend and confidant of reclusive billionaire Howard Hughes, and owner of the New York Yankees from 1945 to 1964. Highly organized, with a can-do attitude, he profited from the construction boom during World War II and built a successful casino empire in the 1950s. His company, Del Webb Corporation, became the first gaming establishment to go public on Wall Street in 1960, at a time when the casino industry was suffering from scandals due to mob investments. *Time* magazine even named Webb Man of the Year in 1964.

Despite the success, Webb was taking a calculated risk building retirement communities. The Federal Housing Administration and Fannie Mae were said to be reluctant to provide loans to seniors, fearing they would die before enough principal was paid. Prevailing attitudes of the day also held that seniors should live sedate lives, with little physical activity. Webb's contrarian sales pitch was built around maintaining an "active lifestyle," and his first development had a golf course and recreation center as its centerpieces. Author Marc Freedman, in his 1999 book *Prime Time: How Baby Boomers Will Revolutionize Retirement and Transform America,* also notes that Webb benefited from DEMOGRAPHIC trends. Many Americans were nearing retirement, had bought homes after World War II with low-interest loans and could sell their properties for significant profits. At the same time, the SOCIAL SECURITY program was expanding, giving seniors more economic security and independence.

Freedman and others note that Sun City marked a turning point in aging in America, one in which the elderly became a somewhat segregated class instead of an important part of the social fabric. This social segregation of the elderly has also helped fuel "INTERGENERATIONAL WARFARE" by making it easier for critics to depict the aged as selfish and having an uncaring attitude about the next generation's future. Retirement communities have legal exemptions from federal civil rights laws allowing them to bar residents with children. Residents in Sun City, among other communities, have tried to de-annex themselves from local school districts or vote against school bond measures, arguing that education represents a disproportionate share of state spending. While the phe-nomenon may not be widespread, it demonstrates that retirement is a comparatively recent social development that may need to be rethought to better involve older people at more social and economic levels.

Western Airlines v. Criswell

This 1985 U.S. Supreme Court case *Western Airlines v. Criswell* (472 U.S. 400) clarified what exceptions may be granted to the anti-AGE DISCRIMINATION provisions in the Age Discrimination in Employment Act of 1967 (ADEA) (PL 90-202). The case was brought by two airline pilots who faced being forced to retire due to a Federal Aviation Administration rule that prohibited anyone from serving as a pilot or copilot after they turn sixty. The pilots asked Western Airlines to reassign them to the lesser post of flight engineer, a position not required in some of today's aircraft that at the time involved a person serving as a member of the cockpit crew who did not operate the controls unless the pilot and copilot become incapacitated. The airline turned down the request, saying the age-sixty requirement also extended to its flight engineers, because they may be expected to carry out the same tasks as pilots. The pilots sued the airline, saying the extra flight engineer rule violated the ADEA.

The airline argued that it could use age as a "bona fide occupational qualification," or BFOQ, adding that its age-discrimination was justified because it was a reasonable necessity for the operation of a safe airline. The airline acknowledged that age-related physiological and psychological deterioration varied from person to person, but said testing each employee would not be practical.

A U.S. district court jury disagreed, and an appellate court upheld the verdict.

The Supreme Court, voting 8–0 with Justice Lewis Powell absent, ruled a BFOQ exception did not justify mandatory retirement of flight engineers at age sixty. Employers had to establish whether the challenged job criteria were reasonably necessary to the essence of the employer's business, the high court ruled. Justices added that employers must lay out some factual basis for believing all or most members of certain age categories would be unable to perform the jobs involved.

White House Conference on Aging

White House Conferences on Aging have taken place once every decade since the 1960s and served as catalysts for developing aging policies on federal, state, and local levels. The events attract several thousand attendees, many of whom are selected by governors, members of Congress, and aging organizations. The most recent conference, in 1995, was convened by President Bill Clinton after Congress authorized the gathering in the 1992 amendments to the OLDER AMERICANS ACT. The 2000 reauthorization of the Older Americans Act makes provisions for another conference in 2005.

President Harry S Truman is credited with calling the first national conference on aging in 1950, though it lacked the "White House" imprimatur. That gathering addressed shifting DEMOGRAPHICS that already were pointing to an increase in the elderly population, but delegates took no formal action. The next gathering, in 1961, was authorized by Congress in the White House Conference on Aging Act (PL 85-908) and

designed to be a nationwide forum to address problems and concerns of the elderly. The meeting helped spur the political advocacy of such groups as AARP and the NATIONAL COUNCIL OF SENIOR CITIZENS and began to lay the groundwork for passage of the Older Americans Act and the creation of the MEDICARE and MEDICAID programs, all in 1965.

White House aging conferences in 1971 and 1981 involved more interest groups, including representatives of black, Hispanic, and disabled groups, and led to changes such as the 1983 amendments to the SOCIAL SECURITY ACT (PL 98-21), which, among other things, mandated that BENEFITS be subject to federal income taxes for the first time. The 1995 conference, attended by more than 2,200 delegates, was notable for a strong call to protect SOCIAL SECURITY and current benefits, and to study ways to keep the program solvent for the next generation of beneficiaries. Conferees registered similar support for Medicare and Medicaid—especially for provisions for home- and community care—while opposing the practice of using block grants to award states their share of Medicaid funds. Conferees also called on Congress to reauthorize the Older Americans Act and the services it funds, especially MEALS ON WHEELS, transportation services, HOME HEALTH CARE, and ELDER ABUSE prevention.

Windfall reduction

The windfall reduction, officially known as the "windfall elimination provision," was enacted as part of the 1983 amendments to the SOCIAL SECURITY ACT (PL 98-21) in order to reduce Social Security BENEFITS for workers who also have pensions from work not covered by SOCIAL SECURITY. This mainly applies to federal workers, who are covered under the Federal Civil Service Retirement System. The provision was seen as necessary because some uncovered workers who earned significant income during their working lives could have qualified for sizeable Social Security benefits, because of the formula used to calculate the benefits. Since the income the workers earned during their years in noncovered jobs did not factor into the benefit calculation, the formula could mistakenly regard them as low-paid workers for a substantial portion of their working lives. Social Security's benefit calculation is weighted to provide proportionally higher payments to workers who spent most of their careers in low-paying jobs. Hence, before the changes, some workers who only spent part of their careers in Social Security-covered employment also qualified for such treatment under the weighted formula.

The windfall reduction works by lowering one of the mathematical factors in the benefit calculation that is applied to a worker's AVERAGE INDEXED MONTHLY EARNINGS from 90 percent to as low as 40 percent, depending on the number of years of his or her Social Security coverage. That could substantially reduce the monthly benefit of an annuitant. The National Association of Retired Federal Employees, which opposes the windfall reduction, said it can reduce a worker's earned Social Security benefit by as much as 55.6 percent. However, workers with thirty or more years of Social Security–covered employment are exempt from the provision. Those with twenty-one to twenty-nine years of coverage would have the windfall reduction implemented on a sliding scale. The windfall reduction was phased in over five years and affects those workers eligible for both Social Security benefits and noncovered

pensions after 1985. Proposals are introduced annually in Congress to soften the blow of the reduction by making a certain amount of earnings exempt from the calculation. But passage of any of these measures is viewed as something of a legislative long shot, because they are viewed as possibly helping highly compensated federal employees get richer.

Worker-beneficiary ratio

The worker-beneficiary ratio, sometimes also called the dependency ratio, is a measurement often cited in debates over SOCIAL SECURITY and refers to the number of workers paying taxes into the system compared to the number of elderly people taking payments out of it. The figure is often used by proponents of changing or scrapping the system to suggest that tomorrow's workers will be overburdened by DEMOGRAPHIC aging, especially the surge of retiring BABY BOOMERS. According to the Social Security Board of Trustees' 1997 assumptions, the worker-beneficiary ratio has declined over the past four decades, and is expected to continue to do so. In 1960, there were 5.1 workers for each beneficiary. In 2000, the figure stood at 3.3. By 2020, projections are there only will be 2.4 workers per beneficiary, and by 2040, the ratio is expected to fall to 2.0.

Conservatives and other program critics argue this is cause for alarm because Social Security was envisioned as a contributory pension system to provide the elderly with a safe cushion of retirement income—not a welfare program aimed at redistributing wealth from one generation to another. Critics also note the numbers show younger generations will be unfairly burdened at a time when they may be experiencing slower wage growth and a tightening national economy.

However, the numbers may be misleading. Most economists judge an economy's health by broader criteria, taking into account the total dependency of a society by including all elders, children, disabled, and other nonworking people. In the United States, this ratio was tightest during the baby boom years of the early 1960s, when couples were experiencing some of the century's highest birth rates, and older children were just entering college. Demographers say, in the decade from 1960 to 1970, the ratio came close to approaching one worker per one nonworker. Far from using the statistic as a rationale for curtailing social services, policymakers at the time viewed it in terms of future growth and responded by building new schools and making other accommodations.

Some observers believe one has to take into account this broader view when gauging how Social Security will fare in the twenty-first century. While there surely will be more elderly people, birth rates are simultaneously expected to decline as younger generations have fewer children, offsetting some of the anticipated stresses on the system. Indeed, even taking into account the growing number of retirees, as well as increased LIFE EXPECTANCIES, the ratio is only expected to reach 1.2 by about 2075, according to some projections.

Workforce Investment Act

See JOB TRAINING PARTNERSHIP ACT.

Index